Environmental and Natural Resource Economics

ENVIRONMENTAL AND NATURAL RESOURCE ECONOMICS

An Encyclopedia

Timothy C. Haab and John C. Whitehead, Editors

Associate Editors
Jill L. Caviglia-Harris
Paul E. Chambers
Matthew G. Interis
Lea-Rachel Kosnik
David M. McEvoy
Daniel R. Petrolia
Peter W. Schuhmann

 GREENWOOD

AN IMPRINT OF ABC-CLIO, LLC
Santa Barbara, California • Denver, Colorado • Oxford, England

Library of Congress Cataloging-in-Publication Data

Environmental and natural resource economics : an encyclopedia / Timothy C. Haab and John C. Whitehead, editors ; associate editors, Jill L. Caviglia-Harris, Paul E. Chambers, Matthew G. Interis, Lea-Rachel Kosnik, David M. McEvoy, Daniel R. Petrolia, Peter W. Schuhmann.

    pages cm

    Includes index.

    ISBN 978-1-4408-0119-8 (hardback) — ISBN 978-1-4408-0120-4 (e-book)

1. Environmental economics—Encyclopedias.   2. Natural resources—Encyclopedias. I. Haab, Timothy C., 1969–   II. Whitehead, John Claiborne, 1963–   III. Caviglia, Jill L., 1970–

    HC79.E5E7434   2014

    333.703—dc23   2013044942

ISBN: 978-1-4408-0119-8
EISBN: 978-1-4408-0120-4

18   17   16   15   14   1   2   3   4   5

This book is also available on the World Wide Web as an eBook.
Visit www.abc-clio.com for details.

Greenwood
An Imprint of ABC-CLIO, LLC

ABC-CLIO, LLC
130 Cremona Drive, P.O. Box 1911
Santa Barbara, California 93116-1911

This book is printed on acid-free paper ∞

Manufactured in the United States of America

The views expressed in these entries are those of the authors and do not represent the views of their employers.

CONTENTS

LIST OF ENTRIES

GUIDE TO RELATED TOPICS

BASIC CONCEPTS

Market Failure

Asymmetric Information
Cartels
Common Pool Resources
Externality
Green National Accounting
Natural Monopoly
Public Goods
Tragedy of the Commons

People

Baumol, William J.
Boulding, Kenneth
Ciriacy-Wantrup, S. V.
Clawson, Marion
Coase, Ronald
Crocker, Thomas D.
Daly, Herman E.
d'Arge, Ralph C.
Hardin, Garrett
Hotelling, Harold
Jevons, William Stanley
Kneese, Allen V.
Krutilla, John V.
Malthus, Thomas Robert
Ostrom, Elinor
Pearce, David W.
Pigou, Arthur C.
Rosen, Sherwin
Schelling, Thomas C.
Tolley, George S.

Events

Benefit–Cost Analysis of the Clean
    Air Act
Clean Air Act
Clean Water Act
Cuyahoga River Fire
Deepwater Horizon Oil Spill
Earth Day
Environmental Justice
Executive Order 12291
Exxon *Valdez* Oil Spill
Guidelines for Preparing Economic
    Analyses
Montreal Protocol
NOAA Panel on Contingent
    Valuation
Sulfur Dioxide Trading
Toxics Release Inventory
Trans-Alaskan Pipeline

Movements

Association of Environmental
    and Resource Economists
Behavioral Economics
Books
Ecological Economics
Environmentalism
Fisheries Economics
    Associations
International Association for Energy
    Economics

Journals
Philosophy
Sustainability

United States Society for Ecological
Economics
University Economics Departments

ENVIRONMENTAL ECONOMICS

Policy

Coase Theorem
Conservation Reserve Program
Corporate Average Fuel Economy
Corporate Environmentalism
Emissions Trading
Experimental Methods and Policy
Information Disclosure
International Environmental Agreements
International Trade
Monitoring and Enforcement
Offsets
Payments for Environmental Services
Pigouvian Taxes
Precautionary Principle
Property Rights
Regulation
Safe Minimum Standard
Subsidies
Trade Policy

Environmental Topics

Agriculture
Air Pollution

Brownfields
Drought
Environmental Kuznets Curve
Food Safety
Hazardous Waste
Health
Invasive Species
Municipal Solid Waste
Natural Hazards
NIMBY and LULU
Noise
Nonpoint Source Pollution
Recycling
Water Pollution

Climate Change

Adaptation
Carbon Pricing
Climate Change and Forests
Climate Change Impacts
International Climate
    Agreements
Sea Level Rise
Technological Innovation

RESOURCE ECONOMICS

Allocation

Catch Shares
Complexity in Fisheries
Exhaustible Resources
Fisheries Management
Forestry
User Cost

Energy

Alternative Energy
Biofuels
Energy Efficiency
Energy Policy
Forecasting
Nuclear Power

Peak Oil
Renewable Energy

Resource Topics

Biodiversity
Coastal Resources

Land Use
Groundwater
Tropical Rain Forests
Water Conservation
Water in Development
Wetlands

APPLIED WELFARE ECONOMICS

Basics

Benefit–Cost Analysis
Discounting
Green Jobs
Nonmarket Valuation
Pollution Abatement Costs
Risk and Uncertainty
Welfare
Welfare and Equity

Valuation Methods

Averting Behavior
Benefit Transfer
Choice Experiments

Contingent Behavior
Contingent Valuation
Experimental Methods and Valuation
Hedonic Price Method
Meta-Analysis
Travel Cost Method

Valuation Topics

Amenity Values of Forests
Ecosystem Services
Endangered Species
Outdoor Recreation
Passive Use Value
Value of Statistical Life

PREFACE

What can we do about climate change? How do we reduce pollution? Is reducing pollution worth it? What will we do when we run out of oil? Why haven't we switched to renewable energy yet? Does government involvement help or hinder solutions to these problems? How do we measure the costs and benefits of environmental projects? These and many other questions can be answered with a broad understanding of economics as applied to environmental and natural resources.

Economics is the study of stuff. Who has stuff? Who wants stuff? How is stuff made? How is stuff sold? Who buys stuff? Who sells stuff? Where does the stuff to make the stuff come from? How do we get the most out of our limited stuff? And, where does the leftover stuff go? Economics is the study of the decisions, the institutions, the rules, and the laws that result in how our stuff is made and consumed and ways to make people better off.

Critical to the study of economics is the simple fact that all stuff either comes from or is returned to the environment. Ignorance of this fact, and the blind pursuit of personal well-being, results in markets misallocating stuff and society being worse off than it can be, today and in the future. Failing to understand economics and the role the economy plays in creating and solving environmental problems leads to bad decisions and bad policies. Just as economies cannot exist without depending on environmental and natural resources, environmental and natural resource problems cannot be solved separate from the economy. To paraphrase Homer Simpson, the patriarch of the cartoon Simpson family, who once said, "Beer. The cause of, and solution to, all of life's problems," economics is the cause of, and solution to, all of our environmental and natural resource problems.

Environmental and Natural Resource Economics: An Encyclopedia offers the critical information needed to understand environmental and natural resource issues, presented in an objective and accessible manner. With entries written by the top thinkers in the field, this encyclopedia serves as a general reference on all aspects of environmental and natural resource economics. It focuses on the key concepts, movements, events, people, and organizations relevant to the study of environmental and natural resource economics.

This encyclopedia is a comprehensive reference of all aspects of environmental and natural resource economics, organized topically by the most common way the subject is taught at the college level: market failure, environmental policy, natural resource economics, and applied welfare economics. It is intended for advanced high school students, undergraduate students at two- and four-year institutions, teachers of economics, non-specialist scholars, researchers in other disciplines (such as political science, geography, and history), practitioners, policy makers and general readers. The encyclopedia can enhance the basic economic literacy of anyone involved with environmental and resource issues; and that includes everyone.

We begin the encyclopedia with an introductory essay on environmental and natural resource economics. We encourage you to start with this overview as it will provide a context for many of the entries that follow. In choosing authors for each entry, we sought out those who not only know something about the topic, but are known as a thought-leader on that topic. Following the introduction are over 140 entries on topics ranging from critical historical events to current theories on environmental and natural resource issues. We believe that exploring these topics will provide you an entry into the vast field of environmental and resource economics. And we believe that after delving into *Environmental and Natural Resource Economics: An Encyclopedia*, you too will come to understand that economics is the cause of, and solution to, all of our environmental and natural resource problems.

Timothy C. Haab and John C. Whitehead

ACKNOWLEDGMENTS

We would like to thank a number of people who helped move this project along. First, Brian Romer, our original editor, had the idea and talked us into the project. Hilary Clagget, who took over as editor, provided guidance and was patient while we tried to do almost everything at the last minute. Our associate editors, Jill Caviglia-Harris, Paul Chambers, Matt Interis, Lea-Rachel Kosnik, Dan Petrolia, and Pete Schuhmann provided an initial editing of about half of the entries and also provided some last-minute comments on the introduction. The contributors were timely, sharp, and amazingly able to provide a wealth of knowledge to a broad audience in a short space. Finally, on behalf of Brian Murray, we thank William Boulding, Dean of the Fuqua School of Business at Duke University and Kenneth Boulding's son, for his participation in a personal interview with Brian to inform the entry on Boulding.

INTRODUCTION

Environmental and natural resource economics is a subfield of economics that borrows from traditional fields of microeconomics such as public finance, industrial organization, and international trade. Its roots are in the market failure theory of negative externalities, public goods, and common pool resources. Much of the focus is on the economics of pollution control, the intertemporal allocation of exhaustible and renewable natural resources and applied welfare analysis (that is, benefit–cost analysis). The philosophical underpinnings of environmental and natural resource economics lie in standard microeconomic principles. In this context, the environment is important because producers use it for profit and households benefit from its use for activities that generate happiness such as health and recreation.

Environmental issues also pervade macroeconomics. For example, green national accounting incorporates environmental and natural resource principles into the measurement of the gross domestic product (GDP) and regulation may have macroeconomic effects on employment, inflation, and productivity. The related field of ecological economics takes a broader and more eclectic view of environmental and natural resource problems. In particular, there is a focus on sustainability and inclusion of alternative approaches to traditional economic analyses.

At the heart of the field of environmental and natural resource economics is the question of whether markets contribute to, are the primary cause of, or are potentially the solution to environmental and natural resource problems. Most economists view markets as the ideal tool for allocating society's scarce resources. Scarcity matters because consumer satisfaction stems from the quest for more; more is preferred to less. Due to scarcity, decisions must be made as to how to allocate society's scarce resources. Left alone, the forces of supply and demand will generate a market that distributes scarce resources among participants in an economy in a way that maximizes the total well-being (welfare) of the market participants, if all of the costs and benefits of consumption and production accrue to the consumers and producers in the market. But in the case of environmental and natural resources, that's a big "if".

When markets fail to effectively allocate scarce resources, there is said to be a market failure. There are five types of market failures: externality, public goods, common pool resources, market power, and asymmetric information. Each of these is prevalent to varying extent when dealing with environmental and natural resource issues.

In many cases, markets fail to account for costs or benefits of consumption or production that pile up to those outside of the market. For example, it is fairly obvious that gasoline manufacturers and drivers all benefit from the production and consumption of gasoline (otherwise gas would not be produced, and cars would not be driven). But when a driver drives, the consumption of gasoline produces emissions (hydrocarbons, nitrogen oxide, carbon monoxide, carbon dioxide) that, when accumulated, impose costs on nondrivers; for example, asthma and bronchial incidence from ozone and smog or social costs of climate change due to greenhouse gas emissions. These external costs, called negative externalities, are a real part of the costs of producing and consuming gasoline and in a well-functioning market would be captured by the consumers and/or producers. Unfortunately, market participants have no incentive to pay these costs (when was the last time you paid for someone else's health care costs caused by an asthma attack?) and the market fails to capture the full costs and benefits of consumption and production. The result is too much gas consumption/production relative to the amount that would be produced if the market captured these external costs, and a misallocation of society's scarce resources such that society is worse off than if the market had worked properly. In short, if markets fail to capture the full benefits and costs of production and consumption, society is worse off than if those costs are fully accounted for and markets create an outcome in which societal welfare (or well-being) is not maximized. Other examples of negative externalities include air pollution, water pollution, invasive species, and noise.

Not all externalities are bad. Positive externalities arise when the external third party effect is positive. Suppose a consumer buys a hybrid car for the gas mileage benefits. This purchase also reduces pollution but that may have not factored into the consumer's decision. When a market good produces these positive externalities the market fails to allocate resources efficiently. Too few of these goods are produced and the market price is too low since it does not capture all of the benefits that that good generates to society.

Public goods are those goods for which consumption is nonrival and nonexcludable. When my consumption does not keep you from consuming, goods are nonrival. The good is nonexcludable when it is produced and the producer cannot prevent a consumer from consuming. Together these public good properties create an opportunity to consume without paying. This free-rider problem causes markets to fail to allocate resources efficiently. Markets do not form because producers have little incentive to make something that can be consumed without payment. Important global public goods are climate change and biodiversity.

Common pool resources, such as fisheries and groundwater, are rival but nonexcludable goods. Fisheries are rival since once one fisherman catches a fish it cannot be caught by another. Once a unit of groundwater is pumped to a community another community cannot capture that same unit. These resources are nonexcludable because one user cannot prevent another from harvesting the same resource stock. Since all users have an incentive to extract the resource before competitors do, too much tends to be extracted too fast.

Market power can arise in retail and wholesale natural resource markets. Market power results when there are not enough buyers or sellers for markets to be competitive. A natural monopoly is a market structure where a single firm can most efficiently sell the product. Unfortunately, once a natural monopoly has market power, the monopolist can take advantage of that power and underproduce (and overprice) the good relative to the socially efficient amount. Regulation is necessary to reduce the impact of the market power. Retail electricity is a natural monopoly where pricing is regulated. A cartel is a group of firms that make pricing decisions together as a monopoly. The Organization of Petroleum Exporting Countries, more commonly known as OPEC, is an example. Environmental and natural resource markets created by government policy, such as catch share and emissions trading markets, can also suffer from market power.

Asymmetric information is a market failure that results when one party to a transaction has more information about a product's attributes than another party. An example is food safety where the producer knows more about health risks than the consumer. The demand for risky food will be greater than if information about the health risks were available. Hazardous and toxic wastes are other examples. Residents who live near facilities that emit these wastes do not have perfect information about their risks and thus make uninformed, and perhaps costly, decisions. Markets require complete information to allocate resources efficiently.

The field of environmental and natural resource economics is dedicated to identifying those markets that are not efficiently allocating society's natural assets. In cases where those assets are misallocated by unregulated markets, the goal is to identify the lowest cost solutions (policy) for remedying the market's misallocation. The subfield of environmental economics is primarily the economics of pollution and environmental policies designed to confront the pollution problem. Events such as the Cuyahoga River fire and Earth Day and the environmental movement coincided with the emergence of environmental regulation at the U.S. federal government level. The Clean Air Act and Clean Water Act were enacted in the early 1970s and are the two major U.S. federal environmental laws. The approach taken with both of these laws and others, when enacted, was command-and-control regulation.

Command-and-control is a type of top-down regulation where the government or regulatory agency specifies how a regulatory target is to be met. For example, technology-based standards are requirements that businesses and consumers use a certain product to reduce pollution. A criticism of command-and-control regulation is that it often imposes uniform standards across industries or geographic areas that increase the cost of meeting environmental quality goals and reduce the efficiency of policy.

The first consideration among economists is whether a private market can solve the market failure problem. Many environmental problems stem from ill-defined property rights. A market-based environmental policy is based on the explicit assignment of property rights. Commonly known as the Coase theorem, assignment of explicit property rights may allow bargaining between those who impose and suffer from negative externalities. Compensation may lead to the optimal environmental quality when transactions costs are low. Government programs can be used to encourage voluntary corporate environmentalism to supply public goods and reduce negative externalities. Information provision, such as the Toxics Release Inventory and food safety labeling laws, can be used to correct asymmetric information problems.

When these market-based solutions fail to fully solve the problem, economists often advocate incentive-based environmental policy over command-and-control regulation. Incentive-based environmental policies include subsidies, Pigouvian taxes, tradable emissions permits, offsets, and payments for environmental services. Subsidies are a payment from the government to a polluter to reduce the activity causing the pollution. Pigouvian taxes are a requirement that a polluter pays the government a per-unit fee in exchange for the right to pollute. Both subsidies and taxes can be designed to achieve the efficient pollution level but the implicit property rights assumed by the two programs differ. Subsidies confer property rights for a healthy and functioning environment to the polluter while taxes confer property rights to those who are negatively affected by the pollution. Government policies such as the Acid Rain Program assign property rights to the environment and allow this property, in the form of emissions permits, to be traded. Offsets and payments for environmental services involve compensation for practices that reduce negative externalities. The success of incentive-based environmental policy has led some command-and-control policies, such as Corporate Average Fuel Economy standards, to incorporate trading.

Climate change and other global public goods issues provide special challenges for environmental policymaking. Incentive-based policies have been designed to encourage technological innovation and adaptation. Carbon pricing, such as carbon emissions trading and carbon taxes, have been advocated by many economists. Tradable carbon permit markets have been implemented in Europe and, regionally, in the United States. Carbon taxes, a Pigouvian tax on carbon, have been implemented in Canada. In the area of climate change, offsets tend to be payments from rich countries to poor countries. For example, rich countries might provide payments for environmental services that protect forests or wetlands.

Environmental policy to address climate change is complicated by the global nature of the public good. International climate agreements, such as the Kyoto Protocol, have largely been unsuccessful. Yet, other types of global public goods have been successfully addressed with international environmental agreements. A notable example is the Montreal Protocol, which addressed protection of the ozone layer.

International trade in goods, services, and factors of production is another complicating factor for environmental policymaking. One country's strict environmental policy can lead to international capital flows to less strict countries that become pollution havens. Trade policy, such as green tariffs, can be used to offset these flows but can lead to other inefficiencies.

Environmental policy in developing countries poses another set of complications. Environmental policy may constrain the development process. The economics of the environmental Kuznets curve (EKC) suggests that weak environmental policy is likely during the initial stages of development. According to this hypothesis, once a developing country's income reaches a certain level, the demand for environmental policy increases and environmental quality improves. There are at least two problems with using this as evidence for growing out of any environmental problems. First, the EKC does not apply for all types of environmental quality. Second, weak environmental policy can, in certain cases such as tropical rain forests, lead to irreversible destruction of natural resources.

The subfield of natural resource economics is separate from environmental economics in that the most efficient intertemporal allocation of natural resources is the dominant concern. In contrast to most environmental problems where the analysis is static, or conducted for a fixed time period, the analysis of natural resource allocation is dynamic. Economists must consider the effects of resource use today on the future.

Natural resources are generally categorized as exhaustible or renewable resources. Exhaustible resources are nonrenewable, that is, there is a fixed resource stock and any usage of that stock reduces the amount of the stock available for the future. Examples include fossil fuels (such as oil, coal, and natural gas) and the biodiversity in tropical rain forests. Exhaustible resources bring the economic concept of scarcity to the forefront, because once some resource is extracted and consumed, it is gone and cannot be regenerated. The opportunity cost of usage today is known as user cost. Early attempts to understand the economics of exhaustible resource use include the work of Harold Hotelling, who developed a theoretical rule based on the concept of user cost. Hotelling's rule states that as an exhaustible resource is depleted, with well-functioning markets, the price of that resource will continually increase at the rate of interest. It is this price increase that provides incentives for conservation, exploration, and investments in alternative resources. Policymakers often focus energy policy on forecasting future resource availability, encouraging conservation, maintaining well-functioning markets, identifying and encouraging opportunities for investments in alternatives, and encouraging exploration. In the United States, local, state, and federal governments have invested heavily in exploration and infrastructure needs for transport of oil through projects such as the Trans-Alaskan pipeline.

Recognizing the exhaustible nature of, and the overwhelming reliance on, fossil fuels, some believe that widespread economic catastrophe is imminent once the peak extraction rates (called peak oil) have been achieved. Hotelling's rule offers an alternative explanation for how the transition between exhaustible and renewable fuel sources will occur. Alternative energy sources such as solar and wind are renewable, nondepletable resources since they are replenished by natural processes. These energy sources are an important backstop fuel for exhaustible resources. The price of these and other substitute backstop fuels, such as nuclear and biofuel, caps on the price of the exhaustible energy source. As an exhaustible resource is depleted its price rises but no higher than the renewable substitute price.

Fisheries are renewable common pool resources that, without government regulation, are allocated with open access. Open access resources are subject to a race for extraction called the Tragedy of the Commons. Open-access fisheries management attempts to achieve the optimal sustainable yield of catch with a variety of measures, while not directly confronting the open-access problem. Examples are gear restrictions or trip limits. The regulation constrains the technology available to catch fish but does not limit the number of fishers who wish to use the technology. Catch shares are an attempt to regulate fisheries using the assignment of property rights through the creation of markets in the right to fish.

Some resources such as groundwater are both renewable and exhaustible. While groundwater aquifers can sometimes recharge after extraction, depending on the local geology, due to the common pool nature of groundwater, aquifers can also suffer from the Tragedy of the Commons.

Forests are renewable resources that are generally privately owned, except, for example, in the case of tropical rain forests. The optimal rotation considers the most beneficial time to cut a stand of trees. The trade-off between the growth of the forest, the growth of timber revenue, and growth of new standards of timber are considerations. Market failures result because forests provide amenities such as recreation, biodiversity, and climate change mitigation. Tropical rain forests, which are important for biodiversity, are most appropriately managed as exhaustible resources due to their slow growth.

Land and water are natural resources that do not fit neatly within simple exhaustible and renewable categories. The principle economic problem is how to use these resources with competing urban, rural, and agricultural uses. Each type of land and water resource has its own allocation issues. Negative externalities such as disposal of municipal solid waste, hazardous waste, and other by-products of the production process can create not in my back yard (NIMBY) and locally unwanted land use (LULU) problems. Agricultural use of land can create water pollution problems with nonpoint source pollution. Coastal resources and wetlands can be even more problematic in terms of efficient use with provision of public goods, such as recreation and scenic amenities, natural hazards, and sea level rise. Water has agricultural, drinking, industrial, and recreational uses. These alternative uses can create conflicts and overuse when water is not priced efficiently.

Another consideration for policymakers who must make environmental and resource allocation decisions is whether the benefits of the policy exceed the costs of the policy. Benefit–cost analysis is the practical application of welfare economics, the study of the well-being of individuals and, ultimately, society. Benefit–cost analysis can be used to determine the most efficient level of environmental quality or natural resource use. In 1981 Executive Order 12291 mandated that major federal regulations pass a benefit–cost test. The U.S. Environmental Protection Agency's benefit–cost analysis of the Clean Air Act is one of the most comprehensive and extensive analyses ever conducted, providing guidelines and a framework for future studies.

In benefit–cost analysis of environmental quality and resource use policy, the major benefits are nonmarket benefits. In other words, they occur outside the normal functioning of markets. For example, reductions in air pollution improve human health and visibility. Reductions in water pollution improve ecological health and provide greater outdoor recreation opportunities. The measurement of nonmarket benefits is a considerable challenge. In addition to this challenge, benefit–cost analysis must also consider the measurement of pollution abatement, monitoring, and enforcement costs. These costs are rarely accurately measured with simple accounting methods.

So-called nonmarket valuation methods are used to estimate nonmarket benefits. Nonmarket valuation methods can be separated into two categories: revealed preference and stated preference approaches. The revealed preference approaches use information on actual behavior to uncover values for the environment and natural resources. Examples of revealed preference approaches are averting behavior, the hedonic price method, and the travel cost method. Stated preference approaches use information on hypothetical behavior to uncover nonmarket values. The primary stated preference approaches are choice experiments, contingent behavior, and contingent valuation. Other valuation approaches include benefit transfer, meta-analysis, and laboratory and field experiments.

One considerable valuation challenge is the measurement of passive use values, those environmental values that are not revealed by any type of behavior— sometimes referred to partially as nonuse values, existence values, option values, among other names. Debates continue about whether passive use values exist, whether they should be included in benefit–cost analysis and, if so, how to accurately measure them. A major event in the development of valuation methods was the Exxon *Valdez* oil spill. The state of Alaska commissioned a contingent valuation study to estimate the lost passive use values of the spill. The resulting contingent valuation controversy led to the Report of the NOAA Panel on Contingent Valuation and extensive development of both stated and revealed preference methods. The *Deepwater Horizon* oil spill could lead to similar concentrated research efforts.

Benefit–cost analysis is a tool used to help achieve the economic goal of efficiency. Economists recognize that other goals are important to society and that these can supersede efficiency in policymaking. Some natural resources are so important, so scarce, development is so irreversible, or there is so much risk and uncertainty that the precautionary principle or the safe minimum standard should be applied. Equity and environmental justice are other considerations for society and policymakers.

Timothy C. Haab and John C. Whitehead

Further Reading

Cropper, Maureen L., and Wallace E. Oates. 1992. Environmental Economics: A Survey. *Journal of Economic Literature* 30(2): 675–740.

Devarajan, Shantayanan, and Anthony C. Fisher. 1981. Hotelling's Economics of Exhaustible Resources: Fifty Years Later. *Journal of Economic Literature* 19(1): 65–73.

Fisher, Anthony C., and Frederick M. Peterson. 1976. The Environment in Economics: A Survey. *Journal of Economic Literature* 14(1): 1–33.

Pearce, David. 2002. An Intellectual History of Environmental Economics. *Annual Review of Energy and the Environment* 27(1): 57–81.

Adaptation

The year 2012 was one of the hottest on record. The United States suffered from extreme drought. Climate scientists have argued that rising carbon dioxide concentrations can increase the probability of low-probability weather events, such as drought, tornadoes, and category five hurricanes. Economists are concerned that an unintended consequence of continued world population growth and per-capita income growth will be further increases in global carbon dioxide levels. Such economic growth is likely to translate into more emissions if credible carbon mitigation agreements are not enacted. If greenhouse gas producers faced a positive price for contributing to this social externality, this is expected to induce behavioral responses such as purchasing more fuel-efficient vehicles and trigger innovation to create products that use less fossil fuels. In the absence of such an incentive, greenhouse gas emissions will rise and the risk of climate change impacts increases. How will extreme climate shocks such as heat waves, droughts, and the increased occurrence of natural disasters impact economies in the developed and the developing world? How much will individuals in rich and in developing nations suffer from such changing conditions? Will the price of food soar? Will many more people die in natural disasters? Will day-to-day life be miserable because of heat waves? If we could answer these questions, we could begin to understand how climate change will affect our quality of life and our standard of living.

Note that the broad topic of climate change adaptation requires both climate science and social scientists to work together. An interdisciplinary group of scientists specialize in studying how climate change will impact weather, agricultural production, the oceans, trees, and different creatures. It is the job of the economists to study the direct and indirect impacts of climate change on the choices made by households, firms, and governments.

Adaptation can be defined as how we individually and collectively cope with the new challenge of climate change. The economic approach for studying climate change adaptation focuses on how self-interested individuals, profit-seeking firms, and local and national governments respond when confronted by the known unknown called climate change.

To offer a concrete example, consider heat waves. Suppose that in the past Chicago had a 4 percent chance of a heat wave in the summer while Los Angeles had a 1 percent chance of such a heat wave. In this new age of climate change, assume that people now believe that Chicago's chance increases to 12 percent while Los Angeles's chance increases to 4 percent. How will the economy adapt to this new news?

Self-interested households that are susceptible to heat are increasingly likely to migrate to Los Angeles. The relative shift in probabilities of extreme heat waves has made Chicago a relatively riskier city than Los Angeles. Mobile people will respond by moving to higher ground (i.e., less risky Los Angeles). We know that migration rates are higher for younger, more educated people. Are the less educated, elderly doomed to die from heat waves in Chicago? An optimist would say "no." Given that we anticipate that Chicago faces increased risk of extreme heat waves, individuals have access to coping strategies such as accessing improved air conditioned areas.

Richer people will be better able to access such spaces than poorer people. The desire to protect the poor against climate shocks creates a redistributionary role for local government. In a Rawlsian sense, government could take some tax revenue and use such revenue to build cooling centers and public pools where people who have fewer resources can beat the heat. In this sense, a richer society is better able to adapt to climate change because such a society has a higher level of per-capita income to allow for private adaptation and it is possible to raise greater tax revenue for redistribution to protect the poor.

For-profit firms will anticipate that Chicago's heat waves offer new opportunities for them. Firms that can produce cooling products such as energy-efficient air conditioners can grow rich. There are many low-tech ways to keep cool. Such firms will be more likely to engage in costly research and development to create new ways to stay cool once they anticipate that there will be a market for such innovations.

Note that in this simple example, household decisions, firms' decisions, and government choices all facilitated adaptation to the new climate shock. But, this optimistic case may not always hold. Consider the case of increased flood risk in a coastal city such as New Orleans. To counter such climate change–induced risk, government may build sea walls to protect the populace. An unintended consequence of the public feeling safer in the flood-prone area is that more people may move in and fewer may move out. In this case, public investment in adaptation crowds out private self-protection (i.e., spatial mobility). Whether public and private investment in adaptation are complements or substitutes is an important (and open) research question.

A second relevant research question related to climate adaptation is risk perception. In the example sketched earlier, everyone in Chicago and Los Angeles agreed about how climate change had shifted the probabilities of the extreme heat wave. But, what happens if some people in the economy are behavioral and do not update their probability assessments? Aren't they doomed because they will take no action to protect themselves? An intuitive example of this point is to contrast the smart Vulcan Mr. Spock from *Star Trek* with the average Joe Homer Simpson. We expect that Spock will be more likely to make the right investments but is Homer doomed? An optimist would counter that some for-profit firms will anticipate Homer's misery and will innovate to help him to adapt because he will be willing to pay a great deal for products that will help him cope with the new realities posed by climate change.

These two examples highlight the evolutionary role that markets can play in helping us to adapt to climate change. This ambiguous threat poses different challenges for different cities around the world. In a world with 7 billion people, we may soon launch many field experiments to see which ideas do and do not work for helping us to adapt. The good ideas we discover will broadly diffuse and help all of us to cope with the new reality we have created.

Matthew E. Kahn

See also: Behavioral Economics; Climate Change Impacts; International Climate Agreements; Technological Innovation

Further Reading

Kahn, Matthew E. 2010. *Climatopolis: How Our Cities Will Thrive in the Hotter Future.* New York: Basic Books.

Agriculture

Agriculture both affects and is affected by the environment. Agriculture affects the environment mainly because agricultural lands comprise over a third of the world's land area. At the same time, agricultural productivity is directly tied to the environment through the quality of topsoil, climate, and weather. Air and water pollution can also affect agricultural productivity. Given the direct importance of climate on agriculture, it has been a key focus of studies on the potential impacts of climate change.

Land dedicated to agricultural production is comprised mainly of pasture, range, and croplands. Except for Africa and parts of Latin America, the vast majority of arable land on the planet is now used as cultivated pasture or in crop production. In more developed nations, a relatively small portion of arable land has been converted to urban and suburban uses. The physical scale of agriculture shows farmers are indeed key stewards of our environment.

Agricultural production affects environmental quality in many direct and indirect ways. Many native landscapes, like the tall grass prairies of the Midwestern United States, nearly vanished generations ago as they were displaced with some of the most productive cropland in the world. Regular tilling of former grasslands has contributed to widespread erosion of topsoil.

Aside from loss of soil and some key wildlife habitats, agricultural production is a source of many nonpoint source water pollutants, especially nitrogen and phosphorus fertilizers, but many other chemicals as well. New crop varieties were bred to take advantage of these chemical fertilizers, which allowed plants to better harness the sun's energy and soil moisture in photosynthesis. These advances created a green revolution that grew crop yields three- to fourfold over the last 75 years. This growth in productivity has helped to feed a rapidly growing human population that possesses an ever-growing appetite for resource-expensive foods like meat and dairy products.

An externality from fertilizer applications is that crops or other plants in photosynthesis never absorb a portion of it. In time, the fertilizers leach out of the soil into streams and rivers, which upsets natural aquatic ecosystems. Livestock animal waste can also leach into waterways. Altogether, agriculture is perhaps a principal source of water pollution, especially in developed nations. These excess nutrients feed algae blooms that rapidly absorb oxygen in the water, giving rise to vast aquatic dead zones that are nearly devoid of sea life. The broader ecological consequences of such dead zones remain unclear and is an active research area.

In her famous book *Silent Spring*, Rachel Carson made the general public aware of the loss of habitats and vast chemical use. The book helped to inspire early environmental movements that were probably instrumental in banning of dichlorodiphenyltrichloroethane (DDT), establishment of the Environmental Protection Agency, and enacting of the Clean Water Act.

Over the last decade or so, a fair amount of controversy has erupted over the emergence and rapid adoption of genetically modified crops, or genetically modified organisms (GMOs). The most prevalent kinds of GMOs include a gene that makes crop plants resistant to glyphosate (brand name Roundup), a popular herbicide developed by Monsanto. These so-called Roundup-ready crops make it much easier and less costly for farmers to control weeds. Although there has been no evidence or scientific rationale for how these crops could cause direct harm to humans, widespread use of the seed and glyphosate has bred weeds that are resistant to the herbicide. Farmers and seed companies are now looking toward new herbicides to control weeds that have become resistant to the herbicide.

While it is easy to see some of the environmental harm from modern chemical-intensive agricultural production, there are also great, if indirect, environmental benefits. Were it not for the great advances in productivity, principally brought about by chemical use, much more land would need to be cultivated to feed burgeoning human populations and their appetites. Agricultural commodity prices would be much higher than they are today. Millions and perhaps billions more would be hungry and malnourished, and remaining forest and grasslands areas would be even less prevalent.

Of course, environmental attributes also affect agriculture. Soil depth, soil acidity, nutrient content in soils, precipitation, temperature, carbon dioxide concentrations, and solar radiation are all fundamental to plant development and photosynthesis, from which nearly all food and life are ultimately derived. To some extent human activities can augment these characteristics of the environment, but doing so can be costly.

Land is allocated to various crops, livestock, and other land uses depending on the geophysical attributes that determine its greatest comparative advantage. Wheat is mostly grown in relatively cool climates; corn and soybeans in warmer climates; rice in warmer regions with access to plentiful and inexpensive irrigation water.

Pollution affects crop outcomes too. High ozone concentrations are known to reduce grain yields, and reduced concentrations in the United States may have contributed significantly to productivity growth over the past few decades.

Burning of fossil fuels and deforestation have rapidly risen atmospheric carbon dioxide concentrations, which are warming the earth's climate and are probably changing rainfall patterns. All of these changes affect agricultural production. Higher carbon dioxide concentrations can increase water and radiation use efficiency in some plants, possibly boosting crop yields and drought resistance. At the same time, warmer temperatures may lengthen growing seasons and open up new areas in northern latitudes to crop production.

But warmer temperatures may also increase water loss through evaporation and evapotranspiration, and may cause other heat-related stresses. While total rainfall is expected to increase, its spatial and temporal patterns could change markedly. Episodes of flooding are expected to increase.

While considerable uncertainty remains about the net global influence of climate change on agricultural production, early optimism about global gains now seems more dubious, as mounting evidence and recent experience suggests that extreme heat can be very damaging and benefits from carbon dioxide may be less than previously believed.

Michael J. Roberts

See also: Air Pollution; Climate Change Impacts; Land Use; Water Pollution

Further Reading

Carson, Rachel. 1962. *Silent Spring*. Boston, MA: Houghton Mifflin.

Field, Christopher B., Vincente Barros, and Thomas F. Stocker. 2012. *Managing the Risks of Extreme Events and Disasters to Advance Climate Change Adaptation*. A report by the Intergovernmental Panel on Climate Change. June.

Long, Stephen P., Elizabeth A. Ainsworth, Andrew D. B. Leakey, Josef Nosberger, and Donald R. Ort. 2006. Food for Thought: Lower-than-Expected Crop Yield Stimulation with Rising CO_2 Concentrations. *Science* 312(5782): 1918–1921.

Schlenker, Wolfram, and Michael J. Roberts. 2009. Nonlinear Temperature Effects Indicate Severe Damages to US Crop Yields under Climate Change. *Proceedings of the National Academy of Sciences* 106(37): 15594–15598.

Air Pollution

Air pollution typically results from negative production externalities—where some activity like driving, generating power, or manufacturing creates a spillover that affects third parties. Excessive levels of airborne chemicals—typically broken down into two categories, criteria pollutants (e.g., lead, ozone, sulfur dioxide) and toxics (i.e., carcinogens)—can cause adverse health outcomes as well as other harmful impacts like limestone deterioration, crop damage, and unsightly skylines. Unpriced in markets, these negative effects offer prime examples of market failures or incomplete markets as their producers do not take the external harm into account in their decision making.

The resulting overproduction of air pollution also has textbook remedies including conventional command-and-control (CAC) regulations, Coasian property rights–based approaches, and Pigouvian-style emissions taxes. Rigid CAC mandates traditionally dominate air pollution policy. Pollution control via CAC occurs by regulating the technologies used to emit or abate (e.g., catalytic converters, smokestack scrubbers) or setting performance standards (e.g., New Source Performance Standards, ambient ozone concentration limits). Most notable of these efforts is the 1970 Clean Air Act (CAA) and its subsequent amendments. Significant reductions in emissions and improvements in air quality followed many of these regulations in the United States.

Incentive-based approaches like emissions charges or tradable emissions permits are increasingly popular alternatives to CAC for air pollution control. Permits and charges have different strengths and design issues, although in principle either can achieve efficient air quality. Tradable permits or cap-and-trade programs serve to create markets and promise cost-effective abatement. The theoretical advantages of this approach to curbing air pollution actually got tested when the SO_2 Trading Program of the 1990 CAA Amendments was implemented. (SO_2 stands for sulfur dioxide.) This cap-and-trade program found success in both environmental and economic terms. Southern California also successfully implemented an extensive NO_x cap-and-trade program, the Regional Clean Air Incentives Market (RECLAIM).

Basic regulatory tools of permits, charges, or standards get applied to air pollution emissions or ambient concentrations. Permits, tradable or not, target quantity controls whereas charges address prices. Standards-based approaches typically mandate technologies for emitting or abating or set thresholds for emissions or ambient concentrations that might require additional efforts to attain them. Standards have proven popular among policymakers despite the disconnect with the fundamental nature of air pollution externalities. Restricting polluters' choices is an inefficient substitute for aligning their private costs of pollution with social damages.

The economics of air pollution control distinguishes between uniformly and nonuniformly mixed pollutants. Lower-atmosphere pollution involves nonuniformly mixed pollutants, where the emissions' harm depends on the location of the source of emission. Cost-effective control policies for these pollutants require spatially differentiated rules or penalties (and typically dispersion modeling to predict source-specific impacts at one or more receptor sites).

Measuring the economic value of air pollution damage helps us understand the scope of the problem and design policy solutions. For example, Pigouvian taxes derive from these marginal damage estimates. Some of the earliest research in non-market valuation involved air pollution. Economists frequently use hedonic pricing to identify the implicit value of air quality improvements from variation in housing sale prices. Another revealed preference method, averting behavior, measures economic value by observing how people invest in things like air filters to avoid pollution damage. Economists also use the contingent valuation method to directly measure the value individuals place on air quality improvements. Recent valuation work has emphasized responses to air quality variation across markets in a general equilibrium sense (e.g., people's willingness to pay for cleaner air may change after they relocate and housing prices change in response to air quality changes).

For nonuniformly mixed pollutants, this local variation in air quality implies that the damage caused by emissions depends on their time and place as much as the quantity emitted. Properly designing a Pigouvian tax scheme or a permit market to account for this spatial and temporal complexity can complicate matters. That cap-and-trade that allows pollution in some areas to rise has recently halted the SO_2 trading market. Cost-effective policies, possibly leading to localized air pollution hot spots, pose thorny environmental justice considerations, especially in light of how people cluster nonrandomly. Recent studies, however, find no evidence that minorities or the poor fared worse under the SO_2 or RECLAIM trading schemes.

Polluters respond to changes in air pollution regulations by reducing emissions and also by relocating their activity. Regions with stricter regulations under the CAA see business move to locations with lower restrictions, which act as pollution havens. Grandfathering or exempting older technologies may enhance political feasibility of some regulations, but it also results in more inefficiencies and environmental damage. The flexibility under cap-and-trade facilitated switching to low-sulfur coal and shifting pollution control efforts to plants with lower abatement costs. As expected, innovation under CAC focuses on reducing compliance costs (e.g., scrubbers with lower operating costs) while innovation under cap-and-trade advances environmental effectiveness (e.g., better removal efficiency for scrubbers).

Producing information as a public good has also been used to address air pollution externalities. Local air quality advisories, for instance, both inform averting behavior and offer opportunities to voluntarily curb emissions on peak days. Unsurprisingly, the strongest behavioral impacts occur for sensitive populations reducing exposure, while altruistic emission reductions are harder to detect. The Toxic Releases Inventory also informs the public about toxic air releases of firms, letting them adjust their home-buying choices or investment decisions to avoid toxic assets.

Air quality trends reflect that, despite the growing scale of economic activity, activities can shift to greener ones and the dirty industries that remain can operate more cleanly. The frontiers of air pollution control involve difficult challenges, such as better addressing mobile sources, air toxics, indoor air, and interactions among various pollutants (e.g., NO_x and SO_x, criteria pollutants, and greenhouse gases) and among regulatory regimes. Economic analysis shows how major efficiency gains can be achieved through adopting incentive-based policies. Yet these approaches are limited in practice, especially where transaction and information costs are high. Moreover, as air pollution remedies initially focused on cleaning the air, and then reformed to do so more efficiently, they seem under increasing pressure to do other things like advance equity, jobs, and climate change goals.

Douglas Noonan

See also: Averting Behavior; Clean Air Act; Coase Theorem; Contingent Valuation; Emissions Trading; Environmental Justice; Externality; Hedonic Price Method; Information Disclosure; Pigouvian Taxes; Property Rights; Sulfur Dioxide Trading; Toxic Release Inventory

Further Reading

Chay, Kenneth Y., and Michael Greenstone. 2003. The Impact of Air Pollution on Infant Mortality: Evidence from Geographic Variation in Pollution Shocks Induced by a Recession. *The Quarterly Journal of Economics* 118(3): 1121–1167.

Schmalensee, Richard, and Robert N. Stavins. 2013. The SO_2 Allowance Trading System: The Ironic History of a Grand Policy Experiment. *The Journal of Economic Perspectives*, 27(1): 103–121.

Stavins, Robert N. 1998. What Can We Learn from the Grand Policy Experiment? Lessons from SO_2 Allowance Trading. *The Journal of Economic Perspectives* 12(3): 69–88.

Alternative Energy

Alternative energy is a catch-all term that encompasses any new form of energy generation used or promoted in order to avoid the negative consequences of energy forms currently in use. Historically, there has never been a perfect energy source. All forms of energy production have exhibited some negative conse-quences, be they bads such as waste and garbage outputs, or negative externalities including air pollution and unpleasant visual effects. The search for an alternative energy source that alleviates the most harmful negative consequences of whatever energy source is currently predominant has been an ongoing quest.

The first alternative energy source can be considered to be coal, as a substitute for wood. Prior to the Industrial Revolution, wood was prevalent, cheap, and easy to burn, but its overuse devastated entire forests in Europe. In addition, burning wood in small, often windowless abodes led to pollution and safety hazards. At different times in history coal, whale oil, and petroleum have all been seen as alternative en-ergy sources and as solutions to then-prevalent energy problems.

The most popular alternative energy sources today are solar power (includ-ing photovoltaics and solar thermal power) and wind power. They are consid-ered alternatives to fossil-fuel-based energy generation (from coal, petroleum, and natural gas), which predominate worldwide energy production at the start of the 21st century. Both solar power and wind power solve what is seen as the most prevalent negative consequence of fossil-fuel-based energy generation: air pollution. This includes air pollution from chemicals, particulate matter, organic compounds, toxic materials, and the emissions that lead to climate change. Solar power and wind power are also popular because they are renewable sources of energy production, and so do not suffer the negative consequence of diminish-ing supplies. They are also domestic sources of energy production and so are not dependent on imports from what may be hostile countries. Finally, solar power and wind power have the technical capability to be distributed, or what is some-times referred to as decentralized energy generation sources. They can be placed on individual homes and in small areas and do not rely on large, single generation stations that can be susceptible to large-scale blackouts, terrorist attacks, or other centralized vulnerabilities.

Other alternative energy sources that are popular today include geothermal, hy-drogen, fusion, algaeoleum, and tidal power production. Geothermal, algaeoleum, and tidal power are all renewable energy resources and so they relieve the negative air pollution consequences of today's fossil-fuel-based energy production tech-niques. They are also, for the most part, domestic-based energy resources and so help to alleviate national security concerns. None of them are necessarily decentral-ized forms of energy generation, however, and their relative technical immaturity (as compared to solar and wind power) is a drawback. Hydrogen and fusion are not officially renewable energy resources. Hydrogen could be considered a renewable if a renewable energy source was used to power the electrolysis process involved in production, but this is not always the case. While both hydrogen and fusion may be domestic-based energy resources, they are based on relatively immature tech-nologies and so suffer from that drawback as well.

There are some renewable energy technologies that are only controversially considered alternative, and they include nuclear power and hydropower. Both nuclear power and hydropower are emission-free, and so alleviate the most common negative consequence of fossil-fuel-based energy production, air pollution. However, they suffer from other environmental problems that make them unattractive to some advocates of alternative energy solutions. Nuclear power produces highly radioactive wastes that must be stored and safely disposed of for long periods of time, and hydroelectric power traditionally comes from large dams that block free-flowing rivers and disturb natural riverine ecosystems. Newer forms of smaller, run-of-river hydroelectric plants avoid the negative consequences of large dams and reservoirs, but their potential physical implementation is limited and so they will never serve as the predominant solution to worldwide energy needs. Nuclear power and hydropower therefore, as with most alternative energy sources, solve some problems but not others. In the end, the bottom line remains that there still is not a clear winning alternative energy solution.

The viability of any particular alternative energy source is also greatly tempered by practical implementation considerations. Large-scale switching to any of the alternative energy solutions mentioned would be extremely costly. Capital costs would be incurred building the new generation plants (and retiring the old fossil-fuel-based plants, especially if they were to be retired early) and it is likely that energy distribution mechanisms (for example the electricity grid or the network of automobile refilling stations) would have to be revamped or entirely rebuilt as well. Such switching costs are not given as much attention in the academic literature (or the press) as the basic R&D and generating costs for producing alternative energy, but they are likely to be considerable and would hamper efforts to switch to any true alternative energy solution before the technology and benefits of doing so are absolutely certain.

This therefore involves a bit of a chicken-and-egg problem. In order to switch to an alternative energy solution more consumers need to demand it to make the switch cost-viable. But until the alternative energy solutions are cost-viable, few cost-conscious consumers will demand them. Overcoming the high burden of substantial switching costs will be difficult for any single potential alternative energy solution, or any proposed combination of solutions.

This implies that, as has historically been the case, alternative energy solutions tend to penetrate the market slowly, over many decades, and often in companion with traditional energy solutions. They rarely disrupt entire markets, but instead slowly infiltrate them. Alternative energy solutions, when developed, are long-term goals, not quick-term salvations.

Lea-Rachel Kosnik

See also: Air Pollution; Biofuels; Climate Change Impacts; Energy Policy; Externality; Nuclear Power; Renewable Energy

Further Reading

Dresselhaus, M. S., and I. L. Thomas. 2001. Alternative Energy Technologies. *Nature* 414:332–337.

Kruger, Paul. 2006. *Alternative Energy Resources: The Quest for Sustainable Energy.* Stanford, CA: Wiley.

Amenity Values of Forests

Forests provide a myriad of market and nonmarket services that are of value to society. The most obvious values of forests are associated with market values for timber and minerals. Economists refer to valuable nonmarket services as amenity values. Forest amenity values include ecosystem services, recreation, esthetics, and heritage. Forests provide watershed ecosystem services such as capturing, storing, and purifying water. Forests help stabilize soils, thus preventing erosion. Trees help clean the air and act as carbon sinks. Forests provide habitat for species, including those that are threatened and endangered, and protect biological diversity. Some of these services are of value because they represent avoided costs (e.g., water purification). Other ecosystem services are valued for motives that are not associated with use. For example, people value the existence of animal habitat, even if they themselves will never visit a particular forest.

In addition to values derived indirectly from ecosystem services, there are a variety of recreational activities that can take place in forests, providing direct benefit to different user groups by providing opportunities for activities such as hiking, hunting, and cross-country skiing. Visitors and surrounding communities value scenic views provided by forests. Certain forests may also have historical values, containing remnants of old dwellings or migration trails. Specific forests may have spiritual and cultural value for Native American tribes.

The specific menu of amenities provided by a forest, and the human value of these amenities, can differ with its vegetative/ecosystem characteristics, its legislative designation, and its proximity to communities. For example, a review by Pearce finds wide variation in values, depending on whether forests are tropical or temperate; some of the largest nonmarket values are for carbon storage (based on the estimated price in the carbon market) and recreation and existence values for unique forests.

Effective and efficient management of forests requires consideration of the benefits of all goods, services, and amenities provided by forests. The value of natural resource extraction is easily established by markets for these goods. However, the many amenity values associated with forests typically do not have a market value. Ignoring the value of these amenities will result in decision making that does not maximize social welfare.

There are a number of ways in which values can be placed on forest amenities. For example, hedonic studies can be used to estimate the value that homeowners place on proximity to forests. In these types of studies, econometric analysis is used to estimate how the value of residential real estate changes with distance from a forest, controlling for a variety of other factors that affect housing values, such as school district, housing characteristics, etc. This type of analysis can be combined with hedonic wage models to estimate the marginal impact of forest proximity on both wages and housing costs. Travel cost methods can be used to estimate recreational values associated with forests. In these types of studies, one uses trip costs to visit forest recreation sites to estimate the value of the activities at these sites. Stated preference surveys are particularly useful for valuing passive use services provided by forests. For example, one might use contingent valuation or choice experiment methods to estimate habitat values. Amenity values can also be considered in the context of optimal rotation models.

To understand the importance of amenity values from a policy perspective, it may be helpful to consider the issue of inventoried roadless areas (IRAs). IRAs are public forests or grasslands of 5,000 acres or more that meet the criteria for a wilderness area (e.g., undeveloped federal land that is primarily shaped by nature and not man and which offers outstanding opportunities for recreation or solitude), but are neither categorized nor managed as wildernesses. In practice, IRAs are areas that have historically had no roads and thus little logging.

An important policy question for IRAs is how they should be managed. Should future road building be prevented, meaning that these areas would effectively be managed as wilderness areas? Or should these areas be managed similar to other forests, allowing the building of roads, and thus probable resource extraction? It should be clear that the decision of whether or not to allow road building directly pits resource values against amenity values. In 2001, the U.S. Forest Service (USFS) adopted the Roadless Area Conservation Rule, better known as the Roadless Rule, which generally prevented road construction and related activities (logging and mineral extraction) in IRAs. This rule impacted about 30 percent of national forest land.

Early analysis of the Roadless Rule by the USFS and Office of Management and Budget identified significant costs from implementation of the rule related to foregone timber and mineral income and employment. There was no accounting for the amenity values provided by keeping the areas roadless, perhaps reflecting the challenges of valuing nonmarket goods. Secondary analysis by Loomis and Richardson in fact found significant benefits associated with recreation, passive use, carbon sequestration, and waste treatment services, suggesting that a strong economic argument existed for prohibiting road construction in IRAs.

The legislative and court history of IRAs is a convoluted one. Implementation of the Roadless Rule was delayed and the rule was subsequently replaced with a rule that created a state petition process for managing IRA areas. The issue was then tied up in the courts for many years. In March 2013, the courts dismissed a lawsuit by the state of Alaska and ruled that no further challenges to the Roadless Rule were allowed because the statute of limitations had passed. Thus, after many years of litigation, the Roadless Rule now stands.

Jennifer A. Thacher

See also: Benefit–Cost Analysis; Ecosystem Services; Forestry; Nonmarket Valuation; Passive Use Value; Welfare

Further Reading

Krieger, D. 2001. *Economic Value of Forest Ecosystem Services: A Review.* Washington, D.C.: The Wilderness Society.

Loomis, J., and R. Richardson. 2000. *Economic Values of Protecting Roadless Areas in the United States. An Analysis Prepared for the Wilderness Society and the Heritage Forest Campaign.* Washington, D.C.: The Wilderness Society.

Office of Management and Budget (OMB). 2002. Stimulating Smarter Regulation: 2001 Report to Congress on the Costs and Benefits of Regulations and Unfunded Mandates on State, Local, and Tribal Entities. Washington, D.C.: Office of Information and Regulatory Affairs, OMB.

Pearce, D. W. 2001. The Economic Value of Forest Ecosystems. *Ecosystem Health* 7(4): 284–296.

U.S. Forest Service (USFS). 2000. Roadless Area Conservation: Final Environmental Impact Statement. USDA Forest Service, 1 B-4.

Association of Environmental and Resource Economists

The Association of Environmental and Resource Economists (AERE) is an international association for economists working on environmental and natural resources issues. AERE was founded in 1979 and has about 1,000 members. Most of the members hold the doctorate degree and work in academic institutions. AERE's goal is to promote communication among economists who are interested in environmental and natural resource economics. The major activities of the association are joint sponsorship of the World Congress of Environmental and Resource Economists, the AERE Summer Meeting, sponsorship of sessions at other conferences, the publication of two journals and the *AERE Newsletter*, and various honors and awards. AERE is governed by a president, president-elect, past president, vice president, secretary, treasurer and six elected board members. The AERE's Web address is http://www.aere.org.

The World Congress of Environmental and Resource Economists is jointly sponsored by AERE and the European Association of Environmental and Resource Economists. Locations alternate between North America and the rest of the world. It has been held in Venice (1998), Monterey (2002), Kyoto (2006), Montreal (2010), and Istanbul (2014). It is a large conference with over 500 paper presentations and participants from more than 50 countries. The annual AERE Summer Meeting is an extension of the AERE Workshop. Twenty-two workshops were held between 1985 and 2009. The workshops were small conferences with 10 or more paper presentations that focused on a specific topic such as energy, fisheries, or health. The first AERE workshop was held in Boulder and the last was held at Washington, D.C., and hosted by Resources for the Future in 2009. The inaugural AERE Summer Conference was held in Seattle in 2011 with 340 attendees. The AERE workshop lives on with thematic sponsored sessions within the summer conference. AERE also sponsors sessions at the Allied Social Science Associations annual meeting, Agricultural and Applied Economics Association annual meeting, and regional economics conferences such as the Southern Economic Association and Western Economic Association International.

The *Journal of Environmental Economics and Management* (JEEM) began publication in 1974 and it became official journal of AERE in 1983. JEEM publishes theoretical and empirical papers devoted to environmental and resource issues and is widely considered the top journal in the field. The November 2013 issue of JEEM was the last published as the official journal of AERE as the association plans to launch a new official journal, the *Journal of the Association of Environmental and Resource Economists*. *The Review of Environmental Economics and Policy* (REEP) publishes nontechnical articles that "fill the gap between traditional academic journals and the general interest press." Articles include symposia on a focused topic, those that survey the literature, and features such as policy monitor and individual reflections on the literature. The *AERE Newsletter* is published twice each year and contains a president's column, announcements, and essays.

AERE honors and awards are the Distinguished Service Award, Fellows, Outstanding Publication in JEEM, and the Publication of Enduring Quality. There have been eight recipients of the AERE Distinguished Service Award including founding members, JEEM editors, and the executive secretary. In 2005 AERE began to recognize members who have made significant contributions to the field with the AERE Fellows Award. Six members were awarded fellowships in 2005, 2006, and 2007 and three members have been awarded fellowships annually since. The Publication of Enduring Quality award is given to a publication that has had a lasting and significant contribution to the field. There have been 30 articles and books receiving the Publication of Enduring Quality Award since 1989. In 2009 AERE began to recognize the Outstanding Article in JEEM. All past recipients of AERE awards can be found on the AERE website (www .aere.org).

John C. Whitehead

See also: Fisheries Economics Associations; International Association for Energy Economics; Journals; United States Society of Ecological Economics

Further Reading

Krutilla, John V. 1980. Activation of the Association of Environmental and Resource Economists. *Journal of Environmental Economics and Management* 7(2): 77–80.

Russell, Clifford S. (compiler). 1995. *An Early History of the Association of Environmental and Resource Economists*. AERE Handbook, http://www.aere.org/about/documents/AEREHandbook2010.pdf

Asymmetric Information

Asymmetric information describes the situation where some agents have information relevant to a particular economic transaction that other agents do not. For example, consumers often do not have information about the sources of food products (i.e., where and how produced, genetic modification, etc.); regulators have less information about pollution control costs than do emitters of pollution; consumers' willingness to pay for public goods is important information in determining the optimal provision of these goods, but consumers are the only ones to know their own willingness to pay. These are only a few examples of situations where asymmetric information may be used strategically by the possessor. Such informational asymmetries may result in market failure, a situation where a free (unregulated) market does not provide the socially optimal allocation of resources. Relatively small informational asymmetries can have large impacts on market equilibria. Effective policy requires understanding and accounting for these asymmetries.

While early economists discussed asymmetric information issues, many dismissed the importance of the concept as simply a problem of transactions costs, arguing that the application of general economic principles would suffice in eliminating information problems. That is, the solution to the asymmetric information problem was to incorporate the costs of acquiring information into the traditional models, and previous welfare conclusions would remain valid.

However, information is not simply a transactions or input cost for a commodity that can be purchased in a market analogous to other goods and services. Information is similar to a public good in that it is nonrivalrous (one person's consumption of information does not prevent others from consuming the same information). It is also something that cannot be fully examined prior to being purchased. After all, once the information is known, what incentive is there for anyone to then decide to purchase the already known information?

Asymmetric information problems are pervasive in economics, including finance, public goods, industrial organization, health, labor, as well as natural resource and environmental economics. In environmental economics, for example, pollution control can be complicated by asymmetric information as the polluter may have superior information concerning pollution control costs and/or actual emissions.

How does asymmetric information reduce efficiency in markets? It can inhibit trades that would be most beneficial to involved parties. Akerlof's used car (lemon's) market is the classic example. Used car buyers do not know if a car is high or low quality, but the seller does, so there is an asymmetry in information. Of course the seller of the higher quality car signals high quality, but the problem is that the sellers of low quality cars have a profit incentive to signal that they are high quality. How does the consumer know the higher quality product? Buyers rationally pay a price based on expected quality of the car, leaving sellers with higher quality cars underpriced to the extent that sellers take higher quality used cars off the market (because the average compensation will be less than their actual value). The average quality of cars in the market is now lower, the prices buyers are willing to pay is now less based on this lower expected quality, and the cycle continues, potentially undermining the existence of the market. That is, gains from trade to both parties may be foregone due to the asymmetry of information, or trades that do occur may not be the best trades for the parties involved. This *adverse selection problem* is a result of asymmetric information related to a characteristic or quality.

How might efficiency losses due to informational asymmetries be mitigated? Akerlof suggested two potential solutions to the problem: screening and signaling. Screening includes direct expenditures on verification (e.g., used car inspection). Signaling involves expending resources to convince others of the quality (e.g., a college degree may signal the ability to learn). Other ways of mitigating the information problem include warranties (guarantees), licensing practices, chains, and designing mechanisms to align incentives to mitigate the informational asymmetry. Regardless of the incentive mechanisms, regulations, and/or ancillary markets (e.g., used car inspection, home inspection), the bottom line is that there is likely to be some efficiency loss due to the asymmetry of information. Those with superior information may have the opportunity to earn a rent as a result of this information. Understanding the nature of the asymmetry is critical to mitigating the efficiency loss through the design of rules in the market, the property rights structure, and/or government regulation.

Specific to environmental economics, consider a regulator who is tasked with designing a pollution control mechanism because the emissions impose a negative externality on those outside the transaction. Under perfect information, the optimal design would result in a level of pollution such that the marginal benefit from pollution control is equal to the marginal cost of control. But when the polluter has superior knowledge about the cost of abatement, not only can the optimum be impacted, but also the appropriate mechanism of regulating pollution quantities or prices. The regulator is then left to design policy or regulation based on his or her limited information. Through suitably designed regulation, the regulator may induce the firm to use its superior knowledge in the social interest, or at least mitigate rents from this information, and provide incentives for efficiency improvements.

Suppose pollution is emitted from numerous sources and aggregate emissions are capped to reduce emissions. Who should reduce pollution and by how much? Pollution control costs to society are minimized if those with the lowest abatement costs are the ones to reduce pollution. However, the regulator cannot observe the firms' costs of reducing pollution and all polluters have a profit incentive to claim they would face high emissions reductions costs. To ameliorate the information asymmetry, a policy that provides choice may be effective. An emissions permit market enables interested parties to buy and sell the right to pollute, but the number of permits in the market is restricted to meet the emissions cap. Those with abatement costs that are less than the market permit price reduce their pollution emissions. Those with relatively high abatement costs buy permits to pollute. If the permit market is perfectly competitive, the equilibrium permit price will equal the marginal abatement cost. With this approach the regulator delegates the pollution control decisions to the polluting firms and the firms will minimize costs of meeting the cap through buying and selling permits in the market. A U.S. policy example is the Clean Air Act Amendments (CAAA) of 1990, which, among other things, introduced marketable emission allowances (pollution permits) for SO_2 emissions. This departed from the traditional command-and-control type of environmental regulations through the mechanism of an allowance market.

In addition to the adverse selection form, where the information involves a characteristic or type, there are important asymmetries in information that may be affected by unobservable actions or choices of participants. This is the *moral hazard problem*. The classic example is insurance markets. The problem is that once something is insured, the insured may not have the incentive to exercise the appropriate level of care. In terms of pollution control, there are situations where the pollution source is unobserved (e.g., nonpoint source pollution). Conservation is another example. In both cases, without corrective action, the agent has the incentive to underperform. Adverse selection and moral hazard often occur in combination (e.g., pollution control and conservation). The CAAA provided incentives for electric utilities to control pollution and promote conservation (conservation also naturally controls pollution).

Robert H. Patrick

See also: Emissions Trading; Food Safety; Nonpoint Source Pollution; Regulation; Sulfur Dioxide Trading; Welfare

Further Reading

Akerlof, George A. 1970. The Market for Lemons: Quality Uncertainty and the Market Mechanism. *Quarterly Journal of Economics* 84(3):488–500.

Laffont, J. J., and J. Tirole. 1996. Pollution Permits and Environmental Innovation. *Journal of Public Economics* 62(1–2):127–140.

Shortle, J. S., and R. D. Horan. 2001. The Economics of Nonpoint Pollution Control. *Journal of Economic Surveys* 15(3):255–289.

Spulber, D. F. 1988. Optimal Environmental Regulation under Asymmetric Information. *Journal of Public Economics* 35(2):163–181.

Stiglitz, Joseph E. 2000. The Contributions of the Economics of Information to Twentieth Century Economics. *Quarterly Journal of Economics* 115(4):1441–1478.

Averting Behavior

When threatened with damage from environmental hazards, people sometimes act to reduce the damage that they are likely to incur. They may stay indoors on smoggy days or otherwise adjust daily activities to reduce exposure to ambient air pollution. They may purchase bottled water to avoid drinking from contaminated local water supplies. Aside from trying to reduce exposure to hazards, people may act to mitigate the damage caused by a given amount of exposure, for example by using medication or medical treatment to offset health effects of pollution exposure. Averting behavior (or defensive, mitigating, or protective behavior) refers to actions taken to defend against hazards, whether by reducing exposure or by offsetting effects of exposure. Defensive behavior can influence the effectiveness of some policies or programs. For instance, the success of hazard warnings such as smog alerts hinges on whether and how people adjust their behavior in response to information about hazards.

The existence of defensive behavior presents both a problem and an opportunity for estimating economic benefits of environmental improvement (or economic damages of environmental degradation). Ignoring averting behavior when it is present causes biased estimation, probably underestimation, of the physical and economic damages of pollution. But, in some situations, accounting for protective behavior can provide a means of estimating the damages of pollution or the benefits of pollution control.

To see how ignoring defensive behavior can bias estimation of pollution damages, consider estimating the economic damages of ambient air pollution. One component of the damage is the value of the asthma attacks caused by increased air pollution—some air pollutants exacerbate asthma. Estimating the resulting economic damages requires an estimate of the number of asthma attacks caused by air pollution. This estimate normally would be obtained by observing how many additional asthma attacks occur when air pollution worsens. If people with asthma engage in defensive behavior, however, and if the defensive behavior is effective, then some of the asthma attacks that pollution would otherwise have caused are averted. Asthma attacks that do not occur are not observed, and consequently the number asthma attacks attributed to air pollution is understated. With the number of asthma exacerbations underestimated, the economic damages are understated as well.

The conclusion that ignoring averting behavior can bias estimates of economic damages of pollution has prompted economists to investigate the extent to which people actually take action to defend against pollution hazards. Researchers have examined (1) whether people restrict outdoor activities in response to increased air pollution or to public information about air pollution hazards; (2) whether people take averting actions when water supplies are contaminated; (3) whether homeowners mitigate hazards from radon gas; and (4) whether survey respondents report that they change their behavior when pollution is high. Results of these studies suggest that many people take averting actions; defensive behavior increases when pollution increases, and estimators of effects of pollution that ignore averting actions are biased. One recent study estimated that adjustments in outdoor activities in response to smog alerts reduced the number of hospital admissions for asthma caused by an air pollutant by 60 percent.

Whereas ignoring averting behavior can bias estimation of economic damages of pollution, accounting for protective behavior sometimes can provide a means of estimating damages. To illustrate, suppose that an individual spends $500 in money and time to boil water and buy bottled water during a temporary but extended incident of contaminated water supplies. Assume rational behavior: that people will defend against pollution as long as the subjective benefits of defensive action exceed the costs. Then momentarily ignoring the joint production problem discussed later, the resident's averting behavior reveals that avoiding the water contamination is worth at least $500 to her. In short, expenditure on averting action provides information about the economic damages of water contamination.

Economists have estimated benefits of avoiding water contamination based on costs of averting actions such as purchasing bottled water, boiling or treating water, hauling water from an alternate source, or installing water filtration systems. They have estimated benefits of reduced air pollution by examining expenditures on medical care that mitigate adverse health effects of air pollution exposure. They have estimated benefits of reducing risks of skin cancer from stratospheric ozone depletion based on averting expenditures for sunscreen lotion. In related work, economists have estimated benefits of reduced risk of death by considering consumer purchases and use of safety equipment like motorcycle and bicycle helmets.

Although information on averting behavior has been used to estimate economic benefits in a variety of contexts, there are three serious obstacles to obtaining accurate benefit estimates in this way. The first is the joint production problem that occurs when a protective behavior jointly produces additional benefits or costs beyond its impact on mitigating pollution damages. For example, people may have motivations for buying bottled water, such as taste or convenience, that have nothing to do with avoiding contaminated water supplies. Spending on bottled water overstates averting expenditure, because part of the spending is attributable to the joint benefits of taste and convenience rather than to the avoidance of contamination. Benefit estimation requires isolating the part of expenditure that should be attributed to avoidance, but doing so is difficult in the presence of joint production.

The second obstacle to accurate benefit estimation based on defensive behavior is that many averting actions do not have an easily determined price, complicating measurement of averting expenditure. For example, protective behavior may require time, and value of time is uncertain, particularly for persons not in the labor force. The price of medical care also is difficult to determine, and it is even less clear what price would apply when a person avoids ambient air pollution by limiting outdoor activities.

The third obstacle concerns estimating the effectiveness of averting behavior, for example estimating how many asthma attacks are avoided by adjusting daily activities, or how many cases of illness are avoided by defending against contaminated water supplies. To illustrate the problem, suppose that persons who for unobserved reasons are particularly susceptible to experience poor health outcomes are more likely than others to take averting action. In that case, one would expect the association between defensive behavior and health to understate the true effect of defensive behavior.

Mark Dickie

See also: Air Pollution; Benefit–Cost Analysis; Nonmarket Valuation; Health; Information Disclosure; Risk and Uncertainty

Further Reading

Blomquist, G.C. 2004. Self-Protection and Averting Behavior, Values of Statistical Lives, and Benefit Cost Analysis of Environmental Policy. *Review of Economics of the Household* 2(1): 89–110.

Dickie, M. 2003. Defensive Behavior and Damage Cost Methods. pp. 395–444 in *A Primer on Nonmarket Valuation*, P.A. Champ, K.J. Boyle, and T.C. Brown (editors). Dordrecht: Kluwer Academic.

B

Baumol, William J.

William Baumol was born February 26, 1922, in New York City. After receiving his BSc from the College of the City of New York in 1942, he undertook graduate study at the London School of Economics, earning his PhD in 1949. He taught at Princeton University for 43 years, where he is now professor emeritus and senior research economist. He has also taught at New York University for over 36 years, where he currently holds the Harold Price Professorship of Entrepreneurship in the Stern School of Business. Professor Baumol is the author of more than 40 scholarly books, and has written over 500 articles published in peer-reviewed journals as well as the popular media. Among his many honors and awards, he was elected fellow of the Econometric Society in 1953, fellow of the American Academy of Arts and Sciences in 1971, and distinguished fellow of the American Economic Association in 1982.

Baumol's research in economics has covered diverse areas of the discipline, including, among others, entrepreneurship and innovation, economic growth, industrial organization, and antitrust economics and regulation. His seminal contributions include a model of the transactions demand for money, the sales-revenue maximization model, an analysis of cost disease, the theory of contestable markets, and the concept of super-fairness. Most recently, Baumol has focused on entrepreneurship and innovation, *The Economist* magazine remarking that, "Thanks to Mr. Baumol's own painstaking efforts, economists now have a bit more room for entrepreneurs in their theories . . ." (March 9, 2006).

In the field of environmental economics, Professor Baumol is best known for his textbook on the theory of environmental policy, coauthored with Wallace Oates. First published in 1975, this book has become a standard reference in many graduate-level classes in environmental economics due to its comprehensive coverage of both the theory of externalities and the design of environmental policy, with chapters on topics such as imperfect competition and externalities, optimal pricing of exhaustible resources, marketable emissions permits, and international environmental issues.

Specifically, Chapter 8 of the book, drawing on his joint work with David Bradford concerns Professor Baumol's major contribution to environmental economics— understanding the relationship between externalities and the technical concept of nonconvexities in production sets. If an industry imposes a large enough negative externality on another industry, the normal conditions for maximizing social welfare break down due to the fact that the production set becomes non-convex, that is, the production possibilities frontier is no longer concave in shape. Instead of the normal unique equilibrium where market-clearing prices ensure that a concave production possibilities frontier is tangent to a convex community indifference curve, there are potentially many local equilibrium outcomes in the presence of externalities. In such a setting, market processes may not result in a socially optimal outcome; instead the point at which an economy ends up will have to be chosen collectively. As a consequence, Pigouvian taxes, designed to internalize the social costs of an externality, may actually move the economy away from a social optimum.

Ian M. Sheldon

See also: Externality; Pigouvian Taxes; Welfare

Further Reading

Baumol, W. J. 2010. On the Increasing Role of Economic Research in Management of Resources and Protection of the Environment. *Annual Review of Resource Economics* 2(1): 1–11.

Baumol, W. J. and D. F. Bradford. 1972. Detrimental Externalities and Non-Convexity of the Production Set. *Economica* XXXIX: 160–176.

Baumol, W. J. and W. E. Oates. 1988. *The Theory of Environmental Policy*, 2nd ed. Cambridge: Cambridge University Press.

Behavioral Economics

Environmental economics, more so than other areas of economics, faces the problem of allocating scarce resources with little to no help from markets. Indeed, environmental economics is largely defined by market failures—when missing and incomplete markets lead to outcomes that are not efficient and not socially optimal. The task for environmental economics is to use economic theory to prescribe cost-effective environmental policies that improves upon the failure of markets. The efforts have led to meaningful improvements in environmental management, but the prescriptions have relied heavily on theories that assume people behave in a perfectly rational and self-interested manner. However, research has demonstrated quite clearly that people's behavioral patterns can be quite different than those predicted by so-called rational choice theory. People are not perfectly rational, do not possess unwavering willpower, and are not absolutely self-interested.

If these attributes only caused people to deviate from theory in a random manner, theory could still provide accurate predictions on average. But in many settings, particularly those related to environmental policy, behavior deviates from theory in systematic and predictable ways. For example, we tend to care are too much about small chances and too little about future outcomes, we are concerned with others and about our relative standing to them, and our decisions are substantially influenced by cues, frames, and default options. Such behavioral tendencies might not matter too much in some situations, but to the extent that actual behavior patterns deviate from theoretical predictions, policies that are guided by theories assuming perfect rationality and self-interest will be less effective and possibly counterproductive.

Behavioral economics seeks to close the gap between behavior and theory by understanding the imperfect behavior that theory tends to ignore and using the knowledge to improve the precision of theory and effectiveness of policy. Increasingly, researchers and policymakers are recognizing the importance of augmenting economic models to incorporate behavioral elements. In 2010, the British government established the Behavioral Insights Team to help apply knowledge from research in the behavioral sciences to improve public policies. Results have been very positive. Using behavioral insights, projects have increased household investment in energy efficiency measures, improved the rate of regulatory compliance, and dramatically shortened the time for people using unemployment services to find a job. With such success, the government moved to require that behavioral science be included in the required curriculum for civil servants.

Behavioral economics has a lot to say about how society works, but it is particularly relevant to the concerns of environmental economics because the gap between behavior and theory is exacerbated by missing and incomplete markets. This is because rationality is not an individual concept based on self-reflection; rather it is a social construct that relies on active exchange that aggregates and diffuses information. In the absence of well-functioning markets, decisions are more isolated and therefore more susceptible to our cognitive limits and biases. Indeed, if environmental economics is concerned with imperfect markets, behavioral economics is concerned with imperfect behavior. And the two imperfections are not autonomous. Researchers and policymakers have increasingly recognized the need to consider both market and behavioral imperfections simultaneously, which has led to the emergence of research at the confluence of behavioral and environmental economics. This work, generally referred to as behavioral environmental economics, attempts to improve our understanding of how to design better mechanisms and policies by compensating for market imperfections while also accounting for behavioral imperfections.

To illustrate the relevance of behavioral environmental economics, consider the well-documented energy paradox. Research and field studies consistently find that people buy fewer energy conservation products than predicted by standard models. The energy paradox corresponds to behavioral research that finds that people discount the future too much, exhibit a bias for the status quo, and rely on heuristics for complicated calculations. The policy implication is that people might not respond as expected to changes in energy prices, which implies that a carbon tax based on standard models likely will fall short of its goals. Behavioral research can help identify the best way to make the policy more effective—higher tax rates, complementary mechanisms like energy efficiency labels, or alternative approaches like energy efficiency standards.

Behavioral economics has also revealed relevant insights about how people perceive and respond to environmental risk. Research shows that people systematically misjudge risk, in particular those with small chances and severe outcomes. Also, people tend to dismiss risk too easily if it is shared by society, revealed gradually and realized in the future. These misperceptions about risk can lead to inefficient levels of insurance and protection, as well as incorrect valuations for environmental risks. And considering the risk characteristics of climate change, these behavioral tendencies help explain the difficulty of implementing meaningful climate policy.

A success story for behavioral environmental economics is the successful implementation of a congestion charge in Stockholm. The consistent public opposition to Pigouvian instruments is striking. Energy taxes were rejected by the United States in 1993 and by Switzerland in 2000, while a congestion charge was rejected by Edinburgh in 2005 and by New York City in 2008. These outcomes could be a result of rational economic and political calculations, but experimental research indicates behavioral biases play a significant role in the opposition. By considering people's tendencies, Stockholm policymakers were able to implement a congestion charge via a public referendum in 2006. To mitigate behavioral biases, the policy prescribed a six-month trial period before the referendum to allow people the opportunity to experience the effects of the mechanism. It worked. The trial run shifted public support by nearly 20 percentage points, which led to an approval that seemed unlikely prior to the trial run.

Behavioral research has contributed a great deal to our general understanding of environmental management and policy. People are influenced by context and framing, and they care about their relative standing in addition to their absolute position. Consequently, the prospects of policy can depend on labels, reference points, cultural and social norms, and the distribution of costs and benefits. Research also finds behavioral responses can differ across different types of incentives; in particular, people's good intentions can be diminished with the introduction of monetary incentives. Such behavioral findings have broad implications. For instance, management of local environmental resources often can benefit from granting more authority to local stakeholders who participate in a collaborative and shared process, and conversely, can be harmed by exogenously imposing incentives and institutions.

In the end, behavioral environmental economics recognizes that things are complex. Neither people nor markets live up to the ideals presumed by standard theory.

Ignoring either of these facts makes things easier, but it leaves the door open for ineffective and counterproductive policies. The challenge for behavioral environmental economics is to gain a more comprehensive understanding of the complexities that exist in people and markets, and in turn use that knowledge to refine theory and improve policy.

Todd L. Cherry

See also: Carbon Pricing; Energy Efficiency; Ostrom, Elinor; Pigouvian Taxes

Further Reading
Ostrom, E. 1998. A Behavioral Approach to the Rational Choice Theory of Collective Action. *American Political Science Review* 92(1): 1–22.

Shogren, J., and L. Taylor. 2008. On Behavioral-Environmental Economics. *Review of Environmental Economics and Policy* 2(1): 26–44.

Benefit–Cost Analysis

The notion that a zero pollution objective is not necessarily ideal policy is one of the more difficult concepts for environmental economists to convey. After all, if pollution is bad should we not design policy to completely eliminate it? The answer lies in understanding scarcity: we have unlimited wants, but live in a world with limited means. Economists in general study how people make decisions when faced with scarcity. Scarcity implies that resources devoted to one end are not available to meet another; hence there is an opportunity cost of any action. For both individuals and societies scarcity necessitates trade-offs, and the reality of trade-offs can make the complete elimination of pollution undesirable. Once this is acknowledged the pertinent question becomes how much pollution should be eliminated. To help provide answers economists use an analytical tool called benefit–cost analysis.

Benefit–cost analysis provides an organizational framework for identifying, quantifying, and comparing the costs and benefits (measured in dollars) of a proposed policy action. The final decision is informed (though not necessarily determined) by a comparison of the total costs and benefits. The benefits of environmental regulations can include, for example, reduced human and wildlife mortality, improved water quality, species preservation, and better recreation opportunities. The costs are usually reflected in higher prices for consumer goods, higher taxes, and direct government expenditures. The costs are market effects readily measured in dollars, while the benefits are nonmarket effects for which dollar values are not available.

Environmental economists tend to favor benefit–cost analysis because of the discipline and transparency it provides in evaluating policy options. It is easy to evaluate absolutes. Most would agree that reducing nitrogen contamination of groundwater wells, limiting the occurrence of code red ozone alerts, and preserving habitat for grizzly bears are worthy goals. Determining the relative merits of any one of these compared to the others, or compared to nonenvironmental goals such as improving public education, is much more daunting. Because policymaking is ultimately about evaluating the relative merits of different actions some mechanism is needed to rank the alternatives. Without the discipline of benefit–cost analysis it is not clear how the interests, claims, and opinions of parties affected by a proposed regulation can be examined and compared. Criterion such as moral or fair do not lend themselves well to comparison and are subject to wide-ranging interpretation. Benefit–cost analysis is far from perfect, but it demands a level of objectivity and specificity that are necessary components of good decision making.

In theory, the process of benefit–cost analysis is straightforward. In evaluating any environmental action or other public intervention we need only list out the potential costs and benefits of the action, assign monetary measures for each category in the list, add them up and compare them, and if the benefits are greater than the costs the action is worth it from an efficiency perspective. In practice each of these steps is fraught with difficulty. In some respects qualitatively listing the categories of benefits and costs is the easiest part. For example, consider the benefits and costs of dam removal from western streams. The benefits can include improved stream ecology, enhanced wildlife populations, and better moving water recreation opportunities. The costs include loss of electricity generation, flood control, and flat water recreation. These lists, however, are almost certainly incomplete. Most policy actions have some degree of uncertainty and unintended consequences. In listing the categories practitioners try to focus on the first order effects, while acknowledging ex ante uncertainty.

Assigning monetary values to the categories is the most difficult and controversial of the steps in benefit–cost analysis. It is necessary, however, for comparison of benefit and costs in the same units. Since many, often most, of the benefit and cost categories are nonmarket—which is to say they are not bought and sold at market prices—an extra step is needed to assess the dollar values indirectly. Research in nonmarket valuation has developed fairly sophisticated theoretical and empirical methods for describing and measuring nonmarket values. Economic research has examined, for example, the value of flat water versus moving water recreation, the existence of particular wildlife populations, and benefits of ecosystem services such as flood control. Estimates of these types of environmental services are the building blocks needed for assigning monetary values to nonmarket services.

Once the benefits and costs are measured in dollar terms an additional difficulty must be addressed. Typically benefits and costs do not occur at the same time. Again referring to the dam removal example, electricity generation will be lost immediately but wildlife populations may take years to recover. In this case the cost occurs right now, but the benefit is not available until later. Compare this to a monetary transaction. A hundred dollars awarded today is not the same as a hundred dollars awarded two years from today. To compare the two, adjustment for the interest potential is necessary. This is similarly needed for benefit–cost analysis. If we want to compare benefits and costs occurring at different time scales discounting is needed to express future costs or benefits at today's equivalent value. The practice of discounting is straightforward, but no agreement exists on what the correct discount rate is. The choice of discount rate can often determine whether net benefits are found to be positive or negative.

Once each step in the process has been addressed and the discounted costs and benefits calculated, there remains the challenge of interpretation. Benefit–cost analysis uses a very narrow criterion for determining the desirability of an action. The focus is on efficiency, and nothing is said about distribution or fairness: from an economic theory perspective an action would pass the benefit–cost test if all of the benefits accrued to one wealthy person and the costs were borne by the most disadvantaged members of society. Most members of society would agree this would not be a desirable outcome. Thus benefit–cost analysis should not be the sole determinant of a decision, but rather one of several used to summarize available information.

So how is benefit–cost analysis done in practice day to day? There is a large reliance on off-the-shelf benefit and cost estimates rather than original studies due to time and money constraints. Much of the work is qualified: since it is usually impossible within time limits to account for all potential costs and benefits analysts provide monetary estimates for categories that can be determined and acknowledge those that cannot be measured. Thus a full accounting of even the efficiency properties of an action is usually beyond reach. Nevertheless, the structure and transparency the benefit–cost analysis process provides when conducted carefully can organize and help discipline public decision making.

Dan Phaneuf

See also: Discounting; Executive Order 12291; *Guidelines for Preparing Economic Analyses;* Nonmarket Valuation; Welfare; Welfare and Equity

Further Reading

Atkinson, G., and S. Mourato. 2008. Environmental Cost–Benefit Analysis. *Annual Review of Environment and Resources* 33:317–344.

Boardman, A. E., D. Greenberg, A. Vining, and D. Weimer. 2010. *Cost-Benefit Analysis*, 4th ed. Upper Saddle River, NJ: Prentice Hall.

Benefit–Cost Analysis of the Clean Air Act

The Clean Air Act Amendments of 1990 made several important changes to U.S. clean air laws. Most notably, the 1990 amendments introduced the innovative sulfur dioxide emissions trading system with the goal, at the time, of substantially reducing acid rain. The amendments also instituted a new technology-based mechanism for regulating emissions of many cancer-causing and otherwise highly toxic pollutants, known as air toxics, and imposed new requirements to help cities and counties make further progress toward meeting federally established ambient air quality standards for the six pervasive air pollutants commonly referred to as the Clean Air Act's criteria pollutants.

Along with these major changes, the 1990 amendments required the U.S. Environmental Protection Agency (EPA) to develop, for the first time, a series of comprehensive benefit–cost analyses of the historical and prospective Clean Air Act provisions, and report the results formally to Congress and the public. The question Congress asked was: "How do the overall health, welfare, ecological, and economic benefits of Clean Air Act programs compare to the costs of these programs?" The resulting studies have been among the most far-reaching and innovative benefit–cost analyses ever conducted, and they showed that the investments the country has made (and will make) in air quality have yielded (and will continue to yield) economic benefits through improvements in human health, visibility, and ecological health that far exceed their costs. The study series applied the best techniques and data available to economists, epidemiologists, engineers, and policy analysts, and received thorough and public review by multiple panels of independent experts.

The sheer scope of the series of analyses, known widely as the Section 812 studies in reference to the section of the 1990 Clean Air Act Amendments requiring the studies, is unprecedented in U.S. environmental law. The series of reports cover provisions authorized by federal action over a five-decade period, including the landmark Clean Air Act of 1970, major amendments in 1977, and all provisions of the 1990 amendments as implemented through 2020. The economics of air quality over this 50-year period are addressed through three reports: the Retrospective Analysis addressed benefits and costs from 1970 to 1990, the First Prospective addressed the period 1990 to 2010, and the Second Prospective addressed the period 1990 to 2020; each of which adopted the formal title "The Benefits and Costs of the Clean Air Act . . ." plus a reference to the time period covered. The historical perspective of the Retrospective Analysis allowed EPA to use a survey of incurred direct compliance costs for the Act, and to employ a computable general equilibrium model to assess broader macroeconomic implications. The prospective analyses relied on projections of compliance costs based on modeling of least-cost compliance strategies and (mostly) current technologies.

Developing scenarios for the benefit–cost comparison is one of the most important aspects of large cost–benefit studies: benefits and costs should be measured with respect to carefully defined and internally consistent scenarios representing two alternative states of the world; in this case, with and without a set of Clean Air Act provisions. The analytical sequence then involves estimation of direct costs, which is typically based on reported compliance expenditures—or projected estimates of costs for technologies and consumer adjustments in behavior—necessary to achieve requisite reductions in air pollutant emissions. Estimating benefits is typically more laborious, and includes modeling air quality under alternative emissions scenarios; estimating changes in health (e.g., reduced mortality and sickness) and welfare (e.g., enhanced visibility) outcomes associated with air quality differences; and economic valuation of these health and welfare changes.

In the second prospective study, "The Benefits and Costs of the Clean Air Act from 1990 to 2020," annual direct costs for the central case were estimated to be about $65 billion, but benefits were estimated to be approximately $2 trillion, exceeding costs by more than 30 times. Most of the benefits represent reductions in premature mortality, which is associated by epidemiologists with reduced exposures of populations to fine particulate matter, very small particles that can penetrate deeply into the lungs. The study estimates that the 1990 Clean Air Act Amendment programs achieve reductions in premature mortality risks equivalent to saving approximately 235,000 individuals by 2020. These premature mortality risk reductions were characterized in economic terms using EPA's standard value of statistical life of $7.4 million for 1990 (which when adjusted for growth in income yields an estimate of $8.9 million in 2020). Critics of the study question the magnitude and the valuation of the estimated reductions in premature mortality risk. Some claim one or both of these estimates are too high, though other critics argue one or both factors could be too low.

In the report, EPA acknowledges that an ideal measure of the value of reducing premature mortality would take into account certain characteristics of the individuals most susceptible to succumbing to air pollution, such as advanced age and compromised health status, as well as elements of the air pollution risk, such as its involuntary nature. EPA notes that a survival curve approach might provide a theoretically preferred method for valuing the economic benefits of reduced risk of premature mortality associated with reducing air pollution, but that alternative approach is currently infeasible because it does not align well with current estimates of individual willingness to pay to avoid mortal risks.

Three other aspects of the study are unusual in benefit–cost analysis of regulations. First, the comprehensiveness of the study provides an ability to look at synergistic and antagonistic effects in physical systems, an effect which is important in atmospheric chemistry. For example, nitrogen and sulfur oxides interact in complex ways to form fine particles in the atmosphere; and nitrogen oxides are a precursor of ambient ozone but, when nitrogen oxide concentrations are high, can actually destroy ozone. As a result, benefit–cost analysis for air pollution is not as simple as developing a marginal damage curve for each pollutant—instead, the marginal effect of additional emissions depends critically on where on the curve a given policy's effects are manifest, with respect to multiple pollutant concentrations.

Second, the studies were consistently reviewed by leading environmental economists and other specialists organized by EPA's Science Advisory Board as a panel specifically charged with providing peer review of the Section 812 reports. Known as the Advisory Council on Clean Air Compliance Analysis (Council), the review board carefully considered such issues as the economic valuation and health effects estimation approach for premature mortality, and ultimately supported EPA's approach. Third, the 1990 Clean Air Act Amendments required EPA to attempt to value benefits wherever possible, and to avoid assuming a default value of $0 for benefit categories where data are thin. This led to a high degree of exploration of benefits valuation in areas where it is more difficult to be fully confident—for example, cancerous effects of air toxics and ecological service flow valuation. Some of these explorations also led to improvements in the standard benefits valuation approach used at EPA, such as incorporating the longitudinal effect of income on willingness to pay (WTP), designing new benefits transfers techniques for visibility valuation, and incorporating the effect of learning by doing in estimating compliance costs.

Key challenges and frontiers established by the studies include use of macroeconomic models (computable general equilibrium models) to look at economy-wide economic impacts, for both compliance costs and key benefits categories, and development of a population simulation approach as a first step in improving estimation and valuation of avoided premature mortality. The study has proved useful to EPA in many areas, both for current practice of regulatory economic analyses and establishing new methods and data to support EPA's activities.

Jim DeMocker and Jim Neumann

See also: Benefit–Cost Analysis; Benefit Transfer; Clean Air Act; *Guidelines for Preparing Economic Analyses;* Pollution Abatement Costs; Sulfur Dioxide Trading

Further Reading

U.S. Environmental Protection Agency, *The Benefits and Costs of the Clean Air Act* main website: http://www.epa.gov/oar/sect812.

U.S. Environmental Protection Agency. 2011. *The Benefits and Costs of the Clean Air Act from 1990 to 2020: Full Report.* Washington, D.C. April.

U.S. Environmental Protection Agency. 2011. *The Benefits and Costs of the Clean Air Act from 1990 to 2020: Summary Report.* Washington, D.C. March.

Benefit Transfer

Benefit transfer is the use of research results from preexisting primary studies at one or more sites or contexts (often called study sites) to predict welfare estimates such as willingness to pay or related information (e.g., benefits, costs, elasticities, marginal effects) for other, typically unstudied sites or contexts (often called policy sites). Benefit transfer provides a means to generate information required for policy analysis when primary research is infeasible. Examples might include estimates of demand responses to price changes in recreation, the public's willingness to pay for cleaner water, the passive use value of whales, or the social cost of obesity or climate change, among many others. Benefit transfers are most often used when process constraints (e.g., time, funding, or informational needs) preclude original research, so that off-the-shelf estimates must be used instead. For example, benefit–cost analyses required for U.S. government rulemaking often occur under time, funding, and regulatory constraints. As a result, benefit transfer is often used to provide needed information.

There are many types of benefit transfer; these are generally grouped into the broad categories of unit value transfer and function transfer. Unit value transfers include the transfer of a single unadjusted value, a value adjusted according to attributes of the policy context (e.g., income or time), a measure of central tendency (e.g., mean or median value), or a range of estimates from a set of prior studies. Function transfers, in contrast, derive needed information using an estimated function from original research, a meta-analysis function that synthesizes results across multiple research studies, or a preference calibration approach that constructs a structural utility model linking results from two or more prior studies. In all function transfers, additional information on the policy context is needed in order to adjust the transferred function from the study context to the policy context. To date, the transfer literature generally favors function transfers over unit value transfers given they provide greater flexibility in adapting existing information to new contexts, although unit value transfers can perform well if the study and policy contexts are very similar.

Most benefit transfers begin by defining the informational needs and characteristics of a policy site, including the type of value needed, the affected resource and population, and the ways in which resource changes affect the relevant population. The literature or other sources are then searched for studies with similar characteristics and contexts that provide the needed information. Once these studies are located, models are developed to transfer information from the existing studies to the needed policy context.

Benefit transfers are subject to a variety of potential errors. These are grouped into two categories—measurement error and generalization error. Measurement errors occur when the value estimated by original research, based on a sample from a population, does not reflect that population's value—these errors are associated with the original research from which transfer estimates are derived. Generalization or transfer errors, in contrast, are associated with the transfer process itself. Generalization errors are related to such factors as differences between study and policy sites (and populations), the commensurability of nonmarket goods and policy contexts, and the transfer method applied. Most evaluations of benefit transfer focus on transfer error since it is assumed that original research provides unbiased estimates, or that biased estimates have been filtered out during the selection of studies for transfer.

Transfers are generally evaluated in terms of predictive accuracy and transfer validity, both of which involve the size of transfer errors. A transfer accurately predicts a value estimate when the transfer error is small. In contrast, transfer validity requires that value estimates or other characteristics (e.g., parameter estimates, resources, and markets) are statistically the same (i.e., there is no statistically significant transfer error). For example, predictive accuracy is achieved when the consumer surplus estimate from recreation demand curves at a study site and policy site are similar. Transfer validity is achieved when this surplus estimate, or related estimates, such as the income elasticity from the demand curves, are statistically identical.

In actual transfer applications the true value of the topic of interest is unknown. For this reason, out-of-sample predictive performance, or convergent validity testing, has been the focus of past assessments of validity. That is, transferred estimates are compared to an estimate provided by original research on the situation in question. Results from such tests are mixed, with an average transfer error of 35 percent. Because the need for predictive accuracy and transfer validity can vary across applications, there is no universal test or acceptable error level that dictates the suitability of benefit transfer. For example, some contexts might require a high degree of accuracy (e.g., in litigation), while other contexts require statistical validity. In still other cases a lower degree of accuracy might be acceptable (e.g., in prescreening of available projects).

Some patterns in benefit transfer performance have emerged—errors are often smaller in cases where sites and populations are similar. This requires similarity across multiple relevant dimensions. For example, the definition of the affected commodity (i.e., the good, service, or resource) between the study context and the policy context should be consistent—apples should generally be compared to apples. However, given the ways in which nonmarket values are formed, expressed, and measured, original research outcomes over seemingly similar commodities can sometimes have very different value estimates; or conversely, seemingly dissimilar commodities may have value estimates that are consistent with each other. Other factors that can affect original research outcomes include the underlying policy process through which change is realized, available substitutes and complements, attributes of local historical or cultural context, and other factors. Thus, scaling up and scaling down of transferred estimates is often subjective.

There must also be similarity in the scope of the market being evaluated (e.g., as it pertains to the spatial distribution of values), or adjustments must be made to account for any differences. Unfortunately, this is one area that the literature often fails to consider in sufficient detail. For example, original research often provides information on a per person or a per household basis for a predefined and sampled population, but does not evaluate the extent of the market or the total size or geographic extent of the population that holds those values.

Ultimately, the quality of benefit transfers depends not only on the availability of accurate and valid transfer methods, but also on the quality of the underlying valuation research from which these transfers are drawn. Confidence in and applicability of benefit transfer is limited by the quality, breadth, and depth of existing valuation research. Benefit transfer practitioners must also be able to identify and interpret relevant primary studies. For individuals less familiar with economic methods and models, it may be difficult to identify, access, and interpret suitable original research. Hence, improvements in benefit transfer require improvement in the quality and extent of valuation research, as well as benefit transfer practitioners' abilities to access and interpret the provided information. Although valuation databases such as the Environmental Valuation Reference Inventory can help practitioners identify research studies suitable for transfer, these databases are only as good or as comprehensive as the research studies they include. Conditions are improving, however, as analysts are becoming increasingly aware of the challenges to conducting valid and accurate transfers, the literature continues to suggest solutions and improved methods, and valuation databases have made relevant valuation results increasingly available.

Randall S. Rosenberger and Robert J. Johnston

See also: Benefit–Cost Analysis; Meta-Analysis; Nonmarket Valuation

Further Reading

Johnston, R. J., and R. S. Rosenberger. 2010. Methods, Trends and Controversies in Contemporary Benefit Transfer. *Journal of Economic Surveys* 24(3): 479–510.

Rosenberger, R. S. and J. B. Loomis. 2003. Benefit Transfer, in P. A. Champ, K. J. Boyle and T. C. Brown (editors), *A Primer on Nonmarket Valuation*, pp. 445–482. Dordrecht: Kluwer.

Biodiversity

Biodiversity does not have a single, clear definition. The United Nations Convention on Biological Diversity defines biodiversity as the variability among living organisms from all sources including, inter alia, terrestrial, marine, and other aquatic ecosystems and the ecological complexes of which they are part; this includes diversity within species, between species, and of ecosystems. Genetic diversity is a range of genetic characteristics within a species and species diversity is the measure of different types of organisms at the community level, ecosystem, or higher level of ecological organization. Commonly, species diversity serves as a proxy for biodiversity. Species diversity has two major components: species richness and species evenness. Species richness is the total number of species within a community. Species evenness is the relative abundance with which each species is represented in an area.

In addition to definitional difficulties, there exists great uncertainty with regard to the estimate of the number of species. This level of uncertainty is nontrivial. Approximately 8.7 million species exist globally with only 14 percent or 1.2 million species described. Given this high level of uncertainty, taxonomic surveys are important instruments in the understanding of biodiversity. Unfortunately, taxonomic surveys are time-consuming and costly.

Economists are interested in biodiversity because variability among living things provides important benefits but is threatened by human activity. Cultural values, especially for indigenous peoples, recreational opportunities, regulation of nutrient cycles, carbon sequestration, natural pest control, pollination, genetic resources, food, and fuelwood are among the benefits derived from biodiversity. In addition to the use value motives for biodiversity preservation, there are preservation motives that are based on passive use value and future unknown use values. With passive use value, individuals are better off by simply knowing that certain species and ecosystems exist, unrelated to any current or expected future usage. Because future needs are unpredictable, there is also a significant option value associated with biodiversity. For example, the Pacific yew tree, once considered to be tree of little commercial value, was crucial in the development of the anticancer drug Taxol. The irreversible destruction of species, such as the Pacific yew tree, would have precluded the discovery of the previously unknown benefits.

Similar to the definitions and measures for biodiversity, the threats to biodiversity are also numerous and include habitat destruction, invasive species, overexploited resources, pollution, and climate change. Habitat destruction, or modification due to expansion of human populations and human activities, is the greatest threat to biodiversity. Habitat destruction may be carried out in a complete form where an area of land is directly developed or may be done in a partial form (fragmentation). Habitat fragmentation occurs where relatively continuous geographic areas are split into smaller discontinuous areas, which may be too small to maintain viable native populations. Invasive and alien species can be extremely detrimental to biodiversity. For example, the introduction of the Nile perch to Lake Victoria was the cause of possibly the largest single vertebrate extinction occurrence in the 20th century. Mainly due to Nile perch predation, it is estimated that 200 of 300 of the endemic *Haplochromine cichlids* species have gone extinct or are threatened by extinction. Climate change adversely affects biodiversity by altering the distribution or range of many terrestrial species and causing stress on other species. It also impacts marine systems by changing the timing and length of the spring bloom of phytoplankton and ocean chemistry. Finally, biodiversity is threatened by pollution. For example, pollution in the form of agricultural runoff, especially nitrates, is responsible for the decline and/or the extinction of certain amphibian species.

In an ideal world, decisions regarding biodiversity would be addressed with benefit–cost analysis with certainty and complete information. Unfortunately, this is not the case. There is evidence that biodiversity expenditures are based on intuition or the ranking of the projects without the consideration of costs. Also, conservation efforts are greatly affected by the characteristics of the species and the public's knowledge of the species. Individuals are more willing to donate to conservation efforts if they are familiar with the species or perceive the species to be attractive. As a result, certain threatened species, including many invertebrates that play critical roles in ecosystem function, are underrepresented in conservation efforts.

Although the preservation of biodiversity and climate change are considered to be the two most significant environmental issues today, both are also plagued by underprovision and the complexities associated with global public goods. Since biodiversity is a normal good, richer countries have a greater willingness and ability to preserve biodiversity and poorer countries have the incentive to convert areas of biodiversity into pasture and arable land. However, areas of rich biodiversity (e.g., rainforests and coral reefs) tend to be located in poorer countries. This discrepancy in the distribution of monetary and species wealth has prompted various nations and nongovernmental organizations to engage in environmental assistance in the form of financial transfers and technical expertise. However, many biodiversity projects are beset with the weak enforcement of property rights, poor monitoring, and other factors that reduce the effectiveness of these efforts.

Paul E. Chambers

See also: Climate Change Impacts; Invasive Species; Passive Use Value; Public Goods; Tropical Rain Forests

Further Reading

Ferraro, Paul J. 2003. Assigning Priority to Environmental Policy Interventions in a Heterogeneous World. *Journal of Policy Analysis and Management* 22(1): 27–43.

Ferraro, Paul J., and Subhrendu K. Pattanayak. 2006. Money for Nothing? A Call for Empirical Evaluation of Biodiversity Conservation Investments. *PLoS Biology* 4: e105.

Metrick, Andrew, and Martin L. Weitzman. 1998. Conflicts and Choices in Biodiversity Preservation. *Journal of Economic Perspectives* 12.3: 21–34.

Solow, Andrew, Stephen Polasky, and James Broadus. 1993. On the Measurement of Biological Diversity. *Journal of Environmental Economics and Management* 24: 60–68.

Weitzman, Martin L. 1992. On Diversity. *Quarterly Journal of Economics* 107: 363–405.

Biofuels

A biofuel is any fuel produced from biomass. Biomass is any plant or plant-derived material, and includes, but is not limited to, corn, corn residue (cobs, stalks, and leaves), forest residue (branches and leaves), animal manure, algae, and urban waste. In the United States, the leading biofuel feedstock is corn (for ethanol), but in Brazil it is sugarcane (for ethanol), and in Europe, it is canola (rapeseed, for biodiesel).

Biofuels are a subset of the more general class of alternative fuels, which includes solar, wind, and other sources of energy that do not derive from fossil fuels. Although fossil fuels are technically biofuels as well, given that they were produced from decomposed plants and animals buried in the ground for millions of years, the term biofuels as typically used refers only to those fuels produced from plants grown today. Unlike other alternative fuel sources, biomass can generally be converted directly into liquid fuels. The two most common types of biofuels are ethanol and biodiesel, but other examples include biobutanol and biogas. In fact, even firewood qualifies as a biofuel. Biofuels are sometimes further segmented into first-generation biofuels, which are those derived from plant carbohydrate components (sugars and starches), and second-generation biofuels, which are derived from fibrous parts of plants (cellulose and hemicellulose).

As of 2012, ethanol is the world's leading biofuel (estimated by the OECD/FAO at 113 billion liters for 2012). Ethanol is an alcohol, typically produced via fermentation of biomass carbohydrates, in the same way that beer and wine are produced. As of 2012, the leading producer of ethanol is the United States, where almost all fuel ethanol is produced from corn. Brazil, which is the second leading producer of ethanol, relies primarily on sugarcane for its ethanol feedstock. Although current technology allows for commercial production of ethanol from biomass from the plant's carbohydrates only, research is ongoing that may allow for commercial production of biofuels from the relatively more abundant fibrous parts of plants. Ethanol can also be produced via gasification. This process utilizes high temperatures in a low-oxygen environment to convert biomass into synthesis gas. This syngas is a mixture of hydrogen and carbon monoxide, and can be converted chemically into ethanol (and other fuels). The lion's share of ethanol produced in the United States is blended with petroleum gasoline to improve engine performance and reduce emissions. For most vehicles, the blend is generally no more than 10 percent, from which derives the term E-10 fuel, but an increasing number of vehicles have flex-fuel engines, which allow for greater proportions of ethanol. Although the allowable blend is anywhere along the spectrum, the typical blend is 85 percent ethanol and 15 percent petroleum gasoline, hence the term E-85. Brazil's vehicle fleet boasts a large share of flex-fuel vehicles, and consequently, ethanol is generally blended at higher levels in that country.

Biodiesel was the second-most consumed biofuel in the world as of 2012. OECD/ FAO estimates worldwide biodiesel production in 2012 at 25.8 billion liters. Biodiesel is made through a chemical process called transesterification whereby glycerin is separated from fat or vegetable oil. The process leaves behind two products—methyl esters (the chemical name for biodiesel) and glycerin (a valuable by-product used in soaps and other products). It is generally used as an additive to conventional diesel, up to 20 percent, but can also be used exclusively in diesel engines. Europe is currently the leading producer and user of biodiesel, where canola (rapeseed) is the leading feedstock. In the United States, biodiesel is produced primarily from soybean oil. Argentina, Malaysia, and Thailand are expected to become major players in the biodiesel market, where palm oil plays a major feedstock role. Biodiesel can also be produced from other agricultural oils such as sunflower, as well as from recycled cooking grease and animal fats.

A variety of policies worldwide have been used to promote the production and use of biofuels, including the Renewable Fuels Standard in the United States, the Renewable Energy Directive in the European Union, and blending mandates in Canada and Australia. Among developing nations, Argentina, Brazil, India, Indonesia, Malaysia, and Thailand all have a variety of blending mandates and/or export incentives in place.

The promotion of biofuels is not without controversy, which is primarily concerned with the alleged carbon reduction benefits of biofuels. The basis for the claim that biofuels are carbon neutral is that the carbon emitted during combustion of the fuel will be absorbed again by the subsequent year's crop. This is referred to as the feedstock carbon uptake credit. There is, thus, no addition of new carbon to the atmosphere, in contrast to fossil fuels. However, this credit does not account for the potential for increased carbon emissions due to the clearing of forests and other land for biomass production. When land-use changes are accounted for, biofuels can increase carbon emissions relative to fossil fuels.

Related to the earlier discussion is the food versus fuel debate. This refers to the relationship between grain and fuel markets caused by the diversion of land traditionally devoted to food crops, and the crops themselves, to fuel production. This relationship results in grain prices being more closely tied to the price of oil, leading to increased price volatility, and has triggered a debate on whether the diversion of grains to fuel production results in reduced supplies (and higher prices) for food and feed needs.

Because biofuels can substitute for petroleum-based fuels to some extent, production and use of biofuels is a function of feedstock prices, biofuel prices, and prices of their substitutes. As oil (and by extension, gasoline and diesel) prices rise, ethanol and biodiesel become cost competitive, providing incentives to increase the amount of biofuels blended with conventional fuels. This is generally constrained, however, by legal blend limits. For example, in the United States, ethanol can be blended with conventional gasoline up to 10 percent, but efforts are underway to increase the blend limit to 15 percent. Biodiesel faces no such legal blending limit; however, biodiesel currently faces both real and perceived vehicle performance obstacles. Biodiesel generally provides better engine performance and lubrication, but a small decrease in fuel economy. Biodiesel vehicles can also have problems starting at very cold temperatures, but this is more of an issue for higher percentage blends.

Daniel R. Petrolia

See also: Alternative Energy; Energy Efficiency; Energy Policy; Externality; International Association for Energy Economics; Renewable Energy

Further Reading

Daschle, T. 2007. Food for Fuel? Myth versus Reality. *Foreign Affairs* 86(5): 157–160.

Fargione, J., J. Hill, D. Tilman, S. Polasky, and P. Hawthorne. 2008. Land Clearing and the Biofuel Carbon Debt. *Science* 319: 1235–1238.

OECD/FAO. 2011. *OECD-FAO Agricultural Outlook 2011–2020.* New York: OECD Publishing and FAO.

Runge, C. F. and B. Senauer. 2007. How Biofuels Could Starve the Poor. *Foreign Affairs* 86(3): 41–53.

Searchinger, T., R. Heimlich, R. A. Houghton, F. Dong, A. Elobeid, J. Fabiosa, S. Tokgoz, D. Hayes, and T. Yu. 2008. Use of U.S. Croplands for Biofuels Increases Greenhouse Gases through Emissions from Land-Use Change. *Science* 319(5867): 1238–1240.

Books

Academic textbooks have served as gateways to the field of environmental and resource economics to countless generations of graduate and undergraduate students. Pearce and Turner's 1990 text provides a comprehensive overview of the field of environmental and resource economics. Its popularity is likely due to its effective targeting of undergraduates with and without a strong background in general economics. It is more heavily adopted in the European classroom, since most undergraduates at U.S. universities learned from AERE fellow Tom Tietenberg's 1996 classic *Environmental and Resource Economics,* which provides a comprehensive and extremely clear overview of the workings of various policy instruments (Lynne Lewis was added as a coauthor with the eighth edition in 2009). The 2003 book by Perman, Common, Mcgilvray, and Ma provides a comprehensive overview aimed at upper-level undergraduates or master's students. It provides a clear textual and mathematical treatment of all major areas of the field. The 1992 Turner, Pearce, and Bateman text could be regarded as a more elementary version of the Pearce and Turner text discussed before. The Pearce, Markandya, and Barbier 1989 book *Blueprint for a Green Economy* was aimed at a popular audience, but was quickly adopted for lower division courses in both environmental studies and environmental economics. It is very accessible to the more general science and policy audience as it offers solutions from an economic perspective to many of the problems that were identified in these fields.

On the research front, the field of environmental and resource economics has been heavily influenced by a small number of technical books. The Stern Report, which is mostly a synthesis of the literature on the economics of climate change, has rapidly become the single most highly cited book in environmental economics. It serves as the backbone textbook in a number of quickly evolving courses on the economics of climate change and has given a new life to the literature on discounting in environmental and resource economics. In terms of original scientific work, the most highly cited book remains the 1989 Mitchell and Carson book on contingent valuation. Freeman's 1993 book helped codify what was known about nonmarket valuation more generally. Baumol and Oates helped to synthesize what was known about instruments for pollution control. Clark's *Mathematical Bioeconomics* has played a significant role in defining the modern approach to the economics of renewable resources. Two classic books on the economics of climate change, one by Nordhaus and one by Cline, set out the main issues in thinking about the economics of climate change. Daly's book, *Steady State Economics,* was instrumental in starting the subfield of ecological economics that he further helped codify in his *Beyond Growth: The Economics of Sustainability.* Bromley's 1991 book is a classic in the area of property rights, institutions, and the political process as they influence environmental policy.

While it is impossible to survey all books in the field, a group of books stand out in terms of their collective citation counts. Resources for the Future (RFF) published a set of volumes over two decades starting with Barnett and Morse's *Scarcity and Growth* in 1963, which changed the prevailing view on the nature of resource scarcity, followed by Clawson and Knetsch's 1966 *The Economics of Outdoor Recreation*, which proposed the travel cost model, Mäler's 1974 *Environmental Economics: A Theoretical Inquiry* strengthened the ties between environmental economics and welfare economics, Krutilla and Fisher's *The Economics of Natural Environments*, which provided fundamentally new insight as to how natural systems and public lands were viewed from an economic perspective, and Tietenberg's 1985 *Emissions Trading: An Exercise in Reforming Policy*, which laid out issues related to marketable permits from a policy perspective.

Another set of books examines environmental and resource issues in the developing country context. Norgaard's 1994 book, *Development Betrayed*, introduces the concept of coevolution of human and natural systems. Repetto and Gillis focused attention on the economic forces driving tropical deforestation. Other important works are Bromley (1989 and 1992), Pearce, Markandya, and Barbier (1990) and Costanza (1992).

Nonmarket valuation is another literature where books have had a significant impact. Important works here are Cummings, Brookshire, and Schulze (1986); Hausman (1993), Pearce and Moran (1994); Bateman and Willis (1999); and Haab and McConnell (2002).

Maximilian Auffhammer

See also: Journals

Further Reading

Auffhammer, Maximilian. 2009. What Has Mattered in Environmental and Resource Economics: A Google Scholar Perspective. *Review of Environmental Economics and Policy* 3(2): 251–269.

Barnett, H. J., and C. Morse. 1963. *Scarcity and Growth: The Economics of Natural Resource Availability*. Baltimore, MD: Resources for the Future.

Bateman, I., and K. G. Willis. 1999. *Valuing Environmental Preferences: Theory and Practice of the Contingent Valuation Method in the US, EU, and Developing Countries*. New York: Oxford University Press, USA.

Baumol, William J., and Wallace E. Oates. 1975. *The Theory of Environmental Policy: Externalities, Public Outlays, and the Quality of Life*. Englewood Cliffs, NJ: Prentice-Hall.

Bromley, D. W. 1991. *Environment and Economy: Property Rights and Public Policy*. Oxford: Blackwell.

Bromley, D. W. and D. Feeny. 1992. *Making the Commons Work: Theory, Practice, and Policy*. San Francisco, CA: ICS Press.

Clark, Colin W. 1976. *Mathematical Bioeconomics: The Optimal Management of Renewable Resources*. New York: Wiley-Interscience.

Clawson, M., and J. L. Knetsch. 1966. *Economics of Outdoor Recreation*. Baltimore, MD:.The Johns Hopkins Press.

Cline, William R. 1992. *The Economics of Global Warming*. Washington, D.C.: Institute for International Economics.

Costanza, R. 1992. *Ecological Economics: The Science and Management of Sustainability*. New York: Columbia University Press

Cummings, R. G., D. S. Brookshire, W. D. Schulze, R. C. Bishop, and K. J. Arrow. 1986. *Valuing Environmental Goods: An Assessment of the Contingent Valuation Method*. Totowa, NJ: Rowman & Allanheld.

Daly, Herman E. 1996. *Beyond Growth: The Economics of Sustainable Development*. Boston, MA: Beacon Press.

Dasgupta, Partha S., and G. M. Heal. 1979. *Economic Theory and Exhaustible Resources*. New York: Cambridge University Press.

Freeman, A. Myrick. 1979. *The Measurement of Environmental and Resource Values: Theory and Methods*. Washington, D.C.: Resources for the Future.

Haab, T. C. and K. E. McConnell. 2002. *Valuing Environmental and Natural Resources: The Econometrics of Non-Market Valuation*. Northampton, MA: Edward Elgar.

Hausman, J. A. 1993. *Contingent Valuation: A Critical Assessment*. Amsterdam and New York: North-Holland.

Krutilla, J. V., and A. C. Fisher. 1985. *The Economics of Natural Environments: Studies in the Valuation of Commodity and Amenity Resources.* Resources for the Future.

Mäler, K. G. 1974. *Environmental Economics: A Theoretical Inquiry.* Baltimore, MD: Johns Hopkins Press.

Mitchell, Robert C., and Richard T. Carson. 1989. *Using Surveys to Value Public Goods: The Contingent Valuation Method.* Washington, D.C.: Resources for the Future.

Nordhaus, William D. 1994. *Managing the Global Commons: The Economics of Climate Change.* Cambridge, MA: MIT Press.

Norgaard, R. B. 1994. *Development Betrayed: The End of Progress and a Coevolutionary Revisioning of the Future.* London: Routledge.

Pearce, D. W. and D. Moran. 1994. *The Economic Value of Biodiversity.* London: Earthscan.

Pearce, D. W., and R. Kerry Turner. 1990. *Economics of Natural Resources and the Environment.* Baltimore, MD: John Hopkins University Press.

Pearce, D. W., Edward B. Barbier, and Anil Markandya (editors). 1989. *Blueprint for a Green Economy.* London: Earthscan.

Pearce, D. W., E. Barbier, and A. Markandya. 1990. *Sustainable Development: Economics and Environment in the Third World.* Northampton, MA: Edward Elgar.

Perman, Roger, Yue Ma, Michael Common, David Maddison, and James Mcqulvray. 2012. *Natural Resource and Environmental Economics,* 4th ed. New York: Addison Wesley.

Repetto, R. C., and Gillis, M. 1988. *Public Policies and the Misuse of Forest Resources.* Cambridge: Cambridge University Press.

Stern, Nicholas Herbert (editor). 2006. *The Economics of Climate Change: The Stern Review.* Cambridge: Cambridge University Press.

Tietenberg, T. H. 1985. *Emissions Trading: An Exercise in Reforming Pollution Policy.* Washington, D.C.: Resources for the Future.

Tietenberg, T. H. 1996. *Environmental and Natural Resource Economics,* 2nd ed. New York: HarperCollins.

Turner, R. Kerry, D. W. Pearce, and Ian Bateman. 1992. *Environmental Economics: An Elementary Introduction.* Baltimore, MD: Johns Hopkins University Press.

Boulding, Kenneth

Kenneth E. Boulding (1910–1993) was an economist with a very broad disciplinary and topical sphere of influence. Born the son of a plumber in Liverpool, England, in 1910, Boulding was the first in his family to receive more than an elementary education. He was classically trained in politics, philosophy, and economics at Oxford, after an initial brief foray into chemistry. Upon receiving his undergraduate degree in 1931, his paper on displacement costs was published in *The Economic Journal*, then edited by John Maynard Keynes. He held a postgraduate fellowship at Oxford and then received a Commonwealth Fellowship to study in the United States, primarily at Harvard and Chicago, where he was influenced by luminaries such as Joseph Shumpeter, Frank Knight, and Jacob Viner. And he influenced them as well. Knight's article titled "The Theory of Investment Once More: Mr. Boulding and the Austrians" was published in the *Quarterly Journal of Economics* in 1936, when Boulding was a mere 26 years old.

From the beginning, Boulding's work challenged conventional assumptions on a range of topics such as capital theory, pricing, and income distribution. Although a strong theorist to the core, he was averse to economic canon that failed to capture the complexity of real-world problems. While mathematically competent himself, he decried what he viewed as economics' overemphasis on mathematization in the mid-20th century. As his career evolved, he dedicated more attention to a fully integrative model of social science that drew heavily from psychology, sociology, and philosophy, as well as economics. This interdisciplinarity may reflect the influence of his wife, Elise, a distinguished scholar of sociology, but it also revealed a curious mind stimulated by the complexity of life. His topics of inquiry evolved as well from an early emphasis on conventional matters of capital, markets, and income to more unorthodox topics (for the time) of peace, conflict, population, and the environment. A Quaker, Boulding was deeply committed to the ideals of social justice.

Boulding's work on the environment first became evident in his text, *A Reconstruction of Economics* (1950), which proposed an ecological framework for the workings of society and the economy, and somewhat later with his work on evolutionary economics and principles of entropy, which comingled with the work of Nicholas Georgescu-Roegen and K. W. Kapp. His attention to population dynamics was unique for its time and his emphasis on *homeostasis*, sustaining the condition of stocks—manufactured or natural—over the enlargement of flows as a determinant of human welfare was and remains controversial within economics. His 1966 essay, "The Economics of the Coming Spaceship Earth," argued that standard economics texts failed to recognize the transition of earth from an open system, "a virtually limitless plane" from which humans can draw materials and into which humans can expel wastes, to a closed system in which "the outputs of all parts of the system are linked to the inputs of other parts." This tied back to the foundations laid in *Reconstruction,* which established a basic conflict between consumption necessary to sustain full employment and the drawing down of stocks (in this case the natural environment) necessary to enrich human lives.

Boulding experienced success and recognition in mainstream economics for much of his career. Knight's remarkable call out to Boulding in the title of his 1936 article perhaps foretold his destiny as a winner in 1949 of the John Bates Clark medal for an economist under the age of 40. Two generations of economists trained in the mid-20th century cut their teeth on his text, *Economic Analysis*. He was voted president of the American Economic Association in 1968, and was purported to be nominated for the Nobel Prize in both Economics and Peace. Yet it may also be fair to say that he was a man whose views were widely respected, but often ignored in the economics profession. His own writings suggest an awareness of this juxtaposition, but one that did not embitter him so much as motivate him to push the boundaries of economic thought and application. In later life, he still viewed himself as an economist, even if there were some within the field who may have assumed he had launched to another intellectual island. Despite any questions about the extent of Kenneth Boulding's acceptance by the economics mainstream, his influence on the development of environmental economics on topics such as sustainability, population, and green national accounts is both clear and profound.

Brian C. Murray

See also: Ecological Economics; Environmental Justice; Green National Accounting; Philosophy; Sustainability

Further Reading

Boulding, Kenneth. 1950. *A Reconstruction of Economics.* New York: John Wiley and Sons.

Boulding, Kenneth. 1966a. *Economic Analysis,* 4th ed. New York: Harper and Brothers.

Boulding, Kenneth. 1966b. The Economics of the Coming Spaceship Earth, in A. Markandya and J. Richardson (editors), *Environmental Economics: A Reader.* New York: St. Martin's Press.

Boulding, Kenneth. 1971. In Fred Glahe and Larry Singell (editors), *Collected Papers,* vol. 1, Boulder, CO: Colorado Associated University Press.

Knight, Frank. 1936. The Theory of Investment Once More: Mr Boulding and the Austrians. *Quarterly Journal of Economics* 50(1): 36–67.

Mott, Tracy. 2000. Kenneth Boulding: 1910–1993. *The Economic Journal* 110(464): 430–444.

Brownfields

The term brownfield or brownfield site means an industrial or commercial site that is idle or underused because of real or perceived environmental pollution. Examples of brownfield sites include factories, chemical plants, old dumps, rail yards, abandoned hospitals, dry cleaning facilities, and by some classifications, former gas stations. Contamination may be actual (confirmed by tests) or perceived (based on past uses of the property). Some jurisdictions now designate property contaminated with controlled substances—such as meth labs—as brownfields.

Brownfield sites exist worldwide. Between one-half million and one million brownfield sites exist in the United States alone, depending on whether or not former gas stations are included. There are many more contaminated properties that have not been officially designated as brownfields, as well as more severely contaminated properties that fall under the Comprehensive Environmental Response, Compensation, and Liability Act of 1980 (CERCLA); these severely contaminated properties are better known as Superfund sites.

The U.S. Environmental Protection Agency (EPA) has the responsibility of regulating contaminated properties. In 1995, during the administration of President Bill Clinton, the agency announced its Brownfields Action Agenda after it recognized that owners were abandoning less-contaminated properties in fear of being held liable under the existing Superfund legislation. The Superfund liabilities included holding past, present, and future property owners responsible for all cleanup costs. In addition, the EPA cleanup standards often resulted in the property being restored beyond its original, predevelopment condition. The potential cost involved in such efforts discouraged any type of redevelopment or reuse. The EPA responded by granting the states considerable freedom to establish programs to evaluate and clean these less-contaminated properties as a way to encourage their redevelopment. The EPA, sometimes in conjunction with other government agencies, also provided small grants for evaluation, cleanup, and redevelopment of these sites. These funds attracted a few developers to participate in cleaning and reusing these properties.

Eight years after brownfields legislation was first proposed, Congress created the designation at the federal level by amending the CERCLA statute to add Title II, Brownfields Revitalization and Environmental Restoration Act of 2001. President George W. Bush signed the act into law in 2002. Title II codified those parts of the EPA program that were deemed successful. The brownfields designation, and exemption from CERCLA standards, sought to further encourage redevelopment by providing the following: limiting the financial liability for certain innocent owners and purchasers of the property as well as owners of adjacent properties; treating prospective redevelopers differently than the owners under whom the contamination originally occurred; authorizing the EPA to provide funding for site assessment, cleanup, technical assistance, and insurance for revitalization programs; and setting different cleanup standards depending on the planned use of the revitalized property, including the use of engineered barriers to allow leaving contamination in place instead of requiring the removal of all contamination. Brownfield site redevelopment projects continued to be regulated by the states—many of which have their own brownfields legislation and state environmental agencies—with assistance from the federal government.

Revitalizing and reusing brownfields is of great consequence because these properties have a potentially large impact on their communities. Brownfields that are not redeveloped may become eyesores, dragging down neighboring property values and discouraging other revitalization programs in the surrounding area. Additionally, brownfields may become safety and health threats to the neighborhood, which typically are already lower income and disadvantaged. Another consideration is that developers will build on previously unused properties (greenfields) typically far from city centers, contributing to sprawl. On the other hand, without the potential Superfund-type cleanup costs looming, brownfield sites have much to offer potential developers. Most brownfields are along existing transportation corridors, with utilities already in place, and many sites are near city centers, making the property attractive for infill development. Redeveloping brownfields has the potential to revitalize depressed areas, provide jobs during cleanup and at the businesses established after redevelopment, increase the neighborhood tax base as well as increase property values around the revitalized property, and redress possible environmental inequities.

Redeveloping brownfields is not without controversy. The biggest question is whether the costs of cleaning and reusing brownfield sites are greater than the associated benefits. Currently, there is no way to generalize the successes since each property presents its own challenges to cleanup and redevelopment. Because insurance companies are increasingly willing to cover at least a portion of the developer's risk of unknown liabilities, another economic consideration is whether the use of federal and state funds to help in the evaluation and cleanup of these properties is an efficient use of scarce resources or whether to encourage a more market-based approach to revitalizing these sites. There is also a question about whether the legislation favors redeveloping brownfield sites that offer the largest return on investment as opposed to removing contaminated sites from impoverished areas. Finally, there is not yet enough experience with redeveloped brownfields to examine possible long-term health effects, as well as how to ensure that cleanup measures will be monitored and enforced over time.

Although the brownfields designation was intended to encourage redevelopment and reuse of such properties, obstacles still remain. Many property owners resist the brownfields designation due to the perceived stigma. Private developers are often unwilling to take on the potential financial and market risks associated with redeveloping brownfields, especially in lower income communities. Many nonprofit and community organizations that have attempted to redevelop brownfields in these neighborhoods have had difficulty obtaining the funding needed for assessment and cleanup due to the investment risk perceived by some lenders and investors. In addition, some sites may be too small for profitable redevelopment. Furthermore, conflicts may arise over the proposed reuse and the community may ultimately resist the plans for redevelopment. For example, developers may favor industrial and commercial uses, while nearby residents may prefer parks.

The EPA has stated that cleaning and reusing brownfield sites provides economic, environmental, and social benefits. However, the costs of redeveloping brownfields must be measured against the benefits of such an undertaking. In addition, future efforts need to focus on removing any lingering obstacles. For example, expanding the role of the private sector and market institutions—such as insurance—should not be neglected. Encouraging increased public–private collaboration and funding may also spur additional redevelopment projects. Finally, a more transparent method of prioritizing contaminated sites would help to ensure that those areas having the greatest potential value for redevelopment also have the greatest opportunity to attract the needed attention and funding.

Peter M. Schwarz and Gwendolyn L. Gill

See also: Benefit–Cost Analysis; Externality

Further Reading

American Planning Association, Creating Community-Based Brownfields Strategies. http://www.planning.org/research/brownfields/

Public Law 107-118 (H.R. 2869), Small Business Liability Relief and Brownfields Revitalization Act, signed into law January 11, 2002.

Public Law U.S. Environmental Protection Agency, Brownfields and Land Revitalization, http://epa.gov/brownfields

Stromberg, Edwin. 2010. Guest Editor's Introduction. *Cityscape: A Journal of Policy Development and Research* (Special Issue on Brownfields) 12(3): 1–5.

Carbon Pricing

Global climate change may be one of the most important challenges facing policymakers in the 21st century. If left unchecked, scientists project that rising atmospheric accumulations of greenhouse (i.e., heat-trapping) gases—primarily CO_2 emissions from the combustion of fossil fuels (coal, petroleum products, natural gas)—will raise the earth's average temperature by several degrees Celsius by 2100. Temperatures today are currently 5°C higher than at the peak of the last Ice Age when the climate was radically different. The associated risks with dramatic temperature increases are substantial.

In responding to this challenge, it is critically important to use policy instruments that are effective in exploiting opportunities for emissions reductions. For energy-related CO_2 emissions, these opportunities include fuel-switching in power generation—shifting from coal-fired generation (which is very carbon intensive) to natural gas (which involves less CO_2 emissions) and from these fuels to zero-carbon sources like nuclear power, hydro power, and wind. CO_2 emissions can also be reduced through reducing the overall level of electricity demand, reducing the demand for transportation fuels (e.g., through people driving less and using more fuel-efficient vehicles), and reducing fuels used directly in homes and factories (mainly for heating purposes).

A carbon tax (i.e., a tax applied to fossil fuels in proportion to their carbon content) is an especially effective instrument—as the tax is passed forward into the price of fuels and electricity, all of the possibilities for reducing CO_2 emissions will be exploited. Carbon taxes also provide across-the-board incentives for the future development and deployment of technologies to improve energy efficiency, lower the cost of cleaner energy sources, and so on. They are also fairly straightforward to administer: for example, taxes can be levied on the output from coal processing plants, while for many countries extending existing motor fuel taxes to all refinery products would be relatively simple.

Other regulatory policies (imposed in isolation) are by definition far less effective than carbon taxes, as they exploit a much narrower range of emissions reduction opportunities. For example, a subsidy for renewable generation does not reduce emissions outside of the power sector, nor does it reduce electricity demand, or encourage switching from coal to natural gas or from these fuels to nuclear power.

Carbon taxes are also, potentially, beneficial in other ways. Carbon taxes raise significant amounts of government revenue, thereby reducing the need for other taxes—particularly taxes on personal and corporate income and value-added taxes—to finance the government's budget. Lowering the rates of these other taxes has significant economic benefits in terms of improving incentives for labor force participation, effort on the job, investment in physical and human capital, and so on.

Through appropriate choice of the tax level, carbon taxes can also strike the right balance between the environmental benefits of emissions mitigation and costs imposed on the broader economy. With revenues used for the general budget, the appropriate tax level is (approximately) the environmental damages per ton of CO_2 emissions. A careful assessment by the U.S. government suggests these damages (e.g., costs to future world agriculture, costs of sea level rises, health impacts, risks from more extreme warming, etc.) are around $35 per ton (though some would argue for higher damage estimates).

Emissions trading systems are another promising approach though, insofar as possible, they should be designed to mimic the potential advantages of carbon taxes. This means they should comprehensively cover emissions and include price stability provisions like price floors and ceilings to keep the emissions price in line with environmental damages per ton. Importantly, allowances should also be auctioned. If revenue opportunities are foregone—for example, through giving away free allowances or diverting revenues to unproductive earmarks under a carbon tax—other burdensome taxes must be higher (or other valuable spending lower) for a given government budget.

Implementing carbon taxes—or tax-like instruments—has proved very challenging politically: more than 90 percent of global greenhouse gas emissions are not yet covered by formal pricing schemes (though a number of country-level programs are in the pipeline) and prevailing emissions prices (e.g., in the EU Emissions Trading System) are often well below environmental damages. One explanation for this is that higher energy prices hurt households. In fact, rather than tax fossil fuel energy, some countries (especially oil producers) heavily subsidize it—according to International Monetary Fund (IMF) estimates, the worldwide fiscal cost of such subsidies amounted to $480 billion in 2011.

But the first point to emphasize is that holding down energy prices below levels warranted by production costs plus environmental damages is a highly inefficient distributional policy, as only a minor fraction (typically around 5–10 percent) of the benefits accrue to the bottom income quintile—most of the benefits leak away to higher income groups. Distributional concerns call for far more targeted policies—progressive adjustments to the broader tax and benefit system, spending on basic education and health services, etc. And in many Organisation for Economic Co-operation and Development (OECD) countries (though not the United States) the problem is not so much that energy is under-taxed, but that these taxes are poorly targeted at externalities. Much of the burden on households from higher prices for electricity and motor fuels could be offset through scaling back taxes on electricity use and vehicle ownership, as carbon pricing is introduced.

While domestic initiatives to price carbon (especially in the United States) would help to kick-start broader climate mitigation efforts, international coordination is also important. Harmonizing emissions prices across countries can strengthen environmental effectiveness while alleviating, to some degree, country concerns about their international competitiveness positions. One possibility would be for the major emitting countries (the 15 largest emitters account for 80 percent of global CO_2 emissions) to agree on a carbon tax floor. This would avoid the need (which has hampered international climate negotiations to date) to agree on individual emissions targets for numerous countries and any country would have the flexibility to set higher carbon taxes than the agreed minimum. Monitoring the agreement, however, would require safeguards against fiscal cushioning (i.e., the possibility that a country might reduce the effectiveness of carbon pricing through adjusting broader fiscal provisions affecting the energy sector).

Participation of large-emitting developing countries in pricing agreements is also important—projections suggest that India and China together, for example, will be responsible for a third of global CO_2 emissions by 2030. Although some developing countries (including China) are planning some pricing initiatives, these efforts could be reinforced by promoting international financial flows for mitigation projects in these countries.

One promising way to achieve this would be to allow entities covered by carbon taxes or trading schemes in developed countries to earn credits by paying for verifiable mitigation projects in developing countries. Another possibility is to channel project funds directly through the Green Climate Fund (GCF). A natural source of finance for the GCF would be internationally coordinated charges on international aviation and maritime emissions, given that these emissions are currently underpriced and that the claim of national governments on the tax base is less obvious than for domestically consumed fuels.

Even under optimistic scenarios for the future progress of mitigation policy however, we are already committed to significantly warming the planet for future generations. There is some—hopefully extremely remote—chance of catastrophic climate change in the future (due, for example, to unstable feedback mechanisms in the climate system). Mitigation efforts therefore need to be complemented with efforts to develop last-resort technologies (e.g., technologies to directly remove CO_2 from the atmosphere, or deflect incoming solar radiation) as possible insurance against extreme outcomes.

Ian Parry

See also: Climate Change Impacts; Emissions Trading; International Climate Agreements; Offsets; Pigouvian Taxes

Further Reading

Interagency Working Group on Social Cost of Carbon, 2013. *Technical Support Document: Technical Update of the Social Cost of Carbon for Regulatory Impact Analysis under Executive Order 12866*. United States Government, Washington, D.C. Available at: www.whitehouse.gov/sites/default/files/omb/inforeg/social_cost_of_carbon_for_ria_2013_update.pdf

IPCC, 2007. *Climate Change 2007: The Physical Science Basis*. Contribution of Working Group I to the Fourth Assessment Report of the Intergovernmental Panel on Climate Change. Cambridge University Press, Cambridge.

Joseph A., A. J. Krupnick, R. G. Newell, I. W. H. Parry, and W. A. Pizer. 2010. Designing Climate Mitigation Policy. *Journal of Economic Literature* 48: 903–934.

Parry, I. W. H., R. Mooij, and M. Keen (editors). 2012. *Fiscal Policy to Mitigate Climate Change: A Guide for Policymakers*. International Monetary Fund.

Cartels

A cartel is an explicit arrangement among suppliers in an industry to manage output and prices in order to capture additional profit. The presence of an explicit arrangement distinguishes cartels from other forms of strategic interaction in oligopoly environments. A successful cartel must (1) identify a profit-enhancing level of sales for the cartel, (2) assign output or sales quotas to cartel members, (3) monitor cartel member sales, and (4) be able and willing to punish excessive sales by cartel members.

Since, at least, Adam Smith's *Wealth of Nations* in 1776, economists have taken note of cartel behavior. Smith wrote, "People of the same trade seldom meet together, even for merriment or diversion, but the conversation ends in a conspiracy against the public, or in some contrivance to raise prices." Given the widespread benefit to suppliers from a successful cartel, it is perhaps surprising that many industries are not so organized. The lack of widespread cartelizing may be evidence of the difficulties of maintaining a cartel, evidence of the success of public policies against cartels, or both.

Because the profit-enhancing level of sales is below the competitive level of output, cartels will require some or all of its members to reduce sales. The resulting higher prices will then leave members curtailing sales in a position in which the marginal revenue from added output is greater than the marginal cost, presenting cartel members with the constant opportunity for short-run gain at the expense of other cartel members. The chief challenge a cartel faces is in maintaining member compliance with quotas given the constant temptation to cheat. Diversity of positions among cartel members—high cost producers vs. low cost, short term time horizon vs. long term, and so on—will further complicate cartel operations.

When discussing natural resource cartels, economists have an easy example: the Organization of Petroleum Exporting Countries (OPEC). Unfortunately, OPEC is a bad example. OPEC only loosely satisfies the conditions of a rigorous definition of cartel, and most serious studies of the organization find it has failed to sustain world oil prices at higher than competitive levels. But there are several examples of durable natural resource cartels, and certain natural resource industries may be particularly susceptible to cartelization. In addition, successful cartelization reduces industry output. If, as Robert Solow said, "the monopolist is the conservationist's best friend," a successful cartel may be the conservationist's *next* best friend. Natural resource economists have taken special interest in cartelization for these reasons.

Historically, several natural resource industries have experienced attempts at cartelization and some industries have sustained cartels for several years. Over the 20th and 21st centuries, cartels have emerged for diamonds, bauxite (aluminum ore), tin, magnesium, and yellowcake (uranium ore), among others. Unsuccessful or disputed cases of cartelization include petroleum and copper.

OPEC attracts the most attention, both among the public and among professional economists, likely due to the high value of petroleum and the association between OPEC and the energy crises of the 1970s. The organization formed with five members in 1960, largely as a defensive response among exporting nations in reaction to a price cut imposed by the large, international oil companies that then exercised significant control over the world market. Little public notice of the organization was taken until Arab members of OPEC imposed a boycott on exports to the United States in October 1973 and a subsequent tripling of world oil prices to over $12/ barrel in 1973 dollars. OPEC became a convenient scapegoat for politicians in oil importing nations such as the United States. Publicly, little notice was taken at the time of how U.S. price controls and associated policies created the domestic energy crisis and, because lower prices discouraged domestic production and encouraged consumption, boosted OPEC's economic power. Repeal of petroleum price controls in the United States along with the high-price-induced supply response by non-OPEC producers diminished OPEC's economic influence after 1980. Although economic analyses of OPEC continue to support a variety of views of the organization's influence and success, many analysts have concluded that the apparent influence of OPEC is largely due to the actions of Saudi Arabia.

Cartelization in the diamond industry presents a clear contrast to the petroleum market experience, with the international diamond cartel perhaps being the most successful and longest-lasting cartel. The De Beers family of companies began in South Africa in 1888, at a time when over 80 percent of the stones were produced in that company, successfully dominating marketing channels that took South African diamonds to European markets. Over the 20th century the company expanded horizontally as diamond mines in other countries were developed, to maintain some control over supply, and vertically, to better manage distribution. The company quite willingly built up a large stockpile of diamonds to accommodate purchase agreements with suppliers while controlling the supply, and therefore the price, of diamonds reaching the consumer market. The stockpile also represented a potential threat to any supplier who wished to bypass the cartel, as it could easily flood the market with the quality and color of stone the supplier had to offer. At the beginning of the 21st century, increasing supply from producers who remained outside of the De Beers organizations, principally from Australia, Canada, and Russia, and the increasing political taint associated with conflict diamonds led the company to reduce its scale and shift its marketing strategies. However, the company remains in the business of promoting orderly competition in diamond markets.

In between examples of, at best, the periodic market influence of OPEC in petroleum and the long-enduring market dominance of De Beers in the diamond business, other producer groups have struggled to capture the excess profits available through cartelization and sometimes succeeded. The International Copper Cartel created in 1935 controlled about half of world production, but non-cartel supply was too elastic in response to price increases and the cartel was unable to significantly increase price. A cartel in mercury production was sustained by formal agreement from 1928 until 1950 and continued less formally afterward, aided by low cost conditions in Spain and Italy and cartel-supporting government policies in those two countries. The formal agreement was dissolved after an Italian mining company violated marketing restrictions. The informal cartelization continued to have influence through the 1960s, but faded as low-cost production emerged in numerous other countries around the world. The uranium ore (yellowcake) market was cartelized by a secret arrangement in 1972 among the largest non-U.S. producers, some privately owned and some state-owned, in the face of inelastic and readily predictable demand driven by the growth of nuclear power. The cartel was aided by international agreements monitoring movements of uranium as well as by the enthusiastic support of the governments of exporting nations. When the agreement became public, however, it was rapidly abandoned in the face of pressure from importing nations.

Michael Giberson

See also: Exhaustible Resources

Further Reading

Alhajji, A. Fayçal, and David Huettner. 2000. OPEC and Other Commodity Cartels: A Comparison. *Energy Policy* 28(15): 1151–1164.

Levenstein, Margaret C., and Valerie Y. Suslow. 2006. What Determines Cartel Success? *Journal of Economic Literature* 44(1): 43–95.

Spar, Debora L. 2006. Markets: Continuity and Change in the International Diamond Market. *Journal of Economic Perspectives* 20(3): 195–208.

Taylor, June H., and Michael D. Yokell. 1979. *Yellowcake: The International Uranium Cartel.* New York: Pergamon Press.

Catch Shares

If a fishery is managed under a catch share or rights-based program, individual entities (e.g., harvesters, associations, or communities) have a secure privilege to harvest in a specific area or to harvest a fixed share of a seasonal or annual total allowable catch (TAC). How much each harvester can harvest each season or year depends directly on the size of the TAC, which will vary with biological estimates of sustainable harvest levels. The term catch shares is relatively new and refers to a suite of programs that essentially assign partial rights to an asset. For example, under individual quota programs, individual harvesters have a right (or more aptly a privilege) to a share of the net stock growth while the underlying stock remains owned by the commons. As such, catch share programs do not guarantee the same harvest in each year or even any harvest in each year, but they do provide an incentive for efficient decision making since—as an owned asset—the catch shares are a mechanism for capturing resource rents.

Consider the alternative. Without a catch share program, fishermen compete for a share of the TAC at sea in order to maximize the catch per trip. This type of management system is often referred to as open access, which creates a race to fish and all the intendant effects such as overinvestment in vessels and gear, short seasons, low-quality product, and suboptimal economic performance. Under a catch share program, the objective of the fishermen becomes one of maximizing the long-run value of the catch share. As such, fishermen would consider, for example, the benefits of reducing habitat damage, releasing juvenile fish to allow for subsequent growth and spawning, or improving the storage of fish on board to increase product quality and market value.

Catch share programs are considered mechanisms to improve the efficiency and value of fisheries, not to improve the health of the underlying stock directly. This is because catch share programs can change who catches the fish, not the TAC. While catch shares alone can generate resource rents, it is the transferability of the shares that can improve the overall economic performance of the fishery. When shares are transferable, like cap-and-trade markets for pollutant emissions, the market for shares can incentivize the more efficient producers to buy shares from their less efficient competitors. The voluntary exchange between more and less efficient producers benefits both parties and creates economic value. The process of a fleet becoming more efficient through the exiting of less efficient harvesters is commonly referred to as rationalization.

In theory, catch share programs with transferability—often referred to as individual transferable quotas (ITQs)—solve the property rights problem experienced by fisheries that are managed as open access resources. As such, catch share programs are increasingly being used to help manage commercial fisheries around the world, especially in countries that seek to manage fisheries to generate resource rents and profits for fishermen. These countries manage nearly all species with harvester rights systems (e.g., New Zealand, Australia), while countries that seek to maximize catch—such as the United States—have relatively few.

In practice, the implementation of catch share programs has been met with controversy, primarily over equity concerns associated with the initial distribution of shares. While there are many potential approaches (most notably auctions or lotteries), the most prevalent is granting of rights without charge based on historic participation in the fishery. Basing the initial distribution on historic participation is perceived as equitable to fishermen, and rewards those that worked to develop a market for the fish. Equity considerations have also motivated restrictions on transfers. Examples include restrictions on the maximum shares owned (to prevent market concentration) and the transfer of shares between regions (to support community stability) or between gear types (to retain traditional or recreational fishing practices). Trading restrictions can improve equity but also reduce anticipated gains in economic performance expected from the program.

Key decisions with regard to the implementation of catch share programs include the duration of the right, owner requirements, and fees. In theory, the rights should be granted in perpetuity to provide the incentives necessary for efficient long-run decision making. In practice, however, some programs have been time-limited and subject to continuation only after review, which can undermine the potential effectiveness of a catch share system. Owner requirements should permit open participation in the ITQ market. In practice, however, use-it-or-lose-it provisions often require the share owner to be on board or on site to ensure sustainable practices are being used (e.g., minimize bycatch release mortality and habitat damage). Other provisions may prevent leasing to other fishermen, sales to non-fishermen (e.g., NGOs), and brokers who do not fish. Short-term quota leasing has been an unintended outcome in some fisheries and has been criticized for causing lease-dependent fishermen, who are often those who do not have the funds to purchase shares. Lastly, theory would also suggest that resource rents should be continuously collected on behalf of the owners of the common resource. In practice, such charges are explicitly prohibited in some countries although transfers can be subject to taxes and or administrative charges.

Catch share programs with tradable rights (be it for quota or regions) share many similarities with cap-and-trade programs with one major difference; a central exchange market for catch shares does not exist. Parties that wish to trade are often left to find a trading partner and negotiate a price, a process that can be time-consuming and costly. Many fisheries lack the basic structure of information sharing that is usually provided in a formal market, including that of price discovery. In addition, some markets are thin with few traders. As a result, achieving the efficiency objective of catch share systems is hindered.

To date, catch share programs have improved efficiency and market value, and have provided other benefits associated with stopping the race to harvest (e.g., improved safety at sea and elimination of other open access regulations). Controversy will continue as long as efficiency and equity goals remain, but more attention to both the markets and the transfer restrictions will provide the transparency needed to ensure successful catch share management regimes.

Sherry L. Larkin

See also: Common Pool Resources; Emissions Trading; Fisheries Management

Further Reading

Arnason, R. 2002. A Review of International Experiences with ITQs: An Annex to Future Options for UK Fish Quota Management. CEMARE Report No. 59, Centre for the Economics and Management of Aquatic Resources, University of Portsmouth, Portsmouth, U.K., p. 64.

Buck, E. H. 1995. Individual Transferable Quotas in Fishery Management. Congressional Research Service (CRS) Report 95-849, U.S. Library of Congress, Washington, D.C. http://cnie.org/NLE/CRSreports/Marine/mar-1.cfm

Huppert, D. D. 2005. An Overview of Fishing Rights. *Reviews in Fish Biology and Fisheries* 15: 201–215.

Squires, D., J. Kirkley, and C. A. Tisdell. 1995. Individual Transferable Quotas as a Fisheries Management Tool. *Reviews in Fisheries Science* 3(2): 141–169.

Sutinen, J. G. 1999. What Works Well and Why: Evidence from Fishery-Management Experiences in OECD Countries. *ICES Journal of Marine Science: Journal du Conseil* 56(6): 1051–1058.

Choice Experiments

When people are choosing a product like a new TV set they often compare the features of the TVs available. They compare features like brand, screen size, warranty length, price, and other attributes of the various alternatives available to them. Similarly when people are choosing hiking trails or fishing sites as part of a recreational experience they may compare the trails or sites on the basis of the attributes. Some of the attributes will be quantitative (how far away is it, how many camping spots are there at the site, what is the fish catch rate) and some may be qualitative (how is the water quality, is the scenery nice). Environmental economists are often interested in knowing what people would be willing to pay for improvements in environmental quality attributes, like better water quality. Knowing how an individual would trade-off an extra unit of water quality (measured in some specific way) for an extra unit of travel cost or an increase in entrance fee would provide insight into the value of the environmental amenity. When trying to measure these trade-offs using real-world data, however, we often find that there is not enough variation in the attributes, or all the attributes are highly correlated (e.g., better water quality sites have better fish catch rates). That makes it difficult to identify the impact of a particular attribute because its impact cannot be identified uniquely in a statistical model. Alternately it may be the case that the impact we are trying to measure is outside the range of the current attribute levels. For example, we may wish to know the value of increasing the clarity of water beyond the level it is at any fishing site in our region. In cases like these we may use stated preference methods—asking people which fishing site they prefer—where the alternatives presented to them are hypothetical and are based on attributes that are usually considered important in the choice of the alternative. This is what is commonly referred to as a choice experiment.

One of the most confusing aspects of the literature on choice experiments is the terminology around the name. A *contingent valuation* question could be considered a choice experiment as it typically involves a yes or no question (a choice) and the main attribute is the cost. A more typical example of a choice experiment is the presentation of multiple alternatives (e.g., three fishing sites), where each alternative is described by attributes (e.g., distance from home, catch rate, water quality, etc.) at specific levels (100 miles or $45 in round-trip travel cost, expect to catch one fish per hour, poor water quality, etc.). The respondent is asked to choose one of these alternatives from the set, thereby revealing information on what they prefer and implicitly their trade-offs between the various attributes. The respondent makes a discrete choice from a choice set that is experimentally designed to help identify the trade-offs by combining the alternatives, attributes, and levels in a very specific way. A number of variants of this approach also exist including rating or ranking alternatives, identifying the best and worst alternatives or indicating how many trips the respondent would make to each alternative. A myriad of names have been applied to these methods including attribute based choice experiments, stated choice, conjoint, choice based conjoint, and others. Furthermore, in most applications of choice experiments respondents are asked repeated questions (many sets of three fishing sites) to help identify preferences. These cases are called repeated discrete choice experiments or a sequence of discrete choices. For the remainder of this description the word choice experiment will be used to describe a multinomial choice sequence (two or more alternatives where each alternative is based on attribute and levels, and respondents are asked to make a choice from each of multiple such tasks).

How do choice experiments provide information on the value of environmental amenities? There are several steps in the use of choice experiments. First, the research problem needs to be defined. In the example mentioned earlier it could be the measurement of the economic (monetary) value of an improvement in water quality at the fishing site. The good needs to be characterized in ways that respondents can relate to them. In this case it means determining the relevant attributes for a fishing site and trip, the range of levels that each attribute should have, and decisions about how many alternatives to present and how many replications to ask people to respond to. Once the attributes, levels, and alternatives have been determined an experimental design is required so that combinations of attributes and levels are presented to respondents in ways that facilitate the measurement of preferences (or trade-offs). This area of the choice experiment literature has exploded recently. Specific combinations of attributes and levels may be chosen to minimize the variance of the statistical measures of the preference parameters, or to achieve some other design objective. The possible combinations of attributes and levels becomes very large quickly as the number of attributes, levels, and alternatives increases thus experimental designs are required to gather information efficiently. These efficient designs often require some information (or priors) about preferences, but that information can be captured from other studies or from pretests. These two steps—determination of attributes and levels, and experimental design—are critical steps that require significant attention to detail (some qualitative, some quantitative).

The next step in a choice experiment is to design the data collection process. Just as in any questionnaire based project decisions about survey mode (e.g., mail surveys, Internet panels, telephone surveys, etc.), sampling strategy, sample size, and questionnaire design must be addressed. Finally, after implementation of the questionnaire and data collection has been completed, econometric analysis of the data can occur. Most applications of choice experiments use random utility theory in which the consumer is assumed to choose the alternative that generates the highest utility. The researcher observes the systematic components of preferences (the attributes) but assumes that there is also a random component known to the respondent that affects the choice of each alternative. Specific assumptions about this random component allow the researcher to estimate preferences for the attributes employing econometric models. Often these preferences are simply the weights in a linear expression of utility as a function of the attributes. These preference weights provide the basis for the analysis of how much one would be willing to pay (in additional travel costs or entrance fees) for an increase in water quality.

The choice experiment described earlier is a stated preference version of the *travel cost method* that employs random utility theory. The theory is the same as discrete choice recreation demand, but the data generating mechanism is stated, rather than revealed, data. Extensions of the very simple choice experiment described earlier include allowing for heterogeneous preferences over the population sampled, examining more complex forms of the utility function, examining different forms of the random component, and other extensions. These changes in model structure will also affect the way that willingness to pay is calculated. In addition, these hypothetical data could be used in combination with actual data from recreation sites so that the actual data help ground the analysis in actual choices while the hypothetical data help introduce variation into the attributes and improve estimation of preferences.

Choice experiments can also be used to measure *passive use or existence values* by presenting people with choices of policy outcomes that are described by attributes. For example, people may be asked to choose between alternative endangered species management programs that are described by alternatives like the impacts on various species at risk and the costs. Choice experiments have been used to measure the *value of statistical life* by asking respondents to choose between programs that reduce different health risks but cost different amounts of money. Finally, choice experiments have been used to explore impacts of environmental quality changes on property choices, somewhat analogous to *hedonic price methods* by presenting respondents with a set of hypothetically designed properties and asking them to choose their preferred house.

Choice experiments have become very popular in the academic literature and are probably the most widely used stated preference technique. The same approach is used in marketing to measure product demand (among other things), in transportation to measure preferences for transport alternatives, and in health economics to measure preferences for treatment alternatives.

W. L. (Vic) Adamowicz

See also: Benefit–Cost Analysis; Contingent Valuation; Nonmarket Valuation; Passive Use Value; Travel Cost Method; Value of Statistical Life

Further Reading

Carson, R., and J. Louviere. 2011. A Common Nomenclature for Stated Preference Elicitation Approaches. *Environmental and Resource Economics* 49(4): 539–559.

Champ, P., K. Boyle, and T. Brown (editors). 2003. *A Primer on Nonmarket Valuation.* Dordrecht: Kluwer.

Kanninen, B. J. (editor). 2007. *Valuing Environmental Amenities Using Stated Choice Studies.* Berlin: Springer.

Ciriacy-Wantrup, S. V.

In his seminal book, *Resource Conservation: Economics and Policies*, and in other early publications, S. V. Ciriacy-Wantrup (1906–1980) anticipated several directions that environmental and resource economics would take through the second half of the 20th century. John Krutilla, in his own seminal work on preservation of natural environments, included a footnote stating, "It must be acknowledged that with sufficient patience and perception, nearly all the arguments for preserving unique phenomena of nature can be found in the classic on conservation economics by Ciriacy-Wantrup." Wantrup (as he was commonly known except as the author of his publications) also anticipated the development of contingent valuation. He developed a primitive version of dynamic optimization and explored the theoretical effects of changes in economic parameters such as interest rates, uncertainty, tenure arrangements, and price expectations. In his book and later work, he helped to develop a more nuanced understanding of resource use under open access (which he referred to as fugitive resources) and common property. The prescience of his life's work justifies his place as one of the founders of environmental and resource economics.

In all his work, Wantrup combined rigorous economic analysis with a firm understanding of the physical and biological sciences and an appreciation for the roles that institutions play in economic life. He also insisted that the work of resource economists should seek to be relevant to public policy. For example, water resource policy, with emphasis on the western United States, was a recurrent theme in his research throughout his career.

Wantrup has been cited most often in recent years for his concept of the safe minimum standard of conservation (SMS). He devoted particular attention to those renewable resources that have critical zones measured in terms of their current stock. If a stock falls within its critical zone, there is a risk of irreversible loss of the resource itself. For a species of plant or animal, for example, the critical zone would be encountered if there are so few remaining members of the species that near-term extinction is likely. He defined the SMS this way: "a safe minimum standard is achieved by avoiding the critical zone—that is, those physical conditions, brought about by human action, which would make it uneconomical to halt or reverse depletion." Wantrup saw the SMS as a strategy to avoid the large, though uncertain, future losses that might result from extinction of species and irreversible depletion of other renewable resources.

In his book, he explored in a preliminary way how the SMS would apply to soils, groundwater, grazing lands, forests, and other resources. In later research, he applied the SMS to the threatened California tule elk, prime agricultural land, and water quality.

Though the SMS has yet to be fully integrated into mainstream environmental and resource economics, a significant branch of the literature has grown up around it and it continues to receive attention in textbooks. Logically and on an intuitive level, it has much in common with the precautionary principle.

Wantrup was born in Langenberg, Germany, in 1906, the son of a clergyman. Growing up, he spent summers on his grandfather's farm, where he acquired a life-long interest in agriculture. He attended the University of Berlin, the University of Vienna, and the University of Bonn, and received an M.S. degree from the University of Illinois in 1930 and a Doctor of Agriculture degree from the University of Bonn in 1931. Wantrup stayed on at Bonn as a faculty member until 1936. He left Germany for good in response to the rise of the Nazis and moved to the United States, working at the Rockefeller Foundation before joining the faculty of the Department of Agricultural and Resource Economics, University of

California-Berkeley, in 1938. He spent the rest of his career there doing research and teaching. He chaired more than 20 doctoral theses, most in the 1960s and 1970s, when student interests shifted from more conventional agricultural economics to environmental and resource economics. His approach to teaching was decidedly Teutonic, leaving little doubt about who was the professor and who was the student, but he was also fiercely loyal to his students and seemed to revel in the attention they gave his work during the last two decades of his career. He died in Berkeley in 1980.

Wantrup's legacy extends beyond his written work and students. In his will, he endowed the S. V. Ciriacy-Wantrup Postdoctoral Fellowships in Natural Resource Economics and Political Economy at the University of California-Berkeley. At last count, more than 40 young scholars have held Wantrup Fellowships. Many have been associated with the Department of Agricultural and Resource Economics, but in keeping with Wantrup's broad interests, fellows have also worked in geography; environment sciences, policy, and management; energy resources; international studies; and other fields.

Wantrup was a man who practiced what he preached. He owned two rural properties in California, one on the Mendocino coast and the other in Napa County. With his blessings, the Mendocino property became a state park in the early 1970s. In his will, he donated the other property to the Land Trust of Napa County and it became the Wantrup Wildlife Sanctuary.

Richard C. Bishop

See also: Common Pool Resources; Contingent Valuation; Krutilla, John V.; Precautionary Principle; Safe Minimum Standard; Sustainability

Further Reading

Ciriacy-Wantrip, S. V. 1968. *Resource Conservation: Economics and Policies,* 3rd ed. Berkeley, CA: University of California Division of Agricultural Sciences. (Originally published in 1952 by the University of California Press.)

Ciriacy-Wantrip, S. V. 1985. *Natural Resource Economics: Selected Papers.* Richard C. Bishop and Stephen O. Anderson (editors). Boulder, CO, and London: Westview Press.

Clawson, Marion

Marion Clawson was a giant in the field of resource and environmental economics. Over his long career that spanned almost 70 years, he produced over 30 professional books and hundreds of papers. Marion Clawson was a product of western America, growing up on a small ranch in Nevada. His early memories were of life on the ranch where his father was a rancher and miner. Marion's interest in ranching was reflected in his academic work. He received his Bachelor of Science in Agriculture in 1926 and a Master of Science in Agricultural Economics in

1929, both from the University of Nevada. He would go on to have, in essence, two full careers. His first career was as a civil servant, initially in the Department of Agriculture, where his early years were spent doing agricultural research in the west. During World War II, Clawson earned a Ph.D. in economics from Harvard University. In 1947 he joined the Bureau of Land Management and served as its director from 1948 to 1953.

Clawson began his second career in 1955 as a researcher with Resources for the Future (RFF), an independent Washington-based policy research institute. During the first part of his RFF career Clawson's work covered a host of topics including agriculture, soil conservation, and urban land policy with his principal focus on land issues and outdoor recreation.

In 1973, Clawson had his first major involvement in forestry as one of several authors of the "Report of the President's Advisory Panel on Timber and the Environment," a report much of which was personally written by Clawson. Although the report was not overwhelmingly influential, years later Clawson opined that he believed that the report had a significant influence on the development of the National Forest Management Act of 1976.

The experience marked a defining point in Clawson's already diverse and illustrious career. After that panel report, Marion went on to write 11 more books, 8 of them on forestry. Perhaps his most influential book on forestry is *Forests for Whom and for What?* In this 1975 book, Clawson not only addressed issues of economic efficiency but he also covered cultural and social acceptability, and the income distributional consequences of forest production. In many respects this modest book was an early primer on forest economics, forest issues, and forest policy.

Much of Clawson's work on forests focused on the public forestland and on the National Forest System. His books in this area include *Forest Policy for the Future* (1974), *The Economics of National Forest Management* (1976), and *The Federal Lands Revisited* (1983). Marion's concerns involved questions of to what uses lands should be put and how best to manage lands for those ends. In this context the mix of federal, state, and private lands is important.

The peak of Clawson's influence on forestry probably came during the late 1970s with two very influence articles in the journal *Science*. In the 1976 article, Clawson argued that the National Forest Service devoted too many resources to poor lands and too few to high-productivity sites. In the 1979 article, Clawson showed how the nation's forests had recovered, far beyond what had been anticipated even by the most optimistic analysts, from earlier logging and land-clearing abuses. His argument was that the American forests were in far better condition than was commonly supposed, in large part due to their natural resiliency, which he felt was consistently underestimated.

Clawson continued his writings on forestry into his late eighties. He passed away in 1998 at the age of 92.

Roger A. Sedjo

See also: Amenity Values of Forests; Ecosystem Services; Forestry; Outdoor Recreation; Public Goods

Further Reading

Clawson, Marion. 1976. The National Forests—A Great National Asset Is Poorly Managed and Unproductive. *Science* 191(4227): 762–767.

Clawson, Marion. 1979. Forests in the Long-Sweep of American History. *Science* 204(4398): 1168–1174.

Sedjo, Roger A. 1999. Marion Clawson's Contribution to Forestry. Resources for the Future Discussion Paper 99-33, April.

Clean Air Act

The Clean Air Act (CAA), one of the most significant U.S. environmental protection laws, authorizes the Environmental Protection Agency (EPA) to issue regulations affecting almost every sector of the economy. The Office of Management and Budget (OMB) prepares a report to Congress each year on the costs and benefits of all federal regulations and they have consistently found that air pollution regulations issued by EPA's air program account for the largest share of both costs and benefits across all federal regulations. In their 2012 report, OMB notes that the annual benefits of air regulations are between $82 and $557 billion (the large range is based partly on OMB assumptions about uncertainty in the value of mortality risk reductions) and annual costs are between $22 and $28 billion. These benefits and costs are primarily associated with reduced public exposure to just one air pollutant: fine particulate matter.

The CAA, although passed in 1970, was significantly influenced by earlier legislation, including the Air Pollution Control Act of 1955, the CAA of 1963, and the Air Quality Act of 1967. These early laws began the process of defining the roles of federal and state governments in addressing air pollution, especially when it crosses state boundaries. The 1970 CAA was the first environmental legislation to grant far-reaching powers to the federal government to regulate air pollution sources and to establish ambient air quality standards that apply nationwide.

The 1970 CAA established National Ambient Air Quality Standards (NAAQS) to protect public health in polluted areas. To allow states some autonomy in addressing their own unique circumstances, the CAA gave state agencies flexibility in defining how the national standards would be achieved. This was accomplished by authorizing each state to prepare its own State Implementation Plan, although federal approval of the plan was still required. The CAA also requires New Source Performance Standards to limit air pollution emissions from stationary (industrial) sources, National Emission Standards for Hazardous Air Pollutants to reduce emissions of particularly toxic air pollutants (air toxics), and a mobile source pollution control program.

The CAA Amendments of 1977 established a New Source Review program for areas of the United States not attaining the levels of the NAAQS. This program mandated stringent controls on new industrial sources and required emissions to be offset by emissions reductions from other industries in the area. Similarly, a Prevention of Significant Deterioration (PSD) program was established for areas attaining the NAAQS, with the goal of preventing air quality in these areas from deteriorating to levels that would exceed the NAAQS. PSD generally requires new or modified emissions sources to install modern emissions controls, workplace practices, or a combination of both.

The CAA Amendments of 1990 were developed to address several deficiencies that had been identified as the original CAA was implemented. In crafting the CAA Amendments of 1990, Congress wanted, in particular, to address three major environmental threats: acid rain, urban air pollution, and air toxics. Also, there was considerable interest in making the nation's air pollution permit program more workable and in improving compliance with regulations through a strengthened enforcement program. The 1990 Amendments included six major Titles: Air Pollution Prevention and Control (Title I), Emission Standards for Moving Sources (Title II), General Provisions (Title III), Acid Deposition Control (Title IV), Permits (Title V), and Stratospheric Ozone Protection (Title VI).

One notable feature of the amendments was its reshaped air toxics program, which required the EPA to publish a list of source categories responsible for emissions of 189 air toxics and to issue Maximum Achievable Control Technology (MACT) standards for each category (the air toxics list was subsequently reduced to 188 when one air pollutant was determined to be nontoxic). A distinction was made between major sources, defined as facilities that emit at least 10 tons per year of any single air toxic or 25 tons per year of any combination of these pollutants, and area sources, which have toxic emissions that are less than these amounts. Examples of area sources are auto body shops and dry cleaners, which individually do not emit much pollution, but taken together, represent a large source of air pollution.

MACT standards for new sources are based on the application of emission control technology equivalent to the best controlled similar source found anywhere in the United States, although EPA is allowed to take into consideration costs, other environmental impacts, and energy requirements when considering whether to go beyond the required level of control. For existing sources, the standards are based on the average of the best performing 12 percent of existing sources. To control emissions from area sources, EPA may elect to establish standards based on generally available control technologies or operating practices. Note that while MACT standards are technology-based, EPA must examine health risk levels at regulated facilities after eight years and tighten the standards if necessary to reduce any remaining unacceptable risk (referred to as residual risk).

Another prominent feature of the 1990 amendments was the new permitting authority. Previously, a new facility's pollution control requirements may have been scattered among numerous state and federal regulations, some of which could be hard to identify or contain conflicting requirements. The amendments attempted to simply this process by incorporating all of a source's permit obligations into a single permitting document (called a Title V Permit) and by having the source pay a single permit fee to cover agency administrative costs. This program was designed to simplify permitting requirements for both the source and the agency, to ensure compliance with all applicable requirements, and to facilitate enforcement.

The amendments addressed mobile sources in several ways. Tighter emission standards were established for both automobiles and trucks, and manufacturers were required to reduce emissions from gasoline evaporation during refueling. Fuel quality was also controlled by reducing gasoline volatility and the sulfur content of diesel fuel, by requiring cleaner (reformulated) gasoline for cities with serious ozone problems, and by specifying higher levels of alcohol-based oxygenated fuels to be produced and sold during the winter months in areas exceeding the federal carbon monoxide NAAQS.

The 1990 amendments added a number of market-based provisions to reduce emissions. The most successful of these provisions was the Title IV program to reduce emissions that cause acid rain. The Acid Rain program established a federally managed cap-and-trade program that capped sulfur dioxide and nitrogen oxides (NO_x) emissions from power plants and set up a market for trading of pollution allowances. In addition, Title I allowed for the use of economic incentives in developing regulations to reduce emissions of volatile organic compounds (VOCs) from consumer and commercial products. Any fees collected are to be placed in a special fund in the U.S. Treasury to carry out the activities of emissions reduction. An example of how this has been implemented in regulations is an EPA rule to reduce VOC emissions from manufacturing of coatings (e.g., paint). In this rule a market-based option was included that enables a company to continue manufacturing architectural coatings with VOC contents higher than the limits included in the final rule through payment of a per gallon exceedance fee amounting to approximately $2,500 per ton of excess VOCs. The CAA Amendments also provided for a fee-based incentive to encourage attainment of the national ozone standards. Severe or extreme ozone nonattainment areas that do not attain the standards by their attainment dates can be assessed a fee of $8,900 per ton of NO_x and VOC emitted (where exceeding 80% of a base amount).

Bryan Hubbell and Richard Crume

See also: Air Pollution; Benefit–Cost Analysis; Emissions Trading; Externality; Health; Pigouvian Taxes; Pollution Abatement Costs; Regulation; Sulfur Dioxide Trading; Value of Statistical Life

Further Reading

Hubbell, Bryan J., Richard V. Crume, Dale M. Evarts and Jeff M. Cohen. 2010. Regulation and Progress under the 1990 Clean Air Act Amendments. *Review of Environmental Economics and Policy* 4(1): 122–138.

Office of Management and Budget, Office of Information and Regulatory Affairs. 2013. 2012 Report to Congress on the Benefits and Costs of Federal Regulations and Unfunded Mandates on State, Local, and Tribal Entities. April.

Clean Water Act

The principal law governing surface water pollution in the United States is the Federal Water Pollution Control Act, commonly referred to as the Clean Water Act, listed in Title 33, Chapter 26 of the United States Code. Originally enacted in 1948, this law was significantly revised and expanded in 1972 with its goal "to restore and maintain the chemical, physical, and biological integrity of the Nation's waters." Major amendments to the act were passed in 1977 and 1987.

Federal action to control water pollution can be traced as far back as the Refuse Act, a section of the Rivers and Harbors Act of 1899, but this law was primarily aimed at promoting water navigation. The 1948 Federal Water Pollution Control Act was the first federal law designed specifically to reduce water pollution. It authorized the federal government to engage in research into water pollution, but the states remained responsible for their own local water quality. However, in 1972, growing public awareness and concern for controlling water pollution led to amendments that consolidated the authority to regulate surface water pollution within the newly created Environmental Protection Agency.

The 1972 law established a still unmet national goal of eliminating the discharge of pollutants into navigable waters by 1985, with an interim goal of establishing water quality sufficient for recreation and the protection and propagation of fish, shellfish, and wildlife by 1983. It also set the national policy of prohibiting the discharge of toxic pollutants in toxic amounts and it provided for federal financial assistance for the construction of publicly owned waste treatment works. Industries were required to install the best practicable control technology, and municipal wastewater treatment plants were required to meet secondary treatment standards by 1977. Industries were required to meet a stricter standard, the best available technology economically achievable (BAT), by 1983 (later extended to 1989).

In 1977, the law was amended and given its moniker, the Clean Water Act. These amendments established three categories of pollutants: conventional, nonconventional, and toxic pollutants. The BAT requirement was still applied to toxic and nonconventional pollutants, but a new level of treatment called the best conventional technology was created to deal with conventional pollutants (total suspended solids, biochemical oxygen demanding materials, fecal coliform, pH, and oil and grease). In 1987, another set of major amendments phased out the construction grants program, replacing it with the State Water Pollution Control Revolving Fund. Under this program, states contribute matching funds to a revolving loan fund for wastewater treatment, which is then repaid and made available for future construction in other communities.

The 1972 amendments shifted the authority for pollution control to the federal government and allowed EPA to set technology-based, numerical effluent limits on the amount of discharges that can come from point sources (discrete conveyances of pollution such as pipes or man-made ditches). The limits are enforced by requiring point sources to hold a discharge permit specifying the pollutants that the source must control, numerical or narrative limits on those pollutants, and time periods for how often the source must monitor for that pollutant.

States are required to submit to EPA the designated uses for navigable waters (e.g., recreation, fish and wildlife propagation, public water supply, industrial and agricultural uses, etc.), and to submit water quality criteria identifying the maximum concentrations of various pollutants that support these designated uses. If the technology-based effluent limits do not achieve the designated use for a water body, then the EPA may set a Total Maximum Daily Load (TMDL), which is the maximum amount of a pollutant from all sources that may be discharged into that water body. If all water quality standards are met, then antidegradation policies and programs are required to keep the water quality at acceptable levels.

The Clean Water Act is primarily designed to control pollution from point sources (i.e., pollution that comes from readily identifiable sources) but has done little to address nonpoint source pollution. Nonpoint sources may be contributing more than 50 percent of total water pollution today, but most of them are not subject to effluent guidelines. The 1987 amendments directed states to develop and implement nonpoint pollution management programs and did provide some limited federal financial assistance, but it did not require federal pollution limits and there is no federal enforcement mechanism for these sources. States (but not the EPA) may require nonpoint sources to implement the best management practices to meet a TMDL.

The Clean Water Act continues to evolve, not only through Congressional amendments, but also through court action. In 2009, the Supreme Court held that the EPA could use benefit–cost analysis in establishing technology-based standards for cooling water intake requirements for power plants. In 2012, the Supreme Court unanimously ruled that property owners had the right to challenge the government's threats to fine them for alleged Clean Water Act violations without waiting for the EPA to attempt enforcement.

The success of the Clean Water Act can be measured by the water quality benefits it produces. Since 1982, the EPA has valued the monetizable benefits of its actions under this statue using benefit–cost analysis. Over time, this valuation has improved and utilized more sophisticated water quality models, but the EPA is currently not able to value all of the benefits that it produces. Benefit transfer has proven difficult because of the lack of a single measure of water quality across states. Estimating benefits based improvements in ecological outputs rather than water quality is possible, but requires ecological production functions that are often difficult to estimate. In addition, more recent stated preference techniques may be needed to adequately measure the passive use values that can contribute substantially to the total economic value of water quality improvements.

Charles W. Griffiths

See also: Benefit–Cost Analysis; Clean Air Act; Externality; Monitoring and Enforcement; Nonmarket Valuation; Nonpoint Source Pollution; Passive Use Value; Regulation; Water Pollution

Further Reading

Copeland, Claudia. 2010. Clean Water Act: A Summary of the Law. Congressional Research Service 7-5700.

Freeman, Myrick. 2000. Water Pollution Policy, in Paul R. Portney and Robert N. Stavins (editors), *Public Policies for Environmental Protection*, 2nd ed. Washington, D.C.: Resources for the Future.

Griffiths, Charles, Heather Klemick, Matt Massey, Chris Moore, Steve Newbold, David Simpson, Patrick Walsh, and William Wheeler. 2012. U.S. Environmental Protection Agency Valuation of Surface Water Quality Improvements. *Review of Environmental Economics and Policy* 6(1): 130–146.

U.S. Environmental Protection Agency. Introduction to the Clean Water Act. http://cfpub.epa.gov/watertrain/pdf/modules/IntrotoCWA.pdf

Climate Change and Forests

From boreal forests in the northern reaches of North America and Asia to tropical rainforests in the heart of the Amazon and Congo basins, the world has about 4 billion hectares of forest land. In the past several centuries, these forests have been threatened by land conversion and timber harvesting. In the future, climate change could present new and unique challenges to forests and the people who rely on them, including changing productivity levels, increasingly large forest fires, and the movement of forests across the landscape.

For a world that relies on forests to sequester carbon from the atmosphere, filter water, create unique habitats, and provide fuel, fiber, and shelter, the potential impacts of climate change have important implications. Each year, about $140 billion in timber is harvested across the world for industrial uses, and about $63 billion is harvested for fuelwood uses. Despite losses from deforestation and timber harvesting, recent estimates suggest that forests globally are still accumulating net carbon at about 4.4 billion tons of CO_2 per year, amounting to net sequestration of $31 to $132 billion per year, depending on the value of carbon. Just considering timber and carbon, forests provide an annual flow worth $230 to $330 billion per year. This means that on a per hectare basis, forests provide annual timber and carbon service flows in excess of $58 per hectare per year.

The impacts of climate change on forested ecosystems can be analyzed in three categories: changes in forest growth, dieback effects, and shifts in species distributions. Forest growth will benefit from rising carbon dioxide levels in the atmosphere, which will aid plant growth. There is some evidence that historical increases in atmospheric carbon dioxide concentrations already have enhanced forest growth. These increases, however, may be tempered by increasing forest dieback, due to drought stress and increased fire incidence. Some ecosystem models suggest that forest losses due to dieback may be large enough to offset enhanced growth, causing forests to become a net source of carbon to the atmosphere in the future. Species movement across the landscape will reduce the effects over time as species better adapted to climate change move into a region, but these changes could take very long time periods if naturally driven.

Economic models must account for these ecological changes. Most studies have concluded that the impacts in timber markets, however, are not likely to be large. The reason for this is that economic models account for human adaptation, which includes salvaging dead timber, harvesting forests in anticipation of future potential dieback, regenerating new species that can better tolerate a changed climate, regenerating faster-growing species in order to reduce the time to harvesting, and potentially fertilizing forests to take advantage of higher levels of atmospheric carbon.

In fact, climate change is likely to strengthen an important trend that has been building over the past half century—the shift in timber production away from extracting old growth and toward sustainable plantation forestry. Most regions that are currently increasing their timber output are doing it with fast-growing, nonindigenous species, rather than native forests. These plantations are highly adaptive, and as a result, regions that are taking advantage of them will gain competitive advantage with climate change. Although the regional distribution of timber output globally may vary with climate change, the global flow of timber or fiber for markets or fuel wood is unlikely to decline.

While timber harvesting is unlikely to be imperiled by climate change, the flow of other ecosystem services, including carbon, could be heavily affected. A key reason for this is that a large portion of the world's forests have little or no timber value, and thus, little or no management. Even if climate change causes dieback or other impacts in unmanaged regions, landowners are unlikely to perform even the most rudimentary adaptations. Because most nonmarket values are public, there is little opportunity for markets to help compensate landowners for the public benefits they provide. Of course, government may intervene and reserve lands with particularly high ecosystem values, but government intervention of this sort usually makes management more, not less, difficult.

Aside from the potential impacts of climate change, forests could play a vital role in reducing the impacts of climate change via carbon sequestration, or the storage of carbon in forest biomass. One estimate suggests that forests could reduce net global carbon emissions by up to one-third of the total reduction needed across all sectors for an abatement policy that equates benefits and costs. Managers can do this by increasing the world's forest area, changing forest management, and storing more wood in forest products. Putting policies in place to do this, however, would not be easy, as it would take substantial coordination across all levels of government, from country to country, and within countries.

In addition to coordination problems, several other substantive contractual issues could get in the way of implementing carbon sequestration, such as additionality, permanence, and leakage. Additionality refers to the difficulties associated with determining whether an individual action to increase carbon storage in forests is truly additional, or in other words, something that was done for the sole purposes of increasing carbon. If the action would have taken place anyway (e.g., if the landowner had already decided to increase their forest area), then there would be no net carbon gain for the atmosphere. Permanence refers to potential reversals that could occur if the forest under contract is subsequently harvested, or undergoes a disturbance like fire. Leakage occurs when carbon sequestration actions in one location cause an increase in carbon elsewhere. For instance, if land is converted to forests in one region, land prices could rise, providing incentives for landowners elsewhere to cut down their trees. Leakage could occur locally or, if carbon policies are widespread it could occur across international boundaries.

So far, policy makers have not agreed on the best way to handle these contractual issues, but there would be a massive payoff associated with doing so. Estimates of the annual value of carbon sequestration in forests would are around $64 billion per year for a global climate change policy that balances benefits and costs. This would increase the annual service flows in forests to over $290 billion per year, or more than $75 per hectare per year. Given that the value of carbon sequestration in forests is much further spread out than the value of timber, a carbon sequestration policy would provide significant value for areas that are lightly managed.

Brent Sohngen

See also: Adaptation; Amenity Values of Forests; Climate Change Impacts; Forestry; Tropical Rain Forests

Further Reading

Boisvenue, C., and S. W Running. 2006. Impacts of Climate Change on Natural Forest Productivity—Evidence Since the Middle of the 20th Century. *Global Change Biology* 12: 862–882.

Intergovernmental Panel on Climate Change. 2007, *Mitigation of Climate Change*. Intergovernmental Panel on Climate Change. Cambridge: Cambridge University Press.

Norby, Richard J., Evan H. DeLucia, Birgit Gielen, Carlo Calfapietra, Christian P. Giardina, John S. King, Joanne Ledford, et al. 2005. Forest Response to Elevated CO_2 Is Conserved across a Broad Range of Productivity. *Proceedings of the National Academy of Sciences of the United States of America* 102(50): 18052–18056.

Sohngen, B., and R. Mendelsohn. 2003. An Optimal Control Model of Forest Carbon Sequestration. *American Journal of Agricultural Economics* 85(2):448–457.

United Nations Food and Agricultural Organization. 2010. Global Forest Resources Assessment Main Report. Forestry Paper 163. Rome, Italy.

Westerling, A.L., H. G. Hidalgo, D. R. Cayan, and T. W. Swetnam. 2006. Warming and Earlier Spring Increase Western U.S. Forest Wildfire Activity. *Science* 313(5789): 940–943.

Climate Change Impacts

Human emissions of CO_2 and other greenhouse gases are often referred to as a planetary experiment with uncertain impacts. As climate scientist Wallace Broecker allegedly put it, "The climate system is an angry beast and we are poking it with sticks."

One source of uncertainty comes from the inevitable limitations of scientific knowledge. For example, the 2007 Intergovernmental Panel on Climate Change estimates that maintaining a heavy reliance on fossil fuels through 2100—what is called the A1FI emissions scenario—is likely to raise global temperatures during the 21st century by anything from 2.4° to 6.4°C (4.3° to 11.5°F). This is an extremely wide range.

It is worth noting that the IPCC's best estimate is 4.0°C (7.2°F), meaning that the high-side range (4.0°–6.4°C) is 50 percent larger than the low-side range (2.4°–4.0°C). This asymmetry, which is caused by scientific uncertainty concerning positive feedback loops in the climate system, results in a fat tail of improbable-but-not-impossible outcomes with very large temperature increases. Some economists—notably Martin Weitzman at Harvard—argue that buying insurance against the risk of fat-tail outcomes is the best reason to reduce greenhouse gas emissions.

Perhaps even more uncertain than the science, however, are the social and economic aspects of climate change. Three challenges are worth emphasizing: a theoretical issue about the economics of risk, an empirical issue about economic development, and an interdisciplinary issue about climate change impacts.

The theoretical issue is that economists have a hard time dealing with situations involving low-probability-but-catastrophic outcomes. This is easy to see from a thought experiment called the St Petersburg paradox. In one version, you flip a coin until the first appearance of Heads—say, on the nth flip—and then must give up 2^n dollars: \$2 if the first appearance of Heads is on the first flip, \$4 for the second flip, \$8 for the third flip, etc. Ask yourself how much you would pay to avoid playing this game (or for an insurance policy that will cover you against losses) and your answer is almost certainly different than the expected value of the game, which is infinite (!): Expected Value = 1/2 (2) + 1/4 (4) + 1/8 (8) . . . = 1 + 1 + 1 + . . .

Economists are of course not the only people who struggle with low-probability-but-catastrophic outcomes, and it is not at all clear that any other perspective—for example, an ethical approach based on the precautionary principle—will provide a greater degree of enlightenment. Nonetheless, we are left with the uncomfortable fact that we are skating on thin ice.

The second challenge—about economic development—is that we do not know what the world will look like 100 years from now. Perhaps we will have the technology to pull carbon out of the atmosphere, or to adapt to climate impacts, or (who knows?) to move to another planet if we destroy this one. In a fascinating 1992 address to the American Economic Association on "Some Economics of Global Warming," Nobel laureate Thomas Schelling asks readers seeking insight into the world of 2100 to consider how hard it would be to imagine the present day from the perspective of Americans a century earlier, in 1900: "Most of us worked outdoors; life expectancy was 47 years (it is now 75); barely a fifth of us lived in cities of 50,000 or more."

If the impressive growth in living standards over the past century continues in the new century, it will be hard to argue that current generations should make large sacrifices for the sake of future millionaires. Per-capita economic growth of, say, 2 percent per year means that the generation 100 years from now will be eight times richer than we are, and the generation 250 years from now will be 140 times richer. But that is a big if, and in fact this source of uncertainty is closely connected to the controversy about discounting future damages from climate impacts. The fundamental question, often overlooked in the heated rhetoric about discounting, is how future living standards will compare with present living standards.

The third and final challenge—about climate impacts—is that we are uncertain about how climate change will affect our economy and society. Will a business as usual approach to climate change lead to the catastrophes suggested by natural scientists? Or will the results be more modest, perhaps more akin to the damages from smog in Los Angeles in the 1970s or in Beijing in the 2000s?

Many but not all economists take the latter view, arguing that the costs from climate change will probably be only a few percentage points of global gross domestic production (GDP), that human societies are resilient and adaptable, and that even poor countries are likely to get rich before they get hot. This is certainly possible—history shows that many societies have damaged their natural environments on a massive scale while simultaneously increasing living standards—and it is this fairly blasé view of 2°–4°C temperature increases that causes economists like Weitzman to focus on fat-tail risks.

But it is also possible that this blasé view of our planetary system is fundamentally mistaken, akin to our rosy view of the financial system prior to the crash of 2008. Indeed, a good way to think about uncertainty surrounding climate impacts is to ask if the best analogy is financial markets, which appear to be prone to systemic risk and catastrophic failure, or normal markets like those for agricultural products, which adapt and respond to changing circumstances without collapsing.

In summary, economists face a daunting series of questions when it comes to the welfare impacts of climate change: How hot will it get? How bad is it to get hot? How rich will we get before it gets hot? And how should uncertainty about all of these issues affect economic analysis and policymaking?

Yoram Bauman

See also: Carbon Pricing; Discounting; Precautionary Principle; Risk and Uncertainty

Further Reading

Nordhaus, William D. 2009. An Analysis of the Dismal Theorem. Cowles Foundation Discussion Paper No. 1686, January.

Schelling, Thomas C. 1992. Some Economics of Global Warming. *American Economic Review* 82(1): 1–14.

Tol, Richard S. J. The Economic Effects of Climate Change. *Journal of Economic Perspectives* 23(2): 29–51.

Weitzman, Martin L. 2007. A Review of *The Stern Review on the Economics of Climate Change. Journal of Economic Literature* 45(3): 703–724.

Coase, Ronald

Ronald Coase was the Clifton R. Musser Professor Emeritus of Economics at the University of Chicago Law School. Coase received the Alfred Nobel Memorial Prize in Economic Sciences in 1991 for his contributions to the role of transactions costs and property rights for resolving problems of externality.

Coase was born in a London suburb on December 29, 1910, received a Bachelor of Commerce degree from the London School of Economics (University of London) in 1932, where he was greatly influenced by professor of commerce Arnold Plant. He then traveled to the United States on a Sir Ernest Cassel Travelling Scholarship, where he studied how (and why) American industries were organized in different ways. From this experience came his interest in the concept of transactions costs and why firms exist, resulting in the publication of his seminal work, "The Nature of the Firm" (1937). Once back in London, he taught at the Dundee

School of Economics and Commerce, the University of Liverpool, and the London School of Economics, where his work focused on public utilities. During the war, he worked as a government statistician, and afterward, returned to his previous work, focusing on the postal service and broadcasting.

Coase migrated permanently to the United States in 1951, first working at the University of Buffalo, then at the Center for Advanced Study in the Behavioral Sciences at Stanford, and later at the University of Virginia. In 1959 he continued to study the broadcasting sector, particularly the U.S. Federal Communications Commission, where he suggested the use of a pricing system to allocate the radio frequency spectrum and further developed his argument for the rationale of a property rights system. The meeting between him and members of the economics faculty at the University of Chicago in which his arguments were initially dismissed by leading economists is now famous. At their urging, he published his argument as the monumental work "The Problem of Social Cost" (1960). From this article came the now-famous Coase theorem that states that under sufficiently low transactions costs, interested parties will internalize externalities through private negotiations. This theorem has, however, been overapplied and abused at times by free-market advocates as ammunition against government intervention. Abandoning government intervention was never the point of Coase's argument, but rather that efforts to mitigate externality should focus less on arguments over liability and more on reducing transactions costs.

Coase moved to the University of Chicago in 1964 and became the editor of the *Journal of Law and Economics,* for which he served until 1982. Under his leadership as editor, the law and economics subdiscipline was born and flourished. He was the founding president of the International Society for New Institutional Economics (1996–97), and was the research advisor to the Ronald Coase Institute. Throughout his career, Coase urged economists to "write about the way in which actual markets operated and about how governments actually performed in regulating or undertaking economic activities." He passed away on September 2, 2013.

Daniel R. Petrolia

See also: Coase Theorem; Property Rights

Further Reading

Coase, R. 1959. The Federal Communications Commission. *Journal of Law and Economics* 2: 1–40.

Coase, R. 1960. The Problem of Social Cost. *Journal of Law and Economics* 3: 1–44.

Coase, R. 1991. Autobiography. Nobelprize.org: The Official Web Site of the Nobel Prize. Accessed online May 22, 2012: http://www.nobelprize.org/nobel_prizes/economics/laureates/1991/coase-autobio.html

Farber, D. A. 1997. Parody Lost/Pragmatism Regained: The Ironic History of the Coase Theorem. *Virginia Law Review* 83: 397–428.

Stigler, G. 1988. *Memoirs of an Unregulated Economist.* New York: Basic Books.

Coase Theorem

The Coase theorem is a nonmathematical description of the conditions under which two (or more) parties can bargain their way to a socially efficient allocation of disputed resources. In his 1960 article in the *Journal of Law and Economics*, "The Problem of Social Cost," Nobel Prize winning economist Ronald Coase lays the foundation for this oft-discussed and oft-misinterpreted theorem. Because Coase himself did not set out to define a mathematical theorem, there are multiple ways to think about the Coase theorem and its implications for how economists think about property rights and markets and their role in the socially efficient allocation of environmental and natural resources.

While perhaps far from Coase's original intent in outlining the role of property rights in bargaining situations over a local externality (think a local factory polluting a small community), the starting-point version of the Coase theorem in economics usually addresses the role of free markets in solving a local property rights dispute. A firm pollutes because it feels like it has the right to produce, with emissions as a natural by-product of production. The victim feels she has the right to clean air. At issue is both parties believe they have the property right—a situation ill-suited to bargaining. If I believe I am in the right, and you believe that you are in the right, neither party has the incentive to give up anything to get what they want. Without a resolution of the property rights dispute, there will be no bargaining or market transactions and there will always be a socially inefficient amount of pollution produced. If property rights are well established, regardless of to whom they are assigned, then both parties have incentives to bargain to the socially desirable outcome.

This free-market version of the Coase theorem goes something like this:

> As long as both parties are free to bargain, the final amount of pollution will be independent of the initial allocation of property rights.

The problem is not that the polluter is polluting. Pollution has its benefits—to the producer and to the consumer of the produced product. The problem is that both the polluter and the third-party victim think they have ownership (the property right) and no legal authority has stepped in to clearly define the property rights. Markets operate efficiently only when ownership is clearly defined. So who owns the clean air? In the free-market version of the Coase theorem, the role of the legal system is to decide who gets the property rights and then get out of the way; bargaining between the two parties will achieve the socially optimal outcome.

In simplest form, if the polluter is assigned the property right, then the victim of the pollution has the incentive to pay the polluter to not pollute. The polluter will accept payment to not pollute until the cost of preventing additional pollution exceeds the willingness to pay from the victim for additional pollution reductions. Likewise, if the victim is assigned the legal property right to clean air, the polluter has an incentive to pay the victim to allow it to pollute and the victim will accept payment as long as the payment exceeds the additional damages caused by additional pollution. In either case, the final amount of pollution is the same, and only the distribution of wealth is different. Because bargaining is assumed to be free, it does not matter to whom the property rights are assigned, just assign them to either the polluter or the victim and let bargaining (or the market) work. The result will be an efficient solution.

The free-market version of the Coase theorem fits nicely with other market-based solutions to externality problems, like Pigouvian taxes and subsidies. A properly set Pigouvian tax on emissions, or a properly set Pigouvian subsidy on pollution abatement, will result in the same final amount of pollution; the tax or the subsidy act as a social price for pollution. The free-market Coasian bargaining solution does the same thing; only it allows bargaining to set the price for pollution. The market solves the problem. This version of the Coase theorem serves as a foundation for emissions trading schemes in which tradable pollution permits serve as a proxy for the property right to pollute.

There are a lot of assumptions embedded in the simple free-market version of the Coase theorem that render the theorem unrealistic in its simple form. In "The Problem of Social Cost," Coase's intent was to clarify the conditions under which bargaining might or might not resolve a property rights dispute efficiently. A more realistic fair-market version of the Coase theorem makes explicit one of the conditions that might keep the free market from efficiently solving the pollution problem: transactions costs, or any other impediment to bargaining. The fair-market version of the Coase theorem is:

> In the presence of transactions costs, the final amount of pollution depends on the initial allocation of property rights.

The focus here is on the transactions costs. If the victim is assigned the property right, the free-market version of the Coase theorem says that the victim will be willing to sell that right up until the point where the monetary damage from one more unit of pollution exactly equals the amount the polluter is willing to pay for it. With transactions costs, the victim must also recoup the transaction costs in addition to the damages. The result is less pollution than we would get without the bargaining (transaction) cost. But, if the polluter has the property right, the transaction costs cause more pollution relative to the free-market version. The result is a different amount of pollution depending on who gets the initial property rights.

The legal system now has a bigger impact. The outcome ends up tilted toward the side with the initial property right. In this case, the free-market version of the Coase theorem is a corollary—created by assuming away transactions costs.

These are probably the two most common versions of the Coase theorem. They focus attention on property rights and transactions costs, and the debate usually turns on whether we can assume away transactions costs in a bargaining situation. But the debate should not stop there. The Coase theorem serves to focus attention on a number of assumptions that need to be looked at before we declare a victory for the free market. Here's a brief discussion of two:

The two versions of the Coase theorem presented earlier ignore the possibility that the bargaining outcome creates wealth for the owner of the property right. If I have the right to clean air, any income I receive from selling that right might increase my demand for clean air. Just like getting a raise at work increases my demand for eating out; getting more money from selling my right to clean air might increase my demand for clean air. Likewise, increased profits to the polluter from selling pollution rights might increase the demand for emissions. Similar to the transactions cost case, the final emissions outcome depends on the initial allocation of property rights.

Further, the increase in profits from selling the property right might lead others to want to take advantage. If firms are free to enter the market, the assignment of property rights to the firms and the resulting profits from the sale of those rights creates an incentive for other polluting firms to enter the market. Similarly, assigning property rights to the victim, and creating wealth through bargaining, creates incentives for new victims to enter the market—for example, more people might move into a polluted neighborhood as a result of the increased wealth from the sale of property rights. The simple versions of the Coase theorem assume away entry—by both new firms and new victims.

The Coase theorem is usually presented separately from other incentive-based solutions to environmental problems. However, the real beauty of the Coase theorem is that it focuses attention on the assumptions needed to make incentive-based solutions work—or fail. Wealth effects are not unique to bargaining solutions: taxes and subsidies have the same problem. Taxes on pollution create potential wealth for the victim and abatement subsidies create wealth for the polluter. If victims are compensated proportionately to their damages, victims have the incentive to incur more damages. Similarly, subsidies create a potential incentive for new firms to enter a polluting industry.

The conditions highlighted by the Coase theorem are not unique to bargaining solutions. And that is the real benefit of talking about Coase. Instead of trying to figure out the right amount of pollution, we now focus our attention on the set of conditions that help or hinder market-based solutions to environmental problems.

Timothy C. Haab

See also: Coase, Ronald; Emissions Trading; Externality; Pigou, Arthur C.; Pollution Abatement Costs; Property Rights; Subsidies; Pigouvian Taxes; Welfare

Further Reading

Coase, Ronald H. 1960. The Problem of Social Cost. *Journal of Law and Economics* 3(1): 1–44.

Coastal Resources

Existing at the interface of land and sea, the coastal zone includes coastal waters and adjacent shore lands. The geographic scope of the coastal zone has been defined to extend seaward to the continental shelf and landward to 100 km of the shore-line. Coastal zones are home to a diverse array of ecosystems, including beaches, wetlands, marshlands, estuaries, mangroves, and reefs. These ecosystems provide a range of valuable services including provisioning services such as production of food, medicine and materials, cultural services such as opportunities for recreation, leisure, and tourism, regulating services such as pollution filtration and shoreline protection, and supporting services such as waste removal and habitat provision. Marine systems have served as the primary means for regional trade throughout human history; hence coastal zones also serve as centers of commerce. Because people are attracted to the coastal zone for these benefits and the esthetic appeal of the land and water nexus, coastal zones are densely inhabited, being home to between 23 and 39 percent of the world's population. Twenty-one of the world's 33 megacities, nearly all of which are growing, are located within 100 km of the coast. Concentrations of human activity around coasts result in numerous anthro-pogenic stressors on coastal ecosystems, including direct habitat alteration, over-harvest of marine species, pollution runoff, nutrient loading, sedimentation, and the introduction of nonnative species. Because these impacts may affect the ability of coastal ecosystems to continue producing ecosystem services, effective manage-ment of coastal resources is therefore of great importance to human well-being. The objective of coastal resource management can be viewed as achieving sustainable stocks and flows of coastal and marine resource goods and services, in combination with a socially acceptable distribution of welfare gains and losses.

Sustainable management of coastal resources presents a unique set of challenges and trade-offs. Coastal zones often include private property on the landward side and open access or common property resources on the seaward side. Potential uses of these common property resources are often conflicting (e.g., commercial vs. recreational fishing, dredging vs. habitat provision). Moreover, markets and behav-iors on the landward side directly impact the quality of nonmarket goods and ser-vices on the seaward side and vice versa. Human populations and physical capital in the coastal zone are also at risk from coastal hazards such as flooding and storms.

Attempts to mitigate the risks of such hazards via habitat modification may reduce the natural resiliency of coastal ecosystems and increase susceptibility to damage. Further, the natural dynamics of coastlines may cause actions in one coastal area to impact flows of goods and services in adjacent or proximate areas.

Overcoming these challenges requires an understanding of the biological and physical processes that provide coastal ecosystem services, as well as the determinants of human behavior and well-being. As such, economic theory and analysis can contribute to coastal resource management in a variety of ways, including modeling how individuals and markets behave in response to changes in resource quality, designing policy instruments that are consistent with the economic incentives faced by resource users, and understanding the range of economic values associated with coastal resources.

The process of economic valuation can play an important role in all of the above-mentioned areas. By monetizing the costs associated with habitat loss, the benefits of conservation and restoration efforts, or the economic dependence on coastal ecosystems, valuation can assist policymakers in making difficult decisions regarding the allocation of scarce resources among competing demands. To date, coastal resources in the United States have been the subject of considerable attention by resource economists compared to other regions of the world. Relatively little is known regarding the economic value of coastal resources in developing nations. Moreover, economic valuation studies have focused largely on measuring benefits from coastal resources that are more apparent and observable, such as those from provisioning and cultural ecosystem services like fisheries production, recreation, and tourism. While the value of shoreline protection services has received some attention by economists, relatively little is known regarding the economic value of the regulating and supportive services provided by coastal ecosystems. For example, the contribution of coastal ecosystems to fisheries production, pollution filtration, climate regulation, and habitat provision, while recognized as economically valuable, are rarely the subject of economic valuation. This is likely due to the difficulty associated with modeling linkages between changes in the quality of these ecosystem services and well-being. Important areas for future research therefore include geographic expansion of economic valuations of coastal resources and the integration of economic valuation efforts with disciplines that address the natural and physical aspects of coastal resources.

Peter W. Schuhmann

See also: Ecosystem Services; Externality; Nonmarket Valuation; Public Goods

Further Reading

Ledoux, L., and R. K. Turner. 2002. Valuing Ocean and Coastal Resources: A Review of Practical Examples and Issues for Further Action. *Ocean and Coastal Management* 45(9–10): 583–616.

Martínez, M. L., A. Intralawana, G. Vázquez, O. Pérez-Maqueoa, P. Sutton, and R. Landgrave. 2007. The Coasts of Our World: Ecological, Economic and Social Importance. *Ecological Economics* 63(2–3): 254–272.

Small, C., and R. J. Nicholls. 2003. A Global Analysis of Human Settlement in Coastal Zones. *Journal of Coastal Research*, 19(3): 584–599.

Turner, R. K., J. Paavola, P. Coopera, S. Farber, V. Jessamya, and S. Georgiou. 2003. Valuing Nature: Lessons Learned and Future Research Directions. *Ecological Economics* 46(3): 493–510.

Wilson, M. A., and S. Farber. 2008. Accounting for Ecosystem Goods and Services in Coastal Estuaries, in Linwood Pendleton (editor), *The Economic and Market Value of Coasts and Estuaries: What's At Stake?* Report for Restore America's Estuaries, NOAA.

Common Pool Resources

Goods and services can be classified based on their degree of excludability and subtractability. Excludability refers to an agent's ability to exclude others from consuming a good or service. For instance, upon purchasing a new vehicle one can exclude others from driving their car via the legal rights conveyed with the purchase and the enforcement of those laws by the government. Subtractability refers to the degree to which one's consumption of a good reduces the ability of others to consume the good as well. For instance, if you have a pack of gum and you consume a piece it reduces the amount available to either you or others by the unit consumed. Goods and services that are excludable and subtractable are defined as private goods and services, ones that are excludable but nonsubtractable are deemed to be toll goods or services, ones that are nonexcludable and nonsubtractable are public goods and services and those which are nonexcludable and subtractable are common pool resources. In environmental economics common pool resources play a central role in the management of the environment. Examples of resources that are conventionally viewed to be common pool resources are fisheries, oil reserves, and the atmosphere—resources that have all received considerable attention with regard to their efficient utilization.

The commons was popularized by Garrett Hardin's "Tragedy of the Commons" in which he outlined the incentive structure that results in the dissipation of resource rents within the commons: "Ruin is the destination toward which all men rush, each pursuing his own best interest in a society that believes in the freedom of the commons" (Hardin 1968, p. 1244). He contextualized the incentive problem present using a grazing area in which agents are free to have as many cattle as they wish graze in the commons. He outlined that there are two components to the decision to add another head of cattle to the grazing area: (1) the utility gain of having another head of cattle to sell after grazing in the commons and (2) the disutility of overgrazing resulting from adding an additional head of cattle to the commons. Given that the disutility of adding an additional head of cattle is shared by all, whereas the utility gains are private and borne solely by the decision agent a rational decision maker will add another head of cattle to the commons. Given this incentive structure he envisioned a commons area becoming overgrazed to a point at which it was not a viable grazing area for cattle; the rents would be completely dissipated.

Hanley, Shogren and White point out an important distinction that needs to be made between a common pool resource and an open access resource. The commons, as referenced in Hardin's work, represents an environmental asset. A common pool resource refers to the governance structure that endeavors to exclude some agents from the commons. On the other hand open access implies a lack of governance that allows agents access to the commons. In Hardin's discussion the rent dissipation is a result of open access to the commons, however in a number of situations governance structures and rights regimes have arisen that limit the dissipation of the resource rents in common pool resources. Central to the development of these governance structures is an effort to create some degree of excludability in the commons because it transforms the commons to a private good.

A resource that well illustrates the tragedy of the commons as well as the problems that arise from open-access and common pool resource governance is fisheries. A seminal contribution in the fisheries literature was H. Scott Gordon's analysis of the incentive structures present in the commons when fishermen have open access to the resource. Gordon illustrated that in the commons a fisherman's objective is to equate total revenues with total cost versus maximizing the difference between the two. He furthermore outlined that in a spatial context the fisherman's primary concern is the average productivity on a fishing ground versus the marginal productivity relative to the other fishing grounds they can fish. In equilibrium the average productivity is equal across fishing grounds and fishermen may actually fish some grounds even when marginal productivity is negative. The incentives problem is well illustrated in his statement, "the fish in the sea are valueless to the fisherman, because there is no assurance that they will be there for him tomorrow if they are left behind today" (Gordon 1954, p. 135). This incentive problem is generated because the resource is not excludable; in the absence of a governance structure a fishery is an open-access resource.

Gordon further discussed that the most efficient utilization of a fishery will occur when there is a sole owner of the resource. This is because the resource becomes excludable and the traditional marginal analysis, that which maximizes the rents derived from the resource, may be achieved. Expanding on the notion of sole ownership Anthony Scott argued that sole ownership was not the only requirement to ensure the efficient use of the fishery. He discussed that the tenure of the rights need to be over the long run and not the short run. If the rights were only for the short run the sole owner would have a similar incentive to overexploit the resource, whereas in the long run the benefits of conservation and dynamic resource management could be ensured. The dynamically optimal use of a fishery was later theoretically illustrated in the seminal work of Colin Clark and Gordon Munro.

Sole ownership does not necessarily imply that only one agent has exclusive control of the resource. The efficient utilization of the resource can be similarly obtained by privatizing the resource using property rights. However, privatization is not the only governance structure that can be used to efficiently govern the commons. Other institutions are Pigouvian taxation and collective governance. The central theme of these governance structures is that they try to invoke some degree of excludability that is enforced via a formal or informal governance structure. The central benefit of privatization is that the owners of the resource can trade among themselves in a Coasian manner in an effort to ensure that the most efficient use of the resource is achieved. On the other hand, Pigouvian taxation seeks to internalize the costs imposed onto others via a tax that aligns the private incentives of an agent in the commons with the incentives generated under sole ownership. Lastly, collective governance has been well illustrated in the work of Elinor Ostrom and it relies on local communities to establish small-scale governance structures to identify the users and management of a resource.

An excellent real-world example of the role that privatization has played in the efficient use of the commons is the recent Bering Sea Crab Rationalization Program (BCRP). The BCRP was enacted in 2005 and it allocated rights (defined as limited access privileges) to those fishermen operating within the federally managed crab fisheries of Alaska. Prior to the creation of this policy there were approximately 250 vessels in the red king crab fishery and nearly 180 vessels in the snow crab fishery and the length of the season was only a few days long. These statistics are indicative of the rampant overcapacity in the race to fish generated by having open access to the commons. Following the creation of the BCRP the number of vessels participating in the red king crab and snow crab fisheries contracted by approximately 65 and 53 percent, respectively, and their respective season lengths began to be measured in terms of months, all generating a more efficient use of the resource (Schnier and Felthoven 2013).

The ability of collective governance to manage the commons has been well illustrated in the work of Elinor Ostrom. She defined a number of key components that are central to the ability of a common pool resource institution to effectively manage the commons. Bergstrom consolidated these factors into eight features that he defined as: (1) clearly defined resource boundaries; (2) appropriation rules defined for the specific community; (3) rules for collective choice; (4) the existence of monitoring and compliance; (5) penalties for noncompliance that vary depending on the gravity of the infraction; (6) access to conflict resolution mechanisms; (7) minimal recognition by national or regional government; and (8) multiple layers of governance for complex commons. Evidence of the effective utilization of collective governance is well illustrated in numerous case studies with contexts ranging from common grazing areas and water allocation regimes to small-scale fisheries.

Kurt E. Schnier

See also: Hardin, Garrett; Ostrom, Elinor; Pigouvian Taxes; Property Rights; Public Goods; Tragedy of the Commons

Further Reading

Bergstrom, T. C. 2010. The Uncommon Insight of Elinor Ostrom. *Scandinavian Journal of Economics* 112(2): 245–261.

Clark, C. W., and G. R. Munro. 1975. The Economics of Fishing and Modern Capital Theory. *Journal of Environmental Economics and Management* 2(2): 92–106.

Gordon, H. S. 1954. The Economic Theory of a Common-Property Resource: The Fishery. *Journal of Political Economy* 62(2): 124–42.

Hanley, N., J. F. Shogren, and B. White. 1997. *Environmental Economics in Theory and Practice*. Oxford University Press. New York.

Hardin, G. 1968. The Tragedy of the Commons. *Science* 162(3859): 1243–1248.

Ostrom, E. 1990. *Governing the Commons: The Evolution of Institutions for Collective Action*. New York: Cambridge University Press.

Schnier, K.E. and R.G. Felthoven. 2013. Production Efficiency and Exit in Rights-Based Fisheries. *Land Economics* 89(3): 538–557.

Scott, A. 1955. The Fishery: The Objective of Sole Ownership. *Journal of Political Economy* 63(2): 116–124.

Complexity in Fisheries

Natural complexity can arise through the biology and behavior of fish and from changing conditions in their environment. Political and socioeconomic systems can also complicate attempts to properly manage fish stocks. Some of the easiest complications to understand can be the most difficult to solve. Consider the example of the Atlantic Bluefin Tuna. Bluefin's fatty belly is highly valued for sushi; an individual fish can command a price of up to $100,000. This fish swims over large portions of the Atlantic Ocean and is harvested by fleets in many different nations. International management of this highly migratory fish stock is through an international organization called the Inter-American Tropical Tuna Commission. But international agreements are difficult to make and even harder to enforce. These complications along with the ability to fly the harvest overnight to the market in Tokyo have led to declining populations and failed attempts to reverse this decline.

The story of the Atlantic Bluefin illustrates international conflicts in fishery management. There are other types of conflict over fishery resources. One increasingly contentious conflict is that between recreational and commercial fishing groups (and in some cases, users of traditional fishing practices). Recreational fishing

groups typically derive a benefit from the fishing experience itself, and have different fishing gear and therefore different cost structures. Economic theory suggests
that a fully tradable catch-share program would lead to optimal allocation in equilibrium. In practice, there is opposition to catch-share programs from some parts of
the recreational community, and the relative share of the allowable catch is often a
source of much debate and conflict between fishing groups.

Another form of recreational use of fish resources is the nonextractive direct interaction with fish populations of activities such as SCUBA dive tourism, snorkel-
ing, and glass-bottom boat tours. The benefits to the consumers of these activities
can be in direct conflict with those of fishing interests. Larger fish populations tend
to improve the recreational viewing experience, while smaller populations may
lead to larger annual yields to the fishing industry.

Environmental complexity can lead to conflict and further complications for
management. The survivorship and reproductivity of many fish species depend
on the conditions of their own and nearby ecosystems. There are many forms of
coastal pollution and alternate uses of coastal habitat bringing other users of the
coastal zone and fishing groups into conflict. A classic example of this conflict is
damage caused by shrimp farming in mangrove swamps to nearby fishery yields.
Managers may also need to consider sources of environmental fluctuation that are
not the result of local economic decisions but result from larger external processes
such as the El Nino—Southern Oscillation or global climate change. These larger
processes can lead to redistribution of species and changes in reproduction and,
most importantly, an increase in uncertainty over a wide variety of management-
relevant factors.

Risk and uncertainty are inherent to wild-capture fisheries. Fish are underwater
and many species move, so current stock size is never known with certainty; the
environmental variations mentioned earlier are likely unpredictable; harvest and
natural mortality are not perfectly observed. Even when the forms of certainty discussed before are dealt with, there remains uncertainty in the reproductive capacity
of a fish stock. Natural growth can be modeled but in order to choose appropriate catch levels, managers must attempt to estimate the particular numerical values (parameters) governing growth and migration but these estimated are always
highly uncertain.

The environments and ecosystems containing fisheries are often highly variable
across their spatial range. Conditions such as water temperature and quality, structure of sea/lake bottom, nature of ecological community, or energy inputs can be
quite different across various patches within the fishery. This spatial variation can
be important for managers to consider. Some patches within the fishery may be of
critical importance to reproduction or as food sources. Areas of biological importance to the fish stock may be relatively more attractive as fishing grounds, leading
to fishing practices that can decrease long-run reproduction.

Managers, ecologists, and economists pay increasing attention to the importance of spatial complexity and this has led to some policies referred to as marine reserves or marine protected areas in the sea and freshwater reserves or freshwater protected areas in lakes. These areas vary in how they are managed, the strictest form being a part of the fishery where all fishing is banned. Studies on the effectiveness of these areas do not all agree, and the direct harvest benefits are still not certain. What is clear is that protecting certain habitats makes sense such as nursery areas (parts of the fishery where younger fish grow larger for later harvest). The benefits for alternate users of fish resources, such as SCUBA and snorkel-swimming observers, are fairly clear as total mass of fish increase with even stronger increases in predator fish (often more highly valued for the viewing experience). It is unlikely that reserves will help with many of the distributional conflicts between nations or fishing sectors but there is some hope that reserves may provide a hedge against some of the uncertainties of fishery management.

To conclude, while property rights are very successful, there are a number of details that may require further attention for policy design. Some difficulties may ultimately be insurmountable but fishery stock assessments and newer spatially oriented policies may prove to complement property rights and lead to improved management outcomes.

Jason H. Murray

See also: Catch Shares; Common Pool Resources; Externality; Fisheries Management; Property Rights; Regulation; Risk and Uncertainty

Further Reading

Sala E., C. Costello, D. Dougherty, G. Heal, K. Kelleher, J. Murray, A. Rosenberg, and R. Sumaila. 2013. A General Business Model for Marine Reserves. *PLoS ONE* 8(4): e58799.

Sanchirico, J. N., K. A. Corchran, and P. M. Emerson. 2002. Marine Protected Areas: Economic and Social Implications. RFF Discussion Paper 02-26. http://www.rff.org/documents/RFF-DP-02–26.pdf

Conservation Reserve Program

The Conservation Reserve Program, commonly abbreviated CRP, is a large, federally funded program that provides payments to landowners and farmers in exchange for taking their land out of production agriculture and planting native grasses, trees, or other vegetation. The United States Department of Agriculture is the primary federal agency that administers the program, but three other agencies contribute to running it: the Commodity Credit Corporation, which is the agency that farmers contract with to enter the program; the Farm Service Agency, which provides support to the commodity Credit Corporation; and the Natural Resource Conservation

Service, which provides expert assistance in implementing conservation practices on CRP lands.

The CRP has its roots in farm programs and policies from the Dust Bowl era and the Great Depression. During this period, farmers were struggling to make ends meet and the devastation wrought by the dust bowl led to the passage of the Agricultural Conservation Program in 1936, which provided support for farmers who planted perennial vegetation (i.e., grasses, shrubs, or trees) on erosion-prone lands. In addition to helping to protect the soil, this had the added benefit of reducing the amount of crops grown and harvested. Thus, this early version of the CRP was intended to do more than conserve soil. It was also seen as an important means to improve farm income and rural livelihoods through directly providing money to rural inhabitants and by reducing the supply of agricultural commodities, thereby keeping prices higher than they would be otherwise.

The modern CRP was begun in the 1985 Farm Bill where the program became more focused on a broad set of environmental endpoints including water quality, wildlife habitat, and general ecosystem health rather than its previous focus on soil erosion and soil quality. It also reduced its official focus on income support and rural development. Over 35 million acres of cropland were enrolled in the CRP across the United States in the years following the programs expansion. The number of acres enrolled hit its peak in 2007 when nearly 37 million acres of land were managed under a CRP contract.

Farmers who are interested in enrolling in the CRP identify the acres they would like to enroll, their characteristics such as the type of soil and whether they are highly sloped, the plantings they are willing to place on the land, and other factors. The information they provide is used to form a score, formally called the Environmental Benefits Index, which is used to determine whether the land will be accepted into the program. Farmers typically sign a contract for 10–15 years where they agree to make the changes to the land specified in their bid in exchange for an annual payment (called the rental rate) and possibly additional compensation to support the costs and maintenance of the new plantings.

There are other conservation programs supported by the federal and state governments that provide payments to farmers to adopt conservation practices on their land. A variety of environmentally friendly agricultural practices can be supported under these programs. Examples include the use of contour farming, buffer strips, and the creation and maintenance of wetlands or other environmentally beneficial open spaces. These programs are sometimes referred to as green payment programs because they pay farmers to adopt land uses that benefit the environment. Some of these programs provide only a portion of the cost of the conservation practices, others pay the full cost of taking the land out of production including payments to cover the installation and maintenance of the conservation practices. The CRP has grown to be the largest of these green payment programs. The Environmental

Working Group reports that nearly $30 billion was spent on the CRP over the period 1995–2011.

Since the primary motivation of the CRP is to provide environmental services to society, an important question is whether it has achieved its goals, particularly given the high cost of the program to the U.S. taxpayer. Studies by the United States Department of Agriculture and others have identified the CRP as a source of significant environmental benefits including impressive reductions in erosion, improved habitat for many birds and animals resulting in larger and more diverse populations, and less agricultural runoff including nitrogen, phosphorus, and pesticides. The planting of native plants contributes to preserving ecological diversity and increases the storage of carbon, a greenhouse gas, in agricultural soils. However, research has also indicated that even greater environmental improvements could be achieved if alternative selection rules were used for choosing which land should be enrolled; the idea of improved targeting of conservation dollars to lands that can provide the biggest bang for the buck is one of the most important ways that the CRP program could continue to be improved.

The CRP has been criticized for declining rural populations since if land is taken out of active production, there may be a need for fewer workers and less business for suppliers of agricultural products such as seed, fertilizer, and machinery. However, studies by the United States Department of Agriculture suggest that such effects are small and that in some areas the additional spending generated by outdoor recreation opportunities more than made up for these economic losses.

In recent years, the competition for land driven by high commodity prices has put pressure on the CRP. Farmers whose contracts are expiring are increasingly finding it more profitable to replant crops on their fields rather than enter into a new contract to keep the land out of production. This has raised concerns about the environmental performance and sustainability of the program as the higher prices mean that successfully retaining large areas of land in the program may become increasingly difficult.

Catherine Kling

See also: Agriculture; Payment for Environmental Services

Further Reading

Cain, Zachary, and Stephen Lovejoy. 2004. History and Outlook for Farm Bill Conservation Programs. *Choices Magazine* 4th Quarter.

Environmental Working Group website: http://farm.ewg.org/progdetail.php?fips=00000&progcode=total_cr

Feather, Peter, Daniel Hellerstein, and LeRoy Hansen. 1999. Economic Valuation of Environmental Benefits and the Targeting of Conservation Programs: The Case of the CRP. Agricultural Economic Report No. (AER-778) May.

Sullivan, Patrick, Daniel Hellerstein, LeRoy Hansen, Robert Johansson, Steven Koenig, Ruben Lubowski, William McBride, David McGranahan, Stephen Vogel, Michael Roberts, and Shawn Bucholtz. 2004. The Conservation Reserve Program: Economic Implications for Rural America. Agricultural Economic Report No. (AER-834) October.

Contingent Behavior

Contingent behavior is a stated preference approach to valuing environmental and natural resources. It is similar to other stated preference approaches, choice experiments and contingent valuation, in that it relies on hypothetical responses to survey questions. Contingent behavior questions ask survey respondents to think about how environmental policies or natural resource allocation changes would change their own behavior. For example, to estimate the benefits of a proposed change in water quality, respondents could be asked how their fishing trips might change in the future with improved catch rates. In order to estimate the benefits of a policy that reduces the risk of a drinking water contamination episode, respondents could be asked about their hypothetical purchases of market goods if the episode were to happen. Survey respondents can also be asked about how their behavior might change if prices were to rise or fall in order to estimate a demand curve.

Contingent behavior differs from contingent valuation and choice experiments. One difference is that contingent behavior questions typically ask for information that could be used to estimate a demand curve: number of trips, number of meals, etc. Another difference is that contingent behavior data is analyzed in the same ways that revealed preference data is analyzed. For example, contingent behavior data on recreation trips would be analyzed with the travel cost method. Contingent behavior data on defensive expenditures would be analyzed with the averting behavior method. Choice experiment and contingent valuation data are analyzed with statistical methods that were developed for that specific purpose.

Yet, in some applications contingent behavior can also be very similar to contingent valuation and choice experiments. The referendum format of the contingent valuation method is a type of contingent behavior where respondents state how they would vote. Choice experiment questions can be framed as a decision among different recreation alternatives. In both of these cases, the contingent valuation and choice experiment survey questions are, in essence, contingent behavior questions because the questions are framed as behaviors.

As with the other stated preference approaches the major advantage of contingent behavior is its flexibility. Revealed preference approaches rely on historical data and environmental policy can lead to behavior beyond the range of historical experience. For example, a water quality improvement could lead to a doubling of recreation trips. Variation of trips and water quality using historical data may not be able to capture this large behavioral response. Contingent behavior questions can be used to construct realistic scenarios for most new policies and credible estimates of expected behavior can be obtained.

Similar to choice experiments and contingent valuation, contingent behavior data also has its drawbacks. Since contingent behavior data is obtained with hypothetical questions survey respondents are sometimes placed in unfamiliar situations where complete information is not available. A respondent's own forecast of their future behavior in hypothetical scenarios can be misleading. Survey respondents may often have good intentions about their future behavior. For example, they may hope to go to the beach every weekend. Also, survey respondents may pay less attention to time and budget constraints when answering hypothetical questions. Both of these realities may lead survey respondents to say that they will participate in a fun activity more often than they have in the past.

Both revealed and stated preference approaches have strengths and weaknesses. Using both types of data at the same time exploits the strengths of both approaches while minimizing their weaknesses. Revealed preference data can be used to estimate the slope of a recreation demand curve with travel costs as the price while contingent behavior data can be used to estimate the magnitude of a demand shift caused by a proposed improvement in environmental quality. By controlling for the differences in the two types of data, the problems caused by the hypothetical nature of the contingent behavior data can be avoided. Problems associated with forecasting beyond the range of historical experience with revealed preference data can also be avoided.

Combining revealed preference and contingent behavior data has addressed a wide range of important issues in nonmarket environmental valuation. For example, one study asked boaters along the Atlantic Intracoastal Waterway in North Carolina questions about boat trips at different depths of the waterway. Many boaters had never had experience with anything other than a shallow waterway. The resulting data was used to estimate the benefits of a dredging policy. Another study asked seafood consumers how many seafood meals they would purchase if they were confronted with a massive fish kill with and without information about seafood safety. The resulting data was used to estimate the value of information provided by the government that seafood is safe to eat. In both cases, accurate estimates of the benefits of environmental and natural resource policy would be more difficult to develop without contingent behavior data.

Using both revealed preference and contingent behavior data can address other nonmarket valuation issues related to the difficulties of data collection. Typical recreation surveys only survey recreation participants. With these, it is impossible to understand the decision to participate in the recreation activity. Surveys of the general population can be used to survey participants and nonparticipants but these data are limited when trying to understand changes in participation in response to environmental or resource policy. Contingent behavior data from surveys of the general population can be used to better understand changes in participation with policy. Also, contingent behavior questions can increase the cost-effectiveness of data collection. A revealed preference survey will often collect only one data point (e.g., number of trips within the past year). Contingent behavior questions can supplement the single revealed preference data point with one or more contingent behavior data points. More information from each respondent can lead to increased statistical precision of environmental benefit estimates.

John C. Whitehead

See also: Averting Behavior; Choice Experiments; Contingent Valuation; Nonmarket Valuation; Travel Cost Method

Further Reading

Whitehead, John C., Timothy C. Haab, and J.-C. Huang (editors). 2011. *Preference Data for Environmental Valuation: Combining Revealed and Stated Approaches.* London: Routledge.

Contingent Valuation

The contingent valuation method (CVM) is a stated preference, survey-based approach to the valuation of amenities and recreational and other behaviors related to environment and natural resources. The CVM is useful for estimating benefits and costs for environmental and natural resource policy analysis and benefit–cost analysis involving nonmarket goods and services. The CVM has been used for major policy analyses associated with the U.S. Clean Water Act, the U.S. Clean Air Act, and the Natural Resource Damage Assessment associated with the Exxon *Valdez* oil spill.

The CVM is one of the most flexible valuation approaches available to policy analysts. The foundation of the CVM approach is a version of the stylized value-elicitation question, "How much are you willing to pay for X?" CVM questions are posed as a hypothetical scenario. Any quasi-public good, for which there are implicit markets for comparison, and pure public goods, for which no implicit market exists, are within the domain of CVM applicability. The only constraint that application of the CVM imposes is that a realistic valuation scenario must be constructed around payment and delivery of the change in environmental quality. Policy analysis often requires valuation beyond the observable range of behavior. The CVM introduces the flexibility to value wide ranges of quality changes. Multiple valuation questions can be used to estimate the value of the incremental benefits of a project to determine the scope at which the net benefits are maximized.

Beyond flexibility, the CVM offers advantages over revealed preference methods in the types of values that can be measured. Willingness to pay is the total value of a policy change and can be decomposed into use and passive use values.

The CVM can be used for measuring the economic value of policy for people who do not experience the changes resulting from policy directly. Direct changes might be experienced through on-site recreation, changes on the job, changes in the neighborhood of residence, or through changes in one's own health.

The components of a contingent valuation scenario include a description of the resource or policy context, a description of the policy or proposed change in resource allocation that will be valued, a payment vehicle and a payment rule. The description of the proposed policy should make explicit exactly what is being valued. A concrete scenario description allows each respondent to understand what good or service would be obtained in exchange for payment. Scenario descriptions must include the baseline level of environmental quality or natural resource allocation and changes to this baseline. These descriptions must be nonpersuasive and neutral.

The payment vehicle and payment rule are closely related. Payment vehicles are the way that respondents would actually pay for the change in resource allocation. Typical payment vehicles include increases in utility bills, increased taxes, increases in prices of related goods, user fees, and donations to special funds. The payment vehicle must be realistic, believable, and neutral. The payment rule makes explicit under what conditions the policy will be implemented. For quasi-public goods for which use is excludable, the payment rule is understood as payment of a fee for service or access. Respondents have little incentive to misrepresent their preferences. Payment rules for public goods are more complex. The payment rule for voluntary contributions is that if donations exceed the program costs then the program will be recommended for implementation. In this case respondents have at least a weak incentive to tell the truth. Since subsequent payment is not enforceable, people who want the policy tend to overstate their willingness to pay. The payment rule with a referendum is majority rule. If 50 percent or more of respondents vote for the policy then it will be recommended for implementation. In combination with an involuntary tax payment vehicle and if the survey is considered consequential there is little incentive for respondents to misrepresent their preferences. A consequential survey is one that has a nonzero probability of influencing policymakers.

Many early CVM applications asked the open-ended willingness to pay question. In practice, this question format is relatively difficult to answer, and respondents may adopt simple valuation strategies or anchor responses. The payment card question asks an open-ended question but provides dollar interval response categories from which respondents indicate the amount that most accurately reflects their maximum willingness to pay. This approach is prone to range bias. If another response category is included the average willingness to pay may change.

The earliest version of the closed-ended question was iterative bidding where everyone in the sample was asked for their willingness to pay a starting dollar amount. If the respondent answered "yes" they would be asked the question again with a higher dollar amount. These questions would continue until the respondent answered "no." If the respondent answered "no" they would be asked the question again with a lower dollar amount until the respondent answered "yes." One problem with iterative bidding is starting point bias where the magnitude of the starting dollar amount influenced final willingness to pay

The dichotomous choice question (often called referendum style in the context of a referendum payment rule) is similar to an iterative bidding question but the starting point is varied across survey respondents and only a single question is asked. The advantage of the dichotomous choice question is that a single valuation question is relatively easy to answer. The major disadvantage is that the answers reveal only whether each respondent is willing to pay is above or below the dollar amount threshold and sophisticated statistical techniques are necessary to estimate the population distribution of willingness to pay.

Since the CVM is based on responses to hypothetical valuation questions, there have been concerns about the accuracy of value estimates. Accuracy of a measure of a theoretical construct (e.g., willingness to pay) is comprised of validity and reliability. Validity is the extent to which a valuation method generates a measure that is unbiased, that is, provides an estimate centered around the true value, if it were known. Reliability is the extent to which a valuation method consistently generates the same measure. While reliability can often be demonstrated through repetition and replication, validity is more difficult to demonstrate when valuing nonmarket goods and services. By their nature, the true value of nonmarket goods and services are unknown. A valid method for estimating these values is thus attempting to provide an unbiased estimate around an unknown and unobservable quantity. It is important that CVM studies demonstrate some degree of both validity and reliability.

Critics of CVM point to the hypothetical nature of the questions, the ability of practitioners to influence results through question format, statistical manipulation, and the often conflicting results on tests of validity as evidence of the inadmissibility of CVM-derived values into policy analysis.

Timothy C. Haab and John C. Whitehead

See also: Benefit–Cost Analysis; Choice Experiments; Contingent Behavior; Experimental Methods and Valuation; Exxon *Valdez* Oil Spill; NOAA Panel on Contingent Valuation; Nonmarket Valuation; Passive Use Value; Welfare

Further Reading

Carson, R. T., and R. C. Mitchell. 1993. The Value of Clean Water: The Public's Willingness to Pay for Boatable, Fishable, and Swimmable Quality Water. *Water Resources Research* 29: 2445–2454.

Carson, R. T., R. C. Mitchell, W. M. Hanemann, R. J. Kopp, S. Presser, and P. A. Ruud. 2003. Contingent Valuation and Lost Passive Use: Damages from the Exxon Valdez Oil Spill. *Environmental and Resource Economics* 25(3): 257–286.

Kling, Catherine L., Daniel J. Phaneuf, and Jinhua Zhao. 2012. From Exxon to BP: Has Some Number Become Better than No Number? *The Journal of Economic Perspectives* 26(4): 3–26.

Mitchell, R. C., and R. T. Carson. 1989. *Using Surveys to Value Public Goods: The Contingent Valuation Method.* Washington, D.C.: Resources for the Future.

Whitehead, J.C., and Timothy C. Haab. 2013. Contingent Valuation Method, in Jason Shogren, (editor), *Encyclopedia of Energy, Natural Resource, and Environmental Economics*, pp. 334–341. Amsterdam: Elsevier.

Corporate Average Fuel Economy

Following the energy crisis of 1973, the U.S. Congress established Corporate Average Fuel Efficiency (CAFE) standards via the U.S. Energy Policy and Conservation Act of 1975 (PL94-163). The National Highway Traffic Safety Administration (NHTSA) was given the authority to determine the average standards for fuel efficiency that U.S. car and light-duty truck (pick-up trucks, minivans, sport utility vehicles up to 8,500 lb gross vehicle weight) manufacturers must meet based on four statutory criteria: (1) technological feasibility; (2) economic practicability; (3) the effect of other federal standards upon fuel economy; and (4) the need for the nation to conserve energy. The intent was to reduce fossil fuel (petroleum) consumption of cars and light trucks by increasing their fuel efficiency.

The CAFE regulations have been updated in response to new congressional laws that broaden U.S. Environmental Protection Agency's (EPA) authority to regulate greenhouse gases (GHGs). EPA was given authority to regulate GHG emissions after the Supreme Court's 2007 *Massachusetts et al. versus the EPA* decision that GHGs are air pollutants covered by the Clean Air Act (549 US 497). Following this decision, in 2009 the EPA administrator signed two findings: (1) the endangerment finding stating that the administrator had determined that the current and projected concentrations of GHGs threaten public health and welfare and (2) the combined emissions of these GHGs from new motor vehicles and new motor vehicle engines contribute to the GHG pollution. Because the primary method to reduce GHGs from vehicles is through improvements in fuel economy, EPA's authority to regulate GHGs is closely related to NHTSA's regulation of vehicle fuel economy. The transportation sector, as a whole, was responsible for 27 percent U.S. GHG (31% CO_2) emissions in 2010. The on-road sector (cars, motorcycles, trucks, and buses) makes up 84 percent of this total.

The EPA and NHTSA now develop harmonized fuel economy and GHG standards. Thus, CAFE regulations, which had an initial justification and focus on energy security and fuel savings, are coordinated with standards for nonfuel economy GHG emissions from such additional factors as air conditional coolants (hydrofluorocarbons) and efficiency factors.

CAFE standards apply to all vehicle manufacturers based on their sales-weighted harmonic average fuel economy, measured in miles-per-gallon (mpg). There are separate standards for cars and light trucks; imported and domestic fleets of cars are tracked separately. The effectiveness of CAFE standards in raising the light duty vehicle fleet's fuel efficiency, and other effects of CAFE regulations has been discussed in a large body of literature. Some debated whether the improvements in average fuel efficiency realized from 1978 (the first year that the CAFE standards went into effect) through 1987 were attained at a reasonable economic cost and whether the CAFE regulations induced undesirable changes in vehicles that could lower their safety. In addition, the CAFE standards themselves, by being less restrictive for trucks than for cars, likely had the effect of encouraging the shift in market share from cars to light-duty trucks. Higher vehicle fuel economy also lowers the cost per mile of driving, which induces additional driving (i.e., the rebound effect). While estimates of this additional driving differ, the EPA and NHTSA have most recently used a 10 percent rebound rate, which implies an increase of 5 percent in vehicle miles traveled when costs of driving are cut in half.

The concerns over safety and changes to vehicle fleets induced by CAFE regulations—as well as a continued national interest in energy security and transportation GHG emissions—have led to a number of reforms and expansions of CAFE regulations.

The Energy Independence and Security Act (EISA) of 2007 required an attribute standard that allowed NHTSA to change the form of the standard from a uniform standard to one based on the sales-weighted footprint (wheel base times track width) starting with model year (MY) 2011. The rationale for moving to this standard is that it reduces the incentive to change the size of vehicles for regulatory compliance. A footprint reduces the incentive to reduce the size of a vehicle since doing so increases the stringency of its fuel economy target. There are separate footprint-based standards for cars and light trucks. Also, EISA broadened CAFE regulations to cover large sport utility vehicles from 8,500 to 10,000 lb gross vehicle weight that were previously exempt from CAFE requirements.

The rules for MY 2012–2016 vehicles require that fleet-averaged fuel economy reach an equivalent of estimated combined average emissions level of 250 grams/mile of CO_2 or 35.4 mpg by MY 2016 (using air conditioning GHG credits by the EPA). Since CAFE standards as measured by NHTSA cannot take into account air conditioning credits this is equivalent to 34.1 mpg as calculated by NHTSA. In 2012 the agencies finalized rules for MY 2017–2025. The final standards are projected to result in an average fleet-wide level of 163 grams/mile of carbon dioxide (CO_2) in MY 2025, equivalent to 54.5 mpg if achieved only through fuel economy improvements and equal to 48–49 mpg (using air conditioning improvement credits). Compared to the standards in place through MY 2016, the EPA and NHSTA estimate that these CAFE standards provide significant savings for consumers in terms of expenditures on fuel. Higher costs for new vehicles will add, on average, about $1,800 for consumers who buy a new vehicle in MY 2025. Those consumers who drive their MY 2025 vehicle for its entire lifetime will save, on average, $5,700 to $7,400 (7% and 3% discount rates) in fuel savings compared to a vehicle meeting the MY 2016 standard.

Technically not part of CAFE regulations is the closely related Heavy-Duty National Program, which, for the first time, reduces GHGs emissions and improves the fuel efficiency of medium- and heavy-duty vehicles. The EPA and NHTSA estimate that the standards will reduce CO_2 emissions by 270 million metric tons and save about 530 million barrels of oil over the life of vehicles built from 2014 to 2018 MYs, providing $49 billion in net benefits.

The details on specific rules have changed over time and differ between the light- and heavy-duty sector. Nonetheless, for compliance, manufacturers are generally allowed to carry back and carry forward CAFE credits in a three- or five-year window around each model year. Thus, the CAFE regulations are one of the first major U.S. regulations to allow for credit borrowing and banking. Other flexibility mechanisms also allow CAFE credit averaging between separate standards for cars and light trucks or within the same regulatory category (heavy-duty) for the same manufacturer and limited trading across manufactures of credits for the same vehicle category.

If a vehicle manufacturer's average mpg for a given compliance category (e.g., domestic passenger car) falls below the applicable standard, and the manufacturer cannot make up the difference by using credits, the manufacturer is subject to civil penalties of $5.50 for each tenth of a MPG that a manufacturer's average fuel economy falls short of the standard for a given model year, multiplied by the total volume of those vehicles in the compliance category. For some manufacturers (predominantly foreign manufacturers of performance vehicles) paying this civil fine is a cheaper alternative than compliance with the fuel economy regulations. NHTSA has collected $844 million from 1983 through 2011 (cumulative, nominal dollars) in CAFE penalties (http://www.nhtsa.gov/fuel-economy).

Jonathan Rubin

See also: Climate Change Impacts; Jevons, William Stanley

Further Reading

Crandall, R. W., and J. D. Graham. 1989. The Effect of Fuel Economy Standards on Automobile Safety. *Journal of Law and Economics* 32: 97–118.

Davis, S. C., S. W. Diegel, et al. 2012. *Transportation Energy Data Book*, U.S. Department of Energy.

Greene, D. L. 1998. Why CAFE Worked. *Energy Policy* 26(8): 595–613.

Kleit, A. 1990. The Effect of Annual Changes in Automobile Fuel Economy Standards. *Journal of Regulatory Economics* 2(2): 151–172.

National Research Council. 2002. Effectiveness and Impact of Corporate Average Fuel Economy (CAFE) Standards, The National Academies Press.

U.S. Department of Transportation, U.S. Department of Energy, et al. 2002. Report to Congress: Effects of the Alternative Motor Fuels Act CAFE Incentives Policy.

U.S. Environmental Protection Agency. 2012. EPA and NHTSA Set Standards to Reduce Greenhouse Gases and Improve Fuel Economy for Model Years 2017–2025 Cars and Light Trucks. Regulatory Annoucement.

Corporate Environmentalism

Corporate environmentalism, or voluntary pollution control by businesses, has become an integral part of U.S. environmental policy, along with the traditional legislative approach to directly regulate emissions, better known as command and control, and market-oriented instruments such as tradable permits. While command-and-control regulation remains the main pillar of U.S. environmental policy, the regulatory landscape has changed since the early 1990s with the increased recourse by federal and state agencies to voluntary pollution control mechanisms to improve environmental protection. These government-sponsored programs encourage businesses to take a comprehensive approach to pollution prevention so as to achieve reductions in pollutants that are not directly regulated and/or lower emissions beyond their targets for regulated pollutants.

In 1990, the Pollution Prevention Act (PPA) was passed to promote widespread adoption by businesses of voluntary pollution prevention (P2) activities. The PPA defines a P2 practice as "any practice which (i) reduces the amount of any hazardous substance, pollutant, or contaminant entering any waste stream or otherwise released into the environment (including fugitive emissions) prior to recycling, treatment, or disposal; and (ii) reduces the hazards to public health and the environment associated with the release of such substances, pollutants, or contaminants." Examples of P2 activities include equipment and material modifications such as substituting less toxic solvents for hazardous solvents, and procedural changes such as self-inspection and monitoring programs to discover spills or leak sources. The U.S. Environmental Protection Agency (EPA) has identified 43 P2 practices that firms can choose to implement voluntarily in order to reduce waste generation.

With the enactment of the PPA, the government's hope is to induce voluntary corporate environmental investments and infuse a pollution prevention ethic within corporate management that stimulate substantial pollutant source reductions across the board. To encourage the adoption of P2 practices and other voluntary environmental investments, the EPA provides matching grants, technical assistance, and access to valuable P2 information exchanges. The EPA has also imbedded in its enforcement settlement process the option of reducing penalties against violators who perform P2 activities above and beyond the mandatory actions required to correct the violation.

In 1991, the EPA created the 33/50 program to reduce emissions of 17 high-priority toxic chemicals—including two ozone-depleting compounds—by a third by 1992 and by 50 percent by 1995, through voluntary action by firms. In early 1991, the EPA invited the 509 companies emitting the largest volume of 33/50 pollutants to participate in the program; these companies were responsible for over three-quarters of the targeted toxic releases. In July 1991, 4,534 other companies were invited to participate as well. With additions through 1995, the EPA invited a total of 10,167 firms to join the 33/50 program, and 1,294 firms accepted. The 33/50 program was purely voluntary, and its pollution reduction targets were not enforceable. Yet, the EPA cites some aggregate statistics as indicators of the program's success. Among reporting firms, total 33/50 chemical releases declined by over 52 percent between 1990 and 1996 compared to a 25.3 percent reduction in non-33/50 toxic emissions over the same period.

In 1992, the EPA introduced Energy Star, a voluntary labeling program designed to identify and promote energy-efficient products to reduce carbon dioxide emissions. To date, more than 20,000 organizations have chosen to participate in the Energy Star program. In the same vein, the EPA partnered with the U.S. Department of Agriculture in 1994 to create AgStar in order to induce voluntary reductions of methane emissions and protect water quality in concentrated animal feeding operations. AgStar promotes the use of anaerobic digesters to capture and combust methane so as to generate electricity.

The number of similar partnership programs between the EPA and businesses has grown rapidly to more than 50 today (www.epa.gov/partners); these programs are designed to address a wide variety of environmental issues related to air and water quality, climate change, energy efficiency, and product labeling. Furthermore, several state agencies have followed the EPA's lead to initiate their own voluntary programs. For example, over 160 businesses joined Ohio Prevention First in 1993, a voluntary program sponsored by the Ohio Environmental Protection Agency (Ohio EPA) to halve emissions generated throughout Ohio by the year 2000. More recently in 2007, Ohio EPA launched the Tox-Minus Initiative, another partnership program with Ohio businesses to achieve meaningful reductions in toxic releases within five years.

In addition to government-sponsored voluntary pollution control mechanisms, many businesses and industries are taking unilateral steps to proactively improve their environmental management by adopting ISO14001 standards and related environmental management systems—such as Total Quality Environmental Management (TQEM)—that enable them to identify the environmental impacts of their products and internalize those impacts in their operational decisions. Many leading firms have shifted away from a regulatory-driven approach to a more proactive and beyond-compliance strategy toward environmental management. For example, in the wake of a tragic gas leak that killed thousands in Bhopal in India, the chemical manufacturing industry responded by creating, on its own volition, the Responsible Care program to enhance environmental performance and occupational safety above and beyond member firms' legal obligations. The apparent success of Responsible Care led the BP Oil Spill Commission to recommend the creation of a like-minded program for the oil and gas industry. Notable examples of firm-led initiatives to rein in waste generation include the multinational conglomerate 3M's Pollution Prevention Pays (3P) program and Chevron's Save Money and Reduce Toxics (SMART) program. More recently, in 2006, DuPont announced that it will increase its spending on research and development of environmentally smart technologies by $400 million while Walmart, McDonald's, and Coca-Cola have all received awards for voluntary efforts to reduce their environmental footprint.

The rise of corporate environmentalism has ignited an ongoing academic debate regarding profit-driven business motives to self-select into costly voluntary programs. Economists have advanced a number of theories to explain this seemingly puzzling behavior. First, firms' overcompliance with environmental norms may be driven by a differentiation strategy designed to attract a growing chorus of green consumers willing to pay a premium for environmentally friendly goods. Alternately, voluntary pollution reductions may shield firms from green political activism, that is, lobbying by environmental interests groups—such as the Sierra Club, the Environmental Defense Fund, the League of Conservation Voters—to enact tighter regulatory standards that could significantly raise costs of doing business. In the same realm, corporate environmentalism may deter boycott campaigns by environmental interest groups. Furthermore, a research-intensive firm may engage in voluntary environmentalism as a strategy to hasten legislative or regulatory action that would ratchet up pollution standards to the detriment of its rivals. A less talked about potential motive is the desire to lessen the scrutiny of environmental authorities, reducing the frequency of costly environmental inspections and enforcement actions. Such rewards, whether promised implicitly or officially, may represent an optimal government policy to promote participation in a voluntary pollution reduction program.

Businesses in developing countries with notoriously weak and/or corrupt environmental enforcement agencies may embrace corporate environmentalism not necessarily to seek green premiums but to reassure upstream customers about their commitment to environmental quality; this is more likely to be the case for businesses in export-oriented developing countries. Indeed anecdotal evidence indicates that many suppliers have faced pressure from their customers in developed countries to seek ISO certification. China, for example, has by far the highest number of ISO 14001–certified businesses in the world.

Researchers have sought to test the empirical validity of the theories listed earlier mostly using data on the EPA's 33/50 program, the Green Lights program, the WasteWise program, the Climate Challenge program, the Energy Star program, and firms' adoption of P2 practices and environmental management systems. Yet, after more than two decades of experience with voluntary pollution control programs and an intense empirical scrutiny, a good deal of controversy remains on how effective these programs have been at curbing pollutant emissions from levels that would otherwise have been produced.

Abdoul G. Sam

See also: Clean Air Act; Emissions Trading; Environmentalism; Monitoring and Enforcement; Regulation

Further Reading

Innes, R., and A. G. Sam. 2008. Voluntary Pollution Reductions and the Enforcement of Environmental Law: An Empirical Study of the 33/50 Program. *Journal of Law and Economics* 51(2): 271–96.

Khanna, M., and L. Damon. 1999. EPA's Voluntary 33/50 Program: Impact on Toxic Releases and Economic Performance of Firms. *Journal of Environmental Economics and Management* 37(1): 1–25.

Koehler, D. 2007. The Effectiveness of Voluntary Environmental Programs—A Policy at Crossroads? *Policy Studies Journal* 35(4): 689–722.

Crocker, Thomas D.

Professor Thomas D. Crocker has been a force behind the development of environmental and resource economics for over four decades. Crocker received his Ph.D. from the University of Missouri in 1967, and taught at the University of Wisconsin and the University of California-Riverside before setting up residency at the University of Wyoming in 1975. Along with Ralph d'Arge, Crocker helped established Wyoming as a forerunner in using economics to understand environmental and natural resource policies. The Association of Environmental and Resource Economists (AERE) inducted Crocker as a fellow in 2008.

Crocker's most influential contribution was his idea of creating a market to trade pollution. The tradable pollution system idea is a concept so familiar today that the phrase cap-and-trade is part of the common vocabulary of pundits, economists, laypersons, and environmental managers. Tradable permit systems have generated more research and applications than nearly any other modern pollution control system. The sulfur dioxide (SO_2) permit system used to control acid deposition was an exemplary application in the United States, and the use of tradable quotas in fisheries is a central management tool worldwide. Cap-and-trade systems are commonly promoted as the centerpiece of climate change policies around the globe, including the European Union's Emissions Trading System (EU ETS). His 1966 paper outlining this idea, *The Structuring of Atmospheric Pollution Control Systems*, received the AERE Publication of Enduring Quality Award in 2001.

Crocker's work on the reciprocal nature of economic and environmental systems has also proven to be far-sighted. He promoted the idea that economists and natural scientists both need to examine jointly determined ecological-economic systems, and he anticipated the current interest in ecological economics well before most economists and ecologists recognized this approach. He argued that economic parameters affect the operations within the natural sciences as much as natural science parameters affect economic policy. His work has shown that systematic applications of choice theory can open the door to addressing how the physical, biological, and economic manifestations of environmental risk mediate each other's behavior.

Crocker is emeritus professor at Wyoming, and continues to explore new ideas in endogenous preferences and risk, and in intra-household health and environmental problems. The foundation for this work is his appreciation that a person's ex ante actions and beliefs influence his or her ex post gains, a concept he has applied to acid deposition control, productivity, groundwater, visibility, health, and non-market valuation. This work led him to explore how private citizens can affect the risk they face through self-protection and self-insurance, and the implications for public policy. Crocker continues to explore the connection between environmental hazards and influences on parents' decisions to invest in children as human capital.

Thomas Crocker has always been interested in a life of the mind—and his vision has helped identify what matters most at the intersection of economics and the environment.

Jason F. Shogren

See also: Association of Environmental and Resource Economists; Catch Shares; d'Arge, Ralph C.; Ecological Economics; Emissions Trading; Health; Sulfur Dioxide Trading

Further Reading

Agee, M., and T.D. Crocker. 2002. Parents' Discount Rate and the Intergenerational Transmission of Cognitive Skills. *Economica* 69:145–154.

Crocker, T.D. 1966. The Structuring of Atmospheric Pollution Control Systems, in H. Wolozin (editor), *The Economics of Air Pollution*, pp 61–68. New York: W. W Norton.

Crocker, T.D. 1984. Scientific Truths and Policy Truths in Acid Deposition Research, T. Crocker (editor), *Economic Perspectives on Acid Deposition Control*, pp. 65–80. Boston, MA: Butterworth.

Crocker, T.D., and J. Tschirhart. 1992. Ecosystems, Externalities and Economies. *Environmental and Resource Economics* 2(6): 551–567.

Cuyahoga River Fire

The Cuyahoga River winds in a U-shape through northwest Ohio, beginning at the confluence of the East Branch and West Branch Cuyahoga Rivers in Burton, Ohio, and ultimately finding its way 100 miles to its termination in Lake Erie in Cleveland, Ohio. Incorporated in 1836, Cleveland's lakeshore location and proximity to canals and railways proved ideal for shipments of raw materials (coal, iron ore) for manufacturers in Pennsylvania and Ohio. The industrial nature of Cleveland's development through the 1800s coupled with little attention paid to environmental concerns at the time led to the Cuyahoga River becoming one of the most polluted rivers in the United States. Choked with toxic sludge and covered in layers of oily industrial residue and debris, by the middle of the 20th century, the Cuyahoga River was void of animal life and frequently caught fire. The most damaging fire occurred in 1952 and caused over $1 million in damage at the time (over $8.5 million today's prices) to boats and riverside buildings. A much smaller fire on June 22, 1969, caught the attention of *Time* magazine, resulting in widespread national coverage and outrage. Often referenced as a landmark event in the establishment of the environmental movement and environmentalism, the 1969 Cuyahoga River fire was, in fact, the culmination of over a century of such events on the river, many of which were larger in scale than the 1969 fire.

Under shadow of the 2010 *Deepwater Horizon* Oil Spill in the Gulf of Mexico, in an Op-Ed in the New York Times marking the 40th anniversary of Earth Day, Nobel Prize winning economist Paul Krugman referenced the 1969 Cuyahoga River fire and the subsequent publicity as a signature event in the founding of the U.S. environmental movement, Earth Day, the establishment of the Environmental Protection Agency, the passage of the landmark 1970 amendments to the Clean Air Act and perhaps most significantly, the passage of the 1972 Clean Water Act (CWA). The CWA established water quality standards for all significant waterways in the United States that would render them fishable/swimmable within a decade. Further, the CWA established a national permitting system for point source pollution (National Pollutant Discharge Elimination System [NPDES]), established national discharge standards for all industrial facilities based on best available technologies, and authorized the U.S. Environmental Protection Agency to work with state environmental agencies to develop and implement state-level plans for addressing local water quality issues. Due to a lack of federal funding to back the mandates, states found it cost prohibitive to meet the fishable/swimmable target for all waterways within the 10-year timeframe—prompting states to rely heavily on benefit–cost analysis to prioritize waterways for targeted cleanup. Despite the lack of recognition of benefit–cost trade-offs in the legislation, the 1972 Clean Water Act provided the foundation for future amendments and legislation, ultimately leading to widespread reductions in water pollution in the United States. Much of this reduction can be traced back to the tipping point of the publicity surrounding the 1969 Cuyahoga River fire.

Today, while still far from clean, the Cuyahoga River is regarded as an environmental success story. The river no longer catches fire, now supports aquatic life along most of its 100-mile stretch, provides recreational opportunities through fishing and boating, and parts of the river are now swimmable.

Timothy C. Haab

See also: Benefit–Cost Analysis; Clean Air Act; Clean Water Act; *Deepwater Horizon* Oil Spill; Earth Day; Nonpoint Source Pollution; Water Pollution

Further Reading

"America's Sewage System and the Price of Optimism." *Time*. August 1, 1969.

"Drilling, Disaster, Denial." *New York Times*. May 2, 2010.

D

Daly, Herman E.

Herman Daly (born 1938) is one of the most influential people in the area of ecological and environmental economics. He has made many seminal contributions, and although retired, he continues to contribute and serves as a mentor to many and an inspiration to even more.

Professor Daly received a Ph.D. in economics from Vanderbilt University in 1967 and came to Louisiana State University (LSU) as an associate professor in 1968. He became a full professor in 1973 and received a chaired professorship (Alumni Professor of Economics) in 1983. Professor Daly remained at LSU until 1988, receiving the Louisiana State University's Distinguished Researcher Master Award in 1976. In 1988, Professor Daly became a senior economist in the World Bank's Environmental Department. In 1994 he became a senior research scholar at the University of Maryland's School of Public Affairs (http://www.publicpolicy .umd.edu/herman-daly), and remains there as an emeritus professor. Professor Daly has had a number of visiting positions including the Federal University of Ceara (Brazil), Yale University, and the Australian National University, as well as a Senior Fulbright Lecturer in Brazil.

Daly's 1968 article "On Economics as a Life-Science" was instrumental in demonstrating that economics could not be viewed as isolated from the ecosystems and the earth system in which the economic system was embedded. In many ways, this could be viewed as the beginning of both environmental economics and ecological economics. His other publications (numbering over 100) have provided a conceptual basis for ecological economics. He also helped develop this new discipline through his role as a founding member of the International Society of Ecological Economics.

His 1973 edited book, *Towards a Steady-State Economy,* in concert with his 1977 book, *Steady State Economics*, were instrumental in demonstrating that economic growth as conventionally defined can actually reduce social welfare, and that there are finite limits to the earth's ability to furnish material inputs and its ability to assimilate waste outputs. Other books include *For the Common Good* (1994), *Valuing the Earth* (1993), *Beyond Growth* (1997), *Ecological Economics and the Ecology of Economics* (1999), *The Local Politics of Global Sustainability* (1999), and *Ecological Economics: Principles and Applications* (2010).

Professor Daly has won a number of prizes and awards, including an Honorary Right Livelihood Award, the Heineken Prize for Environmental Science from the

Royal Netherlands Academy of Arts and Sciences, the Sophie Prize (Norway), and the Leontief Prize from the Global Development and Environment Institute, and the Lifetime Achievement Award from the National Council for Science and the Environment. His Right Livelihood Award Citation (http://www.rightlivelihood.org/daly.html) explains an approach that combines economics, environment, and ethics and

> a masterly synthesis of the application of classical concepts of capital and income to resources and the environment, the laws of thermodynamics, and the insights of ecology, particularly in relation to levels of flows of materials and energy through economic systems. This synthesis has resulted in a quantum leap in understanding as to why the economy is destroying the environment, which has deeply influenced the whole course of the debate as to what should be done about it.

Professor Daly's influence on the development of environmental and ecological economists during the last five decades cannot be overstated. He has clearly shown that it is possible to integrate ecology and economics. While he has never denied the importance of markets, he has shown that the economic performance and environmental preservation are not mutually exclusive, and his work paved the way for our current vision of sustainability.

James R. Kahn

See also: Ecological Economics; Sustainability

Further Reading

Daly, Herman E. 1968. *On Economics as a Life Science. The Journal of Political Economy* 76(3): 392–406.

Daly, Herman E. (editor). 1973. *Economics, Ecology, Ethics: Essays toward a Steady-State Economy.* San Francisco, CA: Freeman.

Daly, Herman E. 1974. *The Economics of the Steady State. American Economic Review* 64(2): 15–21.

Daly, Herman E. 1977. *Steady-State Economics.* San Francisco, CA: Freeman.

Daly, Herman E. 1997. Beyond Growth: *The Economics of Sustainable Development.* Boston, MA: Beacon Press.

Daly, Herman E. 1999. *Ecological Economics and the Ecology of Economics: Essay in Criticism.* Cheltenham, UK and Northampton, MA: Edward Elgar.

Daly, Herman E., and Joshua Farley. 2003. *Ecological Economics: Principles and Applications.* Washington, D.C.: Island Press.

Daly, Herman E., and Kenneth Neal Townsend. 1993. *Valuing the Earth: Economics, Ecology, Ethics.* Cambridge, MA: The MIT Press.

Daly, Herman E., John B. Cobb Jr, and Clifford W. Cobb. 1989. *For the Common Good: Redirecting the Economy toward Community, the Environment, and a Sustainable Future.* No. 73. Boston, MA: Beacon Press.

Daly, Herman E., Robert Costanza, and Thomas Prugh. 1999. *The Local Politics of Global Sustainability*. Island Press, 1999.

d'Arge, Ralph C.

Ralph Clair d'Arge was born in 1941 in Los Angeles. He grew up in the San Fernando Valley nestled at the foot of the San Gabriel Mountains in southern California when the area was still mostly desert, orange groves, and open space. He developed a love of the outdoors, of horses, and of the wide expanses of desert environments. After graduating from Chico State College in 1963 with a degree in agriculture, he attended Cornell to study economics. Ralph graduated with a Ph.D. in economics from Cornell in 1969, specializing in trade and international economics, econometrics, and natural resource economics.

In 1967 Ralph accepted an assistant professor position in the Economics Department at the University of New Mexico where he began a lifelong collaboration with Allen Kneese. In 1969 he was hired at the University of California at Riverside (UCR) where he immediately founded one of the first focused and concentrated Ph.D. programs in environmental and resource economics. The program quickly grew successful in both research and training of Ph.D. students. In 1974, he and Kneese established and became the first co-editors of the *Journal of Environmental Economics and Management* (JEEM). JEEM became the flagship journal for the newly legitimized field of natural resource and environmental economics. At about the same time, d'Arge, Kneese, and number of others were instrumental in founding the Association of Environmental and Resource Economists (AERE), the principal professional association for environmental and resource economists. Ralph's period at UCR was very productive, generating a wide range of innovative and important papers that earned him promotion to full professor before he was 30. His paper with Ayres and Kneese drew on Boulding's spaceship earth metaphor as well as the second law of thermodynamics to depict the biosphere as a contained system in which matter is neither created nor destroyed. Thus whatever is extracted eventually has to return to the ecosystem as residuals that might overtax the assimilative capacity and generate externalities. This simple but powerful metaphor not only was the precursor to modern ecological footprint analysis, but it also linked the two fields of environmental and resource economics and gave justification to economy-wide policy intervention in the face of pervasive externalities. During this period Ralph also initiated the first integrated climate assessment modeling to assess the consequences of flying supersonic transports in the upper atmosphere. Much of that work foreshadowed the more recent work on global warming, employing similar principles of linked atmospheric-economic system models. Ralph's vision for the new resource/environmental economics field saw it firmly integrated with the sciences, a view articulated in the editorial statement for the first issue of JEEM.

In the mid-1970s, Ralph, Tom Crocker, and others from UCR relocated the environmental/resource economics program to the University of Wyoming. This period saw him turn attention to important ideas in valuation of ecosystem services, including the audacious *Nature* article that attempted to value the entire biosphere's services. Ralph and colleagues at Wyoming were instrumental in early contingent valuation techniques, including incorporation of concepts from cognitive psychology that underlie modern developments in behavioral economics. Ralph and colleagues pioneered early work in laboratory experiments and field experiments that presented respondents with real choices. Ralph retired from Wyoming in 1996 and moved to Kentucky, where he returned to his early interests in horses. Ralph passed away in 2009, from complications following lung surgery. He left a legacy that included an inclusive framework for the newly legitimized field of resource and environmental economics, a number of important ideas that predated subsequent work, and students whose careers he touched in numerous ways.

James Wilen

See also: Association of Environmental and Resource Economists; Journals

Further Reading

Costanza, Robert, Ralph d'Arge, Rudolf De Groot, Stephen Farber, Monica Grasso, Bruce Hannon, Karin Limburg, Shahid Naeem, Robert V. O'Neill, Jose Paruelo, Robert G. Raskin, Paul Sutton, and Marjan van den Belt. 1997. The Value of the World's Ecosystem Services and Natural Capital. *Nature* 387(15): 253–260.

Kneese, A., R. Ayres, and R. d'Arge. 1970. *Economics and the Environment: A Materials Balance Approach*. Washington, D.C.: Johns Hopkins Press.

Smith, V. K. 2010. Reflections—Legacies, Incentives and Advice. *Review of Environmental Economics and Policy* 4(2): 309–324.

Wilen, James. 2009. Ralph Clair d'Arge Obituary: June 20, 1941–June 27, 2009. *Journal of Environmental Economics and Management* 58: 251–252.

Deepwater Horizon Oil Spill

On April 20, 2010, an exploratory oil drilling operation located in the northern Gulf of Mexico (approximately 40 miles off the Louisiana coast in the U.S. Exclusive Economic Zone) exploded. The drilling platform, known as the *Deepwater Horizon* (DWH), was owned by Transocean but leased by BP (formerly British Petroleum). At the time of the explosion, the production casing was being cemented at 18,360 feet (5,600 m) below sea level. The explosion was caused by a combination of factors including flaws in the design of the drilling equipment, equipment that malfunctioned, and human error.

On April 22, 2010, the DWH sank and crude oil was first observed. An oil leak was not immediately determined because the leak occurred on the sea floor, which complicated the estimation of the flow and the ability to stop it. The primary leak was contained on July 15, 2010. During the 87 days, at least 4.9 million barrels of crude oil (approximately 205 million gallons) had been spilled, making the DWH the largest accidental marine oil spill in history.

BP was designated the responsible party for damages caused by the DWH explosion under the Oil Pollution Act (OPA) of 1990. The OPA requires compensation of cleanup costs and damages, which include costs to restore natural resources to their pre-spill state and compensation for economic losses that occurred between the time of the spill and when resources are recovered (i.e., interim losses including passive use values). That said, BP is not solely responsible and has sued the owner of the rig (Transocean), the maker of the blowout preventer (Cameron), and the cementer (Halliburton).

The spilled oil caused visible damage to marine and wildlife habitats, killed marine animals, and by extension caused economic damage to the Gulf's fishing and tourism industries. The environmental effects are dependent on the quantity and density of spilled oil and the environmental conditions at the location and time of the spill (e.g., currents, temperature, oxygen levels). Also, BP used approximately 1.9 million gallons of Corexit, an oil dispersant with an unknown environmental impact, to aid the biodegradation of oil.

Due to the lack of an ongoing monitoring system, the large size of the area, and the changing wind patterns and ocean currents, there is no way to know with a reasonable degree of certainty how much oil remains. The use of dispersants and the natural ability of the oil to break down also complicate any attempt to measure the amount of oil remaining. However, during the months following the spill, oil made landfall across approximately 650 miles of coastline, mostly in Louisiana.

Although long-term effects of the DWH oil spill are unknown, past oil spills provide some insights. For example, with the Exxon *Valdez* oil spill, some fish populations did not start to decline until four to six years after the spill. The DWH is the largest spill in U.S. history and is unique in that it occurred subsurface. Long-term threats remain with respect to erosion of coastal marshes due to affected vegetation, the potential existence of large plumes of suspended oil in relation to key marine habitats, and implications for the sea floor since natural assimilation works best on surface oil.

Sherry L. Larkin

See also: Coastal Resources; Exxon *Valdez* Oil Spill; Passive Use Value

Further Reading

National Commission on the BP Deepwater Horizon Oil Spill and Offshore Drilling. January 2011. Deep Water: The Gulf Oil Disaster and the Future of Offshore Drilling. Report to the President, p. 379.

NOAA Restoration Center. 2012. Natural Resource Damage Assessment Status Update for the *Deepwater Horizon* Oil Spill. Silver Spring: NOAA's Damage Assessment, Remediation, and Restoration Program (DARRP). April, p. 91. http://www.gulfspillrestoration.noaa.gov/

Discounting

Suppose a government is considering undertaking one of two possible projects. Both require an immediate expenditure of $100 million. Both produce benefits of $10 million per year for several years. The first project's benefits commence immediately and last through year 15, whereas the second project's benefits do not start until year 16 but they continue for a total of one extra year (through year 31). Which project (if any) should the government undertake? The answer depends on the social discount rate that is used to convert the future values of the benefits into present values (which can then be compared to the present cost of $100 million).

In present value terms, a dollar today is worth more than a dollar in one year because it can be saved and invested. If investments earn a certain rate of return, say 5 percent per year, then a dollar today is worth $1.05 one year from now (one dollar plus five cents interest); it is worth approximately $1.10 in two years (1.05 times 1.05 dollars), and so on. This is the process of compounding and reflects the opportunity cost of consuming more today: you give up the opportunity to save and invest and to consume more in the future.

Discounting is simply this process in reverse: $1.05 a year from now is worth $1 today at a 5% rate, and so $1 a year from now is worth 1 divided by 1.05 dollars today. We discount future values to convert them into present values by multiplying them by discount factors (such as 1 divided by 1.05).

Discounting is a critical part of benefit–cost analysis. Benefit–cost analysis is a tool used to study the effects of various environmental policies (these may be investment projects or regulations). If a policy passes a benefit–cost test then in principle it is possible for those who gain from the policy to fully compensate those who lose and still have something left over. To conduct an analysis, social benefits and costs arising from a policy must be measured and assigned real, inflation-adjusted monetary values. These are weighted by discount factors, with those occurring further in the future given lower weights (discounted more) relative to those which occur sooner. The policy passes the test if the sum of the weighted benefits exceeds the weighted costs. The annual rate at which these discount factors decline is called the social discount rate (SDR).

There is no consensus as to the correct method for choosing the SDR or how to measure it, but the choice is crucial. Many policies and projects incur most of their costs early on and have benefits that occur later. In the cases of climate change abatement, preservation of biodiversity, or storage of nuclear waste, benefits may occur centuries from now. A benefit of one million of today's dollars that occurs 100 years in the future has a present value of over $138,000 at a discount rate of 2 percent, but a value of under $20,000 using an SDR of 4 percent, and less than $500 at an 8 percent rate. A decision to use an SDR that is a few percent higher can mean that many policies will fail a benefit–cost test when they would otherwise pass.

In principle, the SDR should reflect the opportunity cost of funds. However, with many different interest rates to choose from, inconsistencies in individual behavior and credit rationing, it is unclear how to use observed market interest rates to arrive at an SDR. There are two different approaches to obtaining a value for the SDR. One approach is called descriptive. Proponents of this method argue that the SDR should be based on observed market returns to savings and investment. Specifically, the SDR should primarily reflect the before-tax return on private investment, since making public investments means that society gives up the opportunity to earn this return. For example, the federal Office of Management and Budget recommends an SDR of 7 percent because it estimates that this is the marginal pre-tax return on investment for an average U.S. firm.

The second approach is called prescriptive. Its supporters argue that, in principle, the SDR should represent individual preferences for present relative to future consumption.

According to this approach, there are two reasons why an individual prefers present to future consumption: First, people are impatient—they prefer to consume today, possibly because they may not be here tomorrow. This pure rate of time preference may be based on the annual expected chance of death, plus an amount that accounts for simple impatience. Second, members of society may prefer to smooth out their consumption over time. If they expect their income and consumption to keep growing, and if they get decreasing extra satisfaction from extra consumption, then they will prefer to increase present consumption at the expense of the future— they will discount the future.

The UK Treasury now recommends an SDR of 3.5 percent based on the prescriptive method. They prescribe a pure rate of time preference equal to 1.5 percent per year (1% for the probability of death or other catastrophe plus 0.5% for pure impatience), plus a term that equals the expected growth rate of real consumption per person (2% a year) times a parameter that represents how much a typical individual's extra satisfaction falls as their consumption rises (set equal to 1).

Roughly speaking, supporters of the descriptive approach favor much higher numbers for the SDR, and those following the prescriptive approach support lower numbers. Those favoring lower SDRs tend to show greater support for government policies that have costs today and benefits that extend into the future; those who prefer higher SDRs are less supportive of such government interventions.

An extreme case of this difference in viewpoints arises when policies produce most of their benefits for far future generations (such as climate change abatement). Very long-term policy effects will have almost no impact in a benefit–cost analysis if the SDR is much above 2 percent. For example, at an SDR of 7 percent, a $1 million benefit in 100 years is only worth $1,152 today; if it arrives in 200 years it is barely worth $1 today. Many people are uncomfortable with the thought that the same benefit should count for over 850 times more for the present generation than it would for those living 100 years on, and that it should count for over three-quarters of a million times more than for those living in two centuries. But this is the logic of discounting using a constant SDR.

One resolution to this dilemma (which the UK Treasury now recommends) is to use lower and lower rates for discounting costs and benefits that occur further and further into the future—a schedule of time-declining SDRs. One reason to do this is that there is considerable uncertainty as to future returns on investment and growth rates of consumption. To account for this uncertainty, one should average the possible discount factors that would apply to future costs and benefits. This remains a controversial approach. Others have suggested dealing with the issue of intergenerational equity directly rather than through discounting procedures.

Because of the lack of consensus as to the correct approach to use when choosing an SDR, any benefit–cost analysis of an environmental policy should show how the results would differ with higher and lower rates.

Mark A. Moore

See also: Benefit–Cost Analysis

Further Reading

Moore, Mark A., Anthony E. Boardman, and Aidan R. Vining. 2013. More Appropriate Discounting: The Rate of Social Time Preference and the Value of the Social Discount Rate. *Journal of Benefit-Cost Analysis* 4(1): 1–16.

Moore, Mark A., Anthony E. Boardman, Aidan R. Vining, David L. Weimer, and David H. Greenberg. 2004. Just Give Me a Number! Practical Values for the Social Discount Rate. *Journal of Policy Analysis and Management* 23(4): 789–812.

Drought

Winston Churchill's description of Russia—a riddle wrapped in a mystery inside an enigma—could very well apply to the issue of drought. That is, there is rarely agreement or understanding as to when a drought begins or ends (which is why it is often referred to as a creeping phenomenon), nor is there a single definition that can be agreed upon. Indeed, there are a multitude of definitions, including meteorological droughts, hydrologic droughts, agricultural droughts, and socioeconomic droughts, to name a few. There seems to be universal agreement that drought involves a decrease in precipitation relative to an identified norm over an extended period of time. Yet, even here things are not so clear in that what constitutes a drought differs across regions and seasons. For instance, a two- or three-week period of dryness in an arid region such as the Imperial Valley, California, may well be within the norm of weather patterns whereas the same duration and intensity of dryness in Portland, Oregon, or in a tropical region such as Malaysia may trigger serious concerns of drought. Finally, drought is often identified by three characteristics—duration, intensity, and spatial coverage—none of which is known in advance, and for which past experiences are not necessarily good predictors of future events. When coupled with the rarity of drought events within any particular region, the lack of certainty and agreement in what constitutes a drought and its indeterminate impacts pose challenges to planners, particularly with regard to their ability to garner support for adequate planning and preparation for drought.

Despite these challenges, it is easy to find motivation for drought planning in light of the far-reaching and potentially devastating impacts of drought. With respect to the natural environment, the impacts of drought on ecosystems can be dramatic with the capability to change biotic community composition and markedly alter ecosystem function. From an anthropocentric perspective, arguably the most recognized impact of drought is on agriculture, with images of the 1930s Dust Bowl in the United States as memorialized in the writings of Steinbeck coming to mind. And while drought can significantly impact industry, municipalities, and residential households, possibly the largest impacts of drought arise from its impact on hydroelectric power and recreation. Given a future that portends more frequent and intense drought worldwide, the motivation and benefits associated with drought planning and preparation should surely rise.

Of course the necessary amount of planning and preparation for drought, or from an economic perspective the efficient level of mitigation and adaptation, will depend on the benefits—or avoided damages—of strategies to mitigate and adapt to drought relative to the costs of such strategies. These strategies, which vary considerably across regions, can be placed into three general categories: water supply augmentation, demand-side adaptation/mitigation, and institutional adjustments.

Water supply augmentation generally consists of modifying the impact of the meteorological event on water supply availability. Historically, and successfully, water supply augmentation has consisted of the development of water storage and conveyance structures that reduce a region's vulnerability to drought by modifying the spatial and temporal distribution of its available water supply. As such, a region's available water supply is a function of not only the precipitation that falls within that region at any particular point in time, but also of past precipitation events whose excess has been stored. Lake Mead and Lake Powell, which combined can store four times the mean annual flow of the Colorado River, serve such a purpose for the Lower Colorado River Basin, including southern California. Such storage and conveyance structures allow water to move to its highest valued use, temporally and spatially, thereby reducing the economic impacts of drought. While ample opportunity for storage and conveyance still exist in many developing countries, many if not most low-cost opportunities have been appropriated in developed countries. The future usefulness of this approach is therefore limited, with one notable exception—the use of aquifers to store excess water in what is termed conjunctive use. The other historically reliable method to augment supplies has been pumping groundwater. While groundwater will continue to be heavily relied upon, contentious and ill-defined property rights, groundwater overdraft, and increases in groundwater pollution can severely limit its ability to further augment future water supplies in any appreciable manner. Ocean desalinization is an alternative that has been met with some success in particular regions worldwide, although widespread adoption is limited by proximity to the coast, energy requirements, and environmental concerns surrounding air emissions and the potential marine impacts arising from water intake and brine disposal. More recent augmentation opportunities being considered and implemented by governments include storm water capture and wastewater reuse, both of which are viewed as locally reliable and potentially low-cost supply options to reduce drought vulnerability.

Drought planning also can consist of reducing the impacts of drought through increasing resilience and/or decreasing reliance on water. For instance, the development of drought-tolerant crops increases the resilience of agricultural production to drought events by reducing damages on yields. Similarly, agricultural operators and urban residents can implement crop combinations and landscape designs (e.g., xeriscaping) that serve to reduce the effects of drought either directly by reducing impacts on overall farm/landscape production, or indirectly by reducing water requirements. Obviously the change in value associated with altering crop composition or landscape design should be balanced with the benefits such actions provide. In an effort to reduce reliance on water and exposure to drought, water agencies regularly encourage the adoption of water-conserving practices and technologies. Encouragement has often taken the form of subsidies for the adoption of water-efficient technologies such as drip irrigation in the agricultural and landscape settings, or through rebates for the installation of more water-efficient indoor appliances (e.g., shower heads, toilets, and clothes washers). While such nonprice measures have been successful in reducing water use, they can be very costly. As an alternative, agencies increasingly are turning toward water pricing, and tiered-rate pricing in particular, to encourage more efficient water use. A significant benefit of using prices rather than subsidies or rebates for water conservation is that the latter typically leads to losses in revenue—revenue that agencies rely upon to cover their costs—while the former may actually increase revenues given that the demand for water has been shown to be price inelastic.

From an institutional perspective, two strategies that offer potentially large gains in reducing the economic impacts of drought through their ability to facilitate the movement of water toward its highest valued uses are water markets and water banks. Acknowledgment and awareness of possible third-party effects from water trades should be considered when calculating the overall net benefits surrounding the efficiency of water trading. Another equally important development with significant potential from an institutional perspective is the collection and dissemination of real-time information related to drought indictors (e.g., precipitation, evapotranspiration, along with surface, groundwater, and storage supplies). Further development of information systems will allow water users and agencies to have accurate and up-to-date information upon which to monitor their drought risk and base their decisions.

Kurt Schwabe

See also: Adaptation; Climate Change Impacts; Groundwater; Water Conservation

Further Reading

Lord, W., J. Booker, D. Gretches, B. Harding, D. Kenney, and R. Young. 1995. Managing the Colorado River in a Severe Sustained Drought: An Evaluation of Institutional Options. *Water Resources Bulletin* 31(5): 939–944.

Wilhite, D. A. 1993. *Drought Assessment, Management, and Planning: Theory and Case Studies*. Dordrecht: Kluwer Academic.

E

Earth Day

Before 1970 most environmental regulation was conducted at the state level and regulatory activity was influenced by special interests. Competition among states for firm location and other economic differences led to mostly ineffective environmental regulation. Also, the world was a much different place in 1970. In the 1960s the dominant political issues were Civil Rights and the Vietnam War. While publication of Rachel Carson's *Silent Spring* and other events were raising environmental awareness throughout the 1960s, most people were much less aware and concerned about environmental problems in 1970 compared to today.

In this context, the first Earth Day was proposed by Wisconsin senator Gaylord Nelson in 1969. The purpose was to raise environmental awareness with a teach-in similar to peaceful Vietnam War protests. It occurred on April 22, 1970, and was a national demonstration of concern for the environment with 20 million people in the United States participating. The first Earth Day has been credited with raising national environmental awareness and launching federal environmental regulation. Today, Earth Day is celebrated annually in about 140 countries. In many places Earth Day has expanded to Earth Week.

Earth Day was one of several major environmental events in 1970. It was preceded by the National Environmental Policy Act and came before the creation of the U.S. Environmental Protection Agency (EPA) and the Clean Air Act. The increasing environmental awareness of the 1960s, which culminated in Earth Day, launched almost a decade of major federal regulations focused on the environment. In addition to the Clean Air Act, the 1972 Federal Water Pollution Control Act (which was renamed the Clean Water Act with its 1977 amendments), the Endangered Species Act, the Safe Drinking Water Act, and several other major pieces of legislation were implemented.

The environmental regulations of the 1970s focused on goals and approaches that were popular with environmentalists of that era. The Clean Air Act set air quality standards to protect human health and set emissions standards for new cars without regard to cost. The 1972 Federal Water Pollution Control Act proposed a goal of elimination of all discharges into navigable waterways by 1985 and prescribed technology-based standards without regard to cost.

According to Freeman, the Clean Air Act had a significantly positive impact on air quality and the benefits of the Clean Air Act were about 30 percent greater than the costs by 1978. The EPA's retrospective study finds that benefits are much greater than costs from 1970 to 1990. Compared to the Clean Air Act, the Clean Water Act had much less of an impact on water quality but there were a number of success stories. The consensus opinion described by Freeman is that the benefits of the Clean Water Act fell short of the costs. Since the decade of the 1970s federal environmental regulation has moved away from rigid standards and become more incentive-based and flexible.

In 1980 Nelson stated the lesson of the first Earth Day:

> So long as the human species inhabits the Earth, proper management of its resources will be the most fundamental issue we face. Our very survival will depend upon whether or not we are able to preserve, protect and defend our environment. We are not free to decide about whether or not our environment 'matters.' It does matter, apart from any political exigencies. We disregard the needs of our ecosystem at our mortal peril.

In many ways, this lesson is still true. Run through the filter of environmental and resource economics, the efficient management of the earth's resources is still one of the most fundamental issues that society faces.

John C. Whitehead

See also: Benefit–Cost Analysis of the Clean Air Act; Clean Air Act; Clean Water Act; Cuyahoga River Fire; Environmentalism

Further Reading

Freeman, A. Myrick. 2002. Environmental Policy Since Earth Day I: What Have We Gained? *Journal of Economic Perspectives* 16(1): 125–146.

Nelson, Gaylord. 1980. Earth Day '70: What It Meant. *EPA Journal*. April.

Stanton, Timothy J., and John C. Whitehead. 1994. Special Interests and Comparative State Policy: An Analysis of Environmental Quality Expenditures. *Eastern Economic Journal* 20(4): 441–452.

Webber, David J. 2008. Earth Day and Its Precursors: Continuity and Change in the Evolution of Midtwentieth-Century US Environmental Policy. *Review of Policy Research* 25(4): 313–332.

Ecological Economics

Ecological economics can be defined as the transdisciplinary study of the interactions and coevolution of human economy as part of nature's economy. The point of emphasis is the interaction between human economic and social systems, and the larger biophysical system of which they are a part. These interactions can happen on multiple scales, from local, regional, and national, to a global scale as evidenced in growing concerns over climate change. Finally, transdisciplinarity implies the pursuit of a shared perspective for addressing complex problems that transcend traditional lines of inquiry.

Ecological economics is still being defined, and there is no bright line that separates it from related scholarship in environmental and resource economics. Early insights from the 1960s onward included contributions from economists, ecologists, and others concerned with economy and ecology interactions. This was recognized in the shared etymological root -eco- from the Greek word *oikos* meaning household. Influential early thinkers included Kenneth Boulding, Herman Daly, Paul and Anne Ehrlich, Nicholas Georgescu-Roegen, Garret Hardin, C. S. Holling, and E. F. Schumacher. Given its transdisciplinary orientation, the community of scholars engaged in ecological economics should be viewed as a permeable discourse community, with an evolving subject matter. Efforts to create this discourse community moved forward in the 1980s with the establishment of the International Society of Ecological Economics (ISEE) and the research journal, *Ecological Economics*, with Robert Costanza as the founding editor.

Recognizing the interdependence between natural and social systems means that ecological economics is closely connected to issues of sustainable development. Sustainability is an intergenerational justice or equity problem, where a fundamental ethical question is the kind of broad package of capital assets that the current generation is willing to hand over to future generations. What costs in terms of foregone consumption of material goods and lifestyle changes are we willing to pay now to protect natural systems for the future? Thus, in addition to notions of physical (human-made), intellectual, and social capital, ecological economics recognizes natural capital assets, which provide a wide variety of ecosystem services (e.g., provisioning of clean air and water, absorption of waste and pollution flows) upon which sustainable human welfare is dependent. Alternative definitions of sustainability often hinge on notions of how substitutable or complementary different types of capital assets may be with respect to critical natural capital assets (e.g., the capacity of wetlands to absorb waste effluent from farms and cities, or the upper atmosphere to absorb carbon dioxide and other greenhouse gasses produced primarily from the burning of fossil fuels). These different perspectives on substitutability also influence notions of value and the adequacy of economists' approaches to valuing changes in the flows of ecosystems services in present-valued monetary terms. Such nonmarket valuation might facilitate comparisons of alternative preservation or development scenarios in cost–benefit analyses, assessments of damages to natural systems, and the aggregation of expanded measures of human well-being (i.e., beyond standard national income accounting notions of gross national product), sometimes referred to as environmental or green accounting.

Research in ecological economics involves a broad range of topics and tools. Examples range from large complex dynamic simulation models of interactions between ecological and economic systems, to small case studies of indigenous communities and sustained irrigation or grazing systems. The toolkit of the ecological economist might also include game theoretic or behavioral models, experimental laboratory approaches to strategic decision making, and social science survey methods for assessing household preferences. Ecological economics also recognizes the role of governance systems and the diversity of alternative institutional arrangements (the rules of the game, both formal and informal) in affecting human impacts on natural systems. Examples include studies of whether or not social norms and collective actions can be used to avoid negative externalities or degradation of shared common pool resources. While such studies might include investigating small communities to understand indigenous knowledge of local ecologies, they might also range to simulating complex international treaties, such as the pursuit of international agreements over biodiversity protection or global climate change.

Scholarship in ecological economics is open to pluralistic perspectives. For example, within ecological economics there is a spectrum of perspectives on the appropriate social discount rate for actions affecting the further future, and on the limits to substitutability between critical natural capital and other forms of physical and human capital. For some, many human-caused changes in, or degradations of, the natural world are already irreversible, or are subject to true uncertainty surrounding possible catastrophic collapse of life-support systems. It becomes critical from this perspective to depart from mainstream economic thought and political economy prescriptions to maximize standard economic growth measures. This perspective might even eschew attempts at assigning monetary values to the environment, or seeing nature and ecosystem services as commodities (commodification). The focus may turn to notions of carrying capacity, and advocating limits on material affluence dependent on nonrenewable resources, limiting population growth rates, or emphasizing more precautionary principles and notions of safe minimum standards for protecting critical renewable resources (such as threatened and endangered species). For others, while still recognizing the interdependence of natural and social systems, the degree of substitutability is open to inquiry, and can be affected by technological change and innovation, or shifts in social preferences in our lifestyles (e.g., the amount and type of goods we consume and how much we recycle). There may be more emphasis on market exchange systems and utilizing tax and subsidy policy instruments to reduce the social costs of meeting environmental quality goals. Thus, more-or-less questions still predominate the either–or questions of possible catastrophic collapse in life support. Similarly, public sector decision making may consider information on the monetary valuation of changes in ecosystems goods, or even implementing systems of payment for ecosystem services to protect the environment. From this perspective, ecological economics is much closer to environmental and resource economics, and there is considerable overlap in research programs.

Understanding the field can also occur by studying what ecological economists do, as seen in the pattern of research publications and citations. A slight majority of the published research articles in ecological economics are empirical, and although a variety of disciplines are represented, much of the research is still written by one or more authors from a single discipline. Thus, transdisciplinarity is perhaps best seen at the collective level, and as an emerging property or goal. There is considerable overlap in citations analysis of the top journals in ecological economics and environmental and resource economics. However, ecological economics tends to have more citations to the work of natural science journals, and to be less concentrated on particular journals and publications. While nonmarket valuation studies remain common in ecological economics, they are less prominent than in environmental and resource economics. Key topics in ecological economics citations include green accounting, sustainability, and the environmental Kuznets curve studies. The latter includes both theoretical and empirical investigations of the relationship between economic growth indices (e.g., per capita income) and measures of environmental pollution or quality degradation.

Robert P. Berrens

See also: Daly, Herman E.; Discounting; Ecosystem Services; Environmental Kuznets Curve; Externality; Green National Accounting; Journals; Nonmarket Valuation; Precautionary Principle; Safe Minimum Standard; Sustainability; United States Society for Ecological Economics

Further Reading

Common, M., and S. Stahl. 2005. *Ecological Economics: An Introduction.* Cambridge: Cambridge University Press.

Costanza, R. (editor). 1991. *Ecological Economics: The Science and Management of Sustainability.* New York: Columbia University Press.

Costanza. R., D. Stern, B. Fisher, L. He, and C. Ma. 2004. Influential Publications in Ecological Economics: A Citation Analysis. *Ecological Economics* 50(3): 261–292.

Luzadis, V., L. Castello, J. Choi, E. Greenfield, S. Kim, J. Munsell, E. Nordman, C. Franco, and F. Olowabi. 2010. The Science of Ecological Economics: A Content Analysis of Ecological Economics, 1989–2004. *Annals of the New York Academy of Sciences* 1185: 1–10.

Ma, Q., and D. Stern. 2006. Environmental and Ecological Economics: A Citation Analysis. *Ecological Economics* 58(3): 491–506.

Ecosystem Services

Ecosystem goods and services (henceforth, ecosystem services) are defined as the outputs of natural systems that enhance human welfare. Just as humans combine capital, labor, and technology to produce goods and services valued by people, ecosystems combine natural capital and processes to produce valued ecosystem services. Ecosystem services can benefit people in many different ways, either directly or in combination with other inputs (as in the production of market goods).

Examples of ecosystem services include breathable air, surface and ground water suitable for human uses, a climate that supports life, and wildlife valued for consumption, recreation, or existence. Many market products also rely either directly or indirectly on ecosystem services, including those from agriculture, forests, and fisheries. Ecosystem services may sometimes be tangible and easily measured, such as the quantity of timber produced by a forest or drinkable water provided by an aquifer. In other cases ecosystem services are more difficult to quantify, such as the esthetic benefits provided by a natural landscape or the direct and indirect effects of genetic diversity on human health.

Although the concept of ecosystem services gained attention beginning in the late 1990s, the idea that ecological processes provide outputs that have economic value extends back more than four decades. Economists have long recognized the capacity of natural systems to provide measurable market and nonmarket benefits. Valuation of ecosystem services is grounded in the same theoretical structure that underpins all economic welfare analysis. Within this historical context, the primary distinguishing feature of an ecosystem services perspective is greater attention to the linkages between ecological and economic systems that enable ecosystems to enhance human welfare. Ecosystem services perspectives also seek to distinguish benefits provided by natural ecosystems from those provided by human capital, labor, and technology.

Two primary characteristics define an ecosystem service: (1) it must represent an output of a natural system and (2) it must enhance the welfare of at least one person. The latter criterion may be evaluated using the concept of willingness to pay; if a fully informed, rational person would be willing to pay for increases (or to prevent decreases) in an ecosystem output rather than go without, then that output enhances the person's welfare. This does not necessarily mean that the person has to actually pay for the output in the market, only that the person would be willing to do so.

Some ecosystem services—final services—directly enhance human welfare. Other services—intermediate services—benefit humans through effects on other, final services. Ecosystem outputs can also provide final and intermediate services simultaneously, such as high-quality lake water that benefits swimmers directly and recreational anglers indirectly through attendant effects on fish. Both intermediate and final services must be recognized when seeking to understand the total effect of ecosystem changes on human society. Still other ecosystem functions or outputs are not ecosystem services of any type; if changes in a function or output do not influence human welfare directly or indirectly, then the function or output is not an ecosystem service. The sometimes subtle distinctions between ecosystem services and functions, and between final and intermediate services, can be a source of considerable confusion among economists and ecologists.

Concerns about ecosystem services were heightened by the Millennium Ecosystem Assessment, which concluded that human activities have degraded the ability of the earth's ecosystems to provide these services. Many ecosystem services have the characteristics of either public or quasi-public goods; many others (or the ecosystems that provide them) are subject to poorly defined property rights or other causes of market failure. As a result, unregulated actions of free markets will generally lead to a lower level of ecosystem conservation and services than those that would maximize benefits to human society. Recognition of this problem has led to increasing efforts to (1) account for ecosystem service impacts in policy analyses, (2) develop institutional, market, and policy mechanisms to promote ecosystem service provision, and (3) analyze the provision and value of these services.

Economic analysis of ecosystem services can be challenging. These challenges apply to a wide range of research methods, including those that seek to quantify, value and evaluate trade-offs in ecosystem service provision, as well as those that seek to inform the development of markets or payments for these services. Among the primary challenges is the close integration of economics and ecological sciences required for ecosystem services analysis. Another challenge is accounting for the many interrelated ways that ecosystem services influence human welfare. Beyond these challenges, the validity and precision of ecosystem service analyses are influenced by many factors such as: (1) the conceptual and theoretical foundations of the analysis and how these relate to the specific set of ecosystem outcomes chosen for analysis; (2) the validity and precision of the methods used to quantify and value selected services; and (3) the scope or magnitude of changes considered and the geographic scale over which evaluations are conducted.

Unfortunately, many ecosystem service analyses incorporate substandard or invalid methods. Some of these have been published in reputable scientific journals, further adding to the controversy over ecosystem services analysis. Frequent shortcomings of ecosystem service analyses include (1) extrapolating from a small number of unrepresentative studies to entire biomes; (2) using inappropriate measures of economic value such as replacement costs that rarely reflect changes in human welfare, even as approximations; (3) overlooking the dependence of economic values on the scope (quantity) of ecosystem service changes, geographic area over which changes occur, and characteristics of human beneficiaries (i.e., those who benefit from ecosystem services). Some of the most fundamental errors are found in analyses that attempt to value entire ecosystems (e.g., all ecosystem services or natural capital on a planetary, countrywide or other large scale) rather than marginal changes. These studies typically ignore basic economic principles such as diminishing marginal utility.

Beyond research into the ecological supply and economic value of ecosystem services, there is interest in the development of market-based approaches to promote ecosystem service provision. Although such approaches can be more efficient than regulatory or other competing approaches, they are not a panacea. Most current or proposed approaches involve direct government payments or centralized mechanisms, rather than markets driven by underlying economic value. Other approaches rely on indirect ties between consumer decisions and ecosystem outcomes (e.g., eco-certification programs for market goods), or voluntary contributions (e.g., voluntary purchases of carbon offsets for airline flights); these are subject to the same free-rider problem that causes markets to underprovide all public goods. There are fewer examples of cases in which people's willingness to pay for nonmarket ecosystem services has been directly captured through the development of private markets; fee-hunting on private land is an example.

The ecosystem services framework provides a means through which policy analysis can recognize the contributions of natural ecosystems to human welfare. It promotes a more holistic perspective toward the benefits of productive ecosystems. Analysis of ecosystem services also requires interdisciplinary, often complex approaches. Even though the underlying economics and ecology may be well-developed, the integration of these models sometimes requires methodological sacrifices that threaten validity or precision. Given such trade-offs, an ecosystem services framework may not always be the most instructive, nor is it always necessary to promote well-informed policy. Analysts must consider when and where an ecosystem services perspective is appropriate and informative, and when alternative means of policy analysis may provide similar or even superior guidance.

Robert J. Johnston

See also: Choice Experiments; Contingent Valuation; Externality; Payment for Environmental Services; Property Rights

Further Reading

Millennium Ecosystem Assessment. 2005. Ecosystems and Human Well-being: Synthesis. Washington, D.C.: Island Press.

U.S. Environmental Protection Agency. 2009. Valuing the Protection of Ecological Systems and Services: A Report of the EPA Science Advisory Board. Washington, D.C.

Emissions Trading

First emerging as a concept in the 1960s, emissions trading began to be implemented as a component of air pollution control policy in the mid- to late 1970s. It has since been applied to a number of different pollutants in a number of different regions around the world.

The appeal of emissions trading comes from its ability to allocate the control responsibility among emitters so as to achieve a prespecified aggregate emissions target at minimum cost even if regulators have no knowledge about emitter control costs. This rather remarkable policy characteristic flows directly from the relationship between an emissions-trading market and cost-effectiveness.

A cost-effective allocation of control responsibility is achieved when the marginal costs of abatement for all emitters are equalized. Each emitter will minimize his or her own compliance costs by abating up to the point where his or her marginal cost of abatement is equal to the price of an allowance. Since the emissions trading market would yield one allowance price, all emitters would equate their marginal abatement costs to that common price. Hence all marginal costs would be equalized in an emissions trading market, the condition required for cost-effectiveness.

Cost-effectiveness across time is promoted by allowing the banking of any early reductions that exceed current requirements, either to support compliance with future requirements or to be sold. This flexibility allows plants to speed up the timing of the reductions so as to take advantage of the cost savings that might be accrued by coordinating abatement with other investment and maintenance schedules.

In contrast to the cost-effectiveness of emissions trading, theory demonstrates that traditional regulation is in general not cost-effective. Furthermore, subsequent empirical work demonstrated that the degree of inefficiency is typically very large. This remarkably consistent finding was produced for a number of different pollutants and geographic settings. Compared to a traditional regulatory approach to pollution control, it offered the politically salable prospect of using emissions trading to either achieve the environmental objectives at a much lower cost or to obtain a much higher level of environmental quality for the same control expenditure. This research suggested that the gains from reform would be large enough to outweigh any costs associated with moving from traditional regulation to emissions trading.

The mechanics of an emissions trading market are actually rather simple. In the version of emissions trading known as cap-and-trade the first step is to set a cap (or aggregate limit) on the amount of allowable annual emissions (say in tons) from a specified group of emitters in a specified geographic area. Transferable allowances, typically denominated in one-ton units, are then created such that the total amount of emissions authorized by these allowances is no larger than the cap. These allowances are allocated among the emitters either by auction (the allowances go to the highest bidders) or gifting (the allowances are allocated free-of-charge to emitters on the basis of some allocation criterion). At the end of the control period (commonly a year) each emitter must surrender a number of allowances equal to their actual emissions of the covered pollutant during that year. While the total number of allowances is fixed, emitters with too few allowances can buy them from emitters with an excess. Emitters that do not acquire enough allowances to cover their actual emissions by the deadline must pay a penalty.

Two examples of this approach include the Sulfur Allowance Program, part of the U.S. program to control acid rain, and the European Union Emissions Trading System, part of the European approach to control the emission of gases that intensify climate change.

Another version of emissions trading, known as credit or offset trading, is used to promote emissions reductions from sources that may not be covered by an aggregate cap. Once qualifying reductions from a prespecified baseline are certified by a recognized certifying organization, buyers can acquire these credits (popularly known as offsets) and use them, along with their own emission reductions and allowances, to comply with the emission limits imposed by their caps.

To illustrate how it works, consider one credit-trading program, known as the Clean Development Mechanism (CDM), which provides incentives for emissions reductions in developing countries, despite the fact that emissions in those countries are not capped. CDM projects producing quantifiable and enforceable reductions of the greenhouse gases responsible for climate change that are additional to what would otherwise have occurred can, when certified, produce salable credits.

Another credit program, also targeted at developing counties, focuses on reducing emissions from deforestation and forest degradation. Reducing Emissions from Deforestation and Forest Degradation (REDD) is a program of the United Nations. By creating a financial value for the carbon stored in forests, it not only offers incentives for developing countries to reduce emissions from forested lands, but it also provides funds (from the sale of the earned credits) to invest in low-carbon paths to sustainable development.

Emissions trading is an idea that has had a considerable impact on many air pollution control policy areas. From its use to facilitate the phaseout of lead in gasoline, to control both the sulfur and the nitrogen oxide emissions responsible for acid rain and California smog, and, finally, to abate carbon dioxide emissions in Europe and the United States, emissions trading has made its mark. It has also spread not only to other countries such as China and Chile, but also to other related policy areas such as controlling the effluent that is responsible for water pollution.

For more information on selected existing emissions trading programs see: The U.S. Sulfur Allowance Program (http://www.epa.gov/airmarkt/trading/factsheet .html), Regional Clean Air Incentives Market (http://www.aqmd.gov/reclaim/ reclaim.html), European Union Emissions Trading System (http://ec.europa.eu/ clima/policies/ets/index_en.htm), Regional Greenhouse Gas Initiative (http://www .rggi.org/rggi), California Global Warming Solutions Act (http://www.arb.ca.gov/ cc/capandtrade/capandtrade.htm), Clean Development Mechanism (http://unfccc .int/kyoto_protocol/mechanisms/clean_development_mechanism/items/2718.php), and UN's REDD Program (http://www.un-redd.org/AboutREDD/tabid/582/ Default.aspx).

Tom Tietenberg

See also: Coase Theorem; Externality; Offsets; Pigouvian Taxes; Property Rights; Sulfur Dioxide Trading

Further Reading

Tietenberg, Thomas H. 2006. *Emissions Trading: Principles and Practice.* Washington, D.C.: Resources for the Future.

Endangered Species

The benefits of protecting endangered species (and thus their habitats) provide economic value. Value consists of recreational use of endangered species (e.g., wildlife viewing, ecotourism, photography) and nonuse values or passive use values (existence and bequest values) that nonusers have for the knowledge the species continues to exist in the wild and will be available to future generations. These values are measured by economists as the maximum amount of money a person would pay to protect the species and its habitat to provide that particular benefit. For example, the amount a visitor would pay for the opportunity to view sea otters in their natural habitat is a measure of the value to the visitor. The same is true of passive use value. This value is the maximum amount a person would pay to simply know that the species exists in its natural habitat. Likewise for bequest value, the maximum amount a person would pay to know that preservation today will provide the species to future generations.

Currently, one of the accepted methods used to quantify these benefits is the contingent valuation method (CVM), which employs the use of surveys outlining a hypothetical market or referendum in order to elicit people's willingness to pay (WTP) for the preservation of a particular species. It has been found that people are willing to pay a small portion of their income toward the protection of endangered or rare species for the reasons given earlier (e.g., existence value).

A number of studies have estimated willingness to pay to protect different types of endangered species. Households in the United States are willing to pay, on average, $17 annually to preserve land mammals, whereas, the rest of the world is willing to pay $50 annually per household. Similarly, U.S. residents are willing to pay $40 annually to protect marine mammals where the households in the rest of the world are willing to pay $72 annually. When it comes to birds, the willingness to pay for preservation numbers are very similar between the United States ($42 annually) and the rest of the world ($44 annually). While U.S. households are willing to pay somewhat less annually to preserve endangered species, U.S. households are willing to pay more than rest of the world if they are asked to pay a one-time lump-sum payment for species preservation. For land and mammals, U.S. households are willing to make a one-time payment of $61, while the rest of the world is only willing to pay $9. For marine mammals, the corresponding one-time willingness to pay payment is $203 for the United States and $23 for the rest of the world.

Rather than looking at broad categories, examining the willingness to pay of *individual* species derived from studies conducted in different countries allows a comparison of values for the same, or very similar, species. For example, U.S. households are willing to pay $20 to $40 for the preservation of wolves, while residents of Sweden are willing to pay $123. Likewise, residents of Greece are willing to pay $72 for preservation of seals, but U.S. residents are only willing to pay $35. A similar pattern emerges for other species like sea otters and sea turtles. Citizens of other developed countries generally have higher values for the majority of these species than U.S. citizens.

The annual economic value per household of endangered species protection is plausible, representing about one-tenth of 1 percent of annual household income in the United States. However, since the economic benefits from preservation of endangered species is freely available to all households in the United States (and for that matter the world), the aggregate national benefits are in the range of $2–$20 billion dollars per species, depending on the species. One must be careful to recognize that multiplying these per species values times the number of endangered species would greatly overestimate the collective value of all endangered species. This is true for several reasons. First, the contingent valuation surveys asked respondents to value just one species in isolation, not all species at the same time. As such, these values do not take into account substitution effects between species (e.g., for some people, seals, sea otters, and sea turtles might have some substitutability). While the willingness to pay for each species may be less than one-tenth of 1 percent of income, the sum of willingness to pay for the more than 400 endangered animals in the United States and more than 1,200 in the world, WTP in the aggregate would be a sizeable fraction of income. This illustrates the real-world trade-offs that even well-off developed countries, let alone poor developing countries face in determining how much of its scarce resources to devote to protecting endangered species.

John B. Loomis

See also: Biodiversity; Contingent Valuation; Passive Use Value; Willingness to Pay

Further Reading

Richardson, L., and J. Loomis. 2009. The Total Economic Value of Threatened, Endangered and Rare Species: An Updated Meta-Analysis. *Ecological Economics* 68: 1535–1548.

Energy Efficiency

Energy efficiency is achieved by reducing energy use until the costs of further reductions would exceed the benefits. There are several paths toward energy efficiency. Energy consumers can substitute practices that require less energy, such as drying clothes on a clothesline, for practices that require more energy, such as drying clothes in a drying machine. Technological advances such as light-emitting diode (LED) light bulbs can reduce the amount of energy needed for a particular task. The increased use of existing products such as insulation can achieve the same goal. And policies such as fuel economy standards and peak-load pricing can reallocate energy use to more beneficial purposes or to less costly times.

Savings on fuel and electricity bills are the primary incentives for private conservation efforts. For sizable energy conservation projects, a common metric for assessing cost effectiveness is the payback period. The payback period is the time it takes to save enough money to cover the full cost of the project. The simple payback formula is:

Payback Period (in years) = Cost of Project / Annual Savings.

This formula does not account for complicating factors such as inflation, risk associated with the project, alternative investment opportunities, or the discounting of future costs and benefits. Many energy-saving projects continue to provide savings for years after the payback period is reached.

Solar water-heating systems are among many examples of cost-effective products. The payback period for a solar water heater can be as short as two years. Specific payback periods depend on the level of usage, installation costs, local energy prices, and the efficiency of the existing equipment. Other products with a relatively short payback period include high-efficiency windows, geothermal heating systems, fluorescent lighting, and various types of insulation. Successful energy conservation projects come in all sizes. A $13 million energy-saving project at the Empire State Building completed in 2011 will pay for itself in three years.

There are also failures in energy conservation. Decisions to conserve energy can be confounded by imperfect information or improper discounting of future values. Information problems arise when decision makers lack specifics on the costs or benefits of conservation projects, or are poorly informed about goods and services that would facilitate energy conservation. For instance, some people are unaware that solar energy is collected even on cloudy days in winter, or that battery storage allows people with solar systems to use energy all night long. As an example of conservation missteps on a larger scale, there have been great efforts in the United States to reduce gasoline consumption by substituting ethanol made with corn. Unfortunately, it takes almost as much energy to produce ethanol from corn as the ethanol itself provides. Initiatives to produce ethanol from sugarcane, plant stalks, wood by-products, switchgrass, and municipal waste have met with relative success.

The second issue that confounds private conservation decisions, discounting, stems from the timing of costs and benefits. Whether insulating a building, installing a geothermal heat pump, purchasing a hybrid car, or insulating a hot water heater, the major costs are up-front and the benefits come slowly over many years. In order to weigh the benefits against the costs, potential adopters must therefore decide what value to place on future benefits. Essentially, this comes down to choosing a discount rate for future periods. This discount rate is used to determine the value today, or present value, of a future benefit.

The selection of a discount rate depends on the decision maker's preferences, patience, alternative investment opportunities, and feelings for others who might share future benefits. Studies find that individuals apply discount rates that range from extremely altruistic negative values that prioritize future benefits over immediate benefits, to infinite values that treat the present as the only time that matters. The administrations of the past four U.S. presidents applied discount rates between 2 and 10 percent. The U.S. General Accounting Office, the Environmental Protection Agency, and the Congressional Budget Office currently use discount rates in the 2 to 3 percent range.

Even with full information and proper discounting, private incentives typically lead to inefficient levels of energy conservation from a societal standpoint. Society receives benefits from conservation beyond cost savings, only a fraction of which are enjoyed by those who conserve. Fossil-fuel-based energy production is a major source of carbon dioxide, sulfur dioxide, nitrous oxide, and other pollutants that contribute to disease, the loss of wildlife, and global climate change. The extraction of fossil fuels also involves spills, fracking (the injection of water, sand, and chemicals into the ground to release fossil fuels), mountaintop removal, and other potentially dangerous or environmentally destructive activities.

Consider the decision to purchase a $7,000 solar thermal system that heats water using energy from the sun. Because the household does not receive all the benefits of reduced reliance on fossil fuels, the cost of this system may be more than the private benefit, but less than the social benefit. If the private benefit is $6,750 but the total benefit to society is $7,500, the household will decide against purchasing the system. To encourage decisions that provide net gains for society, many countries, including the United States, subsidize solar systems and other products that promote energy efficiency. In the solar thermal system example, a government subsidy of $250 or more would lead the household to purchase the new system. The social benefit not internalized by the household is $7,500 − $6,750 = $750. The government would not want to offer a subsidy in excess of $750, because that could lead to the purchase of systems that cost more than the $7,500 total benefit to society. An alternative way to correctly incentivize private decision making would be to place a tax on energy consumption or production. There is currently a tax on gasoline in the United States. Broader taxes on energy use have been proposed.

Decisions about energy efficiency can be misguided by inadequate information about costs and benefits. It is appropriate to discount any benefits or costs that come in the future at a rate that reflects the preferences of those involved. Additional factors that may warrant consideration include inflation, the risk of project failure, and the availability of alternative investments. Because energy efficiency provides benefits to society, the environment, and future generations, private expenditures on energy efficiency may fall short of the socially optimal level. Subsidies for conservation projects and taxes on energy consumption are among the approaches that, when properly executed, can bring private decisions in line with the best interests of society.

David A. Anderson

See also: Alternative Energy; Discounting; Energy Policy; Externality; Renewable Energy; Subsidies; Welfare

Further Reading

Anderson, David A. 2014. *Environmental Economics and Natural Resource Management.* New York: Routledge.

Empire State Building Company, LLC. *Empire State Building Sustainability Exhibit.* http://www.esbtour.com/d/. Accessed June 9, 2013.

Energy Policy

As an essential input into most economic activity and a long-term driver of economic growth, energy commodities are a focus of politicians and other policymakers. When striving to implement energy policy, these policymakers have different objectives, sometimes even conflicting. They also face incentives and institutional contexts that make achieving a coherent national energy policy difficult.

Energy policy is primarily dominated by concerns about production, distribution, and consumption. A country's energy policy typically focuses on the policy environment surrounding the availability and use of nonrenewable and renewable fuel sources, and the economic, social, and political consequences of that use. Such decisions are usually made through private market processes and transactions, so energy policy sits at the intersection among economics, politics, and science. That intersection can often be uncomfortable because these perspectives can lead to different expectations, time frames, and objectives. Energy policy is also further complicated by its intersection with other areas of policy, such as transportation policy, which can create layers of potentially mutually incompatible objectives.

An overarching goal of energy policy is to implement strategic planning regarding future energy use and availability, with a goal of meeting several subsidiary objectives simultaneously: supply security, environmental quality, and future planning for investment and infrastructure construction. These objectives are frequently in conflict with each other. One of the most substantive challenges in energy policy is bargaining among the various policymakers and other stakeholders (such as the firms whose existence or profitability would be affected by the policy specifics) who prioritize the energy policy objectives differently. Not only do interested parties have different priorities, but they also advocate different means of achieving their preferred objectives. In combination with the ability of specific policies to shift revenues and costs, the competing and sometimes incompatible objectives of energy policy mean that the policy process is usually contentious, and lobbying and rent-seeking are likely.

The instruments of energy policy are those of policy in other areas too—legislation can enable regulation and its enforcement in an attempt to meet policy objectives (such as Corporate Average Fuel Economy standards for vehicles); it can authorize taxation or tax credits to change the incentives of energy producers and consumers at the margin; and it can enact taxpayer funding to subsidize particular activities that legislators see as compatible with meeting the policy objectives, including research. In international transboundary issues, treaties are often used, with varying degrees of success; well-known examples include the Montreal Protocol for the reduction of chlorofluorocarbons (success) and the Kyoto Protocol for greenhouse gas reductions (not a success).

Market design can also be a policy instrument, again with varying degrees of success. The Acid Rain Program's success at reducing sulfur dioxide emissions after the Clean Air Act Amendments of 1990 passed by the Congress did not translate into a similarly successful market for greenhouse gas emission permits in the European Union's Emissions Trading Scheme.

Energy policy is not solely a 21st-century phenomenon. While energy use has always been associated with economic growth and increased living standards, the role of energy in economic activity changed meaningfully in the 19th century, with industrialization and the growing use of steam power. The English economist William Stanley Jevons wrote his seminal book *The Coal Question* in 1865, arising out of concern that England's accelerating industrial activity would be limited by its coal supply. In the burgeoning days of industrialization, the primary energy policy question was supply availability and supply–demand imbalance as a potential limiter of economic growth (a concern that persists to this day in industrialized and industrializing countries).

In the 20th century this supply security question took on a geopolitical dimension, as fuel use shifted toward oil and strategic conflicts at the nation-state level led to such dramatic conflicts as the Organization of Petroleum Exporting Countries (OPEC) embargo of 1974, precipitated by the 1973 Yom Kippur War, and the supply restrictions arising from the Iran–Iraq War in 1979. Increasingly, nation-states with substantial oil reserves saw those reserves as a strategic asset in geopolitical interactions, and through organizations like OPEC they started to act strategically, although incentives to cheat and undermine cartel agreements to reduce output and maintain high prices continue to lead to cartel instability. These actions led to an increasing belief, particularly in oil-importing countries, in the need for national-level energy policy to ensure supply security and enable planning for future economic activity in which oil supplies did not create a material constraint.

While these supply security objectives persist in energy policy, environmental objectives now join them more so than in the 20th century. The environmental consequences of fossil fuel use, and ways to manage those consequences using the policy instruments of regulation, taxation, subsidies, or market design, now form a substantial share of the emphasis of energy policy. Thus energy policy in the early 21st century focuses on balancing the potentially conflicting objectives of maintaining supply security while ensuring that the current and future environmental consequences of fossil fuel use are manageable, both through mitigation and adaptation to global warming. Increasingly policymakers interested in achieving this balance emphasize promoting and accelerating innovation, whether in production, distribution, consumption efficiency, or environmental harm mitigation.

Energy policy involves producers and consumers and their economic interests, legislators and bureaucrats and their interests, environmental interests, and the scientific process, all interacting in a political environment. Not surprisingly, then, the political economy of energy policy is particularly complicated. The combination of self-interested policymakers and firms attempting to influence legislative and regulatory outcomes can lead to rent-seeking and regulatory capture. The combination of firms trying to raise their rivals' costs through regulation and the interest of environmental groups in using regulation to achieve their objectives can lead to a bootleggers and baptists dynamic of coalition formation that may bring regulations into existence that would not pass a benefit–cost analysis. And the presence of concentrated benefits to those interests in combination with diffuse costs of inefficient policies can lead to policies that favor politically powerful groups and do not necessarily achieve one of the general policy objectives outlined earlier. These aspects of the political economy of energy policy can yield persistent unintended consequences and failures to achieve policy objectives of supply security, environmental quality, infrastructure planning, or breakthrough research.

A national energy policy is often presented as a desirable goal, to reduce the extent to which individuals work at cross purposes toward energy development and environmental objectives. In a complex and dynamic world of diverse individuals and constant technological change, though, achieving a stable, coherent national energy policy is unrealistic, and may more often lead to unintended consequences. A better approach to national energy policy may be to focus on reducing transaction costs and reducing distorted investment and innovation incentives. General policies may perform better that align economic and environmental incentives in the face of unavoidable uncertainty about the scientific, economic, and political future.

Lynne Kiesling

See also: Alternative Energy; Carbon Pricing; Emissions Trading; Energy Efficiency; International Environmental Agreements; Jevons, William Stanley; Regulation

Further Reading

Childs, William. 2011. Energy Policy and the Long Transition in America. *Origins* 5(2) (November 2011). http://origins.osu.edu/article/energy-policy-and-long-transition-america. Accessed June 24, 2013.

Grossman, Peter. 2013. *U.S. Energy Policy and the Pursuit of Failure.* Cambridge: Cambridge University Press.

National Commission on Energy Policy. Website. http://bipartisanpolicy.org/projects/national-commission-energy-policy. Accessed June 24, 2013.

Yergin, Daniel. 2012. *The Quest: Energy, Security, and the Remaking of the Modern World.* New York: Penguin.

Environmentalism

Since its inception, the environmental movement has had an uneasy relationship with economics. The environmentalism that arose in the 1970s relied almost exclusively on command-and-control regulations that mandated certain actions by polluters, with little attention paid to issues of economic efficiency, business incentives, or how markets are likely to evolve over time. The movement was populated largely by scientists, lawyers, and activists, many of whom believed that our capitalist system was the main driver of environmental degradation—and that economics was little more than capitalism's enabler.

This skepticism, and sometimes outright hostility, toward economics stemmed from many firmly held beliefs: that the quest for economic growth by definition resulted in the exploitation of the natural world; that private entities with their focus on profit will always degrade the environment; that assigning dollar values to nature was counterproductive, and one of the main drivers of the unhealthy relationship between humans and the environment. The overarching position of the environmental community for much of its first 20 years (roughly 1970 to 1990) was that markets could not be harnessed to benefit the environment, but instead needed to be suppressed and reined in to promote environmental values.

This position still prevails in some environmental circles, but the profound distrust of economics has largely given way to a more balanced and realistic assessment. Environmentalists have discovered that the theory of market failure (the foundation of much of microeconomics) contains a powerful environmental message: private markets alone will *not* fully account for the costs they impose on the environment and human health, nor under many routine circumstances will they promote the sustainable use of natural resources. Environmentalists can now point to classical economic theory for one of their strongest arguments in favor of government action to protect the environment.

This theory not only provides diagnostic criteria to determine when markets work effectively and when they do not; it also offers prescriptive action on how to make markets function better. For example, the rationale for greenhouse gas taxes comes directly from the economic theory of Pigouvian taxation, which posits that polluters should be charged on a per unit basis for the damages they impose on society. Microeconomics can also provide insight into the best stage of the production process to levy the taxes (in order to maximize their efficacy), as well as methods to redistribute the tax revenue to reduce any regressive impact and help transition to cleaner modes of production.

The primary alternative to direct emissions taxation is emissions trading, which allows the government to set an overall cap on total pollution while allowing firms to achieve emissions reduction by buying and selling pollution permits. Cap and trade was successfully implemented in the United States in 1990 for sulfur dioxide emissions (and was adopted by the European Union in 2005 for greenhouse gas emissions), with cost savings to the industry in the hundreds of millions a year, without compromising the target reductions. Environmentalists used to fret about the moral implications of giving polluters a right to pollute; now that cap and trade has a demonstrated record of success, there is growing acceptance that the method can be a powerful environmental policy mechanism.

There is also growing recognition that, where property rights are nonexistent and natural resources are being exploited unsustainably, assigning property rights and limiting access can help reverse the damage. The principle has been applied with significant success in many ocean fisheries; it is also being put into practice to help reverse deforestation in areas where ownership is currently contested.

Sometimes markets fail in subtle ways that have major environmental implications. For example, private entities have little incentive to provide the public with information about their toxic emissions. Consumers, therefore, make purchasing decisions with limited information about what types of production processes their purchases support. Policies that force firms to provide complete information on their toxic emissions can empower users to make better-informed purchases, and more knowingly express their preferences for greater environmental quality.

The examples shown earlier are only a few of the ways in which environmental goals have been advanced by addressing market failures. Assigning dollar values to ecosystems has also been accepted by many environmental organizations, who now view this as an essential ingredient in making sure policymakers and businesses do not overlook, and underestimate, the benefits that nature provides.

New York city decided to purchase its upland watershed because forests could provide water filtration cheaper than a sanitation plant. Costa Rica elected to pay private landowners for the forest ecosystem services their properties provide to the general public. These are just two real-world examples of how placing a dollar value on ecosystems led directly to increased preservation.

The ability of economic theory to advance environmental goals has helped the economics profession win over many once-skeptical environmentalists. The environmental community has come to recognize that market failures are to blame for much of our environmental degradation, along with market distortions—for example, subsidies, tax breaks, and the right to pollute without accountability. These market failures and distortions are the antithesis of healthy capitalism, and are opposed by most economists.

Summing up, over the decades environmentalists have become far more sophisticated in their understanding of economics. Economic theory provides many important tools to analyze when markets work and when they do not, and how to use that knowledge to benefit the environment. Most important, there is a growing recognition that well-functioning markets are not the enemy of the environment, but in fact may be one of its greatest allies.

Jason Scorse

See also: Asymmetric Information; Emissions Trading; Environmental Justice; Externality; Health; Philosophy; Pigouvian Taxes; Public Goods; Sustainability

Further Reading

Scorse, Jason. 2010. *What Environmentalists Need to Know about Economics*. New York: Palgrave Macmillan.

Environmental Justice

Environmental justice is defined by the U.S. Environmental Protection Agency as the "fair treatment and meaningful involvement of all people regardless of race, ethnicity or income." While economic efficiency addresses the benefits and costs of a policy, environmental justice addresses distributional effects, such as how benefits and costs (or burdens) are distributed across the population. Environmental justice is also concerned with issues associated with the siting of undesirable land uses, such as hazardous waste sites and chemical manufacturing plants.

Environmental justice is generally traced back to a social movement in the 1980s when residents protested the siting of polychlorinated biphenyl (PCB) landfill in Warren County, North Carolina, a primarily African American community. While the residents in Warren County were eventually successful in cleaning up this landfill, the protests gave rise to a movement, social science research, and several federal actions to address what has largely been shown to be a correlation between pollution and demographic variables, particularly race, ethnicity, and income.

Economic theory offers several explanations that give rise to the unequal distribution of benefits and burdens across population groups. There are three general theories that have been offered; others exist as well. First, individuals make choices that reflect trade-offs between housing location and location attributes, including environmental conditions. The Tiebout hypothesis has been applied to understand the distribution of pollution across communities, showing that individuals may choose to accept greater pollution in exchange for lower housing costs. Alternatively, pure discrimination has been posited as contributing to the uneven distribution of environmental outcomes across communities. Firms may make deliberate choices regarding facility locations based on the race and income of nearby residents. Finally, profit maximization has been used to explain environmental injustice outcomes. Firms seek to maximize profits by locating in areas where residents are either least likely to provide resistance or where land is cheapest. These are not the only theories that could give rise to unequal distribution of outcomes, but they tend to be the most common.

Empirical research on the existence of and causal factors associated with environmental justice is extensive. Early research tended to use simple correlation coefficients with small sample sizes to support or refute findings of unequal distribution. Methods quickly became more sophisticated as researchers assembled larger data sets enabling the use of regression techniques to control for factors such as type of facility, continuous measures of income, and geographic locations. While not all results point to irrefutable claims, most research shows some evidence of unequal distribution of outcomes across race, ethnicity, and income variables. In an attempt to understand the causal factors, more recent research has introduced a dynamic approach, looking at characteristics before, during, and after the siting of an undesirable location. Examination of the market dynamics associated with facility locations can help determine whether or not an undesirable facility was deliberately located in a poor or minority community or alternatively, whether residential sorting may have occurred (i.e., the characteristics of the community changed after the facility was sited, suggesting residents were making trade-offs between housing choices and pollution).

Regardless of the causal factors, several federal actions have arisen and drawn policy attention to the issue of environmental justice. Most notably, Executive Order 12898, *Federal Actions to Address Environmental Justice in Minority Populations and Low-Income Populations*, was signed by President Clinton in 1994. It requires each federal agency to "make achieving environmental justice part of its mission by identifying and addressing, as appropriate, disproportionately high and adverse human health or environmental effects of its programs, policies, and activities . . ." Former EPA Administrator Lisa Jackson made achieving environmental justice one of the cornerstones of her tenure, prompting a report on the agency's progress, Plan EJ 2014, and setting goals for the future.

Kelly B. Maguire

See also: Brownfields; Environmentalism; Hazardous Waste; NIMBY and LULU; Regulation; Welfare and Equity

Further Reading

Banzhaf, H. Spencer. 2012. *The Political Economy of Environmental Justice.* Palo Alto, CA: Stanford University Press.

Executive Order 12898: *Federal Actions to Address Environmental Justice in Minority Populations and Low-Income Populations*, February 11, 1994.

Ringquist, Evan J. 2005. Assessing Evidence of Environmental Inequities: A Meta-Analysis. *Journal of Policy Analysis and Management* 24(2): 223–247.

U.S. Environmental Protection Agency. 2011. *Plan EJ 2014*, September 2011.

Environmental Kuznets Curve

An environmental Kuznets curve (EKC) is the relationship between pollution and per capita real income (or sometimes per capita real GDP), which is generally assumed to have an inverted U-shape. The idea of an EKC came from Kuznet's study of the inverted U-shaped relationship between poverty and income inequality. General explanations given for the EKC's U-shape are due to scale, composition, and technique effects. As an economy transforms from agrarian-based to industrial-based, the increased concentration of industry causes more pollution. As an economy grows further, the service industry becomes the mainstay, international trade and pollution havens become more prominent, diminishing returns prevail, and more efficient pollution reduction techniques are used in the production process.

The origin of the EKC dates back to the early 1990s. Many theoretical and empirical studies have been conducted related to the EKC's validity, application, and measurement. Applied work has been done in air pollution (PM, SO_2, CO_2, and NO_x), water pollution (nitrogen, phosphorus, dissolved oxygen, BOD, COD, Fecal Coliform), deforestation, hazardous waste, and toxins. However, critics have challenged both the findings (especially those based on cross-sectional data) and policy implications of these studies.

Sophisticated econometric models have been a continuous mainstay in EKC papers published in academic journals. The debates on functional form and explanatory variables to incorporate in the model have been lively. The choice of functional form of income in relation to environmental quality has been questioned because some of the pollutants without assimilative power may continue to increase irrespective of the income level. Other pollutants may first increase, then decrease, and then increase again, resulting in a cubic or N-shaped EKC. To address the functional form of income in the EKC model some studies have included a nonparametric form of income. These use specification tests and find that semiparametric and nonparametric models perform better than parametric models. Therefore, a free functional form rather than an ad hoc specification of income in the regression model has been encouraged.

Data used to assess the shape of the EKC has been primarily panel data consisting of multiple countries over several years. For some air pollutants, studies have utilized a long panel data such as 60 or more years. For other studies related to water quality, a paucity of data has forced authors to look at state-level or Global Environmental Monitoring System data, the latter of which is very patchy. The lack of quality data has been a tremendous weakness to the quality and generalizability of EKC studies. The validity of cross-sectional studies can safely be questioned. The selection of countries used in some EKC studies have been less than systematic, which has caused EKC findings to be sensitive to seemingly minor changes in the selection of countries. The growing trend now is to include as many countries as possible and then identify a unique set of countries that converge. An EKC is then estimated among these converging sets of countries.

Most of the EKC studies utilize a reduced form modeling approach without proper explanation on why one should run a regression with income and pollution in a quadratic form. To overcome the questionability of the reduced form of EKC, several theoretical models have been proposed and advanced. These theoretical models have taken a growth theory approach, for example Solow models and overlapping generation models have both been used to explain the relationship between pollution and income. However, these models are not in agreement in their proposition of why one would observe an inverted U-shaped EKC.

The body of literature on EKCs suggests that a naïve belief that growth will take care of environmental problems should be questioned. Stock pollutants result in cases of irreversible and sometimes catastrophic impact on the environment. In such cases, one may even see a degenerative EKC. Even if growth can address environmental problems, the cost can be significant if the time frame for abatement adoption is too slow. One also needs to consider the intergenerational welfare implications in choosing the optimal abatement time and policy. With the introduction of growth theory–based explanations, the criticism of the EKC being a reduced form model has been addressed. The empirical question on the validity of EKCs will continue to be questioned because the results are sensitive to policy, location, and time perspectives. Heterogeneity across time and space in pollutants means a sophisticated empirical model on a sound theoretical footing will be needed in the future to settle the debate on the existence and shape of EKCs.

Krishna P. Paudel

See also: Air Pollution; Sustainability; Water Pollution

Further Reading
Carson, Richard T. 2010, Environmental Kuznets Curve: Searching for Empirical Regularity and Theoretical Structure. *Review of Environmental Economics and Policy* 4(1): 3–23.

Dasgupta, Susmita, Benoit Laplante, Hua Wang, and David Wheeler. 2002. Confronting the Environmental Kuznets Curve. *Journal of Economic Perspectives* 16(1): 147–168.

Dinda, Soumyananda. 2004. Environmental Kuznets Curve Hypothesis: A Survey. *Ecological Economics* 49(4): 431–455.

Millimet, D. L., J. A. List, and T. Stengos. 2003. The Environmental Kuznets Curve: Real Progress or Misspecified Models? *The Review of Economics and Statistics* 85(4):1038–47.

Stern, David I. 2004. The Rise and Fall of the Environmental Kuznets Curve. *World Development* 32(8): 1419–1439.

Executive Order 12291

Administrative law in the United States governs the process that is used to translate the goals or requirements identified in a law into a set of procedures that define the actions an executive or an independent agency can take to meet those objectives. Presidential Executive Orders allow the president to add to the mandates imposed on these agencies through legislation or past practices. While the Constitution does not specifically allow the president to issue Executive Orders to the agencies within the executive branch of government, they have been issued since the late 1700s. As a rule these orders avoid contradictions with existing laws. Executive Order 12291 is the first, specific mandate requiring regulatory agencies to develop benefit–cost analyses of new proposed rules and include this information with the materials used to evaluate their consequences. It applies to major rules whether they are completely new or they are revisions to existing regulations.

The order identifies several criteria for determining whether a rule is major. The primary basis agencies have used to decide when a rule should be considered major focuses on whether it has $100 million in annual economic impact. The order also can use the estimated increase in costs or prices for consumers, specific industries, levels of government, or geographic regions as a factor in deciding whether a regulation has a major effect. Moreover, it indicates that rules having significant adverse effects on competition, employment, investment, productivity, innovation, or on the ability of the U.S. industries to compete would be reasons for considering it to be major. It was issued by President Reagan in February of 1981, shortly after he took the oath of office.

Most of the federal legislation that regulates private activities leading to air and water pollution establishes processes that define standards for air and water quality. These regulatory procedures preclude using a comparison of the benefits and costs as part of the process used to define those goals. For example, the Clean Air Act requires that the emissions of the criteria air pollutants (i.e., ozone, particulate matter, carbon monoxide, nitrogen oxides, sulfur dioxide, and lead) be established to protect human health with an adequate margin of safety. The legislation does not mention benefits and is specific in suggesting costs should not be considered.

Executive Order 12291 did not officially alter the basis for defining an ambient air quality standard. It does alter the rulemaking process because the information included in the materials assessing the effects of each regulation includes a benefit–cost analysis.

The order has been maintained for over three decades with some modifications to the information that must be included. President Obama, for example, in his version of the order, EO 13563, added a requirement for an assessment of the implications of new rules for values that are difficult or impossible to quantify, including equity, human dignity, fairness, and distributive impacts. It also charged agencies to consider how to promote retrospective analysis of old rules.

EO 12291 transformed the role of economic analysis in the evaluation of regulations, especially environmental regulations. The benefit–cost analysis it required assured a level of consistency in all the information provided as part of the analysis agencies did to evaluate the implications of new regulations. The analysis influenced the environmental regulations in at least three ways. First, those designing rules were induced to consider the full consequences of regulations specifying what would be gained as well as the costs in terms that allowed people to consider the trade-offs implied. This process has become increasingly important as the environmental community together with the general public have realized there is no safe level of pollution. Natural processes along with human activities create risks and policy must treat regulation within the public sector's contribution to the overall process of risk management. The second effect is associated with an increased general role for economic analysis in environmental policy. While it is impossible to document a causal link between the order and new consideration of economics, the history of environmental policy since the order suggests that economists had more opportunities to present alternatives to command-and-control approaches to rulemaking (and successes in getting the alternatives used). Finally, the rule altered the vocabulary used in discussing regulatory policy. There is now a wider appreciation that rules cause resources to be reallocated from some uses to others and it is prudent to consider whether the changes involved are worth it.

V. Kerry Smith

See also: Benefit–Cost Analysis; Clean Air Act

Further Reading

Boardman, Anthony E., David Greenberg, Aidan Vining, and David Weimer. 2010. *Cost–Benefit Analysis*, 4th ed. Upper Saddle River, NJ: Prentice Hall.

Office of Management and Budget, Office of Information and Regulatory Affairs. 2013. 2012 Report to Congress on the Benefits and Costs of Federal Regulations and Unfunded Mandates on State, Local, and Tribal Entities. April.

Smith, V. Kerry (editor). 1984. *Environmental Policy under Reagan's Executive Order: The Role of Benefit Cost Analysis*. Chapel Hill: University of North Carolina Press.

Exhaustible Resources

An exhaustible natural resource is one that cannot be increased in quantity by nature, within a timeframe of human relevance. Fossil fuels (e.g., coal, oil, natural gas), metals, and nonmetallic minerals (e.g., iron, copper, gold, silver) are all exhaustible resources. It takes millions of years for these resources to naturally accumulate in viable quantities. So growth in the resource stock comes through additional discoveries and enhanced recovery methods. For every unit of the resource extracted, at least one less unit is available for future extraction. Relative to the economics of reproducible goods, the nonrenewable aspect implies that there is an opportunity cost to using the resource now rather than saving it for future use, due to its increased scarcity. For the resource producer, that is, the mine owner, optimal production requires a dynamic strategy over the life of the resource.

The idea of scarcity applied to a resource can be traced to Ricardo who developed a static theory of taxes based on land quality. The more productive land would pay a relatively higher tax. This rent represents the increased scarcity value of relatively more productive land. Gray extended this idea to develop a multiperiod example. Hotelling formalized the theory of exhaustible resources in a seminal article in which he developed the concept of scarcity value. This scarcity value is the opportunity cost described in a number of ways in the literature, including user cost, scarcity value, in situ value, or option value.

Hotelling's basic exhaustible resource model assumes a mine owner maximizes profits by optimally producing from a known fixed stock of a homogeneous resource over time. The owner takes into consideration that the reserve is reduced in each time period by the quantity mined, which impacts future profits. Solving this constrained dynamic optimization problem, optimal extraction occurs such that the price in any time period will be equal to the marginal cost of extraction plus the scarcity value of the stock in that time period.

Compare this outcome to that of a perfectly competitive market for a reproducible good where *price equals marginal cost*. The difference is the inclusion of the scarcity value. Thus the optimal production path is found by adjusting production in each time period so that the net value of the last unit produced is equal to the option value of that unit left in the ground; in short, the price of the resource is expected to rise in each time period at a rate equal to the growth in the scarcity value. So under this basic model the scarcity value increases over time as the resource is depleted, resulting in price increasing over time.

Under certain restrictions, Hotelling's basic model results in the market price of an exhaustible resource increasing at the rate of interest. This result, often referred to as *Hotelling's r-percent rule* implies, as a resource becomes increasingly scarce, the price increases at the rate of interest to reflect this scarcity. For optimal production, if the optimal net price (with constant marginal extraction costs) in the initial period were P_0, then the optimal price in the next period would equal $P_0(1+r)$ and in the period after that would equal $P_0(1+r)^2$ where r is the rate of interest. This monotonic price path would be followed throughout the production life of the resource. Hotelling recognized the limitations of this simple model, relaxing some restrictive assumptions to consider the impact of a monopoly market structure, costs as a function of production and resource size, as well as the impact of taxes on production.

Use of the *r-percent rule* (while ignoring the generalizations) has been at the center of several discussions about whether or not the world is running out of key resources like fossil fuels. Barnett and Morse utilized the monotonic price function when empirically considering the question of scarcity. Studying changes in price for a number of commodity groups, they found that in most cases, prices did not increase, but in many cases decreased over the time period. However, the study did not consider many of the complications found in the real world.

To address these complications, researchers have extended Hotelling's model to consider, for example, nonlinear extraction costs and extraction costs dependent on the level of reserves, exploration, recycling, changes in technology, backstop technology (i.e., substitutes), uncertainty, varying quality of the reserve, feedback effects (i.e., mining one unit results in a decrease in the reserve of more than one unit), imperfect competition, common property, and externalities.

These extensions, which relax restrictive assumptions to make the model more applicable to the real world, result in variation in marginal extraction costs and scarcity value, and consequently, the price path and resulting production paths. But basic qualitative result remains the same: optimal production in competitive markets occurs where the market price is equal to the sum of marginal extraction costs and scarcity value of the resource. This implies that the producer who chooses to optimize profits from a deposit will do so by choosing production in each period so that the net value of the marginal unit is the same across each production period.

As computational capabilities have improved the empirical application and the relevance of the theory of exhaustible resources have become a research focus in themselves. A substantial amount of research has been done to see if firms' production decisions are consistent with various specifications of the Hotelling model. Results have been mixed. Different commodities, different econometric tests, different time periods, and different levels of aggregation have made it difficult to compare all of these results, but in general, some of the tests have found support for the theory, while others do not. In general, studies that have found observed production consistent with the theory have tended to be less aggregated, focusing on a single operation, for example, a single well or mine and commodity. Hotelling's theory of exhaustible resources, or the theory of the mine, can be used as a tool to evaluate existing practice or as a prescription to more efficiently utilize resources.

Janie M. Chermak and Robert H. Patrick

See also: Discounting; Hotelling, Harold; User Cost

Further Reading

Barnett, H. J., and C. Morse. 1952. *Scarcity and Growth: The Economics of Natural Resource Availability*. Baltimore, MD: Johns Hopkins Press.

Caputo, M. R. 2011. A Nearly Complete Test of a Capital Accumulating, Vertically Integrated, Nonrenewable Resource Extracting Theory of a Competitive Firm. *Resource and Energy Economics* 33(3): 725–744.

Chermak, J. M., and R. H. Patrick. 2002. Comparing Tests of the Theory of Exhaustible Resources. *Resource and Energy Economics* 24(4): 301–325.

Gray, L. C. 1914. Rent under the Assumption of Exhaustibility. *Quarterly Journal of Economics* 28(3): 466–489.

Hotelling, H. 1931. The Economics of Exhaustible Resources. *Journal of Political Economy*. 39(2): 137–175.

Krautkraemer, J. A. 1998. Nonrenewable Resource Scarcity. *Journal of Economic Literature* 36(4): 2065–2107.

Livernois, John. 2009. On the Empirical Significance of the Hotelling Rule. *Review of Environmental Economics and Policy* 3(1): 22–41.

Ricardo, David. 1821. *On the Principles of Political Economy and Taxation*, 3rd ed. London: John Murray.

Experimental Economics and Valuation

Most environmental goods are nonmarket goods in the sense they are not traded in markets and so do not have market prices. Nevertheless, economists have developed nonmarket valuation methods to measure monetary values for environmental goods and services. How do we know if the estimated values are accurate? How do we know what these methods are measuring? How do we determine best practices? Economists have increasingly relied on the tools of experimental economics to provide answers to such questions.

Experiments in economics, similar to experiments in the physical and natural sciences, involve identifying a causal effect by showing what outcome occurs when some aspect of the study design changes. Two distinguishing features of economics experiments are that they predominantly focus on human behavior and involve economic incentives. The very first contingent valuation study, reported in a dissertation by Davis, can be considered to be part of an experiment of sorts. In studying the demand for outdoor recreation in Maine, Davis compared estimated values from a contingent valuation study with parallel estimates based on the travel cost method. He found the two approaches produced comparable estimates. In this setting we can think of the method (travel cost or contingent valuation) as the lone manipulation in the study design.

Much of the experimentation related to nonmarket valuation is targeted at stated preference methods, such as contingent valuation. One reason for this is that stated preference methods are the most extensively used, as they allow economists to value changes that are beyond the scope of existing data (e.g., a level of air quality in a particular city that has not been experienced in recent years) and further allow for the estimation of passive use values such as the existence value of a rainforest most of us never plan to visit. A second reason is that stated preference methods tend to be the most controversial of nonmarket valuation methods as they rely on stated trade-offs between environmental goods and money rather than based on observed behavior. The primary question of interest has been on validity, and mainly whether stated preferences are in line with our true values for environmental goods.

Experiments related to stated preference methods take place both in laboratory settings as well as in field settings. The virtue of the laboratory setting is the ability to exercise more control over the decision-making environment and further to create a setting where participants can actually pay for goods using a procedure, such as a majority vote rule or auction, that theoretically provides the incentive for participants to reveal their true preferences. It must be noted that many opportunities exist for us to pay for public goods, for instance through charities, but these mechanisms do not truthfully reveal value—many of us value the services of charities yet we do not give money to them.

The most common example of a laboratory experiment is where one group of participants (usually students) are asked, as in a survey, to state their value for an environmental good and another group is presented with an opportunity to actually exchange money in order to fund the same good. The almost universal finding from this type of experiment is that stated preferences overestimate actual values. However, recent evidence suggests that many people in the field survey setting believe that their decisions may be used to help inform policymakers, which is theoretically important for a truthful expression of value. This contrasts the typical experimental analog to a stated preference survey where it is known that there is no chance of payment (or environmental good provision). Experiments where those in the stated preference-type setting face a small chance of actually having to pay suggest that this leads to truthful preferences. Also, participants who believe that their choices may be used to inform policy state values that are closer to those from participants faced with a real payment setting.

Turning to field experiments related to validity of stated preferences, like Davis, there are many comparisons of stated preferences with alternative nonmarket valuation techniques such as hedonic pricing and travel cost. The common finding is that estimates are similar across techniques. As another interesting type of field experiment, some researchers have surveyed people about an upcoming public referendum involving the provision of an environmental change for a price (e.g., a property tax increase) and then compared survey responses with votes on the actual referendum. This type of study has suggested that stated preference surveys do accurately reveal values. This is true even when those surveyed do not already know about the upcoming referendum, as long as they believe the survey might inform the policy decision.

In many instances, stated preference studies are themselves experiments. In the context of a single study researchers often change the type of question used to ask about values, alter the level of the environmental good being valued, alter the information provided about the environmental change, and so on. One advantage of this within-study experiment is that it allows economists to provide policymakers with value estimates tied to many possible changes in an environmental good along with how sensitive these estimates are to subtle changes in survey design. The implementation of other nonmarket valuation techniques, such as the travel cost method, sometimes rely on surveys and in such studies it is likewise common to experiment.

Economic experiments have not only informed the development of nonmarket valuation techniques, they have also aided in our understanding of what determines our environmental valuation. One central finding is that many of us have social preferences in the sense our values depend on the preferences of others. For example, laboratory experiments have demonstrated that people are willing to give up money so that others can be made better off (altruism), pay money so as to reduce the inequality of payoffs between persons (inequality aversion), and alter decisions based on the behavior of others (social norms). One advantage of the laboratory for identifying social preferences is that the experimenter can directly control and manipulate how the decisions of one participant affects not only their earnings but also the earnings of others in the experiment. For instance, the experimenter can force the initial earnings of two persons in the experiment to be different, and then allow one of the persons to pay a price to increase (or decrease) the earnings of the other. With this information in hand, economists, charitable organizations, and others have better harnessed the power of social preferences. Many utilities have started providing information about energy and water use, for instance average consumption, leading those who use more than average to decrease consumption. Charities have increased donations by appealing to social norms—for example, manipulating suggested contributions amounts—and by increasing the benefits of giving—for example, by recognizing donors and establishing contribution matches.

Experiments have further informed us about how people make decisions that involve risk and uncertainty, and how we value consumption today versus consumption in the future—the notion of discounting. Both of these issues are critical for environmental valuation. Most policies related to environmental goods can be characterized as taking us from one uncertain state of nature to another. The value one places on a fishing trip under current environmental conditions, for example, is likely to depend on how well the fish are biting, which will differ from day to day. Now consider a policy intervention that would increase water quality, increasing the health and number of fish. Our anticipated values for the policy are likewise uncertain as we do not know how well the intervention will work or how much more we will enjoy the fishing experience under different conditions. To gain insight, economists have systematically varied the risk and uncertainty associated with decisions in the experimental laboratory to reveal our values. Most of us are averse to risk and uncertainty, which suggests that we value more environmental policies that will reduce risk and favor interventions that is more likely to achieve a particular environmental goal.

Turning to discounting, economists both through laboratory and field experiments have begun to better understand how discount rates change with regard to how far in the future trade-offs are being evaluated. How to discount future benefits and costs is of central importance when evaluating policies where much of the benefits will accrue to future generations such as climate change and ecosystem protection. Experimental economics has the potential to better inform how discounting is used in benefit–cost analysis.

Christian A. Vossler

See also: Benefit–Cost Analysis; Choice Experiments; Contingent Behavior; Contingent Valuation; Discounting; Experimental Methods and Policy; Hedonic Price Method; Nonmarket Valuation; Passive Use Value; Risk and Uncertainty; Travel Cost Model; Value of Statistical Life

Further Reading

Davis, R. K. 1963. The Value of Outdoor Recreation: An Economic Study of the Maine Woods. Dissertation, Harvard University.

Friedman, D., and Sunder, S. 1994. *Experimental Methods: A Primer for Economists.* New York: Cambridge University Press.

Sturm, B., and J. Weimann. 2006. Experiments in Environmental Economics and Some Close Relatives. *Journal of Economic Surveys* 20(3): 419–457.

Experimental Methods and Policy

Al Roth, a storied experimental economist, neatly defines four motivations for conducting economic experiments. One of these is Whispering in the Ears of Princes. The title elegantly describes the dialogue between economists and policymakers. Although Roth's classification is broad, economic experiments are particularly well-suited to inform policies designed to protect environmental and natural resources.

Experiments play an important role in two overarching dimensions of environmental policy. The experimental framework can serve as a test bed for evaluating different policy rules under varying market conditions. It is often the case that data required for assessment of policy initiatives are unavailable and field trials are not economically feasible. In these cases, experiments can be designed to closely resemble, in some important aspects, the real-world conditions that are subject to the proposed policy. In this way, researchers are able to empirically evaluate the effectiveness of specific policy components by analyzing experimental outcomes. For example, a laboratory experiment can be designed to compare the relative effectiveness of an emissions trading system with a uniform emissions tax.

Second, experiments are useful for helping economists more accurately value non-market environmental and natural resources. Environmental policies are almost always supported with cost–benefit analyses that, in part, must put a monetary value on resources that are not bought and sold in traditional markets. One well-established methodology for estimating nonmarket values is the contingent valuation (CV), or stated preference, method. These methods construct a market in the minds of respondents and ask them to report the price they would be willing to pay (willing to accept) for increases (decreases) in an environmental amenity. However, since respondents are not required to actually pay the amount they state they are willing to, the values are subject to being biased because of the hypothetical nature of the questions. In contrast with the hypothetical data from the CV method, a fundamental tenet in experimental economics is that a participant's earnings must be a function of their decisions. A cleverly designed experiment, therefore, can compare revealed values (i.e., observed values) from experiments with stated values from CV. In this way, the experimental method provides a controlled approach used to improve how stated preference questions can be asked to lead to more accurate willingness to pay measures.

Experiments in environmental policy can take many forms, and are often classified in one of four ways. A *laboratory experiment* is one in which a pool of subjects (most often students) participate in a game designed to parallel important aspects of environmental policies, but often in a context separate from the environmental issue at hand. An *artefactual field experiment* is also a laboratory experiment but uses a subject pool that has direct experience with the environmental or natural resource of interest. A *framed field experiment* is the same as an artefactual field experiment except that the context of the experiment is specific to the environmental or natural resource issue. Finally, a *natural field experiment* is one in which subjects interact in their natural environment unaware they are participating in an experiment. Regardless of what form the experiments take, the key element is control. The experimental approach works by conducting multiple treatments, changing only one component at a time. Thus, relative changes between treatments are attributed entirely to the isolated changes in the policy or institution governing the environmental resource.

Environmental economists have found it increasingly useful to apply the tools of experimental economics to contemporary environmental and natural resource policy issues. Experiments have been relied on to evaluate emissions trading systems, environmental taxes, subsidies, tradable fishing quotas, compliance and enforcement incentives, nonpoint source regulation, cooperative agreements, international environmental agreements, conservation of forest resources, water rights, and many more. Moreover, many issues in environmental economics can be classified more generally as public good problems, and the experimental literature in public goods is particularly rich.

The experimental approach also has a well-established record of informing the CV method used to value nonmarket resources. Early studies focused on calibrating hypothetical values from CV by comparing them to real values obtained from controlled experiments. Experiments have also been used to test different ways to frame CV questions with the goal of reducing the gap between hypothetical and real values. Often called cheap talk, these methods include adding script to CV questions reminding participants of their personal financial constraints and informing survey respondents about the problems with hypothetical answers in the hope that they think harder about the questions to avoid potential biases. Other examples include eliciting information about the certainty of hypothetical responses and comparing certain, hypothetical responses to real responses. Many studies have also used experiments to evaluate different survey instruments; for example, open-ended vs. bounded choices and willingness to pay vs. willingness to accept questions.

The link between economic theory and experiments is bidirectional. While economic experiments are guided by theory, experiments focus on observed outcomes, often revealing intricacies of human decision making that are absent from theory. In this way, experiments have the ability to steer policy design in a direction different from that prescribed by theory. Robust experimental results also have the ability to inform new theories regarding how people make decisions. A great deal of what is considered behavioral economics has been triggered by observed anomalies in economic experiments, and public good games in particular. For example, people tend to contribute more to public goods (including environmental goods) than a theory of self-interested agents predicts. They also tend to over comply with regulations. And, perhaps unsurprisingly, people care quite a bit about what others do. We also know that these behaviors are fragile, and highly sensitive to slight changes in the rules of the game or previous interactions between players.

Through experimentation, the environmental economist has the ability to empirically evaluate environmental policies when real-world data is lacking. Of course, the methodology is not perfect, and it requires designs clever enough to parallel important real-world conditions. And while experimental data should not be relied on exclusively to predict whether a particular environmental policy will be effective, it does paint an informative picture. Vernon Smith, a 2002 Nobel laureate in economics, likens experiments to wind-tunnel tests in which alternative policy designs can be tested in the lab before being implemented in practice.

David M. McEvoy, Todd L. Cherry, and Mike McKee

See also: Contingent Valuation; Emissions Trading; Experimental Economics and Valuation; International Environmental Agreements; Public Goods

Further Reading

Kagel, J.H., and A.E. Roth (editors). 1997. *Handbook of Experimental Economics.* Princeton: Princeton University Press.

Cherry, Todd L., Stephan Kroll, and Jason F. Shogren. 2007. *Environmental Economics, Experimental Methods.* London: Routledge.

Externality

When the market works, the incentives of market participants, that is consumers and producers, align with those of society as a whole. In this case, a socially optimal allocation of resources is achieved. An externality occurs when there is a misalignment of these incentives, or in other words when the incentives that drive the choices of consumers and producers are different from those that affect other members of society. In this case, a third party who is external to the market transaction bears a cost (in the case of a negative externality) or receives a benefit (in the case of a positive externality) from the interaction between the consumer and the producer. Because the market participants fail to account for this external cost or benefit when making their choices, they choose to consume and produce at levels that are not optimal from society's perspective. Thus, an externality represents a market failure. In the case of a negative externality, the market outcome (i.e., the outcome that results from the choices of consumers and producers) results in too much of a good being consumed (and produced). With a positive externality, the market outcome leads to too little of a good being consumed (and produced). Externalities can result from consumption or production activities. A consumption externality occurs when there is a misalignment of incentives on the consumption or demand side of the market whereas a production externality arises from misalignment on the production or supply side.

Pollution is a classic example of a negative externality. Firms that generate pollution do not set out to do so; rather pollution is a by-product that results when firms produce other goods and services. How do firms decide how much of a good to produce and therefore, indirectly, how much pollution to generate? When firms seek to maximize profit, they produce at the point where the extra cost of producing one additional unit of a good (the marginal cost) is equal to the additional revenue the firm receives from selling that unit (the marginal revenue). The marginal cost reflects the cost of the materials, labor, etc. that the firm incurs to produce that additional unit of the good. However, from society's perspective, these are not the only costs of producing an additional unit of a pollution-generating good. Air pollution, for example, can lead to adverse health outcomes and poor visibility, among other effects. Water pollution can result in reduced recreational opportunities, negative impacts on aquatic life, and adverse health outcomes. The firm fails to account for these additional external costs when making its production decision to maximize profit and, as a result, chooses to produce too much of the pollution-generating good relative to what would be optimal from society's perspective. The socially optimal outcome involves the firm fully *internalizing*, or taking into account, these external costs when deciding how much of a pollution-generating good to produce.

How does this story change if firms have objectives other than maximizing profit? Many firms now devote significant resources to reducing the environmental impact of their production activities. The motivation for firms to pursue these activities varies; some firms may do so in response to regulatory pressure, others to consumer demands, or even to the preferences of the firm's owners. While these actions may reduce the magnitude of the negative externality associated with pollution, they are unlikely to completely eliminate the externality. Unless these activities result in the firm fully internalizing the external costs associated with pollution, then the externality will remain.

A flu shot is a useful example of a positive externality, albeit one outside the realm of environmental economics. Have you ever considered getting a flu shot? If so, then you likely weighed the costs and benefits of doing so in making your decision (even if you were unaware you were making this comparison). On the cost side, you may have considered the monetary costs of the flu shot (e.g., your insurance copayment or the out-of-pocket cost of the shot), the pain you might feel from the injection, the chance of side effects, and perhaps the forgone time (the time you could spend doing something other than getting a flu shot). The most obvious benefit to you of getting a flu shot is your reduced chances of contracting the flu. In making your decision, you may have even recognized and factored into your decision the reduced chances your roommates or family members would face as a result of you getting a flu shot. If you viewed your *personal* benefits as exceeding your *personal* costs, then you got a flu shot. Otherwise, you did not. From society's perspective, the optimal outcome involves flu shots for those individuals for whom the *social* benefits exceed the *social* costs. The *social* benefits of your getting a flu shot include your *personal* benefits as well as the benefits to *all* other individuals who face a reduced chance of contracting the flu because you received a shot. Thus, the *social* benefits of getting a flu shot are likely to exceed the *personal* benefits. In this case, the market outcome, that is the outcome that results when people make decisions based on their *personal* costs and benefits, results in too few people getting flu shots. Like the pollution example discussed earlier, the socially optimal level of flu shots involves people fully internalizing the external benefits of the activity.

Whether positive or negative, stemming from production or consumption activities, an externality results in an inefficient allocation of resources. The inefficiency is corrected and the socially optimal allocation of resources achieved only when market participants fully internalize the external costs or benefits of their actions. Environmental economists recognize two fixes for externalities. The first applies under specific conditions and relies on coordination among market participants and those impacted by the externality. The second involves regulation, specifically the use of taxes, subsidies, or other instruments, to force internalization of the external costs and benefits. In general, these fixes work by realigning private and social incentives and therefore eliminating the market failure associated with the externality.

Mary F. Evans

See also: Coase Theorem; Emissions Trading; Pigouvian Taxes; Public Goods; Subsidies; Regulation

Further Reading

Aslanbeigui, Nahid, and Steven G. Medema. 1998. Beyond the Dark Clouds: Pigou and Coase on Social Cost. *History of Political Economy* 30.4 (1998): 601–625.

Dahlman, Carl J. 1979. The Problem of Externality. *Journal of Law and Economics* 22(1): 141–162.

Demsetz, Harold. 1996. The Core Disagreement between Pigou, the Profession, and Coase in the Analyses of the Externality Question. *European Journal of Political Economy* 12(4): 565–579.

Exxon *Valdez* Oil Spill

The 1989 Exxon *Valdez* oil spill (EVOS) represented a watershed moment in environmental economics. The spill commanded considerable attention from public and policymakers as oil traveled long distances from the reef hit by the Exxon-owned tanker causing large-scale harm to a wildlife-rich pristine environment. From an economic vantage point, the EVOS brought to center stage the conceptual framework that had been developed for thinking about the economic value of changes to pure public goods where there was no requirement that people directly use the resource in order for there to be a monetary loss. It also focused attention on the survey-based technique, contingent valuation (CV), developed by economists for measuring the monetized value of such changes.

The governmental trustees for injured natural resources, the State of Alaska and the United States, undertook a large-scale CV study of the American public's willingness to pay (WTP) to avoid a future oil spill similar to the EVOS. The government trustees presented the results of the study to Exxon and subsequently, Exxon settled out of court for the roughly $2 billion spent on response and restoration activities plus an additional $1 billion in natural resource damages. The government's CV study had estimated that the American public's WTP to prevent an EVOS-like spill was approximately $3 billion and regulations require that money received for injuries to natural resource go either to restoration activities or to acquire similar resources to those injured. After the settlement, a council of trustee agencies was set up to spend the money received for this second purpose.

There were a number of unsettled issues facing the EVOS case if it had gone to trial, including whether traditional admiralty law took precedence over newer pollution statues, which would have greatly reduced Exxon's liability, what expenditures constituted response that does not count toward liability for natural resource damages and which constituted restoration which does, and on how much weight the court would put on the government's EVOS CV study. The U.S. Oil Pollution Act of 1990, passed in response to the EVOS, codified the positions adopted by government in the EVOS case. From an economic vantage point, these positions largely followed practices of government agencies in conducting benefit–cost analysis, which placed considerable weight on monetizing all benefits and costs of a policy and utilized CV to do this. Violation of the U.S. Clean Water Act was a key component of the government's EVOS case and CV had been used to comprehensively measure the benefits of that act. The last impediment to a government trustee including passive use considerations in a natural resource damage assessment was removed in a major 1989 U.S. appellate court case: *Ohio v. Department of Interior*, 880 F.2d 432, D.C. Cir. 1989. In that case the court ruled that lost passive use value associated with injuries to natural resources was compensable under U.S. law.

The ability to include passive use values illustrates a striking difference between the EVOS and the Santa Barbara oil spill of 1969, which was one of the key events that influenced major U.S. federal environmental legislation enacted over the next several years. The Santa Barbara spill was the largest in U.S. coastal waters until the Exxon *Valdez* and resulted in compensation to government agencies of roughly $15 million. In the EVOS case, the compensation might have been even smaller than this without the inclusion of passive use considerations as Exxon's estimate of the lost nonmarket value was $4 million for the reduction in outdoor recreation in Alaska.

The EVOS CV study used a large in-person survey of a national sample of U.S. households. A detailed description of Prince William Sound where the spill occurred focused on the landscape and impacted wildlife was presented using photographs and show cards. A plan for preventing a future spill similar to the EVOS was put forward that utilized escort ships to prevent a tanker from going off course and which had the ability to quickly lay down a containment boom. The payment mechanism was a one-time federal tax. Respondents were offered a discrete choice between the status quo and paying the specified higher tax to obtain the prevention plan.

Following the settlement with Exxon, the U.S. Coast Guard mandated a prevention plan similar to one put forward in the EVOS CV study. Soon, after a supertanker going down the narrow Straits of Valdez lost power and was drifting toward a reef near the one hit by the Exxon *Valdez* when its escort tugs pushed it away and towed it out for repairs. Subsequently, escort ships have been called upon on several occasions to prevent another potential large oil spill.

Exxon put on a conference after the EVOS settlement in which a set of papers highly critical of CV were presented. In response, the U.S. government sponsored a Blue Ribbon Panel co-chaired by Kenneth Arrow and Robert Solow to assess the use of CV for natural resource damage assessment. The panel concluded that "well conducted CVM studies can produce estimates reliable enough to be the starting point of a judicial process of damage assessment, including lost passive values" and set out guidelines for conducting CV studies for litigation purposes. These guidelines largely followed the procedures used in the EVOS CV study with the exception of requiring a test of whether WTP was sensitive to a change in the scope of the good described. The conflicting views of the Hausman volume and the Arrow et al. report stimulated a substantial amount of research related to CV and nonmarket valuation.

Richard T. Carson

See also: Contingent Valuation; Krutilla, John V.; NOAA Panel on Contingent Valuation; Passive Use Value

Further Reading

Carson, R. T., and W. M. Hanemann. 2005. Contingent Valuation, in K. G. Mäler and J. Vincent (editors), *Handbook of Environmental Economics*. Amsterdam: North-Holland.

Carson, R. T., R. C. Mitchell, W. M. Hanemann, R. Kopp, S. Presser, and P. Ruud. 2003. Contingent Valuation and Lost Passive Use: Damages from the *Exxon Valdez* Oil Spill. *Environmental and Resource Economics* 25(3): 257–286.

Hausman, J. A. (editor). 1993. *Contingent Valuation: A Critical Appraisal*. Amsterdam: North-Holland.

Krutilla, J. V. 1967. Conservation Reconsidered. *American Economic Review* 57(4): 777–786.

U.S. Environmental Protection Agency. 1994. *President Clinton's Clean Water Initiative: Analysis of Benefits and Costs*. EPA 800-R-94-002 (NTIS Document No. PB94–154101). Washington, D.C.: Office of Water, United States Environmental Protection Agency.

F

Fisheries Economics Associations

The International Institute of Fisheries Economics and Trade (IIFET) and the North American Association of Fisheries Economists (NAAFE) are two organizations for individuals interested in fisheries economics, which can be broadly defined to include marine resource economics, fisheries management, seafood trade and markets, aquaculture economics, and fisheries development. Membership of both organizations includes individuals from industry, government, and academia with disciplinary interests ranging beyond economics into other social and biological sciences. IIFET was founded in 1982 under the leadership of Richard Johnston of Oregon State University and as its name suggests was organized as an international organization. It holds a biennial meeting in the even years in locations throughout North and South America, Europe, Asia, New Zealand with the most recent meeting in Africa. IIFET recently instituted a fellows award. The main criterion for selection of fellows is substantial, long-term, ongoing contributions to the advancement and development of economic theory and analysis in the areas of fisheries, aquaculture, and/or seafood trade. Achievements may be evidenced by research, teaching, academic service, and/or policy impact. Anthony Scott of the University of British Columba and James Wilen of the University of California Riverside are the first two IIFET fellows.

NAAFE is an independent organization formed in 2000 primarily under the leadership of Gunnar Knapp of the University of Alaska Anchorage and Walter Keithly of Louisiana State University. It was something of an offshoot of IIFET and much of the impetus for forming the new organization was to focus attention on more local issues and to hold meetings at sites with relatively lower travel costs to allow for more attendance. Meetings are held in odd years and many of the experts in the field attend both meetings. Both meetings span three or four days with many concurrent sessions with academic and policy relevance. *Marine Resource Economics* is the affiliated journal of both organizations.

While the two groups are now fully independent with separate bylaws and officers, the day-to-day business for both is carried out by secretariats hosted by Oregon State University's Department of Agricultural and Resource Economics under the leadership of Ann Shriver. IIFET membership varies between 600 and 800 individuals from approximately 65 countries and attendance at meeting averages about 300. NAAFE's membership is about 150 and attendance at meeting averages about 100. Both are membership organizations open to any interested individual. See the relevant webpages: http://iifet.org and http://naafe.org.

Lee G. Anderson

See also: Association of Environmental and Resource Economists; International Association for Energy Economics; United States Society for Ecological Economics

Fisheries Management

Economists have long understood that the cause of fisheries problems is the inability to exclude users. A resource is open access if users cannot be excluded (or exclusion is costly) and the resource is rival in consumption (also referred to as subtractable), meaning that a fish caught by one individual cannot be caught by another. Under open access, no one owns the fish in the sea. Fishermen thus lack incentives to restrain themselves in order to sustain the biological health of the resource and ultimately the long-term economic health of the fishing industry. Each fisherman races to catch the fish before the other guy. Dynamic resource models, and bioeconomic modeling in particular, demonstrate that open access leads to biological overexploitation (overfishing) and economic losses (rent dissipation).

The degree of excludability is on a continuum. Resources on this continuum are generally referred to as common pool resources, a phrase that sometimes substitutes directly for the phrase open access, and difficulties in solving the exclusion problem is generally referred to as the commons problem. When access is completely nonexcludable and the resource is completely rival, we refer to this extreme case as pure open access. As a practical matter, few fisheries are pure open access because there is often some degree of exclusion. For example, one country may keep other countries from fishing in its territorial waters but fail to exert any control over its domestic fishing fleet. At the other end of the spectrum is complete exclusion under which the resource effectively becomes private property. By definition, a private good is excludable and rival.

In between open access and private property are various institutional arrangements that partially exclude users. Some of these cases are regulatory attempts to limit access. For example, under limited entry—a form of regulated restricted access—the number of participants in a fishery is limited but the level of exploitation of each participant typically is not controlled. Another institutional arrangement between open access and private property is common property resource management whereby communities of resource users self-organize to limit access and sometimes control other aspects of the fishery. Although fisheries contribute significantly to protein consumption, employment, and export earnings in developing countries, many developing countries lack the institutional capacity to manage fisheries with strong government regulations, and common property resource management is seen as a possible alternative. A third option is a hybrid of regulation and common property resource management called co-management, where self-organized resource governance and government regulation reinforce each other; the regulator lacks capacity to manage the fishery entirely on its own, but communities are unable to exclude users (typically users from outside the community) without assistance from the regulator. As globalization of the seafood trade generates more market opportunities for fishery resources, co-management may be necessary to bolster otherwise successful common property resource management.

Rivalry is also a characteristic of open access that is on a continuum. For example, some recreational fishermen like to catch and release fish for sport. Some of the released fish survive and can be caught again. When survival rates are high, the resource is less rivalrous. Combined with nonexcludability, nonrivalry of catch-and-release fish makes the resource more like a public good.

The history of fisheries management is a history of successes and failures in addressing the open access problem. There was a time when even many scientists believed that fishery resources were effectively limitless. Well into the 20th century, fisheries management was aimed primarily at promoting and developing fisheries without recognition of the capacity of humans to affect the availability of fish in the future and with little regard for the problem of open access. By the 1950s, scientific awareness of the finite nature of fishery resources had grown, and the problem of open access was well understood by economists. But the most significant breakthrough on solving the exclusion problem did not come until 1976, when nations agreed to define 200-mile exclusive economic zones (EEZ), which were formally adopted by the UN Convention on the Law of the Sea in 1982. Because the majority of fishery resources exist above continental shelves and in other nearshore environments, the 200-mile EEZ creates the potential for nations to exclude users and manage their fishery resources to sustain the biological resource and generate economic rents. However, to date there is considerable variation in the extent to which nations have addressed excludability within their EEZs. For resources outside of EEZs (ones that are only on the high seas or highly migratory fish that move through the high seas), excludability is limited because it requires an international agreement. For resources that span multiple EEZs (known as straddling stocks), bilateral or multilateral agreements are necessary to address open access.

In the United States, the centerpiece of fisheries law is the Magnuson-Stevens Fishery Conservation and Management Act. At its core is a mandate to end overfishing by setting catch limits in federally managed fisheries. Historically, this mandate has focused on the symptom of the problem, namely biological overfishing, without addressing the cause of the problem. By setting catch limits without addressing the exclusion problem, managers began to control biological overfishing but inadvertently worsened the race to fish. This regulatory approach is known as regulated open access: aggregate catch limits can maintain a biologically healthy stock; fishermen have incentives to build more and bigger vessels to catch fish before their competitors; and managers respond by shortening season lengths, forcing unsafe fishing conditions, gluts of product onto the market, and the need to sell fish frozen rather than fresh. Because the stock of fish is maintained at a healthy level, regulated open access can lead to even more excess fishing capacity and associated economic waste than pure open access. Most notoriously, an economically wasteful derby in the Pacific halibut fishery of Alaska shrunk the season length to less than three days by 1994. In 1995, a solution to address the cause of this problem was introduced: an individually transferable quota program that set the total catch based on biological assessment and divided the catch between resource users into shares that could be traded. Individually transferable quotas were used in only a handful of other U.S. fisheries but appeared to be successful in managing larger numbers of fisheries in Iceland and New Zealand. With the new policy, the Pacific halibut fishery was transformed overnight from a source of tremendous economic waste to one of the great success stories in fisheries management with a season lasting 245 days and a steady flow of fresh high-value product to the market.

The 2006 reauthorization of the Magnuson-Stevens Act provided a means to use new tools like the halibut program in federal fisheries management. These tools are broadly defined as Limited Access Privilege Programs (LAPPs) and include individual fishing quotas (both tradable like in halibut and nontradable) and territorial use rights in fisheries (TURFs). In policy circles, individual fishing quotas have now been renamed catch shares. LAPPs address the cause of overfishing and not just the symptoms by solving the exclusion problem, thus aligning the incentives of individual fishermen with the objectives of fisheries management.

Economists have shown that that problem of open access applies to a broader definition of marine resources than just a single targeted fish stock. A number of innovations have examined spatial heterogeneity of fish stocks and fishing fleets and the potential for closing fishing grounds to increase yields and profits. Here the issue is whether to exclude access to a spatially delineated portion of the stock rather than to the stock as a whole. To some extent, regulators are repeating their mistakes of regulated open access in attempts to control bycatch, the unintentional catch of nontarget species. By setting industry-wide caps rather than individual vessel quotas, regulations create the potential for a race to bycatch. Similar issues arise in the protection of critical habitat and other marine ecosystem services. Proposed solutions to these problems require aligning incentives of individuals with the objectives of management, including spatially delineated management, individual bycatch quotas, and individual habitat quotas.

Martin D. Smith

See also: Bioeconomic Modeling; Catch Shares; Common Pool Resources; Complexity in Fisheries; Dynamic Resource Models; Ecosystem Services; Public Goods; Tragedy of the Commons

Further Reading

Gordon, H.S. 1954. Economic Theory of a Common Property Resource: The Fishery. *Journal of Political Economy* 75(2): 124–142.

Homans, F.R., and J.E. Wilen. 1997. A Model of Regulated Open Access Resource Use. *Journal of Environmental Economics and Management* 32(1): 1–21.

Ostrom, E. 1990. *Governing the Commons: The Evolution of Institutions for Collective Action.* Cambridge: Cambridge University Press.

Smith, M.D. 2012. The New Fisheries Economics: Incentives across Many Margins. *Annual Review of Resource Economics* 4: 379–402.

Wilen, J.E., 2006. Why Fisheries Management Fails: Treating Symptoms Rather than Causes. *Bulletin of Marine Science* 78(3): 529–546.

Food Safety

There are thousands of types of bacteria found naturally in our environment. Some of these are pathogenic microorganisms (pathogens) that enter the food supply and can cause food-borne illnesses to consumers. In recent years, outbreaks of *E. coli 0157:H7, Salmonella, Listeria,* and *Vibrio vulnificus* have caused well-documented incidences of human illness and death associated with consuming everyday products such as tomatoes, eggs, spinach, peanuts, milk, beef, poultry, and oysters. In the United States alone, Centers for Disease Control and Prevention (CDC) data indicate that around 76 million cases of food-borne diseases, resulting in 325,000 hospitalizations and 5,000 deaths, are estimated to occur each year. Further, it is expected that the risks of food-borne illness are likely to increase over time, due to various factors, such as climate (e.g., rising ocean temperatures increase the presence of naturally occurring bacteria that may contaminate the seafood supply chain), continued urbanization of traditionally rural areas (creating runoff that can exacerbate harmful algal blooms in coastal waters), or demographic conditions (rising population levels will continue to place additional pressure on mass production methods of food production that may pose problems in effectively tracing a contamination incident to its source).

As media attention directed at these events has increased public awareness of the risks associated with eating contaminated food, policymakers have attempted to address individuals' risk perceptions by creating new policies designed to reduce the incidence of food-borne illness. These policies come in various forms and at different levels of governance. At the industry level, firms, either voluntarily or mandated by government regulation, may provide safety assurances to consumers. At the federal level, some government agencies attempt to directly control the supply of food products. For example, the U.S. Department of Agriculture's Food Safety and Inspection Service (FSIS) is the public health agency responsible for ensuring that the nation's commercial supply of meat, poultry, and egg products is safe, wholesome, and correctly labeled and packaged. The U.S. Food and Drug Administration (FDA) and Interstate Shellfish Sanitation Conference (ISSC) control the National Shellfish Sanitation Program (NSSP), which is a federal/state cooperative program to promote and improve the sanitation of shellfish produced and sold for human consumption. However, the most significant piece of legislation relating to food safety in the United States for decades came in the form of the 2011 Food Safety Modernization Act (FSMA). While there are several components to the new law, essentially the FSMA shifts the food safety focus from reaction and response to prevention. Under the new law, there are, among others, provisions to provide more frequent and targeted inspections of domestic food production facilities; make importers accountable for verifying that the required controls are in place in foreign food facilities that export to the United States; to grant the FDA authority to issue a mandatory product recall if a company fails to voluntarily recall unsafe food; and to enhance federal, state, and local surveillance systems for food-borne illness so that outbreaks can be identified and controlled more quickly while also gaining the scientific knowledge to prevent future ones.

Since the late 1970s, a significant body of research in the food safety arena has examined the impact of food safety information conveyance on consumer risk perceptions and behavior in the marketplace for a variety of products. Research, using both market-based techniques on actual sales data, and nonmarket valuation techniques, such as choice experiments, averting and contingent behavior, and field experiments, has shown that media coverage of a food-related health scare or contamination event can alter risk perceptions and cause consumers to react defensively, reducing demand for the product even when there is no scientifically supported health risk from normal consumption. Consequently, consumers accrue welfare losses, or avoidance costs. Researchers, interested in examining potential policy implications, have also considered the effect of positive counter information treatments, designed to reassure consumers about the product's safety following a scare event, on risk perceptions and consumer behavior. Generally, studies find an asymmetry in consumer responses to negative and positive product news as consumers place greater weight on negative news concerning a product contamination or health scare event. As such, counter information treatments have a negligible effect on consumer demand, so welfare losses persist.

Since the 1990s, the rising incidence of food-borne illness has also supported a growing area of research examining how consumers value food-borne risk, their preferences for the use of technology in reducing risk, and the role of information in altering risk perceptions. Results from these studies generally indicate that individuals tend to underestimate objective risk of food-borne pathogens, but after receiving information regarding the likelihood of illness or death from consumption, they will pay a premium for safer food. Experimental auction methods have been used to investigate consumers' preferences for food safety technologies, such as freezing, irradiating, or pasteurizing food to reduce food-borne risk. Use of technology in food production presents an interesting trade-off for the consumer. While processing food reduces risk, it can also alter the esthetics (taste, smell, texture) of the product. As such, a consumer's valuation for a new processed food product over a traditional variety is a composite measure of their valuations for actual and/or perceived differences in the individual characteristics of the food. Also, as consumers gain information, either through experience or from external sources, preferences and the resulting valuations are subject to change, so information is likely to be an important determinant of consumers' valuation of processed foods. Research has shown that, in general, consumers will pay a premium for processed foods, but premiums vary across treatment types. However, it has also been shown that processing technologies may degrade the taste of the altered product to the extent that the benefits of risk reduction are overwhelmed by the change in taste, and willingness-to-pay for the processed good declines significantly.

O. Ashton Morgan

See also: Averting Behavior; Choice Experiments; Contingent Behavior; Health; Information Disclosure

Further Reading

Henson, Spencer, and Julie Caswell. 1999. Food Safety Regulation: An Overview of Contemporary Issues. *Food Policy* 24(6): 589–603.

Hoffmann, Sandra. 2010. Food Safety Policy and Economics: A Review of the Literature. Resources for the Future Discussion Paper 10-36.

Forecasting

Forecasting can be defined as making an estimate or statement about outcomes that are currently unknown. Accurate forecasts can be beneficial in many ways. For example, with more accurate forecasts business firms can better plan production and investment in new capital and determine the amount of inventories to hold. Policymakers can benefit from accurate forecasts when designing and implementing policies on energy use, pollution control, and new infrastructure. In addition, many governments receive significant revenue from the ownership or taxation of energy-based resources so that accurate forecasts of energy markets can be critical to government budget plans. Financial market participants may be interested in forecasting energy markets for profit or to lower risk by hedging. Consumers can utilize energy forecasts when deciding what type of automobile or house to purchase.

Forecasting embodies a broad range of possibilities including electricity consumption, coal, oil, natural gas, solar, and wind production. For example, how many kilowatt hours of electricity will a utility company sell tomorrow, next month, or in the coming year? How much wind power will be generated during the next month? In addition to energy consumption and production, energy forecasting can also encompass forecasts of local and global prices of natural resources, such as the price of coal, oil, and natural gas. In a related area, forecasts of carbon dioxide (CO_2) emissions, a component of greenhouse gas, are receiving increasing attention.

Forecasts can be undertaken by selecting from a wide range of options. In the simplest case, one can assume that tomorrow's electricity demand or oil price, for example, will be the same as today. This naïve approach to forecasting, while simplistic, can sometimes be justified on statistical grounds. For example, changes in the inflation-adjusted (real) price of natural gas have been found by some researchers to be unpredictable, which, if true, suggest that the best forecast of the natural gas price tomorrow is the price today. The simplest time series methods of forecasting utilize the past behavior of the data to forecast the future. For example, trends, correlations, and seasonality might be identified in the time series that can be used to forecast the future. More complex time series models might include utilizing the history of multiple time series and/or adopting nonlinear models.

Another approach to forecasting is to construct econometric models that utilize a number of variables hypothesized to impact the variable being forecast. For example, future electricity consumption might depend on population and income growth, among other variables. Other forecasting methods can also be considered or combinations of different methods can be used. The particular forecasting method chosen can depend on factors such as the time period being forecast or forecast horizon (i.e., short-, medium-, or long-term forecasts), the complexity and performance of the model, and cost of creating the forecast.

Another energy-related area of interest is forecasting exhaustible resource prices such as the price of coal, oil, and natural gas. Forecasts of these prices can potentially guide policymakers, households, and private industries in their decision making and impact conservation. The well-known theory of Hotelling generally predicts an upward trend in exhaustible resource prices due to scarcity of the resource. In fact, many exhaustible resource prices have shown price declines for relatively long periods. However, this outcome does not necessarily contradict the theory since technological advances and new discoveries of oil, natural gas, or coal, for example, can counteract the upward price trend predicted by Hotelling.

Some researchers have identified structural change or breaks in energy-related time series that can impact the accuracy of forecast models. Examples of breaks that impact energy markets are the Great Depression, two world wars, and the oil embargo of the early 1970s. Including past structural changes in the forecasting model can potentially lead to more accurate forecasts, while forecasting future breaks is more challenging. For example, the unexpected breakup of the Soviet Union in the early 1990s impacted global energy markets and reduced global carbon emissions. More recently, higher rates of economic growth in China and India will likely have a permanent impact on energy markets. Structural breaks from political instability, major economic events, war, and technological change can all impact energy forecasts in unpredictable ways.

Mark C. Strazicich

See also: Alternative Energy; Discounting; Energy Efficiency; Energy Policy; Exhaustible Resources; Hotelling, Harold; Renewable Energy; User Cost

Further Reading

Hotelling, Harold. 1931. The Economics of Exhaustible Resources. *Journal of Political Economy* 39(2): 137–175.

Lee, Junsoo, John A. List, and Mark C. Strazicich. 2006. Non-Renewable Resource Prices: Deterministic or Stochastic Trends? *Journal of Environmental Economics and Management* 51(3): 354–370.

Taylor, James W., and Antoni Espasa. 2008. Energy Forecasting. *International Journal of Forecasting* 24(4): 561–565.

Forestry

Forestry is characterized by long production periods, and thus one of the key questions addressed by classical forest economics is when to harvest timber. This question is usually posed more specifically as "what is the optimal age at which to harvest a stand (or a forest area with trees of reasonably uniform age, condition, and species composition)?" As a stand ages, the volume of timber available for harvest increases in a sigmoidal pattern. The potential harvest value increases more rapidly than volume, because more valuable products can be cut from larger trees. At some point, the harvest value starts to decline as older trees become diseased, damaged, or die. Clearly, the optimal harvest age occurs before this point, but the question is what harvest age will maximize returns, considering the opportunity costs of capital tied up in the stand.

To build intuition, consider a stand that will be harvested only once through a clear-cut of all the trees, after which the land will be sold. For example, the forest owner might expect to sell the land for farming or development. In each year, the forest owner asks whether it would be more profitable to let the stand grow another year or harvest the timber immediately, that is, whether the marginal benefit of waiting is greater than the marginal cost of waiting. The marginal benefit of waiting is the expected growth in timber value during that year. The marginal cost of waiting is the opportunity cost of keeping capital tied up in the stand and in the land. If the forest owner can earn some annual rate of return on alternative investments, then the opportunity cost is that annual rate of return multiplied by the sum of the stand and the land values. In other words, if the forest owner sells the timber and land immediately, she can put that money in the bank and earn her alternative annual rate of return. If we divide both benefits and costs by the total value of the stand and land, we find that the forest manager should compare the rate of growth in the forest to the rate of return in the market. The rate of growth in the forest falls as a stand ages reflecting the sigmoidal growth pattern. Thus, the optimal harvest age occurs when the rate of growth in the forest falls to the rate of return in the market.

This description of the optimal harvest age omits an important additional feature of forests, which is the joint production of timber and many nontimber benefits or amenities. These benefits, including habitat, recreation, and nontimber forest products, are annual flows generated as long as the forest is left standing. Thus, they constitute an additional marginal benefit of waiting. In the case of a stand harvested once followed by sale of the land, these nontimber benefits imply that the landowner should wait longer to harvest. This is an example of comparative static analysis, which forest economists use to examine how the optimal harvest age changes as a result of changing some characteristic of the case. As another example of comparative statics, it becomes optimal to harvest the stand at a younger age if the market rate of return is higher (and vice versa).

The previous description assumes that the land will be sold after harvest at an exogenous price, which determines an implicit land rental rate. However, if the landowner intends to maintain the land in forest, replanting after each harvest in order to grow a new crop of trees, then the implicit land rental rate depends on the returns to forestry. The starting point for calculating these returns is the bare land after the first harvest, on which a new forest stand will be established and eventually harvested at an age termed the rotation length. The net present value (NPV) of a rotation is calculated by discounting the expected future harvest value at the rotation length and subtracting the up-front cost of reforestation, plus any intermediate costs or revenues appropriately discounted. After the first rotation the land will be reforested at a cost rather than sold for a price. The forest owner chooses the rotation length that sets the marginal benefit (growth) equal to the marginal cost (opportunity costs of postponing harvest and postponing the next rotation) of extending the rotation by one year. This is the Faustmann solution developed by the German economist Martin Faustmann in the mid-1800s for the case of land that will always be managed for timber, in perpetual rotations. As with the case of a single harvest and land sale considered earlier, an increase in the opportunity cost of capital leads to a shorter rotation length. However, with perpetual rotations, a change in the annual value of nontimber amenities generated by the forest does not affect the rotation length, as long as the value of those amenities does not depend on the age of the stand.

Richard Hartman reformulated the Faustmann framework to acknowledge that the flow of nontimber amenities often does change with the age of the stand. When these amenities are valued by the forest owner, for example, in a public forest or a private forest managed for multiple uses, they can have an important impact on when and even whether to harvest. Returning to the case of a single harvest followed by sale of the land, amenity values that increase with age of the stand will make it optimal to delay harvest. If those values are high enough relative to the capital tied up in the timber and the land, it is possible that the optimal choice would be to never harvest timber but rather to manage the forest for those amenity values. In the case of perpetual rotations, the flows of amenity values must be discounted and summed over the rotation length in order to calculate the full NPV of a rotation. Relative to constant amenity benefits, benefits that increase with age of the stand will still lead to a longer optimal rotation length, because the additional marginal benefits of waiting to harvest (another year of high amenity benefits from an old stand) outweigh the additional marginal costs (postponing all future amenity benefits by a year). On the other hand, if younger forests offer greater benefits, for example, for habitat or hunting, then the Hartman formulation may suggest a shorter rotation than the Faustmann solution.

Erin O. Sills

See also: Amenity Values of Forests; Clawson, Marion; Discounting; Land Use; Outdoor Recreation

Further Reading

Abt, Karen, and Jeffrey Prestemon. 2003. Optimal Stand Management: Traditional and Neotraditional Solutions, in E. O. Sills and K. L. Abt (editors), *Forests in a Market Economy,* pp. 41–58. Dordrecht: Kluwer Academic.

Faustmann, Martin. 1849. On the Determination of the Value Which Forestland and Immature Stands Pose for Forestry. Reprinted in *Journal of Forest Economics* 1:7–44 (1995).

Hartman, Richard. 1976. The Harvesting Decision When a Standing Forest Has Value. *Economic Inquiry* 14: 52–58.

G

Green Jobs

The green jobs sector has experienced high growth rates around the world. Its impressive growth is often used to support government policies such as subsidies and other financial incentives to promote further growth in green jobs as a way to generate employment, while improving the environment. Indeed, such sector-specific job growth policies tend to become a main focus of government policies especially when national job growth slows. In the case of green initiatives, policies aimed at improving the environment or mitigating climate change are rebranded as green jobs initiatives, in which gross job creation seems to have replaced the preferred benefit–cost analysis (BCA) in the evaluation of environmental and energy policies.

There are a number of problems that arise when policy impacts are measured by job growth alone. Most importantly, economists have long preached that policy decisions should be based on BCA and not on the simplistic notion of job growth, without consideration of the cost per job. To see this point, it is easy to promote job growth in a given activity by simply encouraging (subsidizing) inefficient technologies that are more costly. We could, for example, use picks and shovels to dig for oil rather than efficient hydraulic fracturing approaches. Such subsidies or incentives have opportunity costs resulting from shifting resources from higher-valued activities to lower-valued activities, reducing aggregate productivity.

One problem of focusing only on jobs is that there is no clear definition of green jobs. What exactly is a green job? Before the number of green jobs can be counted, this definition must be clear and consistent. In the EU-27, only eight countries have adopted official definitions of green jobs (Germany, Austria, Portugal, Bulgaria, France, Ireland, United Kingdom, and Denmark). Eurostat defines the Environmental Goods and Services Sector (EGSS) as "the employment in environmental enterprises but also in public administrations that are involved in the creation of environmental technologies, goods and services and the employment linked to the ancillary activities in the various productive units." The U.S. Bureau of Labor Statistics (BLS) only recently established an official definition of green jobs, which is slightly broader than the Eurostat definition. Using the newly established definition, the BLS generated its first estimate of the total number of green jobs in the United States in 2010 at 3.1 million (2.4% of total employment). Various other countries have similarly estimated the size of their green economy—that, France at 425,882 (2%) and Austria at 178,394 (4.5%) in 2009, and Germany at 101,680

(0.3%) in 2007. Because of the differences in definitions and data collection, estimates between countries are not strictly comparable, making it problematic to perform cross-country studies on the impact of green jobs.

Growth in the green jobs sector does not necessarily imply net job creation. For example, the jobs associated with a manufacturing plant that previously manufactured dishwashers but now manufactures energy-efficient dishwashers would be relabeled as green jobs. Although the number of green jobs increases, the number of jobs in the economy remains the same, and may even decrease if a newer capital-intensive manufacturing technology is utilized. Similar to the relabeling effect, there are also possible significant displacement effects of adopting green technologies. The end product of a solar array or a wind farm is kWh of electricity. Thus, increasing the amount of kWh produced from alternative energy or green energy sources reduces the amount of kWh (and the number of jobs associated with those kWh) that would have been produced from fossil fuels. More direct and indirect green jobs in the supply chain are offset by the loss of direct and indirect jobs in the fossil fuels sector. So net job creation may be zero (or negative) even in cases when a green project passes BCA.

Economic impact studies on green jobs or other industries often miss (or ignore) the relabeling effect and displacement effects. Impact studies typically use an input–output methodology first developed by Leontief in the 1930s and 1940s that measures the flow of resources in an economy. Such analysis has become prevalent among economic development consultants and government agencies through the widespread and low-cost availability of software such as IMPLAN, which provides a simple yet robust set of tools to help quickly model economic impacts. Authors of impact studies regularly fail to distinguish between temporary jobs such as those attributable to the construction phase of a project and permanent jobs that will exist during production, giving the impression that all reported jobs are permanent. In addition, because they do not consider the counterfactual—what would happen in the absence of the activity—impact studies typically ignore the opportunity costs of new projects. Economists have developed a slew of approaches that are superior in measuring the actual net impact such as employing instrumental variable approaches, difference-in-difference approaches, matching approaches, and structural models such as computable general equilibrium.

The benefits and costs of any environmental policy are estimated in two main functions: the damage function and the abatement cost function. For green jobs programs, the abatement cost function typically encompasses the cost of subsidies or financial incentives, as well as the cost of higher energy prices when converting to green alternatives. The opportunity costs of government incentives and subsidies are important because alternatively the tax rates could have been reduced to increase private sector investment or government expenditures could have been increased to support other policies such as infrastructure or human capital development. Labor is incorporated into the BCA cost function through its cost to firms through wages that equal the marginal productivity of labor, or the value of forgone time at other work, household production, or leisure. Labor is associated with an opportunity cost of what that labor could have produced otherwise. Similarly, other costs include the opportunity cost of government funds used to support green jobs. Likewise, BCA analysis would also consider whether there are other methods of abatement such as energy efficiency, reforestation, or cap-and-trade that may be more efficient and less costly. If job creation is the primary goal, then BCA would consider alternative job creation strategies such as tax cuts or expenditures on education and infrastructure. Given the capital-intensive nature of energy development (green or fossil fuels), it is unlikely that this sector would produce as many direct jobs as alternative uses of government support. The benefits would largely accrue to the owners of capital.

Although the benefits may outweigh the costs associated with green jobs programs, it may not satisfy dynamic efficiency as it may not maximize the present value of net benefits from all possible uses of these funds. Green jobs may lower carbon emissions and only moderately increase the demand for labor, but there may be lower cost methods of accomplishing both of these goals separately. The desirability of subsidies for the green jobs sector should be measured using a BCA comparing all alternative strategies, not based on the number of jobs created. Although job growth is often erroneously viewed as a benefit, the fact that the green jobs sector is not likely to be a big job creator (because of displacement effects, small share of employment, and its capital intensity) is potentially the sector's *most* promising aspect because it helps make its costs more competitive with fossil fuels and improves its chances in passing BCA.

Amanda L. Weinstein and Mark D. Partridge

See also: Benefit–Cost Analysis; Carbon Pricing; Emissions Trading; Externality; Subsidies

Further Reading

Bartik, Timothy J. 2012. Including Jobs in Benefit-Cost Analysis. *Annual Review of Resource Economics* 4(1): 55–73.

Partridge, Mark D., and M. Rose Olfert. 2011. The Winners' Choice: Sustainable Economic Strategies for Successful 21st Century Regions. *Applied Economic Policy Perspectives* 33: 143–178.

U.S. Bureau of Labor Statistics. (2012) Measuring Green Jobs. http://www.bls.gov/green/ Accessed July 10, 2012.

Green National Accounting

Current interest in green national accounting has its modern roots in the 1980s when economists, Michael Ward at the Organisation for Economic Co-operation and Development (OECD), Salahi El Serafy at the World Bank, and Robert

Repetto at the World Resources Institute, reflected on the future prospects for a nation, such as Kuwait, living on depleting natural capital (oil for a nation such as Kuwait). The thinking was that when the oil or other important stock of natural capital runs out the nation will have become relatively poor and this prospect should somehow be registered in its current measure of well-being. Current measures of national income such a net national product (NNP) were failing to take account of a large and inevitable future declines. The current NNP was somehow too large. The thinking was that there should be a depletion charge in current NNP to indicate that the productive base of the nation was being eroded year by year since the oil stock was being drawn down year by year. A depletion charge in NNP would be indicating that traditional NNP was unrealistically large. In short, greening the measure of national product for a nation would be registering changes in stock sizes, particularly drawdowns, of significant natural capital in its national income.

This is sound thinking about national accounting and one asks why thinking about adjustments for the current depletion in natural capital emerged only in the 1980s. Modern national accounting was developed in the 1930s in the United States and United Kingdom, nations that were taken to be largely industrial, with fringes of agricultural activity and smaller fringes of mineral extraction. The treatment of mineral extraction in a national accounting framework was left to be handled in something of a back-of-envelope fashion. The size of the mineral extraction sector in, say, NNP was measured simply by the dollar value of its annual product. The depletion-of-stocks issue was left dangling. This is of course appropriate when the values of depletions are small relative to current NNP but not a reasonable procedure when the values of depletions are large relative to current NNP as is the case with Kuwait, a nation essentially living on earnings from annual oil exports.

Another dimension of greening the national accounts is incorporating adjustments for externalities such as pollution in its many forms or excess entry to a fishing ground. Since the measurement of these externalities is so difficult, procedures for carrying out the adjustments have not been standardized. We will leave this class of adjustments aside here and focus our attention on adjustments for depletion of natural capital (disinvestments in natural capital).

Measuring depletions of natural capital in the national accounts is complicated by the fact that a ton of oil extracted from a deposit generally costs something different than a similar ton from another deposit. The difference between market price and extraction cost is referred to as rent per ton. Such rents include a dollar value for scarcity rent (user cost or Hotelling rent) as well as a dollar value for quality rent (Ricardian rent). A marginal ton from a deposit with high extraction costs will typically have only scarcity rent while another ton (intramarginal) from a better quality deposit will have the same scarcity rent plus some quality rent. Formal analysis suggests that scarcity rent captures the value of current depletion. However simply summing up rents for each ton plus all other tons currently extracted generally overestimates the value of depletion, the dollar value we wish to use in adjusting for current using up of natural capital. To measure current aggregate depletion of oil, one wants the rent on the marginal ton multiplied by aggregate quantity extracted over the year. In addition, though current oil extraction is a depletion activity, much activity goes on each year in adding new stock to the current known stock, via exploration. The addition to new reserves represents gross investment (reverse-depletion so to speak) in natural capital and the value of these additions to stock must be entered into the current depletion value as rent multiplied by quantity, with an opposite sign. Hence adjustments for changes in the current value of natural capital can involve entries for investment in natural capital as well as disinvestment.

The sum of dollar values of natural capital is a nation's natural wealth and is typically more difficult to estimate than annual changes in the values of components of national natural wealth. The annual changes (investments and disinvestments) often have realizations in the marketplace and can, roughly speaking, be estimated directly whereas the estimation of the values of stocks themselves usually involves numerous guesstimates.

John M. Hartwick

See also: Exhaustible Resources; Hotelling, Harold; Sustainability

Further Reading

Aronsson, Thomas, Per-Olav Johassson, and Karl-Gustaf Lofgren. 1997. *Welfare Measurement, Sustainability, and Green National Accounting.* Cheltenham, UK: Edward Elgar.

McKitrick, Ross R. 2011. *Economic Analysis of Environmental Policy.* Toronto: University of Toronto Press.

Groundwater

In many parts of the world, irrigation and groundwater consumption are largely dependent on groundwater. Over time, a typical aquifer, or subsurface layer of water-bearing, porous materials, is recharged naturally from precipitation that infiltrates below ground. It can also be recharged via irrigation return flow, due either to canal leakage or excess applied water not consumed by crops. The cost of withdrawing water is a direct function of lift, which is the distance between the water table and the surface. In some cases, water can also naturally discharge from the aquifer to adjacent water bodies, or in the case of a costal aquifer, into the ocean. The management problem is to determine how much groundwater to withdraw over time.

Long before the World Commission on Environment and Development (1987) launched the modern quest for sustainable development, sustainability was a concern to resource managers. A common recommendation was to limit extraction of a renewable resource (e.g., groundwater) to maximum sustainable yield (MSY)—the amount of resource regeneration that would occur at the stock level that maximizes resource growth. Harvesting MSY in perpetuity indeed ensures the convergence of the resource stock to the level that maximizes growth, provided that the initial stock is sufficiently high. However, while the MSY management strategy is straightforward, it generates two sources of waste: ambiguity regarding the transition to the desired stock level and failure to account for the full costs of resource use. These shortcomings led to a search for a sequence of groundwater withdrawals over time that maximizes the present value (PV) of a single groundwater aquifer, or system of aquifers.

Dynamically efficient or optimal resource management entails selecting the sequence of withdrawals that generates the largest PV of social welfare. The solution describes the optimal resource stock in the long run (the steady state)—which may or may not coincide with the MSY stock—as well as the optimal transition path to get there.

MSY may turn out to be eventually optimal in the long run. Managing a resource is a dynamic problem because the stock changes over time in response to natural growth or decay, as well as anthropogenic extraction or replenishment. In the context of groundwater, the volume of stored water in an aquifer is measured by the head level, or the distance from some reference point to the top of the water table. The head level depends on the amount of recharge to the aquifer; the amount of water extracted for consumption; and the amount of groundwater that discharges from the aquifer naturally, for example, to the sea. Each component may vary over time, but the resource stock becomes constant in the steady state, wherein extraction is limited to the recharge net of discharge. The optimal steady-state head level will depend on a variety of factors, including the aquifer's physical characteristics and the demand for water. When water demand is rising, it may be optimal to gradually draw down the groundwater stock to the MSY level, and thereafter supplement with an alternative water source, such as desalinated brackish water. Since discharge is increasing with the head level (a larger volume of stored water means more pressure and a larger surface area through which groundwater can leak), per-period yield is maximized at the head constraint.

Calculating the optimal steady-state head level is generally straightforward, but that level will rarely coincide with the initial state of the system. Optimal extraction in each period is determined by pumping until the marginal benefits of water (MB) fall to equal the full marginal cost (FMC) of withdrawal. The history of extraction determines, in turn, the path of the head level as it transitions from its initial state to the optimal long-run target. Since the FMC is determined only after the solution to the dynamic optimization problem is known, one cannot characterize the extraction and stock paths ex ante. A few general results have been established, however, with respect to time dependence. For a single resource, if the demand and cost functions are stationary over time, the paths of extraction and head will be monotonic. That is, if the initial head level is above (below) the optimal steady-state level, it will fall (rise) smoothly over time until it reaches the target level. If, however, demand is growing over time, a single aquifer should be accumulated initially, then drawn down, and finally stabilized at the optimal steady state level.

Social welfare ideally includes not only the consumption benefits and physical extraction costs of the resource, but also nonuse benefits and environmental damage costs. Thus, the FMC of resource consumption should include any externality cost (e.g., irrigation-induced salinization of underlying aquifers) and user cost, which is defined as the cost of using the resource today in terms of forgone future benefits. In the case of groundwater, extracting a unit of water today lowers the water table—thus increasing stock-dependent extraction costs in all future periods—and forgoes capital gains that could be obtained by leaving the resource in situ to be harvested at a later date. The efficiency condition for resource extraction can be obtained by setting the price (P) equal to the FMC, where FMC includes marginal extraction cost, marginal user cost, and marginal externality cost in PV terms. By consuming along their demand curves, resource users will consume until MB is equal to price. The chance that this welfare-maximizing consumption path coincides with MSY is very slim.

Inasmuch as the FMC exceeds the physical costs of extraction and distribution, a public utility may not be legally allowed to charge the optimal price. Another complication arises from the fact that a price increase across the board may decrease welfare disproportionately for lower income users. One potential solution that addresses both efficiency and equity is an increasing block pricing structure (IBP). If consumers respond to prices at the *margin*, the only requirement for efficiency is that the price for the last unit of water is equal to FMC in every period, that is, the price can be lower for inframarginal units of water. In the simple case of two price blocks, the first-block price can even be set to zero to ensure that all users can afford water for basic living needs. Any units of water beyond the first block would be priced at FMC. If designed properly, the IBP would induce efficient consumption, while returning would-be surplus revenue to consumers via the free block.

In many parts of the world, groundwater is characterized as a common pool resource. In the limit, it is individually rational for competitive users to deplete the groundwater until MB equals unit extraction cost. In this open-access equilibrium, each user ignores the effect of individual extraction on future value. The surprising result that the potential welfare gain from groundwater management is negligible has come to be known as the Gisser-Sanchez effect. Under certain circumstances, the PV generated by the competitive market solution is almost identical to that generated by the optimal solution. Welfare gains may be larger, however, when one or more of the original model's simplifying assumptions are relaxed, for example, when extraction costs are nonlinear, demand is nonstationary, the discount rate is low, and the aquifer is severely depleted at the outset.

Because common pool resources may face overuse by multiple consumers with unrestricted extraction rights, additional governance may be warranted if the gains from governance exceed the costs. The optimal solution may be unattainable when enforcement and information costs are considered. Which of several institutions (e.g., privatization, centralized ownership, user associations) maximizes the net PV of the groundwater resource depends on the relative benefits generated from each option, net of the governance costs involved in establishing the candidate institution. For example, if the initial demand for water is small and the aquifer is large, the gains from management are likely to be small, and open access might be preferred. As demand grows over time and water becomes scarcer, however, a user association, government regulations, or a water market may become efficient.

James Roumasset and Christopher A. Wada

See also: Clean Water Act; Common Pool Resources; Ostrom, Elinor; Sustainability; User Cost; Water Conservation

Further Reading

Gisser, M., and D. A. Sanchez. 1980. Competition versus Optimal Control in Groundwater Pumping. *Water Resources Research* 16(4): 638–642.

Krulce, D. L., J. A. Roumasset, and T. Wilson. 1997. Optimal Management of a Renewable and Replaceable Resource: The Case of Coastal Groundwater. *American Journal of Agricultural Economics* 79: 1218–1228.

Ostrom, E. 1990. *Governing the Commons: The Evolution of Institutions for Collective Action.* Cambridge: Cambridge University Press.

Roumasset, J. A., and C. A. Wada. 2013. Economics of Groundwater, in J. F. Shogren (editor), *Encyclopedia of Energy, Natural Resource, and Environmental Economics* 2: 10–21. Amsterdam: Elsevier.

World Commission on Environment and Development (WCED). 1987. *Our Common Future* (The Brundtland Report). Oxford: Oxford University Press.

Guidelines for Preparing Economic Analyses

The U.S. Environmental Protection Agency's (EPA) *Guidelines for Preparing Economic Analyses* (hereafter the *Guidelines*), last issued in 2010, establishes a sound scientific framework for performing consistent economic analyses of environmental regulations and policies. By design, the *Guidelines* focus on the conduct of economic analysis to support policy decisions and the fulfillment of requirements described by relevant statutes, Executive Orders, and other related guidance materials. Incorporating recent advances in theoretical and applied work in the field of environmental economics, the *Guidelines* provide agency analysts with guidance on analyzing the benefits, costs, and economic impacts of regulations and policies, including assessing the distribution of costs and benefits among the population. The *Guidelines* do not provide a rigid blueprint or a cookbook, but rather summarize analytical methodologies, empirical techniques, and data sources to assist economists at EPA.

EPA first developed guidance for economic analysis in 1983 in response to growing demand for benefit–cost analysis (including President Reagan's Executive Order 12291 requiring benefit–cost analysis for federal regulations with an expected impact on the economy of $100 million annually). In September 2000, the *Guidelines* were substantially revised to reflect the evolution of environmental policymaking and economic analysis since their original release. At the time EPA committed to periodically revise the *Guidelines* to account for further growth and development of economic tools and practices and the best available science. The 2010 edition of the *Guidelines* includes a new chapter on Distributional Analyses and Environmental Justice, and expanded treatments of discounting, baseline definition, stated preference methods, cost estimation, presentation of results, in addition to other revisions incorporating advances in the state of the science. The *Guidelines* were subject to peer review by the Environmental Economics Advisory Committee of EPA's Science Advisory Board.

Many of the topics covered in the *Guidelines* are familiar and typically found in textbooks on environmental economics. However, since the *Guidelines* are used for practical applications of not only benefit–cost analysis but also economic impact analysis, some issues require more attention than would be found in an economics textbook. Key among these are defining baseline conditions, benefit transfer, economic impact analysis, as well as the presentation of the results of economic analyses, including nonmonetary information.

A baseline describes an initial, status quo scenario that is used for comparison with one or more alternative or policy scenarios. Generally, this baseline is defined as the best assessment of the world in the absence of the proposed regulation or policy. While this sounds simple it can be difficult in practice and baseline specification can have a profound effect on the outcome of the analysis. Key concerns addressed by the *Guidelines* include how analyses are affected by noncompliance with prior regulations and how to account for separate regulations that are being developed concurrently.

Benefit transfer, a second best alternative to estimating benefits, is a necessity for many agency analyses where both time and funding are scarce. Ideally, benefits analyses would be informed by original studies tailored to capture the policy scenarios in question. Instead, stated preference or revealed preference estimates are transferred from published studies to the policy context. The transfer is only as good as the original study allows and depends a great deal on the comparability of the study scenario to the policy scenario. It is difficult to characterize the uncertainty associated with transferred benefits estimates. The *Guidelines* describe generalized steps for benefit transfer as well as specific types of transfers (e.g., unit values, function transfers, meta-analyses).

Assessing distributional effects of regulation is an important complement to benefit–cost analysis. The *Guidelines* distinguish between economic impacts analysis, focused on broadly defined economic sectors (e.g., business, government, or nonprofit entities) and distributional analyses that focus on the distribution of effects across individuals and households (e.g., low-income households, children). This distinction is in part driven by requirements from Executive Orders and other policy directives, but also reflects practical considerations. While economic impacts analysis typically estimates changes in profitability, employment, prices, and revenues, distributional analyses address concerns such as environmental justice. Economic methods are generally well-developed to assess economic impacts, but less so for other distributional analyses. For the latter, the *Guidelines* provide a broad overview of options and basic methods that can be applied while introducing greater consistency in these types of analyses.

Presenting the results of an economic analysis of an environmental regulation is not as simple as providing a bottom-line estimate of maximized net benefits. Policymakers rely on quantitative analysis to delineate the costs, benefits, or other impacts of a wide range of control options including some mandated by statute such as the use of best available control technology or lowest achievable emission rate. Whatever the options, the analyses at all stages in the process should be presented in a thorough and transparent manner such that the reader can readily understand the primary conclusions of the analysis; how the benefits and costs were estimated; the importance of nonquantified or nonmonetized effects; key assumptions made; primary sources of uncertainty; and how uncertainty affects the results. All identifiable costs and benefits incremental to the regulation or policy under consideration should be presented, including directly intended effects and costs, as well as ancillary (or co-)benefits and costs. The *Guidelines* provide templates for reporting purposes.

The *Guidelines* are available for download at www.epa.gov/economics.

Chris Dockins and Nathalie Simon

See also: Benefit–Cost Analysis; Benefit Transfer; Executive Order 12291; Discounting; Environmental Justice; Nonmarket Valuation; Pollution Abatement Costs; Welfare; Welfare and Equity

Further Reading

Atkinson, Giles, and Susana Mourato. 2008. Environmental Cost–Benefit Analysis. *Annual Review of Environment and Resources* 33: 317–344.

Boardman, Anthony E., David Greenberg, Aidan Vining, and David Weimer. 2010. *Cost–Benefit Analysis*, 4th ed. Upper Saddle River, NJ: Prentice Hall.

H

Hardin, Garrett

Garrett James Hardin (1915–2003) was a prominent ecologist who enjoyed a long and distinguished academic career at the University of California, Santa Barbara. He is best known for his 1968 essay, "The Tragedy of the Commons," which called attention to the dangers associated with population growth and environmental degradation.

Hardin was born in Dallas, Texas, on April 21, 1915. He was afflicted by polio at an early age, which left him with a shortened right leg and the need to use crutches and then a wheelchair later in life. Physical limitations no doubt played an important role in his desire to achieve success through academic pursuits. Hardin's father was a sales representative for the Illinois Central Railroad, an occupation that forced the family to relocate periodically. His grandfather's 160-acre farm in Missouri was a source of stability and a place where he spent many summers during his formative years. It has been suggested that Hardin's observations of the farm's cat population influenced his views on the need for human population control.

Hardin received a bachelor's degree in zoology from the University of Chicago, where he was mentored by ecologist W. C. Allee, who warned about the perils of overpopulation. Hardin went on to earn a doctorate in microbiology from Stanford. At Stanford he met and married Jane Swanson in 1941. He joined the faculty of the University of California at Santa Barbara in 1946, where he was known as a passionate and thought-provoking teacher. Hardin retired in 1978 after 32 years of service to the university.

Hardin published over 300 scholarly articles and more than 20 books in his lifetime, the last when he was in his eighties. His introductory biology textbook, *Biology: Its Human Implications* (subsequently retitled *Biology: Its Principles and Implications*) was broadly used. Hardin's continued productivity well into retirement earned him the Constantine Panunzio Distinguished Emeriti Award from the University of California system in 1997.

Hardin's ecological training and insight led him to believe that unchecked population growth will lead to environmental devastation. Economists recognize the dilemma Hardin presents as the conflict between what is in an individual's self-interest and what is best for society as a whole. Self-interested individuals will use common pool resources (like the environment) as long as they individually benefit from that use, ignoring the damage that their use imposes on the sustainability of the resource. His writings and lectures addressed the themes of morality and sustainability, and influenced policy debate concerning many controversial topics including population control, immigration, foreign aid, and abortion.

Peter W. Schuhmann and Kate Krause

See also: Common Pool Resources; Tragedy of the Commons

Further Reading

Garrett Hardin Society. http://www.garretthardinsociety.org/

Hardin, G. 1968. The Tragedy of the Commons. *Science* 142(3859): 1243–1247.

Hardin, G. 1993. *Living within Limits: Ecology, Economics, and Population Taboos.* New York: Oxford University Press.

Hardin, G. 1999. *The Ostrich Factor: Our Population Myopia.* New York: Oxford University Press.

Hazardous Waste

Modern societies are pretty wasteful. According to recent estimates, on average Americans generate about 5 pounds of waste each day for a total of around 300 million tons a year. While all waste can cause environmental problems, some waste—known as hazardous or toxic waste—has been singled out for its potential to cause significant environmental damage. If left unregulated, hazardous waste can pollute groundwater, rivers, and lakes, contaminate soil, and kill people, livestock, and wildlife.

While the legal definition of hazardous waste varies across countries, hazardous waste generally includes any discarded material that is toxic, reactive, or flammable and poses a hazard to the health of humans, other living organisms, or the environment. As you might imagine, this definition covers a wide range of materials that are generated by a lot of different companies and processes. This means that big, chemical-intensive companies such as DuPont or Exxon are not the only companies that generate hazardous waste. Much smaller, local companies such as the neighborhood service station, dry cleaner, or even your dentist also generate hazardous waste. In fact, you probably have generated hazardous waste yourself, since leftover paint, some discarded cleaning products, and used batteries all qualify as hazardous waste.

Because waste has no intrinsic value (if it did, we would not waste it), people who generate it want to get rid of it as cheaply as possible. Before hazardous waste was regulated in the United States, most industrial generators just dumped it on unused land. Since many hazardous constituents are persistently toxic, unregulated waste dumps have resulted in damages long after the material has been dumped. Have you ever heard of Love Canal? Probably the most famous unregulated hazardous waste dump, Love Canal was used as a chemical waste dump for a decade before being redeveloped as a neighborhood school site. Twenty years after the dump was closed, unusually heavy rains caused parts of the dump to sink, making the contamination of surrounding groundwater, surface water, and soil apparent. While the full effects of the contamination cannot be easily measured, residents of the area had unusually high rates of cancers, miscarriages, and birth defects. Eventually over 1,000 families were relocated from the area and the cleanup of the Love Canal site cost over $60 million.

Hazardous waste presents a classic case of negative externalities. Unless prohibited by regulation, a generator will decide how and where to dispose his hazardous waste based on private cost, ignoring the effect of that decision on human health and the environment. Economic theory provides three primary solutions to such negative externalities: command-and-control regulation, Pigouvian taxes, and the assignment of property rights. All of these solutions are currently used to minimize the social costs of hazardous waste.

Command-and-control regulation is used in many countries to minimize the externalities associated with hazardous waste disposal by imposing standards for the safe management of hazardous waste. Both the United States and the European Union regulate hazardous waste from the cradle to the grave, that is, from the point of generation until final disposition. Their regulations require facilities that have the potential to generate hazardous waste to test any likely waste streams and if the waste is determined to be hazardous, track, store, and manage it according to particular standards. Such requirements are designed to decrease the potential harm that hazardous waste can cause, and thus the external costs imposed by hazardous waste. Additionally, complying with regulatory requirements significantly increases the private cost of hazardous waste generation and provides incentives for companies to reduce the amount of waste they generate in the first place. Of course, by increasing the cost of legal waste management, command-and-control regulation may indirectly encourage illegal disposal. Thus the enforcement of hazardous waste regulations plays a critical role in their practical effect.

One shortcoming of command-and-control regulation of hazardous waste (and command-and-control regulation in general) is that the regulations are standardized rather than tailored to particular waste streams or generators even though the potential for harm will vary significantly based both on the characteristics of the waste stream and the location in which it is managed and disposed. In some cases, command-and-control regulations may be too stringent from the perspective of maximizing social welfare, while in other cases the regulations may be too lenient.

An alternative solution to the negative externalities associated with hazardous waste is to impose Pigouvian taxes on hazardous waste. In theory such taxes can internalize the costs of hazardous waste disposal and thus provide incentives for generators to reduce the quantity of hazardous waste they produce in the first place. When the costs associated with hazardous waste increase, generators may find it cost effective to change their production processes, use less toxic inputs, or find ways to recycle by-products. Of course, imposing taxes on waste generation or disposal might also lead generators to conceal the amount of waste generated through illegal disposal or dumping.

A final solution to the negative externalities imposed by hazardous waste is the assigning of property rights by imposing legal liability for any damages caused by hazardous waste on the generator of that waste. In theory, assigning legal liability to generators forces them to fully internalize the costs of their waste. This should lead to more careful management of the hazardous waste as well as a reduction in the amount of waste generated in the first place. Additionally, imposing legal liability helps to compensate the victims of pollution, something that neither of the other two solutions accomplishes.

One concern with using legal liability to control for externalities is that generators facing large damage payments might go bankrupt rather than pay a large settlement. If a generator's liability is capped at some level, the generator will not fully internalize the costs associated with its waste and thus legal liability may provide only a partial solution. However, governments can strengthen the liability system by requiring that generators either carry insurance or have the ability to pay reasonable damage awards. For example, in the United States, hazardous waste management facilities are subject to financial responsibility requirements.

While it is difficult to determine the effect of individual hazardous waste regulations as most countries use a number of different policy approaches simultaneously, it is clear that the regulations have made a difference. For example, in 1980 in the United States there were over 50,000 hazardous waste generators, approximately 300 million tons of waste generated annually, and 30,000 unregulated facilities that managed that hazardous waste in some manner. By 2000, only about 20,000 businesses generated approximately 40 million tons of hazardous waste and the 2,000 hazardous waste management facilities were all regulated by the Environmental Protection Agency.

Sarah L. Stafford

See also: Benefit–Cost Analysis; Brownfields; Coase Theorem; Externality; Health; Information Disclosure; NIMBY and LULU; Pigouvian Taxes; Property Rights; Toxics Release Inventory

Further Reading

Jenkins, R. R., E. Kopits, and D. Simpson. 2009. The Evolution of Solid and Hazardous Waste Regulation in the United States. *Review of Environmental Economics and Policy* 3(1): 104–120.

Peretz, J. H., R. A. Bohm, and P. D. Jasienczyk. 1997. Environmental Policy and the Reduction of Hazardous Waste. *Journal of Policy Analysis and Management* 16(4): 556–574.

Porter, R. C. 2002. *The Economics of Waste.* Washington D.C.: Resources for the Future.

U.S. Environmental Protection Agency. 2002. *25 Years of RCRA: Building on Our Past to Protect Our Future.* Washington, D.C.: Government Printing Office (EPA-K-02-027).

Health

The link between human health and the environment is important for at least two reasons. First, environmental pollution is a significant contributor to the global burden of disease. The exact numbers are uncertain, but environmental contaminants and exposures are known to cause a wide range of adverse health effects, including many respiratory, diarrheal, and cardiovascular illnesses and cancers. Second, health concerns are one of the main reasons people care about environmental quality. The public certainly has other environmental concerns, such as protecting natural areas and avoiding the extinction of plant and animal species, but health threats are often a main source of worry.

For these reasons, understanding how the environment affects human health and how these threats can be best managed has been a priority for many researchers and policymakers. Environmental economics contributes to this understanding by addressing the following types of questions: How large are the costs and burden of illness from environmental exposures? What are the benefits and monetary value of preventing illness through policies that improve environmental quality? How are these costs, benefits, and the effectiveness of environmental policies affected by human behaviors?

Answering these questions requires models that integrate environmental science and economics. For example, estimating the loss in human well-being due to health effects from air pollution involves two main parts. The first part is estimating the relationship between elevated air-borne contaminant levels and the increased number (or severity) of illnesses. This concentration–response relationship is typically based on results from environmental epidemiology or toxicology studies; however, it may also require an understanding of how humans change their behaviors in the face of higher pollution levels. The second part is estimating the monetary equivalent of the loss in human well-being due to illness. As with other areas of nonmarket valuation, economists typically rely on willingness to pay measures as the best representation of this monetary equivalent. To answer the questions posed earlier, environmental economists often rely on a household production framework. This framework recognizes that households use their own resources to produce better health outcomes for themselves. First, they engage in averting or defensive behaviors to protect themselves against external harms, such as environmental pollution. For example, if groundwater monitoring indicates higher than usual contaminant levels, households with private wells may purchase bottled water or filtration systems. Second, they engage in mitigating behaviors to reduce the harm and discomfort from illness, for example by buying medicines or staying at home from work. Despite these two types of self-protective behaviors, households may still experience disutility (i.e., pain and suffering) from illness.

Based on this framework, there are four main components for valuing (in monetary terms) the relationship between health and the environment. For a given change in environmental conditions, they involve changes in: averting/defensive expenditures, mitigating (e.g., medical) expenditures, productivity losses (e.g., lost income/wages due to illness), and disutility from pain and suffering.

Health and environmental economists have developed a number of valuation approaches, which can be used to estimate one or more of these components. Cost of illness methods focus on direct medical and other treatment costs (mitigating expenditures) and, in many cases, on indirect costs (productivity losses). They have been widely applied, largely due to data availability, but their main limitation is an inability to capture values associated with changes in pain and suffering. Averting behavior methods focus on the first component. If they only measure changes in averting expenditures, then, like the cost of illness method, they are also limited in scope. However, if they are used with mitigating expenditures to estimate a health production function, then they are capable of incorporating all four components of value. Unfortunately, this combined approach has rarely been used due to its relatively difficult data and technical requirements.

Another approach is to use survey-based stated preference approaches, such as contingent valuation or choice experiments. In health value applications, these methods present survey respondents with hypothetical scenarios involving trade-offs between money and health. Responses are then used to estimate respondents' willingness to pay for better health-related conditions. One of the main advantages of these methods is that they can be used, in principle, to capture all four components of value. However, as with other stated preference applications, one of their main drawbacks is the hypothetical nature of the trade-offs and the resulting difficulty in validating responses.

Economic analysis methods can also designed to address other unique features of environmental health. One such feature is the large variety of health outcomes associated with environmental exposures. These outcomes vary in several dimensions, including the duration, frequency, latency, and severity of illness. Environmental illnesses include a wide range of acute and chronic conditions, both of which can vary in severity from low consequence to high severity and even fatal conditions. Some conditions, such as cancer, can also involve long latency periods between the time of exposure and the development of disease. Using stated preference surveys, in particular, different levels and combinations of these illness attributes can be communicated to respondents and then separately valued.

A second feature is that environmental exposures often result in a risk of illness, rather than a certainty of illness, for exposed individuals. Moreover, policies that reduce environmental contaminants tend to reduce these risks for individuals, rather than to reduce the severity, duration, or other attributes of illness. For this reason, it is important to understand how individuals value reductions in the probability of adverse health outcomes, including death. In addition to using stated preference methods, a variety of revealed preference methods have also been used to explore individuals' trade-offs between money and health risks. Hedonic wage-risk studies, for example, use evidence from labor markets to determine the amount of additional compensation individuals require for taking jobs with higher risks of death. Other studies have examined purchases of safety goods, such as bicycle helmets and fire detectors.

A third, and final, feature is that, when faced with lower levels of contaminants in the environment, individuals may respond by reducing their averting behaviors. For example, after improvements in outdoor air quality, individuals may spend less time indoors where the air may still be cleaner. In these cases, the health improvements or risk reductions are less than they would be without the change in behavior. As previously discussed, accounting for changes in averting behaviors is important for fully valuing improvements in environmental quality. It is also essential for understanding the net effect of policies on environmental health.

George Van Houtven

See also: Air Quality; Averting Behavior; Choice Experiments; Contingent Behavior; Food Safety; Hedonic Price Method; Nonmarket Valuation; Value of Statistical Life

Further Reading

Harrington, Winston, and Paul R. Portney. 1987. Valuing the Benefits of Health and Safety Regulation. *Journal of Urban Economics* 22(1): 101–112.

Prüss-Üstün, Annette, and Carlos Corvalán. 2006. *Preventing Disease through Healthy Environments*. Geneva: World Health Organization.

Hedonic Price Method

The hedonic method is a valuation technique that analyzes consumers' purchases of everyday products to understand the value people place on the various features of the product. The general logic underlying the hedonic method is that we can infer the value of one underlying characteristic of a marketed good by observing how its price changes as its characteristics change. For example, consider two cars that are identical in every way except that one car's fuel efficiency is 24 miles per gallon (mpg) and the other's is 28 mpg. Say we observe the 24 mpg car selling for $22,500 on average and the 28 mpg car selling for $23,300 on average. This observation tells us that the value consumers place on increasing fuel efficiency by 4 mpg is $800, or $200 for each additional mile per gallon.

Since we only indirectly observe the monetary trade-offs individuals are willing to make with respect to changes in any specific characteristic, the hedonic method is referred to as an indirect valuation method. In other words, we do not observe the value consumers have for the characteristic directly, instead we infer it from observable market transactions, such as inferring the value of fuel efficiency to consumers through their automobile purchases. As such, the estimated values from hedonic models are referred to as implicit prices or hedonic prices. In the example shown earlier, the hedonic price that consumers are willing to pay for fuel efficiency is $200 per each additional mpg of fuel efficiency.

Why would we want to understand how consumers value the features of everyday products in environmental economics? Because many things we purchase have environmental quality as either a direct feature of the product or as part of the product's production process. In the example discussed earlier, fuel efficiency of automobiles has important implications for carbon emissions as well as local air quality. Understanding whether consumers value fuel efficiency above and beyond the money it saves them in driving costs is important to understand when trying to quantify one of the many different types of benefits that might arise from policies to increase fuel efficiency standards.

Perhaps the market that economists most focus upon when using the hedonic method to value environmental goods and services is housing markets. The choice of where to live is perhaps one of the most important decisions people make, and this choice tells us a lot about their preferences for being located near to environmental amenities such parks and preserved open spaces or far away from environmental disamenities such as environmentally contaminated properties (known as brownfields or hazardous waste sites). We can determine the value households place on access to a park by comparing the sale prices of houses (or apartments) that are located within walking distance to a public park to those located further away. Similarly, we can determine the value households place on avoiding poor air quality by observing how house prices in areas with better air quality compare to those in areas with poor air quality.

Within the housing market context, hedonic methods have been employed to estimate the value of many types of environmental amenities such as improvements in air quality; access to beaches, parks, and other types of open space; desirable views (i.e., the view of the beach or mountains); tree cover on a property or in the neighborhood; and being located on lakes with higher water quality. Sometimes the focus of a study is to understand the value of avoiding a disamenity. Housing market hedonic models have estimated the value of avoiding: traffic and aircraft noise; proximity to environmentally contaminated properties; proximity to landfills, incinerators and power plants; proximity to odor-producing hog farms; and proximity to wind farms. Housing market hedonic applications provide policymakers with information on the benefits homeowners experience from improvements in their environmental surroundings, such as cleaning up an environmentally contaminated property, improving air quality, or reducing aircraft noise.

Other markets to which hedonic methods have been applied that relate to environmental policy include food, clothing, household appliances, timber, wine, and coffee markets. Typically, these types of applications are interested in understanding the value of organic or environmentally friendly content of the product. Labor markets are another application for hedonic models that has particular importance for environmental policy since a primary policy aim is often to reduce human mortality risks from environmental exposures such as toxics in the air and water. Hedonic models are used to examine how wages vary with characteristics of a job, with a special emphasis on the riskiness of the job. For example, one can imagine that welders working on high-rise buildings might earn more than welders working on one-story buildings, all else equal about the two jobs. By comparing similar jobs, the hedonic method can be used to tease out how people value reducing mortality risks through the wages they are willing to forego to hold safer jobs (i.e., jobs with lower risks of accidental death). Estimates of the hedonic price of reducing risk is then used as an estimate of the benefit of reducing mortality risks through improvements in environmental quality.

Hedonic methods have strong appeal as a nonmarket valuation technique. First and probably foremost, the method is grounded in observed behavior. We look to markets in which lots of consumers purchase lots of varieties of the product and use that rich information to estimate the value of a specific characteristic of interest. In addition, the data needed on purchase prices and product varieties can be relatively easy to obtain. Although hedonic methods are a powerful tool that is widely accepted, they are of course not without limitations. One of the hedonic method's limits relates to one of its main strengths: one must observe a market linked to an environmental good of interest and this is not always the case. And even if a market is available, the hedonic method is only capable of revealing one aspect of the total value of an environmental service—specifically, the use values of the environmental resource for the individuals purchasing the marketed good. For example, the value of proximity to a public park to homeowners is captured by the hedonic method, but the value of the park to nonresident recreationalists is not captured, nor is the value of ecosystems services of any type that accrue to society beyond just the homeowner.

Implementation of a hedonic study has many empirical challenges. In its simplest form, a hedonic analysis regresses prices of a good on its characteristics to estimate the implicit or hedonic price for the characteristic of interest, holding all else constant. To do this, one must obtain accurate measures of prices and characteristic levels. This task is relatively easy in some markets, but can be difficult in housing and labor market applications. For example, capturing all the features of a dwelling's location that contribute to its sales price or rental rate can be very difficult. However, if all the locational features that contribute to a dwelling's price are not observed or captured accurately, the estimated implicit price for an environmental feature of interest may be biased. For example, say a prison facility is located in a neighborhood but it is not known by the researcher, and the facility is located next to an environmentally contaminated property. In a regression analysis, the analyst may incorrectly attribute the impact of the prison on housing prices to the environmentally contaminated property. This is referred to as omitted variable bias and it is an important consideration when undertaking hedonic analysis.

Laura O. Taylor

See also: Brownfields; Hazardous Waste; Land Use; Nonmarket Valuation; Rosen, Sherwin; Value of Statistical Life

Further Reading

Parmeter, C. F., and J. C. Pope. 2013. Quasi-Experiments and Hedonic Property Value Methods, in J. List and M. Price (editors), *Handbook on Experimental Economics and the Environment*. North Hampton, UK: Edward Elgar.

Taylor, L. O. 2003. Hedonics, in P. Champ, K. Boyle, and T. Brown (editors), *A Primer on Nonmarket Valuation*. Dordrecht: Kluwer.

Hotelling, Harold

Harold Hotelling was an American mathematical statistician and economist. He received his bachelor's degree from the University of Washington (UW) where he majored in journalism. His studies were interrupted by his service in World War I, but he returned to complete his degree. According to Darnell, Hotelling said that his interest in economics led him to substitute so many economics classes that his degree might as well have been in economics. After a brief stint as a journalist, he returned to UW to complete a masters in mathematics. He then moved to Princeton to pursue his Ph.D. in mathematics. His goal was to "apply the methods proven so useful in the exact sciences to discover new truth in economics and political science."

While economics today is intimately tied to mathematics, Hotelling was a pioneer. At Princeton his studies included topology, as well as differential geometry, mathematical physics, and astrophysics. Hotelling cited this broad background as contributing to his research. The vast majority of his publications were in mathematical statistics, with relatively few in economics, but many are seminal in these and other fields.

Two of Hotelling's lasting contributions to resource and environmental economics are his 1931 paper in the *Journal of Political Economy,* "The Economics of Exhaustible Resources" and a letter he wrote to the director of the National Parks Service in 1947.

In his 1931 paper Hotelling developed the theory that the price of an exhaustible commodity would increase at the rate of interest. This work drew on his 1925 contribution on economic depreciation, as he recognized the parallel of the finite nature of both purchased capital and exhaustible resources. The formal development relied on the calculus of variations, which was not widely known by economists. This contribution provides the foundation for the vast majority of natural resource economics research that has followed.

In 1947, the director of the National Parks Service asked Hotelling how to economically value national parks. In a response letter, Hotelling noted that people often traveled great distances to these parks and that one could differentiate net satisfaction or value based on the different distances. Hotelling's response suggested the travel cost recreation demand model that is still used today.

Hotelling has also had a lasting impact beyond his research, serving as a catalyst for a great number of economists, statisticians, and mathematicians. He was instrumental in developing statistics groups at both Columbia University and the University of North Carolina, and it has been suggested that through developing these groups, Hotelling almost single-handedly brought statistics into the modern age. While at Columbia Hotelling advised Kenneth Arrow, who was awarded the 1972 Nobel Prize in Economics for insights developed in his dissertation. Arrow writes in his dissertation:

> ... I can't refrain from singling out H. Hotelling ... to whom I owe my interest in economics and my interest in the problem of social welfare.

Harold Hotelling retired in 1960, but continued to teach until 1966. He died in 1973 at the age of 78.

Janie M. Chermak and Robert H. Patrick

See also: Discounting; Exhaustible Resources; Travel Cost Method; User Cost

Further Reading

Arrow, K.J. 1951. Social Choice and Individual Values, Ph.D. Dissertation. Columbia University.

Arrow, K.J., and E.L. Lehmann. 2005. Harold Hotelling 1895–1973. *Biographical Memoirs*, Volume 87, Washington, D.C.: The National Academic Press.

Darnell, A.C. 1988. Harold Hotelling: September 29, 1895–December 26, 1973. *Statistical Science* 3(1): 57–62.

Darnell, A.C. 1990. The Life and Economic Thought of Harold Hotelling, in A.C. Darnell (editor), *The Collected Economics Articles of Harold Hotelling*, pp. 1–28. New York: Springer-Verlag.

Hotelling, H. 1925. A General Mathematical Theory of Depreciation. *Journal of the American Statistical Association* XX: 340–353.

Hotelling, H. 1931. The Economics of Exhaustible Resources. *Journal of Political Economy* 39(2): 137–175.

Hotelling, H. 1947. Letter of June 18, 1947, to Newton B. Drury. Included in the report *The Economics of Public Recreation: An Economic Study of the Monetary Evaluation of Recreation in National Parks*, 1949. Land and Recreational Planning Division, National Park Service, Washington, D.C.

Information Disclosure

Information disclosure policies inform consumers, investors, employees, community organizations, regulators, and other stakeholders about environmental outcomes. These programs are designed to leverage private market and legal forces to achieve policy objectives. Everyday examples in the United States now include toxic releases and carbon emission inventories, energy efficiency labels and eco-labels, advisories for methyl-mercury in fish and radon in homes, environmental performance rankings by *Newsweek* magazine and Greenpeace, and Environmental Protection Agency press releases of violators and penalties. Examples from other countries also abound.

Why are environmental information disclosure policies increasingly common? Transparency programs have several theoretical advantages over alternatives. First, they may be inexpensive relative to other environmental policy instruments. The costs of information dissemination continue to decline. Second, they may be politically expedient. This is especially true when the socially optimal level of the environmental activity is controversial. Third, transparency programs may be implemented even when regulatory authority is absent or unresolved. Recent mandatory greenhouse gas reporting inventories are a notable example. Fourth, they may minimize harm from pollutants emitted abroad or in the past. Environmental authorities cannot directly regulate emissions from other jurisdictions or previous time periods, but authorities can advise constituents about environmental harms from other countries or from persistent contaminants. Fifth, disclosure programs can be flexible, allowing specified at-risk groups to avoid environmental harm without imposing large-scale regulatory costs. For example, household lead warnings may reduce at-risk groups' dangers from lead-based paint without imposing costly uniform mandates like compulsory paint removal. Finally, transparency policies may leverage the benefits of traditional regulatory programs. Environmental authorities regularly publicize fines in order to maximize their deterrence impacts.

How might information disclosure policies influence outcomes? The related literature suggests that key channels may include input market pressures, output market pressures, activist pressures, and regulatory pressures. Firms identified as poor environmental performers may experience: stock divestitures from investors with green preferences; decreased employee loyalty or employee recruiting challenges; lower product demand from consumers with preferences for environmentally differentiated products; fewer business-to-business customers due to requirements for green supply chains; protests, letter campaigns, boycotts, or citizen suits from activist groups; new legal liability claims; intensified public monitoring and enforcement; difficulty obtaining future public regulatory permits; or even new conventional public regulatory burdens. The converses of the statements given earlier are also true; firms disclosed as good environmental performers may experience positive outcomes. An additional mechanism, managerial information, only applies to negative environmental information. Here, disclosed poor environmental performance may inform business managers about wasteful business practices and areas for improvement.

Do information disclosure policies achieve policy objectives in the real world? Present evidence suggests that, despite several theoretical advantages, the effectiveness and cost effectiveness of environmental information disclosure policies in practice remains controversial and context-specific. Some environmental information programs do appear to produce outcomes that are largely consistent with policy objectives. Large community drinking water suppliers that were required to inform residents about regulations and contaminant levels reduced subsequent violations. Eco-labeled products often attract a devoted group of socially responsible consumers. In contrast, some environmental information programs fail to significantly affect behavioral and environmental outcomes. Media campaigns alone did little to encourage radon testing in homes. The impact of unprocessed Toxic Release Inventory (TRI) data on environmental outcomes remains highly contentious. Some disclosure programs even appear to produce counterproductive unintended consequences. Methyl-mercury advisories warning pregnant women and households with young children about the dangers of consuming certain types of fish caused at-risk groups to avoid seafood altogether. Since fish is typically a healthy source of protein relative to alternatives, the net impact of the advisory may well have reduced overall public health. Facilities participating in a recent Department of Energy transparency program experienced worsening overall environmental performance, but selectively disclosed significant improvements to the public.

Why might environmental information programs sometimes fail to achieve policy objectives? The conventional wisdom that information improves welfare requires that stakeholders receive, understand, and carefully process disclosed information. This is often not the case. Evidence suggests that access to information varies considerably across sociodemographic groups. A large and growing body of psychology, marketing, and behavioral economics research suggests that individuals face significant cognitive limitations and bounded rationality. Individuals regularly misperceive risk probabilities and may employ heuristic-based decision-making shortcuts for complex decisions. In short, environmental information may fail to be received, may be misunderstood, or may be processed in a manner inconsistent with policy goals.

What is the take-home message? Environmental information programs can produce effective and cost-effective outcomes, but they are not a panacea. Successful disclosure programs must involve careful ex-ante design, information provision where and when stakeholders make decisions, actionable information, and safeguards against gaming or greenwashing. Disclosure programs must also involve regular ex-post evaluation for effectiveness and cost effectiveness relative to alternatives.

Jay P. Shimshack

See also: Corporate Environmentalism; Health; Monitoring and Enforcement; Precautionary Principle; Risk and Uncertainty; Safe Minimum Standard; Toxic Release Inventory

Further Reading

Bennear, L. S., and S. M. Olmstead. 2008. The Impacts of the "Right to Know": Information Disclosure and the Violation of Drinking Water Standards. *Journal of Environmental Economics and Management* 56(2): 117–130.

Kim, E. H., and T. P. Lyon. 2011. Strategic Environmental Disclosure: Evidence from the DOE's Voluntary Greenhouse Gas Registry. *Journal of Environmental Economics and Management* 61(3): 311–326.

Kitzmueller, M., and J. Shimshack, J. 2012. Economic Perspectives on Corporate Social Responsibility. *Journal of Economic Literature* 50(1): 51–84.

Shimshack, J. P., and M. B. Ward. 2010. Mercury Advisories and Household Health Trade-offs. *Journal of Health Economics* 29(5): 674–685.

Weil, D., A. Fung, M. Graham, and E. Fagotto. 2005. The Effectiveness of Regulatory Disclosure Policies. *Journal of Policy Analysis and Management* 25(1): 155–181.

International Association for Energy Economics

The International Association for Energy Economics (IAEE) was founded in 1977 in response to the 1970's energy crisis. The IAEE is an independent, worldwide, nonprofit organization based in the United States, with over 4,157 members in over 100 nations, providing an interdisciplinary forum for the exchange of ideas among professionals interested in energy economics.

The IAEE's main objective is to bring together professionals from business, government, and academia to advance the knowledge, understanding, and application of economics across all aspects of energy. To achieve this goal, the IAEE strives to facilitate worldwide information flow and exchange of ideas on energy issues, publish high-quality research, and develop and educate students and energy professionals.

The IAEE publishes three periodicals. *The Energy Journal* is the official quarterly journal of the IAEE. It was founded in 1980 to promote the advancement and dissemination of new knowledge concerning energy and related topics. It publishes a blend of theoretical, empirical, and policy-related papers in energy economics. Each quarterly issue contains original refereed articles, short notes, and book reviews. Nontechnical articles on important policy issues are published in the Energy Perspectives section. A Research Forum section reports on the emergence of new analytical methods for economic analysis of energy.

The *Economics of Energy & Environmental Policy,* established in 2011, is a semiannual energy policy publication. It focuses on all policy issues in the interface between energy and environmental economics. EEEP provides a research-based, scholarly, yet easy-to-read and accessible source of information on contemporary economic thinking and analysis of energy and environmental policy. EEEP publishes a blend of policy papers and notes, organized symposia on specific policy issues, feature articles, book reviews, and commentaries on current energy and environment.

The *IAEE Energy Forum* is a newsletter that delivers the latest information on the association, and contains articles that appeal to a general audience interested in the energy field.

In order to meet the association's objectives, periodic conferences are held that focus on energy economics. The IAEE sponsors annual conferences in North America, Europe, Asia, and Latin America. Past meetings have taken place in cities such as San Francisco, Stockholm, Venice, Kyoto, Santiago, Abuja, Moscow, and Taiwan. The conferences attract delegates and speakers from around the world, and from some of the most influential government, corporate, and academic circles.

The IAEE takes pride in developing and educating students in the energy field. There are student chapters in 12 countries, and many student activities are held at the annual conferences, including a Best Student Paper award and student Ph.D. days. A student member also sits on the IAEE Council.

The IAEE operates through a 17-member council of elected and appointed international members. Council and officers serve on a voluntary basis for a term of one to two years.

The IAEE has several awards to recognize exemplary energy economics research. Since 1981, the IAEE has awarded an annual prize for outstanding contributions to the field of energy economics and its literature. Past recipients have included Morris Adelman, Dale Jorgenson, Robert Pindyck, and Jean Tirole. The *Energy Journal* Best Paper Award was instituted in 1989 for the paper designated as the most outstanding of the papers published in *The Energy Journal* the previous year, and the Journalism Award was instituted in 1983 to reward excellence in written journalism on topics relating to international energy economics.

Mine K. Yücel

See also: Association of Environmental and Resource Economists; Fisheries Economics Associations; Renewable Energy; United States Society for Ecological Economics

International Climate Agreements

Climate change is arguably one of the greatest challenges facing the global community. Most scientists agree that our climate is changing as a result of anthropogenic greenhouse gas emissions, and while there remains great uncertainty regarding the effects on our planet, recent studies suggest that the cost of unchecked climate change may be devastating. It is no surprise then that nations have spent significant resources over the past few decades attempting to jointly manage greenhouse gas emissions.

The idea that climate change must be managed jointly is an important one. Carbon dioxide, the most significant greenhouse gas, is a stock pollutant that mixes uniformly in the atmosphere. Thus, the resulting concentration of carbon emissions in the atmosphere is independent of the source of the emissions. This reality means that every country can contribute to the climate change problem through their emissions. It also means that every country can contribute to the climate change solution through emissions abatement activities. In this way, atmospheric concentrations of carbon emissions constitute a transboundary environmental externality.

When externalities cross national borders, unilateral management of carbon emissions is not an effective option. The benefits from actions taken by one country to reduce carbon emissions will be trivial if other countries fail to reduce their emissions (or if they respond by increasing theirs). And if the benefits of emissions abatement are enjoyed by all nations, then there is an incentive for countries to attempt to free ride on the abatement activities of other countries. Moreover, sovereign nations do not answer to a global authority that can ensure all countries participate by externally imposing and enforcing greenhouse-gas regulations. Rather, nations must coordinate voluntarily to negotiate international treaties.

Nations began serious efforts to manage climate change in the early 1990s through the United Nations General Assembly. An Intergovernmental Negotiating Committee was formed to conduct the negotiation process, and in less than two years the body drafted the United Nations Framework Convention on Climate Change (UNFCCC). The objective of the convention (or treaty) was to "stabilize greenhouse-gas concentrations in the atmosphere at a level that would prevent dangerous anthropogenic interference with the climate system." The UNFCCC, however, did not require specific emissions abatement responsibilities for the parties. Rather, it established a framework through which nations convene to negotiate binding protocols that set mandatory emissions limits. The convention entered into force in March 1994. Today 195 countries are ratifying members to the convention.

During the third annual conference of the parties to the UNFCCC in 1997, the Kyoto Protocol was adopted. The treaty, the first of its kind, established binding emissions limits for developed (Annex 1) countries. Through negotiations, Annex 1 countries agreed to reduce their greenhouse gas emissions by an average of 5.2 percent relative to 1990 levels over a period from 2008 to 2012. Although almost all countries signed the treaty soon after its adoption, the treaty only entered into force when certain participation thresholds were met. Specifically, at least 55 of the parties to the conference had to ratify the agreement and those member countries had to account for at least 55 percent of global greenhouse gas emissions. When Russia ratified in late 2004, the treaty satisfied the 55 percent requirement, which triggered Kyoto to enter into force in February 2005.

As of today, the Kyoto Protocol remains the only international treaty requiring binding greenhouse gas emissions limits. Unfortunately, the treaty has been largely unsuccessful. The impending failure of Kyoto can be largely attributed to two major shortcomings. First, the treaty failed to motivate the two biggest greenhouse gas emitters to commit to reducing, or even stabilizing, their emissions. The United States, at the time the biggest emitter (now second biggest), chose not to ratify the treaty. One of the fundamental reasons for the defection was that the United States felt her participation would be futile without having China, then the second biggest emitter (now the biggest), also take on emissions abatement responsibilities. While China is a signatory to the protocol, its classification as a developing country precluded it from any emissions abatement responsibilities.

The second major failure is that the treaty fails to provide the correct incentives to motivate countries to comply with their commitments. The enforcement mechanism for the protocol, established at the seventh conference of the parties in Marrakesh, is essentially nondeterrent. It states that a member country found in violation of their commitments will be required to further limit their emissions during the next commitment period (which began in 2013) to both meet their original target plus an additional 30 percent emissions reduction. In short, the penalty for exceeding emissions limits is more stringent emissions limits. There is no reason to believe that a noncompliant country would take this punishment seriously in the second commitment period of Kyoto. Without an enforcement mechanism that can deter noncompliance, any treaty to reduce greenhouse gas emissions will fall short of its objective.

Economists, through the study of human behavior and institutions, have an important role to play in designing a more effective climate agreement. The underlying incentives that countries face when making emissions decisions are commonly illustrated as a variant of the well-known prisoners' dilemma game. In this game, the collection of countries is strictly better off by jointly limiting their emissions levels. However, individually, countries are better off not restricting their own emissions. The result, or equilibrium, of the game is that all countries choose not to restrict their emissions. They pursue their own self-interests at the expense of the collective interest.

The goal of international climate agreements is to craft a set of rules that align individual interests with the collective interest. Some provisions of the Kyoto Protocol attempted to accomplish this. The minimum participation rule (the 55 percent rule) served as a commitment device in which countries would not take on emissions responsibilities until a critical number of other countries agreed to do the same. However, the 55 percent rule made it possible for the treaty to enter into force without the United States or China taking on any emissions responsibilities. Regardless of whether this was purposeful or coincidental, it is a poor design feature.

Looking beyond Kyoto, an effective international climate agreement must simultaneously address two problems. First, it must address the problem of participation: that is, motivating critical countries to join the agreement (like the United States and China) and take on meaningful emissions abatement responsibilities. Second, it must address the problem of maintaining compliance with the agreement. Economists typically encourage using a combination of carrots (e.g., technology transfers) and sticks (e.g., trade sanctions) as mechanisms to nudge countries in the direction of achieving these goals. Although these problems are challenging, there is reason to be hopeful. Nations are increasingly engaged on the topic of managing climate change. If nations can collectively benefit from mitigating climate change, then it must be possible to design a set of rules that can make it individually worthwhile to participate. The hope is that such a treaty will be created in time to thwart the most costly effects of a changing climate.

David M. McEvoy

See also: Adaptation; Climate Change Impacts; Carbon Pricing; Externality; International Environmental Agreements; Montreal Protocol

Further Reading

Barrett, Scott. 1994. Self-Enforcing International Environmental Agreements. *Oxford Economic Papers* 46: 878–894.

UN General Assembly. 1992. United Nations Framework Convention on Climate Change. FCCC/INFORMAL/84, http://unfccc.int/resource/docs/convkp/conveng.pdf

Weitzman, Martin. 2011. Fat-Tailed Uncertainty in the Economics of Climate Change. *Review of Environmental Economic Policy* 5(2): 275–292.

International Environmental Agreements

There are thousands of international environmental agreements, ranging from relatively straightforward bilateral accords that manage border geographies to global agreements on toxics, endangered species protection, and global climate change. Some manage global commons that do not exclusively belong to any nation, such as deep sea fisheries and Antarctic research and preservation, and others attempt to internalize externalities that cross borders. From an efficiency perspective, it is ideal to have the scale of the agreement equal to the scale of the externality, such that the agreement can cover everyone contributing to and affected by choices in regards to an environmental amenity or problem. This allows for improvements to be made so that those harmed by collectively agreed environmental management choices can be compensated by those who gain (called a Pareto improvement).

There are political complications to reaching economically efficient solutions to international environmental issues. Some nations may see opportunities to free ride on the costly environmental management efforts of others, and participating nations may have incentives to cheat on agreements that can be difficult to monitor and enforce; typically the specifics of implementing agreements are left to the signatories to manage within their own borders, and they report their own compliance to the treaty organization. Selecting relatively easily observed outcomes, even if they do not directly correspond to the environmental benefit the treaty aims to secure, can improve transparency and compliance as well as trust among member countries. If income and development disparities are large within the group of member countries and collective efforts are economically significant, mechanisms to share the costs of compliance and management for poorer countries may be agreed to and implemented. Many such transfer programs are administered by the Global Environment Facility (GEF), initially established by the World Bank but now operating independently.

While the GEF coordinates some administrative work, there is not a single global environmental management organization, so interactions between the environmental and health outcomes of treaties with differing memberships, rules, and procedures present challenges. Climate and ozone, for instance, interact physically—many regulated ozone-depleting chemicals and substitutes are also powerful greenhouse gasses—and decisions made under one agreement can have large effects on outcomes monitored by the other; rules on toxics and invasive species can come into conflict, and global fisheries rules and Antarctic preservation efforts are not harmonized. These conflicts can sometimes be managed on a case-by-case basis, as in the Stockholm Convention decision to allow dichlorodiphenyltrichloroethane (DDT; an insecticide) use that would otherwise be impermissible under the treaty in settings where the danger of malaria outweighed the danger of continued persistent organic pollutant (POP) exposure. More complete integration may be needed for more complex or pervasive interactions.

There are key issues that stand out for environmental agreements in contrast to other international treaties. Typically ecosystems do not have a set and fixed ideal state; they consist of overlapping and interacting dynamic processes, and simple metrics for ecosystem health are not always conveniently available. Success is more likely for agreements that have processes and expertise in place to incorporate new information and scientific assessments over time. The Intergovernmental Panel on Climate Change (IPCC) efforts to update climate science in support of ongoing efforts to reach agreement on global climate policy are a highly visible example, but many major agreements, including the Stockholm Convention on Persistent Organic Pollutants and the Montreal Protocol on Substances that Deplete the Ozone Layer, have relied on ongoing scientific assessments of environmental risks and policy progress to manage global public goods. This can go hand in hand with information and technology dissemination, facilitating burden sharing across member countries.

Since many environmental amenities are nonmarket goods, valuation is important to developing and administering international environmental agreements. When agreements include signatories at different development levels, this can be complicated for both technical and political reasons. Many methods of valuing environmental goods and services, including contingent valuation based on willingness to pay and hedonic estimation based on wage rates, are tied to the income and life expectancy of exposed populations. Where some member states are poor or have large populations who do not work in the market economy, impacts on their populations may be assessed as less valuable using these methods. Alternatives include measuring and reporting outcomes like cases of illness or lost years of life expectancy or acres protected but not aggregating the various categories up into monetized values, which limits the use of benefit–cost analysis but may be more politically palatable.

Many environmental problems are long-term problems, and thus decision makers confront the difficulty of evaluating the wisdom of intergenerational transfers; discounted benefit–cost analysis implicitly assumes that borrowing and saving are possible across the life of the project, but for amenities like global climate those impacted by the choice to invest now or wait for the future are not able to participate in the negotiation of agreements today, and this presents a political and ethical problem without a clear economic solution. Some environmental economists argue for the application of the precautionary principle in such settings. Others argue that this in effect commits societies to the existing system by default even when it is not working to solve the environmental problems at hand.

Catherine S. Norman

See also: Air Pollution; Benefit–Cost Analysis; Carbon Pricing; Contingent Valuation; Externality; Fisheries Management; Health; International Climate Change Agreements; International Trade; Monitoring and Enforcement; Montreal Protocol; Precautionary Principle

Further Reading

Barrett, S. 2005. *Environment and Statecraft: The Strategy of Environmental Treaty-Making.* New York: Oxford University Press.

University of Oregon International Environmental Agreements Database, http://iea.uoregon.edu

International Trade

The complex relationship between trade and the environment can be divided along three broad dimensions: (1) the impact of environmental policy on trade, (2) the effect of trade on the environment, and (3) the impact of trade policy on the environment.

The first dimension relates to the effect of environmental policy on international trade patterns. There exist two primary mechanisms by which this may occur. First, domestic environmental regulation affects the production costs of firms located in the country. Facing higher production costs due to stricter regulation, firms are at a competitive disadvantage relative to firms located in countries with relatively lax regulation. Consequently, net imports may rise as consumers at home and abroad substitute toward products produced more cheaply in environmentally lax countries. The magnitude of this effect depends on the difference in environmental stringency across countries, and the importance of environmental costs in total production costs.

Second, environmental policy may impact trade patterns through foreign direct investment (FDI). FDI occurs when a multinational firm in one country, known as the source, shifts some or all production activities to another country, known as the host. One motivation for FDI is to take advantage of lower production costs in the host. As environmental regulation is one component of a firm's production cost, greater stringency in the source may cause a firm to shift production to a host with relatively lax regulation. Known as the pollution haven hypothesis (PHH), its practical importance again depends on the difference in environmental stringency across countries, and the importance of environmental costs in total production costs. If the PHH holds, environmental policy will affect international trade. For example, if the shift of production activities to the host is limited to the intermediate stage of production and accompanied by shipments of intermediate goods back to the source, then regulation increases the volume of trade.

The second dimension along which trade and the environment intersect relates to the effect of trade on the environment. Such an effect may arise through scale, technique, and composition effects. The scale effect refers to the overall volume of production that occurs. Since production invariably produces some pollution and waste, trade tends to degrade the environment by increasing the volume of production. Production volume may increase, among other reasons, due to the more efficient use of resources when countries specialize in goods for which they have a comparative advantage.

The technique effect concerns the amount of environmental degradation inflicted per unit of production. While trade raises the overall scale of production, the resulting economic growth raises demand for a clean environment. Consequently, stricter regulation is likely to be implemented, resulting in cleaner production processes. In essence, trade raises a country's wealth, and wealthier countries demand a cleaner environment via less damaging production techniques.

The composition effect refers to trade's impact on environmental degradation due to changes in a country's output mix. With trade, countries specialize in the production of certain goods, perhaps those in which they have a comparative advantage, and then trade these goods for products produced elsewhere. If a country specializes in goods that are harmful to the environment (e.g., paper or chemical goods) then the composition effect of trade will result in greater environmental damage. The converse is true if a country specializes in goods that are relatively cleaner to produce (e.g., textiles).

The net effect of trade on a country's environmental quality depends on the relative magnitudes of the scale, technique, and composition effects. Empirical studies indicate that greater trade generally has a modest beneficial impact on environmental quality.

Before continuing, three subtle issues also bear consideration. First, trade entails the transport of goods; this also generates pollution. Empirical evidence highlights the importance of transportation-related pollution. Second, trade may impact the environment through the introduction of so-called invasive species, which may threaten biodiversity, agricultural productivity, marine resources, and other ecosystem services. Third, the interaction between trade and the environment is not limited to international trade. Trade between regions within a country also generates scale, technique, and composition effects. However, one salient difference does arise. With international trade, domestic firms with market power will pass some of the higher production costs due to environmental regulation on to consumers (through higher prices) in foreign countries. For subnational trade, however, higher prices harm consumers located in the same country. Consequently, the technique effect is likely to be weaker, yielding a less beneficial effect of trade on the environment, when trade is across regions within the same country rather than across countries.

The final dimension along which trade and the environment intersect relates to the effect of trade policy, rather than trade per se, on the environment. Trade policies, such as regional trade agreements (e.g., the North American Free Trade Agreement) or membership in the World Trade Organization (WTO), affect the environment via two mechanisms. First, they limit protectionist measures designed to stunt free trade, most notably tariffs or quotas. Consequently, countries may turn to so-called secondary trade barriers, such as environmental regulation, to protect domestic firms from foreign competitors. For example, a country may attempt to circumvent a trade agreement and limit imports of, say, foreign agricultural goods by banning imports of goods using a certain pesticide. Even if this policy has legitimate benefits to the environment, it may be disallowed under existing trade policy as it affects trade. In essence, concern over the unfair usage of secondary trade barriers may prevent countries from implementing desirable pro-environment regulations.

Second, trade agreements may impede environmental protection by prohibiting a crucial enforcement mechanism available to international environmental agreements (IEAs): trade sanctions. IEAs addressing global environmental problems, such as ozone depletion or global warming or protection of the oceans, have few sticks available to punish violators. Imposing trade sanctions on countries in violation of an IEA is one of the few enforcement mechanisms available. However, the fear is that trade agreements in general, and the WTO in particular, will preclude the use of such sanctions. This, in turn, threatens the ability of IEAs to achieve their desired effect.

Daniel L. Millimet and Jayjit Roy

See also: Environmental Kuznets Curve; International Environmental Agreements; Invasive Species; Trade Policy

Further Reading

Antweiler, W., B. R. Copeland, and M. S. Taylor. 2001. Is Free Trade Good for the Environment? *American Economic Review* 91(4): 877–908.

Eckersley, R. 2004. The Big Chill: The WTO and Multilateral Environmental Agreements. *Global Environmental Politics* 4(4): 24–50.

Levinson, A., and M. S. Taylor. 2008. Unmasking the Pollution Haven Effect. *International Economic Review* 49(1): 223–254.

Invasive Species

When species are introduced into new areas, they can change the landscape in at least three undesirable ways. One, they can thrive in the new environment and crowd out existing species, reducing the habitat available to existing species. Reed canary grass is in this category—it can take over wetland habitat and turn it into a less hospitable place for birds. Two, invaders can prey on existing species. An example is emerald ash borer—in its native habitat in Asia, emerald ash borer has natural predators that keep it in check but, in the American continent, its growth is unchecked and is predicted to gradually eliminate all ash trees. A second example of a predator is the black rat, which was accidentally introduced on Anacapa Island, one of the Channel Islands off the coast of California. These rats feed on the eggs of migratory seabirds that nest on the island, reducing the ability of the population to reproduce. Three, invasive species can change the quality of services that the environment provides. For example, common carp stir up sediment on lake bottoms, releasing phosphorus and making lakes eutrophic and less suitable for aquatic life. A complete catalog of invasive species would include terrestrial and aquatic animals, plants, and pathogens and their impact would include a wide range of ecosystem services that humans enjoy and depend upon.

Biologists separate the invasion process into three stages: introduction, establishment, and spread. Economic questions about invasive species can be separated into these stages as well. For the introduction phase, it is worth asking how intensely to screen and regulate the pathways through which species can be introduced. Since invasive species can be thought of as a biological pollutant—a harmful by-product of consumption or production—we can use ideas about pollution abatement and think through the marginal benefits and marginal costs of reducing invasive species introductions. The analogy only goes so far, though, because while small amounts of conventional pollutants can be considered harmless, living organisms reproduce, grow in size, move, and evolve over time. This makes the marginal benefit of complete elimination of the invasive species potentially very large. Thus, a zero-tolerance approach might be the best policy against invasive species damage.

On the other hand, it is easy to look back and say that a benefit–cost calculation would have shown that the introduction of a particular species should have been prevented. If it had been known that damaging species were hiding within the packing material bringing goods from Asia, the packing material could have been treated or other packing material could have been used. In situations where the damage is unforeseen, how much should be spent on prevention? How many limits should be put on international trade, how many shipments should be inspected, and how intrusive should inspections of travelers and their luggage be—particularly if you do not know what you are looking for? The costs of these preventive activities are large and obvious, the benefits less clear. In practice, regulations have been put in place to control introductions through pathways that have already been shown to be problematic. Many wood boring insects have come through solid wood packing material, and now wood packing material must be heat-treated to kill any insects that might be hiding within. Ballast water in ships has been responsible for the introduction of zebra mussels, and now this ballast water must be exchanged out at sea rather than in ports. It is difficult to anticipate the pathway through which the next significant invasive species will slip through.

In the establishment phase, introduced species can gain a foothold in a new environment. The tens rule suggests that approximately 10 percent of species that have been introduced will become established. During this phase, it may be possible to find and eradicate the species. It is important to have a good idea of what to look for and where the species might be located. In the example of emerald ash borer, scientists guess that the species had been introduced about 10 years before it was identified and recognized as a problem. Costs of searching for and controlling established invasive species should be weighed against the expected benefit of those efforts.

In the spread phase, established species start to grow. Not all established species are capable of expanding their territory—approximately 10 percent can—but examples of successful species are dramatic. Zebra mussel, emerald ash borer, gypsy moth, and cheatgrass seem unstoppable with current methods of control. At some point, the question becomes not whether to try to eradicate the species, but how much effort to spend to slow the spread of the species. Often, humans are the culprits responsible for transporting species from one location to another and allowing species to hopscotch across the landscape. Controlling spread may involve changing human behavior through regulations or incentives. For example, inspections of fishing boats to find and remove Eurasian watermilfoil, quarantines on firewood shipments to limit the spread of forest pathogens, and education campaigns to deter the release of earthworms are all policies that can help control the spread of species.

Finally, invasive species may become thoroughly established. Although complete eradication is still feasible in some rare cases, at this point the choice generally becomes how intensely to manage the established population. As an example, sea lamprey is a parasite of fish in the Great Lakes that cannot be eradicated. However, its population has been reduced and kept at a tolerable level through management of spawning grounds. Adaptation to an established population is also an option. New technologies preventing intake pipes from being clogged by zebra mussel insulate power plants and drinking-water treatment facilities. Cities replace healthy ash trees with other species as a way to adapt to the sudden loss of ash trees to the emerald ash borer infestation. An example of complete eradication after establishment is the case of black rats on Anacapa Island, where sea birds are now returning. High up-front eradication costs will yield a long stream of benefits into the future as the island ecosystem is restored.

Frances Homans

See also: Benefit–Cost Analysis; Regulation; Risk and Uncertainty

Further Reading

Costello, Christopher, and Carol McAusland. 2003. Protectionism, Trade, and Measures of Damage from Exotic Species Introductions. *American Journal of Agricultural Economics* 85(4): 964–975.

Leung, Brian, David M. Lodge, David Finnoff, Jason F. Shogren, Mark A. Lewis, and Gary Lamberti. 2002. An Ounce of Prevention or a Pound of Cure: Bioeconomic Risk Analysis of Invasive Species. *Proceedings of the Royal Society of London. B* 269(1508): 2407–2413.

Williamson, Mark, and Alastair Fitter. 1996. The Varying Success of Invaders. *Ecology* 77(6): 1661–1666.

J

Jevons, William Stanley

William Stanley Jevons (1835–1882), a British economist, logician, and mathematician, is recognized along with Carl Menger and Leon Walras as a founder of the marginal revolution in economics. In addition, Jevons contributed some key early insights in natural resource economics. His investigation of the coal industry in Britain highlighted a tension between efficiency in resource use and resource conservation. As Jevons demonstrated, improvements in the technical efficiency of resource use can lead to greater, rather than lesser, rates of resource use.

Jevons was born in Liverpool in 1835 into the family of a prosperous iron merchant. He enrolled at University College in London at age 16, but financial troubles led Jevons to leave school after two years. He became an assayer for the Royal Mint of Australia and moved to Australia in 1854. While in Australia Jevons developed a strong interest in political economy. He returned to England in 1859 and resumed his studies at University College, completing degrees in 1862 and 1863. In 1863 Jevons published a pamphlet, *A Serious Fall in the Value of Gold Ascertained and its Social Effects Set Forth*, his first extended treatment of an economic issue.

After taking an academic position in Manchester in 1863, Jevons turned to the question of coal resource exhaustion, a matter of then substantial political interest. His book on the subject, *The Coal Question,* was published in 1865. The overriding concern of *The Coal Question* was what we now call national competitiveness. Jevons held that ready access to coal had been Britain's great industrial advantage, but that the advantage would wane as coal was mined and additional supplies became increasingly costly.

As compared to more naïve analysts of nonrenewable resources, Jevons focused on increased cost rather than physical exhaustion. Long before the physical limits of the resource were reached, Jevons saw that higher cost would drive energy consumers to alternatives. The alternatives—Jevons examined sun, wind, water, wood, peat, and petroleum as substitutes—were significantly inferior to coal in his estimation, and Britain had less favorable access to such resources than other nations.

The more lasting contribution of Jevons's analysis concerned the relationship between efficiency in use of a resource and demand for the resource. In *The Coal Question* Jevons demonstrated that greater technical efficiency in the use of coal had led to higher demand for coal and concluded greater efficiency would fail to promote conservation. He wrote, "It is wholly a confusion of ideas to suppose that the economical use of fuel is equivalent to a diminished consumption. The very contrary is the truth." This relationship between changing technical efficiency in resource use and changing rates of resource consumption is now termed the Jevons paradox.

When an improvement in technical efficiency in resource use leads to a less than equivalent reduction in consumption, the difference is termed a rebound effect. A rebound effect strong enough to increase resource consumption is called backfire. The rebound effect can be further analyzed into several separate effects: a direct effect, an indirect effect, and an economy-wide or macroeconomic effect. The direct effect involves the added quantity demanded for the resource given that the effective cost of resource use has fallen. The indirect effect involves income-effect-based increases in the consumption of goods and services embodying the resource. The macroeconomic effect arises from the efficiency-based expansion in economic growth. Many analysts focus primarily on the direct rebound effects, but indirect and macroeconomic effects can constitute significant sources of rebound or backfire over time.

The Jevons paradox remains controversial in public policy. Efficiency policies continue to be promoted as conservation measures, for example with automobile fuel economy standards and appliance efficiency standards. Opponents of such policies tend to emphasize the potential rebound, while advocates of efficiency policies tend to ignore or minimize the issue.

Michael Giberson

See also: Corporate Average Fuel Economy; Energy Efficiency; Energy Policy

Further Reading

Jevons, William Stanley. 1865. *The Coal Question: An Inquiry Concerning the Progress of the Nation, and the Probable Exhaustion of our Coal-mines.* London: Macmillan.

Jevons, William Stanley, R. D. Collison Black, and Rosamond Könekamp. 1972. *Papers and Correspondence of William Stanley Jevons.* London: Macmillan.

Journals

Economists disseminate their work in many different ways. In the early stages of research projects they give presentations at conferences and in seminars. Then, as research is finalized, they write research papers that can be the basis of entire books or single book chapters, which are published as draft working papers online as well as in academic journals. Journals are much like magazines but consist of scholarly output: most articles are research papers, but these are accompanied by comments and replies discussing previously published research, editorials, and book reviews. Journal articles are subject to peer review—outside review by other academics who advise journal editors about whether articles are suitable for publication. Peer-reviewed journal articles are important to academic economists in order to get pay raises, promoted, or a better job. In fact, studies have shown that a publication in one of the top few journals can be worth $1,000 to $2,000 in annual salary to a professor.

In economics, journals are usually categorized as being general-interest journals or field journals. General-interest journals, as the name suggests, publish articles on any topic of interest across the entire discipline of economics and are potentially read by anyone in the entire profession. Field journals, on the other hand, focus on one or a few specific areas of interest. For example, environmental and resource economists often will have related interests such as energy or agricultural economics; each of these fields have their own journals and some journals cover more than one related field.

The Econlit database, which is compiled by the American Economic Association (AEA), the primary professional society for economists, can be used to investigate the range of journals in which environmental and resource economists publish. This database indexes journal articles, books, working papers, dissertations, and other publications in economics. It also categorizes all articles by the field(s) covered in the article, so articles in environmental and resource economics can be extracted. In 2011, environmental and resource economists published 2,606 articles from 466 journals indexed in Econlit. The 10 journals with the most environmental and resource economics articles are *Energy Policy; Ecological Economics; Environmental and Resource Economics; Transportation Research: Part D: Transport and Environment;* the *Journal of Environmental Planning and Management; Development; Resource and Energy Economics;* the *Journal of Environmental Economics and Management* (JEEM); *Energy Economics;* and *Climate Policy.* These journals, with the broad coverage of issues by environmental and resource economists, represent the interests of environmental and resource economists as well.

Although the sheer number of journals—and articles published in those journals—is interesting, economists do not judge journals by the number of published articles. Instead, they rate journals by the influence of those journals measured by the number of citations per article, professional surveys, or more complex statistical techniques. The best general-interest journals are the most sought-after outlets in which to publish for economists because of their prestige and wide readership. Because the best general-interest journals are generally considered better publication outlets than the best field journals, all else being equal, an environmental or resource economist would tend to want to publish their work in a general-interest journal. However, all else is not equal: because of their relative prestige and their desirability across all fields of economics, competition to publish in the general interest journals is very high and acceptance rates are relatively low. The general-interest journals also tend to publish articles that are of more general interest, such as widely applicable models or theory. In fact the Econlit data for 2011 showed that other than the *American Economic Review,* the flagship journal of the American Economics Association and one of the most prominent journals in economics, most general-interest journals publish very few environmental and resource economics articles.

No matter what method environmental and resource economists use to rank the influence of their field journals, one thing is clear: JEEM, the official journal of the Association of Environmental and Resource Economists (AERE) until 2014, is the most influential and is one of the oldest journals focusing on the field. In 2014, AERE launched the Journal of the Association of Environmental and Resource Economists with the goal of becoming the top journal in the field. Other journals in the top echelon of the field are (in alphabetical order): *American Journal of Agricultural Economics, Ecological Economics, Energy Journal, Environmental and Resource Economics, Journal of Agricultural and Resource Economics, Land Economics, Marine Resource Economics, Resource and Energy Economics,* and *Review of Environmental Economics and Policy.*

William J. Wheeler

See also: Association of Environmental and Resource Economists; Books; d'Arge, Ralph C.; International Association for Energy Economics; Kneese, Allen V.; Tolley, George S.; United States Society for Ecological Economics; University Economics Departments

Further Reading

Auffhammer, Maximilian. 2009. The State of Environmental and Resource Economics: A Google Scholar Perspective. *Review of Environmental Economics and Policy* 3(2): 251–269.

Brookshire, David S., and David O. Scrogin. 2000. Reflections upon 25 Years of the Journal of Environmental Economics and Management. *Journal of Environmental Economics and Management* 39(3): 249–263.

Kalaitzidakis, Pantelis, Theofanis P. Mamuneas, and Thanasis Stengos. 2011. An Updated Ranking of Academic Journals in Economics. *Canadian Journal of Economics* 44(4): 1525–1538.

Rousseau, Sandra. 2008. Journal Evaluation by Environmental and Resource Economists: A Survey. *Scientometrics* 77(2): 213–223.

K

Kneese, Allen V.

Allen Kneese was an influential scholar and policy advocate in the early years of environmental economics as a discipline. He spent most of his career with Resources for the Future, a prominent independent research organization in American resource and environmental policy, and was the first president of the Association of Environmental and Resource Economists. In addition, he was a founding editor of both the *Journal of Environmental Economics and Management* and the more natural-science-oriented *Water Resources Research.*

During the late 1960s and 1970s Kneese articulated and developed several of the key problem-solving approaches of the discipline of environmental economics. His thinking on the processes of production and consumption led to work showing that externalities, rather than a footnote to microeconomic theory, were pervasive, often large, and intrinsic to the physical transformations associated with production. His emphasis on understanding all the flows of energy and materials in the system led to a focus on recycling and recapturing value that would otherwise be lost in waste streams. These contributions were well ahead of practice of and thinking on manufacturing and waste management at the time.

He is notable for his emphasis on collaborating with natural scientists and engineers to develop a deep understanding of the physical and biological systems involved in environmental problems. While his most broadly known work was on watershed management to protect water quality, his systems approach meant, for example, that he considered the potential impacts on solid waste streams and air pollution of increased regulatory pressure on water pollution. He also highlighted the importance of considering the interactions and net impacts of multiple pollutant streams flowing into a single sink. Kneese made the case that the whole protected environment should be considered when regulating any industry or pollutant that would affect it. Additionally, he showed that least-cost ways of improving environmental quality overall might not involve regulating all polluters the same way.

Kneese's emphasis on understanding the universe of influences on environmental quality led to new insights in the role of institutions and environmental policy. He was a determined advocate for establishing pollution permits and allowing firms to trade in them; despite significant skepticism, he was vindicated by the success of the Acid Rain Program, which was finally implemented in the 1990s. While he did not elaborate the idea of optimal pollution taxes, he did much to popularize them as part of an effort to drive innovation in pollution control. He believed in providing incentives for polluting firms to improve technology rather than simply regulating existing technology by command and control rules, and believed policies that did not incentivize increased production efficiency could not be judged successful. These ideas are generally accepted within the discipline now, largely thanks to Kneese's early work in environmental theory and policy.

Catherine S. Norman

See also: Association of Environmental and Resource Economists; Emissions Trading; Externality; Journals; Pollution Abatement Costs; Sulfur Dioxide Trading; Technological Innovation

Further Reading

Ayres, Robert U. and Allen V. Kneese. 1969. Production, Consumption, and Externalities. *American Economic Review* 59(3): 282–297.

Kneese, Allen V., and Charles L. Schultz. 1975. *Pollution, Prices, and Public Policy.* Washington, D.C.: The Brookings Institution.

Kneese, Allen V., Robert U. Ayres, and Ralph C. d'Arge. 1970. *Economics and the Environment: A Materials Balance Approach.* Baltimore, MD: Johns Hopkins University Press for Resources for the Future.

Krutilla, John V.

Dr. John V. Krutilla, a Harvard University trained economist, was a central figure at Resources for the Future (RFF) from 1955 to 1988. Dr. Krutilla is best known for challenging conventional economic thinking in the 1960s by identifying important inadequacies of economic analysis in dealing with the prospect of conserving the natural environment. At that time, economic analysis dealt exclusively with development alternatives. In 1967, Dr. Krutilla published "Conservation Reconsidered" in the *American Economic Review*. "Conservation Reconsidered" set the agenda for a new research program at RFF, the Natural Environments Program. *The Economics of Natural Environments,* published in 1975, written by Dr. Krutilla and Dr. Anthony Fisher, summarized the accomplishments of the Natural Environments Program.

In these publications, four important and influential themes are emphasized. The first theme is that the benefits provided by the natural environment represent an opportunity cost of development. At the time, elevating preservation as an important and viable alternative to development was a radical departure from conventional thinking.

A second theme is that the welfare economics of price theory, which formed the basis of benefit–cost analysis at the time, does not adequately measure the benefits provided by the natural environment. The preserved environment represents a form of endowment or income to some people, such as the "spiritual descendants of John

Muir," that price theory would not capture. Further current nonusers may value the environment for its mere existence, the option of future use, or as a bequest to future generations. These arguments imply that the preserved natural environment has elements of a public good, which price-based welfare economic analysis cannot capture.

A third important theme is that irreversible development of natural environments requires special consideration in economic analysis. In many instances, the preserved natural environment may be unique and not readily reproduced. In "Conservation Reconsidered," Dr. Krutilla uses the Grand Canyon as an obvious example but further notes that uniqueness need not be absolute. An area that is not globally unique could be locally very unique and the same reasoning applied. One of the primary economic considerations of irreversibly developing and destroying unique natural environments is that consumption goods may not adequately substitute for the loss of these areas. There also exists a dynamic associated with unique natural resources. As more natural areas are developed over time, preserved areas become increasingly scarce. The value for these areas is increasing over time and given their public good characteristics noted earlier, value is also increasing with population growth. Finally, there may be future values associated with these areas that are not currently recognized, such as when areas contain compounds for future drugs. This dynamic, according to Dr. Krutilla, strengthens the case for preservation.

The fourth theme emphasized in "Conservation Reconsidered" and *The Economics of Natural Environments* is the role of resource management in relation to achieving economic efficiency. Resource managers choose not only quantities such as how much land to preserve or how large of a water project to build, but through management choices also choose the quality of the remaining service flows. Analysis of management options is subject to the same considerations as development and hence, the first three themes discussed earlier.

Dr. Krutilla's observations and arguments not only influenced the research agenda of the Natural Environments Program, but also influenced the research agenda for the field of environmental economics. Accordingly, RFF recognizes Dr. Krutilla as the founding father of the modern theory of resource conservation.

Nicholas E. Flores

See also: Nonmarket Valuation; Passive Use Value; Public Goods; Welfare

Further Reading

Krutilla, John V. 1967. Conservation Reconsidered. *American Economic Review* 57(4): 777–786.

Krutilla, John V., and Anthony Fisher. 1975. *The Economics of Natural Environments.* Baltimore, MD: Johns Hopkins University Press.

L

Land Use

For almost as long as there have been urban areas in civilized societies, there have been efforts to preserve certain portions of these areas as parks and green spaces to provide amenities to local residents. It is the mix of land uses in urban areas that forms many of the amenities for local residents. For this reason, over the last century or so, most cities have adopted what are commonly known as zoning ordinances to regulate the types of land uses and development allowed in a given area. A prime motivation for such regulation is to restrict private decision-makers from making land-use decisions that negatively impact their neighbors. In other words, these policies have been developed to reduce the impact of externalities.

Private landowners, like the owners of any other asset, have the incentive to maximize the value of their land. One way in which they do this is by converting it to its highest private value use. The value of a parcel in different uses is determined by market conditions. Areas seeing rapid population and/or economic growth, for instance, are likely to see values for developed land outstrip values for land in agricultural or other uses. In contrast, in areas experiencing slower population or economic growth, there may be little demand for additional development and, thus, relatively low values for developed land vs. other uses. In any case, it is true that in many situations agricultural, forest, or other undeveloped land provides public goods benefits to nearby residents that are not reflected in market prices. Unfortunately, private landowners will not take these public goods benefits into account when managing their land and so we expect that much undeveloped land that, from a social welfare perspective, should remain undeveloped will, in fact, be developed to maximize the private rather than social benefits.

In addition to overconversion of undeveloped land, there are a number of other locally undesirable land-uses (LULUs), which also provide private benefits while imposing costs on neighbors. These include, but are not limited to, landfills, industrial sites, communication towers, and power facilities of all types. Measurement of the value of disamenities from changes in land use and the presence of LULUs is most often done using hedonic analysis.

To solve these market failures, governments at many levels have undertaken a number of policy approaches. The most basic of these is the public acquisition and preservation of land parcels as public spaces. Such acquisition takes many forms, but in urban areas mostly takes the form of public parks, both small and large.

Instead of acquiring the land itself, authorities may separate the development rights from the land and acquire these rights, leaving the land with its existing owner who is now prevented from developing the land he owns, although he retains all other rights. Very often, the funds needed for such acquisitions are raised through increased local property taxes or local bond issues which are approved by the public through voter referenda.

A second common regulatory approach is zoning, which creates zones of parcels designated to contain similar or compatible land uses. For instance, in residential zones, development may be restricted to residential uses of particular density as well as schools, churches, and other similar uses. Similar zoning-based policies have also been used to preserve green space and prevent the spatial growth, or sprawl of urban areas. These are often referred to as urban growth boundaries, or greenbelts. Such policies prevent further development of parcels in a region or belt around existing urban areas. Many other communities require that a certain portion of new development be left as open space. Unfortunately, these approaches may have unintended consequences by increasing property values in the centralized urban area, which, in turn, may drive development to areas beyond those areas set aside, which will increase urban sprawl, commuting, and other costs.

The policies described are based on a command-and-control approach where government regulators dictate development patterns. However, there are also more incentive-based policies that also help to reduce the damages caused by overdevelopment in a more flexible framework. One such policy is development taxes. These taxes, which work like any other Pigouvian tax, charge developers a fee that is increasing in the amount of land developed. Properly designed, such a fee would be set at a level that is equivalent to the social damages caused by the development and could be used to compensate those harmed. It also causes developers to internalize the externalities that development imposes on others and thus reduces the equilibrium amount of development. Another similar approach, which is most often implemented in more rural areas, is a tradable development rights system that separates ownership of the land from the right to develop the land. A set number of development credits are issued and then developers buy and sell these credits as development happens. Such a program minimizes the costs of restricting development while achieving the desired level of total development in an area.

If, as many predict, we continue to see population growth in urban areas, we should expect concerns about land-use to grow, as such growth will put additional financial pressure on property owners to sell their land for development. In this context, there will continue to be a policy debate about how best to preserve undeveloped land so as to provide the associated amenities.

Martin D. Heintzelman

See also: Externality; Hedonic Price Method; NIMBY and LULU; Pigouvian Tax; Public Goods

Further Reading

Brueckner, J. K. 2009. Government Land Use Interventions: An Economic Analysis, in S. V. Lall, M. Freire, B. Yuen, R. Rajack, and J.-J. Helluin (editors), *Urban Land Markets*, pp. 3–23. Dordrecht: Springer.

Glaeser, E. L., and B. A. Ward 2009. The Causes and Consequences of Land Use Regulation: Evidence from Greater Boston. *Journal of Urban Economics* 65(3): 265–278.

Irwin, E. G., K. P. Bell, N. E. Bockstael, D. A. Newburn, M. D. Partridge, and J. Wu. 2009. The Economics of Urban–Rural Space. *Annual Review of Resource Economics* 1(1): 435–459.

Johnston, R. J., and S. K. Swallow (editors). 2006. *Economics and Contemporary Land Use Policy: Development and Conservation at the Rural–Urban Fringe*. Washington, D.C.: Resources for the Future.

Malthus, Thomas Robert

Thomas Robert Malthus (1766–1834), British economist and demographer, perhaps most famously, authored *An Essay on the Principle of Population*. Trained in mathematics at Cambridge and ordained as a curate in the Church of England, Malthus worked independently to publish essays and engage in many of the economic debates of his time. His famous essay was published in six different editions, between 1798 and 1826; the central thesis of the essay is that limits to food production imply limits to the continued growth of human population and the continued improvement of human societies.

An Essay on the Principle of Population is so widely associated with the prediction of famine, war, and disease resulting from food scarcity that such a disaster is often described as Malthusian catastrophe. Malthus begins his argument with two explicit assumptions: food is necessary to humans and human procreation will continue. Malthus further asserts that population will grow exponentially (a geometric ratio) and that food production cannot increase any faster than linearly (an arithmetic ratio). Since exponential growth will always outpace linear growth, these assumptions inevitably lead to predictions of food shortages. Malthus feared a cycle of rapid population growth followed by starvation and death when population outgrew the land's capacity to produce food. Malthus was particularly concerned with the implications for the poor; as food becomes scarce, the poor will suffer greatest. Increased agricultural production and demographic transition (decreased birth and death rates as societies develop) have so far forestalled Malthus's worst fears; technological change in agriculture allowed faster growth in agricultural output than Malthus imagined possible and human populations are growing at less-than exponential rates in most nations and in total globally.

While Malthus's predictions have not yet come true, his central ideas are still influential in modern intellectual and policy debates. Numerous authors in the 20th century revived Malthus's framework replacing or augmenting population growth with economic growth as the push toward catastrophe. Many of these so-called neo-Malthusians argue that economic growth and increasing affluence are the primary drivers of environmental degradation. Neo-Malthusian arguments generally lead to advocacy for strict government policies to limit population and economic growth. Neo-classical economists tend to disagree with both the modeling and policy recommendations of neo-Malthusians. These economists tend to view economic growth as a net positive for societies, bringing increasing benefits to the members of these societies. Both sides still explicitly and implicitly influence many modern environmental policy debates.

Malthus was a devout Christian and moralist sentiments pervaded much of his work. Many of his ideas were founded in a deep concern for the poor. His contributions to the economic notion of rent went beyond theory and informed his initial support of the British *Corn Laws*, a protectionist set of policies intended to benefit British farmers. While ultimately changing his mind on that policy, his groundings in concern for the poor influenced many, including the macroeconomist John Maynard Keynes. Malthus's ideas still echo in many modern economic policy debates on topics ranging from growth and the environment to international trade.

Jason H. Murray

See also: Agriculture; International Trade

Further Reading

Hussen, Ahmed. 2013. *Principles of Environmental Economics and Sustainability: An Integrated Economic and Ecological Approach*, 3rd ed. New York: Routledge.

Winch, Donald. 1987. *Malthus*. Oxford: Oxford University Press.

Meta-Analysis

Meta-analysis in environmental and resource economics may be defined as the systematic review and quantitative synthesis of evidence on a particular empirical outcome, with evidence gathered from prior primary studies. A wide range of empirical outcomes can be evaluated using meta-analysis, including comparable behavioral responses such as the price elasticity of demand for marketed natural resources, value or welfare estimates such as willingness to pay (WTP) for non-market goods and services, hypothesis test outcomes such as the size of a t-statistic for a studied economic effect, and other quantifiable economic phenomena. Meta-analysis in environmental economics is most often accomplished with statistical analysis. The dependent variable in a classical or Bayesian regression model is a comparable empirical outcome drawn from existing primary studies and independent moderator variables represent observable factors that are hypothesized to explain variation in the outcome across observations. Empirical observations used within meta-analysis may be drawn from both the published and unpublished (or peer-reviewed and non-peer-reviewed) literature. Many meta-regression models combine observations from published articles with those from unpublished technical reports, government documents, graduate theses, and other sources.

Meta-analysis is used widely within environmental economics for a variety of purposes. These include (1) estimation of an average or combined effect size for a particular economic outcome, (2) evaluation of the systematic influence of different moderator variables on a studied effect size across studies or contexts, (3) provision of in- or out-of-sample predicted values for purposes such as benefit transfer, and (4) evaluation of publication bias or other systematic patterns in the scientific literature on a specific outcome. Meta-analyses in environmental economics are most commonly used to evaluate systematic influences of study, economic, resource, and population attributes on measures of nonmarket WTP, and generate benefit transfer functions for applied policy analysis. Meta-analyses have also been used in environmental economics to analyze empirical outcomes such as changes in property values, the price and income elasticity of demand for goods such as water, electricity, and gasoline, the effects of environmental regulation on firm location, and the cost of carbon offsets, among many others.

Among the advantages of meta-analysis is an ability to identify and test empirical patterns beyond those available from individual primary studies. Yet meta-analysis must also address potential challenges related to issues such as sparseness of primary research, selection biases in the scientific literature, lack of uniformity in measured effect sizes, heterogeneity of primary study methods and contexts, and insufficient data reporting. The validity of any meta-analysis depends on a variety of factors, including the characteristics of underlying studies and scientific literature, consistency of modeled effect sizes and moderator variables within the metadata, theoretical basis for estimated models, and appropriateness of statistical methods. There is wide variation in these factors across meta-analyses in the literature, leading to concern over the potential use and abuse of meta-analysis in economics. As a result, a number of practitioners have called for standardization of methods and reporting guidelines.

An important consideration is the degree of consistency in modeled empirical outcomes, and the extent to which these outcomes represent comparable constructs according to economic theory. Consistency is often required across multiple dimensions. For example, in meta-analysis of WTP for nonmarket goods, commodity consistency requires that the nonmarket commodity being valued is approximately the same across included studies. Welfare consistency requires that welfare measures represent comparable theoretical constructs. Only observations that satisfy a minimum degree of both welfare and commodity consistency should be pooled within metadata. Similar consistency concerns relate to other types of meta-analyses in environmental economics, and to the definition of moderator variables across observations and studies. While the need for consistency in modeled effect sizes and moderator variables is widely acknowledged, the degree of consistency required has been subject to disagreement. Continuing the valuation example, there is disagreement regarding whether theoretical relationships between Hicksian and Marshallian welfare measures are sufficient to justify the pooling of these measures within metadata for otherwise consistent commodities, whether these measures should be considered inconsistent for purposes of meta-analysis, or whether the consistency of these welfare measures depends on the valuation context.

There is an extensive literature describing statistical methods for meta-analysis. In addition, meta-analyses can only be as good or as unbiased as the sample of data from which they are derived, allowing for the possibility that some measurable biases can be corrected as part of model estimation. The validity of inferences and predictions drawn from meta-analysis requires that the underlying body of literature is a random, unbiased sample of the population of empirical estimates, and that these combined empirical estimates provide an unbiased representation of the true, underlying empirical outcome. When this does not occur, the literature or associated metadata are subject to selection biases. These biases may arise from sociopolitical influences (research priority selection), researcher choices (methodology selection), peer review influences (publication selection), and meta-analyst choices (metadata sample selection). Meta-regression models are often estimated without explicit recognition of the importance of the underlying sample of primary studies. There are a variety of different approaches that may be taken to identify and ameliorate selection biases. These include statistical methods to identify publication and other selection biases and distinguish these biases from genuine empirical effects. Some selection biases can also be partially ameliorated through the use of metadata that include a large sample of observations from both published and unpublished studies. At the same time, it is important to maintain minimum, systematic quality standards for studies in metadata. There is no clear consensus on how meta-analysts should balance the potentially conflicting need for large, unbiased samples of primary studies from both the published and unpublished literature with the need for minimum quality standards for included studies. Because of these challenges, meta-analyses should include clear and transparent reporting of methods for research literature search, compilation, and coding. This includes a complete list of the information coded for each study or estimate, and a bibliographic listing of all included studies.

Ultimately, the validity of meta-analysis depends not only on the use of appropriate statistical methods, but also on the quality, comparability, and extent of the underlying economic literature and an unbiased representation of the literature in the metadata. When appropriate techniques are applied to an extensive, well-reported, and unbiased literature, meta-analyses can reveal systematic patterns that help make sense of the flood of numbers and sometimes conflicting findings from an ever-expanding body of scientific research. It can also provide otherwise unavailable empirical results required for policy or other purposes. When applied incorrectly or to a biased literature, however, meta-analysis can lead to misguided results and inferences. Because of this, it is essential that those conducting meta-analysis are transparent in methods applied for literature search, metadata compilation, and data analysis.

Robert J. Johnston and Randall S. Rosenberger

See also: Benefit Transfer; Nonmarket Valuation; Welfare

Further Reading

Nelson, J.P. and P.E. Kennedy. 2009. The Use (and Abuse) of Meta-Analysis in Environmental and Resource Economics: An Assessment. *Environmental and Resource Economics* 42(3): 345–377.

Rosenberger, R.S. and R.J. Johnston. 2009. Selection Effects in Meta-Analysis and Benefit Transfer: Avoiding Unintended Consequences. *Land Economics* 85(3): 410–428.

Stanley, T.D., and H. Doucouliagos. 2012. *Meta-Regression Analysis in Economics and Business*. Oxford: Routledge.

Stanley, T.D., H. Doucouliagos, M. Giles, J.H. Heckemeyer, R.J. Johnston, P. Laroche, J.P. Nelson, M. Paldam, J. Poot, G. Pugh, R.S. Rosenberger, K., and Rost. 2013. Meta-Analysis of Economics Reporting Guidelines. *Journal of Economic Surveys* 27(2): 390–394.

Monitoring and Enforcement

While the design of an environmental regulation is critical in determining how well it will achieve its objective, people often forget that monitoring and enforcement are equally important parts of an effective environmental program. Rules and regulations that are not actively enforced are often ignored, even by people who otherwise think of themselves as law-abiding. Are you not more likely to obey the speed limit when there are police personnel or a highway patrol car in the lane next to you?

In 1968, economist Gary Becker developed what is now considered to be the classic economic model of crime. In this model, Becker assumes that individuals behave rationally when deciding whether or not to commit a crime. More specifically, in deciding whether to commit a crime, potential criminals compare the expected benefit from committing a crime to the expected cost of committing that crime and only go through with it when the benefit outweighs the cost. This model can easily be applied to environmental regulations with potential violators comparing the expected benefit of violating a regulation to the expected cost and polluting whenever the benefit exceeds the cost. The expected benefit of a violation depends on the resources the company saves by not complying with the regulation. For example, if a regulation requires companies to remove toxic chemicals from wastewater before discharging the water into a river, a company that violates the regulation saves the costs of treating the wastewater. The expected cost of a violation depends on both the probability that the violator gets caught and the penalty the violator faces when caught. If there is no monitoring or enforcement, that is if the probability of getting caught is zero or there is no penalty if you do get caught, any regulation that costs money will be ignored by profit-maximizing companies. As the probability of getting caught or the penalty associated with the violation increases, fewer companies will find it optimal to violate the regulations. Thus monitoring and enforcement can deter environmental violations.

If monitoring and enforcement were free, in theory we could effectively deter all violations by raising penalties to a high enough level that everyone would find it more beneficial to comply with regulations than violate them. Alternatively, if a violator knew her violation would be detected with certainty, then even if she only had to pay a penalty slightly higher than the cost of compliance, she would never find it beneficial to violate a regulation. In practice, however, both monitoring and enforcement are expensive. For many environmental programs, monitoring requires inspectors to visit regulated facilities to determine whether regulations are being followed. Even in those environmental programs where monitoring equipment can be used to determine compliance, someone must maintain the equipment and interpret the records to see whether a regulation has been violated. Penalizing violators also requires resources to do things like determine what the penalties are, issue formal compliance orders, make sure that fines are paid, and in some cases, take the violators to court. If the penalties involve jail time—and some environmental regulations do allow for criminal penalties—there is the additional cost associated with keeping someone in jail.

An optimal monitoring and enforcement program would compare the cost of increased monitoring and enforcement to the benefit such increased deterrence causes—that is the benefit from the increased compliance that results—and continue to increase monitoring and enforcement as long as the benefit outweighs the cost. In designing an optimal enforcement program, you would also want to experiment with varying the mix of monitoring and enforcement to find the combination that provides the highest level of deterrence at the lowest cost. More specifically, you may be able to get the same level of deterrence from very aggressive monitoring that leads to relatively frequent but low penalties as you would from relatively infrequent monitoring paired with very high penalties. If monitoring is expensive relative to enforcement, the second program will provide the same benefit from increased compliance at a lower cost.

Environmental regulations often impose different costs on different types of companies. Since potential violators compare avoided compliance costs (the benefit they get from not following a regulation) to the expected cost of violating the regulation, not all companies are equally deterred by a particular monitoring and enforcement program. In particular, companies that face very high compliance costs will be more likely to violate than companies that face low compliance costs. The cost to society when a company violates a regulation can also differ across companies. Pollution in a highly populated area or a sensitive environment may cause more damage than pollution in a sparsely populated area or impervious environment. Thus an optimal monitoring and enforcement program may need to be different for different companies. For example, penalties could be higher for violations that take place in sensitive environments or companies in highly populated areas could be monitored more closely than companies in less populated areas.

In practice, monitoring and enforcement resources are generally dictated by federal and state environmental program budgets and may be far from the optimal level. Additionally, the penalties associated with violations or regulations may be set or capped by statute. In such situations, regulators may look for other ways to encourage compliance. One alternative that regulators in the United States have used is to harness the power of consumers and investors to penalize companies that violate environmental regulations. For example, if consumers stop buying gas from BP as a protest against the *Deepwater Horizon* oil spill, the loss of profits will reduce the company's bottom line just as a fine from a regulator would. Of course, for consumers to punish polluters by not buying their products or investors by not buying the company's stock, these individuals must be able to get information on a company's environmental record. To help consumers and investors make such decisions, the U.S. Environmental Protection Agency (EPA) provides enforcement and compliance data on all regulated companies in the United States on its website, www.epa-echo.gov.

Sarah L. Stafford

See also: Air Pollution; Clean Air Act; Clean Water Act; Externality; Regulation; Water Pollution

Further Reading

Becker, Gary S. 1968. Crime and Punishment: An Economic Approach. *Journal of Political Economy* 76(2): 169–172.

Gray, Wayne B., and Jay P. Shimshack. 2011. The Effectiveness of Environmental Monitoring and Enforcement: A Review of the Empirical Evidence. *Review of Environmental Economics and Policy* 5(1): 3–24.

Polinsky, A. Mitchell, and Steven Shavell. 2000. The Economic Theory of Public Enforcement of Law. *Journal of Economic Literature* 38(1): 45–76.

Montreal Protocol

The Montreal Protocol on Substances that Deplete the Ozone Layer is a 1987 international agreement to preserve and restore stratospheric ozone, which is degraded by various chemicals used in refrigerants, propellants, and agriculture, which are transported to the upper atmosphere over time. The ozone layer provides a protective shield against ultraviolet radiation, and when it is thinned by ozone-depleting substances (ODS) the increased radiation has effects on human health, including cataracts and skin cancer; agricultural productivity; terrestrial and aquatic ecosystems; and human-made materials like plastics that are used outside.

Emissions of ODS at all locations drive this process, so near-equator emissions impose an externality disproportionately on high-latitude dwellers. Thus an international environmental agreement to provide this global public good was needed to develop a cooperative plan for global elimination of the substances involved.

At the time the treaty was negotiated, the now-famous ozone hole was only a theory, and it was difficult to develop an agreement to phaseout synthetic ODS in settings where there were no clear substitutes. Implementation of the protocol in the face of this uncertainty is often seen as a strong example of the precautionary principle in action. As the scientific evidence of ozone depletion and its anthropogenic origins became stronger and replacement technologies were developed more quickly and at lower costs than first anticipated, phaseout schedules for ODS were accelerated and dozens of new chemicals were added to the agreement.

A key component of the agreement was a system to transfer payments from more developed countries to less developed ones to help them implement costly newer technologies through the Multilateral Fund (MF), and a five-year delayed phaseout schedule for those countries, so that they could benefit from technology development and transfer in richer countries. Also important were three advisory panels, tasked with evaluating new atmospheric science and information about the health and environmental impacts of ozone depletion and the cost and feasibility of alternatives to ODS so that policies could be updated accordingly.

The protocol is broadly considered to be the most successful of the major international environmental agreements. It enjoys near-universal membership, good compliance with phaseout schedules, successful implementation of new technologies (with costs declining over time), and most importantly has stabilized atmospheric concentrations of ODS. Stratospheric ozone levels have stopped their decline and are expected to return to pre-1980 levels in about 50 years. Chloroflourocarbons (CFCs), the primary chemicals of concern in 1987, have been completely phased out, and hydrochloroflourocarbons (HCFCs) and other ODS are greatly reduced.

While the Montreal Protocol focuses on stratospheric ozone, it has also had an impact on climate protection. Many of the regulated ODS are also powerful greenhouse gasses (GHG) that contribute to climate change, and their phaseout has by some estimates done a great deal to slow the rate of warming. On the other hand, many of the replacements for ODS are safe for the ozone layer but are also powerful GHG, and there are trade-offs in accelerating transitions toward these substances that are difficult to solve within the legal framework of the treaty. There is increasing interest in improving coordination between the ozone and climate protection regimes to avoid unintended consequences of ozone protection and reflect the physical interactions between the two in atmospheric systems.

Another issue faced by the protocol is the ongoing series of exemptions for some ODS uses, including methyl bromide used to keep pathogens from spreading with international shipments of food and other goods (quarantine and pre-shipment (QPS) uses), which are not covered by the current rules. Exemptions have proven contentious and have continued past initial cutoffs, and QPS uses are now the largest uses of methyl bromide. There is currently no treaty obligation to eliminate this usage, and many countries have no plans in place to decrease reliance on this process.

Catherine S. Norman

See also: Air Pollution; Externality; International Environmental Agreements; Precautionary Principle; Public Goods

Further Reading

Benedick, Reinhard. 1998. *Ozone Diplomacy*, 2nd ed. Cambridge, MA: Harvard University Press.

United Nations Environment Programme: Ozone, http://www.unep.org/ozone

Municipal Solid Waste

Municipal solid waste (MSW) refers to the accumulation of nonhazardous products and materials discarded by a local community. Put another way, MSW is everyday trash and garbage that every household and firm generates as a by-product of consumption and production.

How can something as ordinary as trash be an environmental problem? Simply put, MSW poses a risk to society in part because so much of it is generated with limited space allocated for disposal. Beyond this fundamental reality, hazardous, or toxic, materials occasionally find their way into the nonhazardous waste stream, which exposes society to significant health and ecological risks. This added risk can occur if, for example, a household or firm discards a toxic item, such as a flashlight battery or mercury thermometer, into the trash instead of properly disposing it with other hazardous wastes to be treated prior to disposal.

As to the accumulation and growth rate of MSW, a few data points are telling. In the United States, MSW generation is currently estimated to be about 250 million tons per year (based on 2010 data), which translates to 4.43 pounds per person per day. That waste generation is growing in the United States is evident from the comparable 1980 values, which are 151.6 million tons in the aggregate, or 3.66 pounds per person per day. Virtually every nation must address the accumulation and growth rate of MSW, but the magnitude of the problem is generally correlated with industrialization, urbanization, and economic advance.

Universally, MSW comprises a wide range of materials. In the United States, these materials are identified as: paper and paperboard, glass, metals, plastics, rubber and leather, textiles, wood, and other. Paper and paperboard represent the majority of wastes generated, accounting for 28.5 percent of the total in 2010. Fortunately, this category has the highest recovery rate at 62.5 percent. Plastics, on the other hand, comprise only 12 percent of the total, but they have one of the lowest recovery rates—about 8 percent in 2010. This low recovery rate is due in part to the challenge of having to sort different types of resins used in plastic products, which adds significantly to the costs of recycling plastics.

An alternative way to characterize MSW is by the products it comprises. The primary categories used in the United States are: durable goods, nondurable goods, containers and packaging, food scraps, yard trimmings, and other. Somewhat predictably, containers and packaging represent the highest proportion of MSW, estimated at 30.3 percent according to recent data. A particularly challenging component of the durable goods category is the collection of electronics waste, or e-waste as it is commonly known. E-waste is a growing problem because of the rising popularity of such products as personal computers, cell phones, and monitors. These contemporary products that have become so integral to everyday life become problematic in the waste stream, not only because of their quantity, but also because these products sometimes contain hazardous substances, such as lead and mercury.

So what happens to all the waste generated in the United States? Some of it is recovered for composting and recycling, some is used to generate electricity through waste-to-energy facilities, and the rest ends up in landfills. In 2010, just over 34 percent of the MSW generated in the United States was recovered, and nearly 12 percent was managed through combustion with energy recovery, leaving about 54 percent, or 136 million tons, discarded in landfills. On a per capita basis, of the 4.43 pounds of MSW generated per day, 2.4 pounds end up in landfills.

Landfill disposal can be problematic, but not because landfill space is running out, even though this has been a common belief. Although declining disposal space might be a reality in selected areas, the truth is that, although there are fewer landfills in the United States, those that do exist are larger in capacity. That said, landfill space *is* limited, due in part to the so-called NIMBY (not in my backyard) phenomenon. Simply put, virtually no one wants to live near a landfill, yet landfills are needed to accommodate all the MSW that is not otherwise recovered or combusted. Another problem is the release of methane gases associated with waste decomposition in landfills, and methane is a greenhouse gas that contributes to climate change. Lastly, landfilled MSW comprises materials and products that could have been recovered and used in place of virgin materials, which contributes to the depletion of natural resources.

In response to these and other environmental risks of MSW generation and landfill disposal, governments sometimes use a command-and-control policy approach, establishing laws and regulations to minimize those risks. Examples include the Resource Conservation and Recovery Act, which outlines criteria for sanitary landfills, and the Pollution Prevention Act of 1990, which promotes source reduction, recycling, and combustion before discarding to a landfill. There are also state and local laws aimed at reducing MSW waste generation or disposal. Some actually mandate a target recycling rate, such as the New Jersey Statewide Mandatory Source Separation and Recycling Act.

An alternative response that governments use to minimize MSW risk is a market approach. This alternative relies on economic incentives to encourage households and firms to reduce MSW risks by engaging in such activities as source reduction (i.e., generating less waste or reducing the toxicity of wastes); designing products and processes that use less packaging; and recycling MSW rather than disposing of it.

A deposit/refund system is a good example of a market-based instrument aimed at minimizing MSW risk. Commonly applied to beverage containers, deposit/refund schemes charge a fee to the potential polluter for the environmental damage associated with improper disposal of the beverage can or bottle. To receive a refund of the fee, the potential polluter must return the container for recycling. Hence, the deposit creates an incentive to recycle without a legislated mandate to do so. In addition to the United States, many countries operate deposit/refund systems for beverage containers, including Australia, Canada, Estonia, Finland, Israel, and the Netherlands. Some nations also use these systems for scrapped motor vehicles and tires, such as Denmark, Finland, the Slovak Republic, and Sweden.

Another example of a market-based instrument used to reduce MSW risk is the pay-as-you-throw (PAYT) program, also known as unit pricing. Municipalities using PAYT programs charge residents a fee for each container of trash to be collected. The fee acts as an incentive to reduce waste generation or to reuse and recycle. The motivation for residents is straightforward. To reduce the fees paid to the city or town, they must generate less trash or recycle. In the United States, there currently are more than 7,000 PAYT programs in operation.

Scott J. Callan and Janet M. Thomas

See also: Climate Change Impacts; Externality; Hazardous Waste; NIMBY and LULU; Recycling

Further Reading

European Commission, Eurostat. 2012. Municipal Waste Generation and Treatment, by Type of Treatment Method. Available at http://epp.eurostat.ec.europa.eu/tgm/table.do?tab=table&init=1&plugin=1&language=en&pcode=tsdpc240 (last updated April 20, 2012).

OECD/EEA (Organisation for Economic Co-operation and Development and European Environmental Agency). 2012. *OECD/EEA Database on Instruments Used for Environmental Policy and Natural Resources Management.* Retrieved from http://www2.oecd.org/ecoinst/queries/index.htm (last updated May 5, 2012).

U.S. Environmental Protection Agency, Office of Solid Waste and Emergency Response. 2011. *Municipal Solid Waste Generation, Recycling, and Disposal in the United States: Facts and Figures for 2010.* Washington, D.C.: U.S. EPA, December 2011.

U.S. Environmental Protection Agency, Office of Solid Waste and Emergency Response. 2012. Reduce and Reuse. http://www.epa.gov/osw/conserve/rrr/reduce.htm (last updated March 12, 2012).

N

Natural Hazards

Natural hazards are large-scale perils associated with irregular but natural environmental events that can harm people, destroy aspects of the natural and built environment, and disrupt social and economic activity. Hazards are often described by frequency of occurrence (often expressed as return interval or probability per unit time) and magnitude of effects (such as level of damage or number of lives lost conditional on an event occurring). Actuarial science focuses on estimating such probabilities and magnitudes for insurance and risk management purposes.

Natural hazards include floods, hurricanes, tornadoes, earthquakes, tsunamis, volcanic eruptions, drought, coastal and riverine erosion, heat waves, blizzards, and other extreme weather events. Some of these hazards are very rare (e.g., tsunamis), whereas others are more frequent. Compared to other risks—like car accidents or house fires—natural hazards tend to have lower frequencies of occurrence and spatially correlated losses. Risk managers associate natural hazards with catastrophe risk or low probability–high consequence (LPHC) risk. Correlated losses make diversification of risk pools difficult.

The occurrence of a LPHC event due to extreme natural conditions is often referred to as a natural disaster, although there is no generally agreed upon definition on what precisely constitutes a disaster. Vulnerability is typically used to describe the potential magnitude of impacts of natural hazards, but can be broken down into endowed vulnerabilities reflecting natural conditions and amended vulnerabilities reflecting the influence of human behavior, the built environment, and policy decisions. Resilience refers to the ability of physical, environmental, social, economic, or governance systems to absorb or resist a perturbation, but research on resilience often recognizes the tendency and ability of systems to change or adapt to evolving circumstances; this makes the study of resilience somewhat challenging.

British political economist John Stuart Mill (1806–1873) opined that disasters could spur innovation and adaptation that would render affected communities better off than before the disaster—a form of creative destruction; his conclusions were based upon comparisons of data before and after disasters that indicated rapid recovery and general improvements in economic indicators. In the *Parable of the Broken Window*, French political economist Frederic Bastiat (1801–1850) argued against such logic, based largely on the concept of opportunity cost—that resources expended to recover from disasters have been diverted from their highest and best use.

While there is no consistent framework within welfare economics that permits assessment of the net economic effects of natural disasters, many authors have explored the macroeconomic effects of such events at the regional and country level. Some find positive linkages between disasters and GDP, total factor productivity and other measures of short- and long-run economic growth, providing tentative support for John Stuart Mill's position. At the regional level, others identified improvements in employment growth rate and stability following hurricanes, tornadoes, and an earthquake. Residential housing stock destroyed by extreme wind events in the United States has been found to rebound very quickly.

Applications of welfare economics to assessment of natural disasters should attempt to distinguish benefits and costs stemming from the event. Costs would include loss of lives, number of days of injury or illness, damages to buildings and infrastructure, damage to locations of historical or social significance, and interruption of business, economic, and social activities. Benefits would include increases in income, employment, output, or other measures of enhanced economic activity. Benefits could also include the opportunity to adapt, augment, and redesign aspects of the built environment or change policy approaches to managing market imperfections, externalities, or public goods—though this latter category of benefits could be very difficult to assess.

Welfare economic approaches can be used to estimate individual's willingness-to-pay for risk reduction. Incremental option value is the theoretical metric used to quantify the value of a change in the level of risk. Studies have used hedonic market data (focusing on real estate or labor) to produce such estimates. Individual values for risk reduction depend upon subjective perceptions of risk, and many studies in behavioral economics have shown that individual perceptions of risk are highly variable, depend upon history and context, and may be labile in some situations. Risk perceptions also influence household, businesses, and organizational behavior in social and economic situations, including where to purchase property; how to develop, fortify, and use property; inventory management; where to work; where to shop, visit, and recreate; and how to prepare for possible disasters.

With regard to natural hazards, important decisions surround planning, adaptation, risk management, mitigation, and insurance. Planning occurs primarily in local governments, with some input from state and federal government. Local officials engage in supervision of land use, zoning, regulation of building and renovation, implementation of community hazard mitigation projects, and management of local economic development initiatives. State and federal governments provide technical assistance, share information, and oversee implementation of state and federal regulations. Risk management occurs at all levels of economic activity, from government to households to businesses. Management of risk includes activities that lessen the probability or magnitude of loss, formal and informal insurance mechanisms, and other ways to diversify exposure.

Hazard mitigation involves measures that ameliorate risk by lowering the probability of hazard or decreasing the conditional expected loss. Mitigation can occur at the community level or individual parcel level.

Insurance is a risk-sharing mechanism that involves transferring income or resources from good states/outcomes to bad ones. Formal insurance markets involve the sale of policies that provide cover for certain unfavorable outcomes in exchange for a regular payment. The viability of formal insurance markets depends upon insurers' ability to identify and analyze risks and market and sell policies to a diverse pool of customers that are averse to the particular risk and willing to pay the required premium. Examples of formal natural hazard insurance include property insurance, wind insurance, flood insurance, and crop insurance. Some levels of government have provided ex post aid in the wake of a disaster in the form of disaster assistance. Humanitarian assistance (temporary food, shelter, necessities) is very common, but disaster assistance sometimes includes payments for individual financial loss. Such schemes can crowd out private incentives to mitigate risk or purchase insurance—a phenomenon known as charity hazard.

Craig E. Landry and Jamie B. Kruse

See also: Asymmetric Information; Coastal Resources; Drought; Hedonic Price Methods; Risk and Uncertainty; Value of Statistical Life

Further Reading

Baade, Robert, Robert Baumann, and Victor Matheson. 2012. Estimating the Economic Impact of Natural and Social Disasters, with and Application to Hurricane Katrina. *Urban Studies* 44(11): 2061–2076.

Bastiat, Frederic. Bastiat.org. 1850. November 2, 2011. www.fee.org/pdf/the-freeman/bastiat0601.pdf

Dacy, Douglas C., and Howard Kunreuther. 1969. *The Economics of Natural Disasters: Implications for Federal Policy.* New York: Free Press.

Rand Corp Santa Monica CA. Disaster and Recovery: a Historical Survey. April 1963. Library of Economics and Liberty. www.econlib.org/Enc/DisasterandRecovery.html

Skidmore, Mark and Hideki Toya. 2002. Do Natural Disasters Promote Long-Run Growth? *Economic Inquiry* 40(4): 664–687.

Natural Monopoly

Use of the term natural monopoly likely began in 1848 when John Stuart Mill used it to describe a characteristic of a resource that resulted in economic rent. That is, a superior quality inherent in the resource would lead to a monopoly that was naturally determined as opposed to being legally granted. More generally, natural monopoly is used to describe industries in which competition does not lead to lower cost production. Instead, the cost of serving the market is lowest with a single firm, and productive efficiency requires single firm production. If that firm sets price above its marginal cost of production (because it naturally faces no competition), allocative efficiency is sacrificed and social welfare declines. This intrinsic trade-off means market forces will fail to produce efficient outcomes, and natural monopoly is an example of market failure.

To illustrate the economic problem of natural monopoly, consider an electric utility supplying service to a small town. The company shares with telecom, cable, and railroad industries the need to invest in a fixed network. The high fixed cost of the network discourages multiple companies from providing electricity to the town once an incumbent is in place. Over some (possibly large) range of output it would be economically inefficient to have competing firms. How large this range of output is depends on the magnitude and type of fixed costs, and the scope for technological advancements.

Total costs of production combine the firm's fixed and variable costs. Variable costs are those that increase with output (e.g., wages paid to labor increase as hours worked increase). Fixed costs do not vary with output. As a result, average fixed costs will decline as more output is produced. As long as the firm's long-run average *total* cost is declining a second producer would only increase the cost of producing the good. Declining average total cost over some range of output is referred to as economies of scale.

More formally, a firm is a natural monopoly if its cost function is subadditive. A firm with a subadditive cost function can serve a single product market at less cost than two or more firms. Declining long-run average total cost is one reason for a firm to have a subadditive cost function for a single product, but it is also possible for a single product firm to have a subadditive cost function over a range of output where its long-run average cost is increasing as long as it is still less costly to have one firm in operation than two.

If a firm produces more than one product (e.g., cable TV and Internet service) subadditivity implies the firm can produce *any combination of* the multiple products together at less cost than the individual products could be produced separately (by different firms). Therefore, economies of scope are necessary for subadditivity when firms produce multiple products. Baumol discusses the complexities of defining a natural monopoly in this context and provides the necessary and sufficient conditions for subadditivity.

If a natural monopoly is operating in a range of output where there are economies of scale, average total costs will exceed marginal cost and pricing at marginal cost will result in the firm making losses. Yet, when price is above marginal cost there are social welfare losses resulting from units that are socially valuable not being produced.

Natural monopolies are often subject to price and or entry regulation in an attempt to minimize welfare losses. Entry regulation occurs when there are few barriers to entry but production costs are minimized when there is a single producer. Price regulation is used to ensure firms cover their fixed cost of production and earn a rate of return to encourage investment. If firms charge a single price and have to breakeven to avoid subsidies then some social welfare will necessarily be sacrificed. Welfare losses result when firms set price equal to average total (to cover their fixed costs) instead of marginal costs. When a natural monopolist produces multiple products, social welfare losses can be minimized by raising prices differentially depending on the elasticity of demand for each product. Because consumers reduce their quantity demanded less the more inelastic their demand for a product, the firm adds more to its revenue with larger price increases for more inelastic demand. This markup method is attributed to Frank Ramsey and known as the Ramsey pricing rule. Some formerly regulated network industries have been fully deregulated (e.g., railroads and airlines) while many others have undergone partial deregulation for portions of the business (e.g., electric utilities, cable television, and the telecommunications). Regulation comes with its own bureaucratic and political costs that can outweigh the social gains. Time and resources are consumed while regulators decide the merits of rate increases, and regulators must rely on imperfect assessments of firms' cost of service. In addition, a judgment must be made about when to reduce or stop regulating an industry. If demand growth or technological change makes competition feasible, movement away from regulation should be considered.

An alternative to regulation of natural monopoly was proposed by Demsetz. He recommended having competition for the market as opposed to in the market. If firms can bid for the right to service the market, the price of service should be bid down to marginal cost if there are a sufficient number of bidders with marginal cost close to the lowest cost. The winner of the bidding process would then have an exclusive franchise for some period of time. On the surface this appears to take care of both productive and allocative inefficiencies, but the franchisor is left with a role not too unlike a regulator. Decisions must be made about rate increases, quality of service, franchise extension, etc. If the franchise is of short duration and bidding is periodic, efforts must be made to ensure bidding parity between the incumbent firm and potential entrants, and arrangements must be made to transfer the franchise if an entrant is the winner in subsequent bidding rounds. Williamson discusses why these are nontrivial complications. Likewise, if the service being provided is very specialized it is possible there will be few low-cost bidders, resulting in a winning bid well above the winner's marginal cost.

In the long run, technological advancements often remove the natural monopoly characteristics of an industry and competition becomes feasible. For example, a local telecommunications carrier may cease to be the lowest cost provider of residential and business telephone services if cable companies can provide those services in addition to television. Other technological advances obviate the need for fixed line networks and reduce barriers to entry. Wireless service is one example.

Also, an innovation that lowers the fixed cost of service will shift down the average cost curve and, as long as there are diseconomies of scale over some range of output, the firm's minimum efficient scale will fall. As the minimum efficient scale is lowered, the range of output that can support multiple firms expands.

Identifying natural monopolies, calculating optimal prices, deciding whether to regulate and deciding when to deregulate are challenging problems especially when firms produce multiple goods. Network industries with natural monopoly characteristics are becoming increasingly competitive following technological advances that have lowered entry barriers and firms' minimum efficient scale of production. In some cases only parts of the industry have become competitive.

Tanga McDaniel Mohr

See also: Energy Policy; Regulation

Further Reading

Baumol, W.J. 1977. On the Proper Cost Tests for Natural Monopoly in a Multiproduct Industry. *American Economic Review* 67(5): 809–822.

Demsetz, H. 1968. Why Regulate Utilities? *Journal of Law and Economics* 11(1): 55–65.

Viscusi, K., J. Vernon, and J. Harrington, Jr. 2005. *Economics of Regulation and Antitrust.* Cambridge, MA: The MIT Press.

Williamson, O. 1976. Franchise Bidding for Natural Monopolies—In General and with Respect to CATV. *The Bell Journal of Economics* 7(1): 73–104.

NIMBY and LULU

The Not in My Backyard (NIMBY) syndrome arises when a facility exhibits a locally undesirable land use (LULU) that lowers property values and diminishes residents' well-being around the land use facility. The NIMBY syndrome occurs when individuals agree that a facility is a good idea for society as long as it is not in their backyard. Examples of local negative externalities that create the NIMBY syndrome include airports that exhibit noise externalities to the local community, landfills that exhibit both smell and safety externalities to the local community, prisons and halfway houses that exhibit safety externalities to the local community and wind farms that exhibit view shed externalities to local residents. Sometimes the negative externality manifests primarily in increased risk to health such as from a nuclear power plant or a hazardous waste disposal facility. One of the major NIMBY issues in the United States is where to locate high-level nuclear waste.

Many times it is efficient for the LULU to be built because the aggregate gains to society as a whole are greater than the cost borne by the local community. The nature of the political process, however, finds that LULUs are often difficult to site because the vocal nature of the small groups affected by the local negative externality. Often in the political process a loud vocal minority that is more likely to be politically active due to the high individual costs find that their preferences influence political decisions more than a majority who receives only small benefits individually and who are less politically active. The efficiency problem occurs when politicians act on the minority preferences even when the benefits are larger than the costs in the aggregate.

To address the problem of inefficiency and to encourage the placement of a LULU, those that receive the benefits could compensate the neighborhood around the site for bearing the external cost. When choosing a location for a NIMBY politicians' concern for remaining in office makes the status quo the default property right due to a reluctance to infringe upon the perceived property rights. When individuals perceive that the status quo defines the property rights then the willingness to accept becomes the appropriate measure of compensation. If an appropriate compensation can be measured LULUs can be located and a Pareto improvement in well-being can occur. Many political mechanisms have been suggested to site LULUs from potential locations bidding on receiving offers of tax breaks for accepting LULUs, to citizen voting in referendums to accept the facilities in their communities. Others, however, suggest that the strategic importance of compensation to solve the NIMBY syndrome is difficult if the local community perceives the compensation as a bribe. Compensation when perceived as a bribe might make local residents less trustful of governments and policymakers suggesting that the solution to the NIMBY syndrome includes both compensation and moral considerations. Public input into the locating decision therefore plays a major role in addition to compensation.

Another problem surrounding LULUs and the NIMBY syndrome is environmental justice concerns. Many times LULUs are located in poor and minority communities, not for efficiency reasons but because these populations have few economic alternatives. In addition environmental justice concerns suggest that poor communities are targeted for LULUs because residents may not be fully aware of the risks involved due to the fact that these communities do not have access to experts who could provide accurate information about benefits and costs. Environmental justice further suggests that a combination of this lack of awareness coupled with low-income residents' lack of political and economic power makes poor communities a frequent target for environmentally hazardous activities. Environmental justice concerns suggest that when poor communities are chosen as a site for a LULU for efficiency reasons the process should be transparent, the company and government must be fully accountable to the community for the potential hazards of the LULU and the process should have full community participation. Environmental justice suggests the equity concerns are as, if not more, important when deciding upon a location for a LULU. In this case compensation for accepting a facility in a neighborhood could address not only the efficiency criterion but also address equity concerns for accepting LULUs in one's backyard.

Peter A. Groothuis

See also: Environmental Justice; Externality; Hazardous Waste; Hedonic Price Method; Land Use; Noise; Nuclear Energy; Property Rights

Further Reading

Frey, Bruno S., Felix Oberholzer-Gee, and Reiner Eichenberge. 1996. The Old Lady Visits Your Backyard: A Tale of Morals and Markets. *Journal of Political Economy* 104(6): 1297–1213.

Inhaber, Herbert. 1992. Of LULU's, NIMBY's, and NIMTOO's. *Public Interest* 107(Spring): 52–64.

Kunreuther, Howard, Paul Kleindofer, and Peter J. Knez. 1987. A Compensation Mechanism for Siting Noxious Facilities: Theory and Experimental Design. *Journal of Environmental Economics and Management* 14(4): 371–383.

O'Hare, Micheal. 1977. Not on My Block You Don't: Facility Siting and the Strategic Importance of Compensation. *Public Policy* 25(4):407–458.

NOAA Panel on Contingent Valuation

In March 1989, the supertanker Exxon *Valdez* ran aground on Bligh Reef in Prince William Sound, Alaska, spilling 11 million gallons of crude oil into the sea. Although a number of natural resource damage cases had been brought by individual states and the federal government up to that time, none of the incidents precipitating the suits had nearly the visibility and impact of that spill. If in addition to the out-of-pocket losses suffered by fishermen, resort owners, tour guides, recreationists, and others directly and indirectly harmed by the accident, Exxon would be forced to pay also for lost nonuse or existence values, the ante would be raised substantially. This possibility focused the attention of Exxon and many other companies on existence values and the contingent valuation method.

The Exxon *Valdez* spill also caught the attention of Congress. It promptly passed an altogether new law, the Oil Pollution Act of 1990, aimed at reducing the likelihood of future oil spills and providing for damage recovery for any spills that should occur. Under the new law, the Department of Commerce—acting through the National Oceanic and Atmospheric Administration (NOAA)—was directed to write regulations governing damage assessment. This became the next battlefield on which to fight about the legitimacy of existence values and the contingent valuation method.

Environmentalists insisted that the NOAA rules embrace lost existence values as fully compensable damages and identify the contingent valuation method as the appropriate way to measure them. Not surprisingly, those upon whom these assessments might one day fall—led by the oil companies—pushed hard to exclude existence values and the contingent valuation method from the regulations. Amid these conflicting pressures, and in recognition of the technical economic nature of the questions at debate, the general counsel of NOAA, Thomas Campbell, took an unusual step. He asked Nobel laureates Kenneth Arrow and Robert Solow if they would chair a panel of experts to provide advice to NOAA on the following question: Is the contingent valuation method capable of providing estimates of lost nonuse or existence values that are reliable enough to be used in natural resource damage assessments? It is important to note that the panel was not asked its opinion on the legitimacy of existence values per se. This may have been because the court of appeals had earlier ruled, in the case of the *State of Ohio vs United States Department of the Interior*, that lost existence values were to be treated the same as other economic losses in damage assessments; whatever the reason, the panel was asked to confine its attention solely to the potential reliability of the contingent valuation method.

The NOAA panel met eight times between June and November 1992. This included an extraordinary all-day hearing in August during which it heard statements from 22 experts, including several of the most prominent names in the economics profession, who either extolled the virtues of the contingent valuation method or condemned it. The panel completed its deliberations in December and, on January 11, 1993, submitted its report to NOAA. The report was published in the Federal Register on January 15, 1993.

The NOAA panel may have managed to upset everyone with its report. Those opposed to the use of the contingent valuation method were disappointed by what many took to be the bottom line of the panel report. This was the phrase, " the Panel concludes that CV studies [applications of the contingent valuation method] can produce estimates reliable enough to be the starting point of a judicial process of damage assessment, including lost passive use values." Not surprisingly, this conclusion was cheered by those government agencies, academic researchers, and others wishing to make continued application of the contingent valuation method in their work.

Nevertheless, the panel reached this conclusion with some reluctance. It would be fair to say that none of its members would have been comfortable with the use of any of the previous applications of the contingent valuation method as the basis for actual monetary damage awards. (To reiterate, none of these studies was intended for this purpose.) For this reason, the panel established a set of guidelines to which it felt future applications of the contingent valuation method should adhere, if the studies are to produce reliable estimates of lost existence values for the purposes of damage assessment or regulation.

These guidelines made a number of proponents of the contingent valuation method quite unhappy. In their view, strict adherence to the panel's guidelines—especially the suggestion that in-person interviews be used to elicit values—would make it very expensive to use the contingent valuation method for damage estimation or regulatory purposes.

Moreover, a number of the guidelines seem intended to ensure that applications of the contingent valuation method would result in conservative estimates of lost existence values—that is, estimates that were more likely to underestimate than to overestimate these values. The NOAA panel created its long list of requirements because it felt strongly that casual applications of the contingent valuation method should not be used to justify large damage awards, especially in cases where the likelihood of significant lost existence values was quite small. By establishing a series of hurdles for contingent valuation studies to meet, the panel hoped to elevate considerably the quality of future studies and thereby increase the likelihood that these studies would produce estimates that could be relied on for policy purposes.

It should be noted that the NOAA panel report had no special legal standing in NOAA's deliberations. Instead, it was one of literally hundreds of submissions pertaining to the contingent valuation method that NOAA received during the time it was drafting its proposed regulations. Nevertheless, when NOAA published its long-awaited proposed rules on January 7, 1994, it said: "In proposing its standards for the use of CV [contingent valuation] in the damage assessment context, NOAA has relied heavily on the recommendations of the Panel."

For instance, the proposed regulations encourage trustees conducting contingent valuation studies to consider using the referendum format and in-person interviews, as the panel had suggested. In addition, the proposed regulations include a requirement that contingent valuation studies test for the sensitivity of responses to the scope of the damage described in the scenario. The NOAA panel had suggested that if respondents were not willing to pay more to prevent more serious accidents, say, other things being equal, the contingent valuation survey was unlikely to produce reliable results. Despite the fact that the panel report had no legal standing, it is worth noting that virtually every contingent valuation study done since makes reference to the respects in which it conforms to the recommendations in the NOAA Panel Report. Thus, it is difficult to deny the impact the report has had.

Paul R. Portney

See also: Contingent Valuation; Exxon *Valdez* Oil Spill; Nonmarket Valuation; Passive Use Value

Further Reading

Arrow, K., R. Solow, P. Portney, E. Leamer, R. Radner, and H. Schuman. 1993. Report of the NOAA Panel on Contingent Valuation. *Federal Register* 58: 4602–4614.

Portney, Paul R. 1994. The Contingent Valuation Debate: Why Economists Should Care. *Journal of Economic Perspectives* 8(4): 3–17.

Noise

Noise pollution consists of all the myriad sources of irritating (and often unhealthy) sounds emanating from other people and other things in the world around us. Loud noises from any source can be physically harmful; chronic exposure to moderate to high levels of noise has been shown in numerous studies to be linked to a wide variety of physical and psychological problems, including hearing loss, aggression, elevated stress, and cardiovascular effects such as hypertension. As a result, a number of studies have tried to measure the impact of living close to a source of noise such as a busy road or airport. In addition, as people increasingly move to large cities where expensive housing translates into dense living conditions, they may be subjected to yet another source of noise that has received much less academic and policy attention: neighbor noise. Some of this noise is caused by inconsiderate behavior, but other noise related to everyday living may more rightly be attributed to poor acoustic insulation from inadequate planning and building.

If you walk on a hard wood floor, practice the drums, or teach your dog to speak on command, chances are you will not chafe at the sound of your own steps, beats, or barks. However noise coming from the outside world that is not under your control may have a very different psychological effect, depending on your tolerance (or *perturbability*) for such things. Thus to the extent that the noisemakers of the outside world do not take into account the full harm inflicted on nearby ears when making decisions about the level of (loud) activity to engage in, noise pollution— like many other forms of pollution—is an *externality*.

In economics there is naturally an interest in calculating the costs of noise pollution and comparing these to the costs of noise abatement policies. However, there is no off-the-shelf observable market price for noise reduction, so researchers must infer a price from people's behavior. One popular approach to valuing noise is to use hedonic house price regressions to analyze the relationship between house prices and proximity to noise sources (usually airports) in order to estimate a shadow price of noise from the market data. All else equal, if similar homes sell for less the closer they are to the airport, the conditional difference in price is interpreted as the market discount attributed to the noise problem. The imputed noise costs found by many of these studies are substantial: for example, one study finds a $200,000 house would sell for $20,000 to $24,000 less if exposed to airplane noise.

In theory, with perfect information and costless mobility, in equilibrium house prices should completely compensate the noise differentials and the average homeowner should be left observationally indifferent between house #1 with noise level x and house #2 with noise level y. In practice, however, information on noise is often difficult to observe (or elicit from sellers), and mobility is far from free. Many people who optimally chose a home 5 or 10 years ago may find themselves in a suboptimal noise situation years later for a number of reasons: increases in local traffic, changes in airplane flight paths, or loud new neighbors next door (indeed, many an excited new urban apartment dweller have faced a rude welcome upon discovering heretofore hidden sources of noise once they move in, a factor which may help explain the popularity of renting in big cities). Furthermore, many housing markets are highly regulated with a large amount of rationing. For all these reasons, house prices may not fully compensate for undesirable characteristics like noise and there will be *residual* welfare costs.

A further complication in using hedonic methods arises due to heterogeneity in individuals' tolerance toward noise, with more perturbable people self-selecting into quieter areas, and more noise-tolerant people self-selecting into louder areas (taking advantage of the lower prices). This self-selection leads to a downward bias in any estimate of the average welfare costs of noise; we cannot necessarily interpret the difference in house prices attributed to noise differentials as the total cost that would be imposed on a particular individual exposed to that noise.

Given these difficulties, several alternative approaches to hedonic models have also been used to measure the welfare impacts of noise. One is to use a contingent valuation or stated choice method where subjects are asked to give their willingness-to-pay for alternative levels of different attributes. These methods are prone to various forms of strategic and recall bias and thus remain somewhat controversial.

A third method that has been used more recently is to use data from the many happiness or life satisfaction surveys that are now available, many of which ask questions about both household income and exposure to various forms of pollution, including noise. Although the use of life satisfaction data is quite a controversial subject in economics, in principle at least it should be possible to estimate the degree to which exposure to noise pollution lowers life satisfaction, and calculate the income transfer required to compensate for this impact. One study finds that exposure to significant levels of noise pollution lowers life satisfaction approximately as much as being disabled, and that noise alone can explain the differences in life satisfaction between urban and rural residents.

In sum, a growing body of evidence suggests that noise pollution is a serious problem that can significantly lower overall public welfare. However as noise is an externality and often not observable before purchasing or renting a home, the free market will not deliver an optimal solution. Instead, urban planners and policymakers should pay more attention to this issue and, when necessary, increase standards of acoustic building codes and/or the enforcement of local noise ordinances. As the world becomes increasingly urbanized, enhanced attention to noise control will ensure that the benefits of city living are more likely to be enjoyed by all.

Diana Weinhold

See also: Contingent Valuation; Externality; Hedonic Price Method

Further Reading

Cohen, Jeffrey P., and Cletus C. Coughlin. 2008. Spatial Hedonic Models of Airport Noise, Proximity, and Housing Prices. *Journal of Regional Science* 48(5): 859–878.

Nelson, Jon P. 2004. Meta-analysis of Airport Noise and Hedonic Property Values: Problems and Prospects. *Journal of Transport Economics and Policy* 38(1): 1–27.

van Praag, M.S. Bernard and Barbara E. Baarsma. 2005. Using Happiness Surveys to Value Intangibles: The Case of Airport Noise. *The Economic Journal* 115(500): 224–246.

Wardman, Mark, and Abigail Bristow. 2008. Valuations of Aircraft Noise: Experiments in Stated Preference. *Environmental and Resource Economics* 39(4): 459–480.

Weinhold, Diana. 2013. The Happiness Reducing Costs of Noise Pollution. *Journal of Regional Science* 53(2): 292–303.

Nonmarket Valuation

Nonmarket valuation refers to a collection of methods used by economists to put monetary values on environmental goods. They are called nonmarket because the goods being valued are not traded in a market. This includes goods like cleaner air, safer drinking water, the closure of beaches, more wetland acreage, and so forth. Economists regard these as goods that matter to people just like cars, candy, and a baseball game. Nonmarket goods simply have no marketplace where people go to buy and sell the good.

Nonmarket values are used in benefit–cost analysis to evaluate government policies and programs and in natural resource damage assessment cases for assessing damages under environmental laws that penalize parties responsible for harming the environment. An example of a benefit–cost analysis is an evaluation of an environmental regulation such as the Clean Air Act. An example of a natural resource damage assessment case is the Exxon *Valdez* oil spill.

Most people are comfortable with putting monetary values on market goods like shoes, bagels, a carnival ride, etc., but not always on nonmarket environmental goods. But, economic principles and good public policy call for measuring environmental goods and services in monetary terms and economists have developed a variety of approaches for doing so. Some of the theories and techniques have been in use for over 50 years.

The field of economics laying out the theoretical foundations for nonmarket and market valuation is called welfare economics. The theory holds that a person's economic value for a good (market or nonmarket) is his or her willingness to pay for that good. This stands to reason, because it reflects what a person is willing to give up in terms of purchasing power over other goods and services for the good in question. Willingness to accept payment is also theoretically acceptable as a measure of value but it has proven to be more difficult in application and so has seen less use.

A few things are worth noting. First, economic values measured using willingness to pay are based on individuals' preferences for a good, not an expert's judgment of value. Second, only people matter in economic value. Flora and fauna matter but only to the extent that people have a willingness to pay to protect nature. Third, since the values are in monetary terms they can be compared with costs and values of other nonmarket goods. This common metric is extremely valuable for policy evaluation.

The goal in valuation then is to find a measure of willingness to pay for the good in question. In the case of market goods this is considerably easier, because we observe what people are willing to pay in actual markets. In the case of nonmarket goods, the task is more difficult, because we have either no observation or only indirect observation in markets. For example, where do we go to observe people buying (and hence making known their willing to pay for) cleaner air?

Economists have devised several approaches for valuing nonmarket environmental goods. Most are classified in one of two broad methodologies: revealed preference (RP) or stated preference (SP). Revealed preference methods use observable behavioral data to make inferences about willingness to pay. For example, people reveal willingness to pay for the environment in how far they travel to visit a recreation site or in how much more they pay for a house if it is located near a lake or if they pay to filter their drinking water. With RP methods analysts use data on actions such as these taken by people to infer economic values.

The common RP methodologies are: the travel cost method for valuing recreational uses of the environment; the hedonic price method for valuing clean air, hazardous waste sites, risk of death, and landscape amenities; and the averting behavior method used to value risk of death and sickness and a variety of other environmental goods.

Stated preference methods, unlike RP methods, are not based on observed behavior. Instead, an analyst constructs a survey in which people are directly or indirectly asked their willingness to pay for an environmental good. Or, alternatively are asked how they might behave vis-a-vis the use of some environmental goods, which, in turn, allows the analyst to infer value. State preference surveys are sometimes simply called willingness-to-pay surveys.

The primary appeal of RP over SP studies is that RP values are based on actual willingness to pay by people in a market-like setting. SP studies, on the other hand, are based on responses to questions in a hypothetical survey where money is not actually paid by individuals. It is one thing to say you are willing to pay $100 to preserve an old growth forest in a survey where circumstances are hypothetical, and quite another to actually pay $100 out of your pocket to visit the site or donate to a fund to protect the site. Actual payment counts for a lot among many economists who tend to treat observed behavior as hard evidence for value.

The advantage of SP studies is that they may be designed to value almost anything. In many policy settings there is no observable behavior that can be used to infer values. For example, one may wish to value the restoration of a river in an urban area where the target level of cleanliness has not been realized in the recent past. How much will fishing and swimming increase on the river? We cannot say for sure because we have not observed people facing such conditions. The most important area where willingness to pay is unobtainable using RP analysis is for estimating the passive use value of an environmental good. Passive use value refers to willingness of people to pay for a good, such as protecting the Grand Canyon or preserving an endangered species, but have no intention of ever using the good (visiting the Grand Canyon or viewing the endangered species). Stated preference analysis is the only approach possible.

The common SP methods are the contingent valuation method, choice experiments, and contingent behavior analysis.

Finally, a growing area in nonmarket valuation is the combining of RP and SP data to take advantage of the strengths of both approaches. This allows the analysis to have grounding in actual behavior offered by RP studies along with the reach of SP studies for valuing goods wherein actual behavior is not observed in market or market-like data.

George R. Parsons

See also: Averting Behavior; Benefit–Cost Analysis; Choice Experiments; Contingent Behavior; Contingent Valuation; Exxon *Valdez* Oil Spill; Hedonic Price Method; Passive Use Value; Travel Cost Method; Welfare

Further Reading

Champ, P., K. Boyle, and T. Brown. 2003. *A Primer for Nonmarket Valuation.* London: Kluwer Academic.

Whitehead, J., T. Haab, and J.-C. Huang. 2011. *Preference Data for Environmental Valuation: Combining Revealed and Stated Preference Approaches.* London: Routledge.

Nonpoint Source Pollution

Pollution that originates from specific, well-defined sources such as sewage outfalls and smokestacks is typically called point source pollution, whereas pollution that comes from diffuse sources such as parking lots and agricultural fields is typically called nonpoint source pollution. Although intuitive, contradictions in distinguishing point and nonpoint source pollution exist. For example, economists typically think of vehicle emissions, which originate from specific, well-defined tail pipes, as a *nonpoint* source problem. The U.S. Environmental Protection Agency (EPA) classifies large animal feeding operations, which tend to dispose of their waste by spreading it on agricultural fields, as *point* sources.

The explanation for these apparent contradictions has both legal and economic components. First, from a legal perspective, the term point source has a specific definition in Section 502 of the U.S. Clean Water Act. The term nonpoint source is used to refer to pollution sources that are not included in this definition. This explains why large animal feeding operations are regulated as point sources: because the EPA has designated them as such. Second, although the term nonpoint source has its regulatory roots in water quality, economists tend to interpret it more broadly. From an economic perspective, the distinction between point and nonpoint sources is that the latter are *prohibitively costly to monitor*. Whereas it is relatively easy and inexpensive to identify and monitor emissions from a sewage outfall, it can be much more difficult and costly to characterize the pollutants entering the environment via agricultural runoff and percolation, or from millions of tail pipes— which explains why economists tend to think of vehicle emissions as a nonpoint source pollution problem. Of course, monitoring cost is a continuous variable and therefore it is best to think of all pollution sources as existing along this continuum, with some easily classified sources at the ends of the spectrum and more ambiguous types nearer to the center. Nonetheless, characterizing all pollution sources as either point or nonpoint persists, even among economists.

Examples of nonpoint source pollution include nutrients and pathogens from septic tanks; heavy metals and petroleum distillates in urban storm water; chemicals, pathogens, and nutrients in agricultural runoff; hydrocarbons and particulate matter from vehicle exhaust; and erosion from construction sites and agricultural fields. Due to the original emphasis on point sources in the Clean Water Act and the difficulties associated with monitoring nonpoint source pollution, more progress has been made on controlling point sources than nonpoint sources. Consequently, the leading cause of surface water impairment in the United States is nonpoint source pollution. Nonpoint source pollution also is a primary contributor to impaired ocean shoreline. The EPA determined not too long ago that the ecological risks posed by nonpoint source pollution are substantially more serious than those posed by pollution from point sources, and the health risks are roughly comparable. It is not surprising, then, that the EPA labeled nonpoint pollution as the "greatest source of water quality problems in the United States today."

Nonpoint sources have received increased regulatory attention recently, but they also present additional challenges compared to point sources. Chief among these is the monitoring problem: when pollutant emissions are readily measured, it is easier to establish limitations or incentives designed to reduce pollution, and to enforce these based on what is measured. Nonpoint source emissions, by definition, are difficult to measure. Largely because of this, regulations typically do not target nonpoint source emissions but rather other aspects of the nonpoint source pollution problem that are easier to measure. The two main alternative targets are the inputs to the polluting activity, and the downstream or ambient environmental quality that is impacted by the pollution. Economists have shown that either approach can, in theory, be implemented to achieve regulations that are as efficient as those that target emissions. However, the information needs are greater and require that the regulator knows a lot about how emissions are produced or what happens to them after they enter the environment.

Input regulation has emerged as the most common approach to reducing nonpoint source pollution in practice, even in cases when the overarching goal is to achieve an improvement in an ambient measure. Inputs may include virtually all aspects of production: raw materials, technologies, management practices, education, etc. Because these things tend to be easier to observe and verify, they can be the basis for regulatory limits and incentives. A prime example is Section 319 of the Clean Water Act Amendments, which, among other things, provides funding to subsidize the adoption of agricultural best management practices (BMPs) to reduce nonpoint source pollution. These subsidies provide an incentive for agricultural producers to switch to less polluting but presumably more expensive production practices. Payment of subsidies is contingent upon installation and maintenance of the required BMPs, which often can be verified relatively easily through site visits or aerial photography.

Input regulation will continue to play an important role in controlling nonpoint source pollution in the future. However, we are also likely to see more common use of two complimentary approaches. The first of these is closer monitoring of emissions. Technological progress continues to reduce the cost of monitoring environmental conditions. Examples include remote sensing and embedded sensor networks that enable huge amounts of spatially and temporally distributed data to be collected. As the cost of monitoring falls, more nonpoint source problems can be moved along the cost continuum and effectively converted to, and managed as, point source problems. The second approach is point–nonpoint trading. Because nonpoint sources have not been regulated as much as point sources, they tend to have lower marginal costs of pollution reduction—in other words, it is often cheaper for a nonpoint source to reduce pollution than it is for a point source. Consequently, if a watershed contains both point and nonpoint sources, and if the point sources are asked to make further emission reductions, it makes economic sense for the point sources to pay the nonpoint sources to make (cheaper) reductions on their behalf.

Kenneth A. Baerenklau

See also: Agriculture; Air Pollution; Externality; Offsets; Water Pollution

Further Reading

U.S. Environmental Protection Agency, 2000. National Water Quality Inventory Report. Washington, D.C. http://water.epa.gov/lawsregs/guidance/wa/305b/2000report_index.cfm. Accessed August 6, 2012.

U.S. Environmental Protection Agency and U.S. Department of Agriculture, 1998. Clean Water Action Plan: Restoring and Protecting America's Waters. EPA-840-R-98-001. Washington, D.C.

U.S. Environmental Protection Agency, OP Regional & State Planning Division, 1989. Comparing Risks and Setting Environmental Priorities. EPA-230-R-89–101. Washington, D.C.

Nuclear Power

A large amount of energy binds the nucleus of an atom. For some isotopes of elements, such as Uranium-235, this energy can be extracted from the atom using a process called fission. In nuclear fission, the nucleus of the atom is split, producing two smaller nuclei, two or three neutrons, gamma rays, and heat energy. The neutrons then strike the nuclei of other atoms, initiating a chain reaction that creates more heat energy. Much like coal- or gas-fired electrical generation facilities, the heat energy is converted to electrical energy using electromechanical generators. The new nuclei, often called the fission by-products, are also unstable and therefore radioactive.

Nuclear energy research was initially aimed at military defense, but in the years following World War II, civilian uses of the atom took priority. The world's first full-scale nuclear electric generation facility was opened in Shippingsport, Pennsylvania, in 1957. By 1971, 22 commercial reactors were in operation in the United States. Meanwhile, Japan, France, and other European countries constructed numerous nuclear power generation facilities and the number of reactors throughout the world climbed steadily until about 1990, when the number of active reactors leveled off. By 2012, roughly 13 percent of the world's electricity was produced by nuclear reactors. Generation facilities in France, Japan, and the United States accounted for half of the electricity produced in nuclear generation facilities.

While nuclear energy is clearly an important source of electricity for the world, doubts about its safety surfaced even before the first reactor went on line. By the early1960s, local opposition to the siting of nuclear power plants was common. These early detractors often were more concerned about siting and esthetics than accidents or waste generation. Local opposition crushed plans to build nuclear reactors in Bodega Bay, California, and Malibu, California. By the 1970s, safety began to be a real concern among opposition groups in the United States and Europe. The 1970s saw large-scale protests against nuclear power generation in the United States and several European countries, particularly Germany. Concerns about the safety of nuclear power grew after the radiation leak at the Three Mile Island nuclear plant in Pennsylvania in 1979 and the Chernobyl nuclear plant disaster in the Ukraine in 1986.

Energy costs are generally stated in terms of total system levelized costs that reflect the cost per megawatt-hour (MW-h) including capital, fuel, fixed and variable operation and maintenance, and financing costs. The total system levelized cost of nuclear power compares favorably to other generation methods: at \$113/MW-h, it is somewhat more expensive than conventional coal (\$99/MW-h) but significantly less than renewable sources such as solar photovoltaic ($157/MW-h) or solar thermal ($251/MW-h).

The levelized cost per MW-h does not include the external costs of producing electricity using nuclear fission. For one, reactors accidents, storage problems, or nuclear waste transport accidents could potentially result in leaks of radioactive material into the environment. Exposure to radioactive material can have a range of detrimental human health effects ranging from a variety of cancers, birth defects, and other abnormalities in children, and even death, depending on the timing of exposure and amount of radiation. There are other external costs of radioactive waste related to the national security. Terrorist activity could target nuclear facilities or waste storage and transport. The market for fissionable materials created by electricity production may make it easier for terrorists or a rogue state to obtain material that could then be used to build a nuclear weapon or a dirty bomb, which combines radioactive material with conventional explosives. While a dirty bomb would not have nearly the mortality and morbidity of a nuclear weapon, the psychological impacts could still be large.

Of special concern when computing the external costs of nuclear energy production is the long half-life of high level radioactive waste, which can range from hundreds to hundreds of thousands of years, depending on the isotopes. And, unlike other forms of electric generation such as coal-fired, humans are only exposed to the radioactive waste products if there is an accident. Thus, the expected external costs of nuclear waste consist of the lost utility from compromised health and environmental damage multiplied by the probability of an accident with human exposure discounted over all the years when exposure occurs. As such, the estimated expected external costs depend on a number of assumptions about the likelihood of an accident, the damages to human health, and the environment, given an accident, and the social discount rate.

Studies have compared the external costs of electricity generated by nuclear reactors to other generation sources. A wide range of estimates have been developed, with differences arising from the assumptions about the externalities related to each fuel source and the effects on human and global environmental health. The external costs of coal-fired generation ranges from $400 to $4200 per MW-h, depending on assumptions. The external costs per MW-h for natural gas range from $300 to $2300/MW-h, whereas the expected external costs of nuclear generation range from $80 to $600/MW-h. The estimated external costs of renewables, averaged over solar PVC, solar thermal, and biomass range from $20 to $400/MW-h. Despite the differences in the estimates, a clear pattern emerges. Coal-fired and natural gas generators have the highest external costs, followed by nuclear power and renewable generation sources.

One of the most important public policy issues related to nuclear energy is what to do with the radioactive waste. The United States generates 2,000 metric tons of nuclear waste per year, mostly from commercial reactors. The total stock of commercial nuclear waste in the United States presently exceeds 60,000 metric tons. Japan and France reprocess nuclear waste to make it less dangerous, then store the resulting by-products in interim aboveground facilities in anticipation of deep geologic burial in the future. The United States currently stores waste on-site at the reactor facilities. For the past two decades, the United States studied a site in the Nevada Desert for permanent deep geologic burial. After 20 years of study, the budget for future research at the site was eliminated. At present, the future of the Yucca Mountain facility is unknown. If the Yucca Mountain facility does not open, the United States will have to find an alternative site for permanent geologic burial or resort to other long-term storage options such as on-site dry cask storage.

Mary Riddel

See also: Alternative Energy; Discounting; Energy Policy; Externality; Precautionary Principle; Renewable Energy; Risk and Uncertainty

Further Reading

Cleveland, Cutler J., and Robert U. Ayers. 2004. *Encyclopedia of Energy*. Amsterdam: Elsevier Academic Press.

Kitson, Lucy, Peter Wooders, and Tom Moerenhout. 2011. Subsidies and External Costs in Electric Power Generation: A Comparative Review of Estimates. Global Subsidies Initiative. International Institute for Sustainable Development.

U.S. Department of Energy, Office of Nuclear Energy, Science, and Technology. The History of Nuclear Energy. DOE/NE-0088.

Offsets

One of the central contributions of environmental economics has been to point out the benefits of achieving societal goals at the lowest possible cost. This has inspired the use of incentive-based policies such as Pigouvian taxes and emissions trading. An offshoot of the emissions trading idea is what is often referred to as offset programs in which sources of pollution that are directly regulated are given incentives to abate. This approach has been most prominently applied in water pollution and climate change mitigation.

As an example, consider the problem of how to reduce the load of nutrients into a watershed. Some of the nutrients come from wastewater treatment plants that are directly monitored and regulated. In addition, nutrients also come from agricultural sources with unregulated pollution loads that are extremely costly to monitor. The cost-effective way to reduce the nutrient loads would achieve reductions from those sources that can abate at the lowest cost, and agricultural pollution is frequently the cheapest to reduce. Offset provisions would allow regulated point sources to satisfy all or a portion of their abatement responsibilities by paying farmers to adopt practices that reduce their pollution load. If the cost to the farmer of adopting such a practice is less than the cost to the wastewater treatment plant of reducing an equivalent quantity of nutrients, then, in principle, a deal can be made—pollution will be reduced at a lower overall cost.

The prototypical example described in the previous paragraph sounds almost exactly like a cap-and-trade type policy—one polluter pays another polluter to take care of part of its abatement responsibility, thus reducing the aggregate cost of achieving an environmental goal. However, there are several important differences here that distinguish offset programs from cap-and-trade schemes. First, the providers of offsets are typically unregulated sources with no obligation to abate pollution. Second, the sources that are given incentives through the offset programs are usually nonpoint in nature, meaning that it is very difficult to know precisely what environmental benefits are actually being created through these payments. These two factors create a suite of challenges that must be taken into account in the design and implementation of offset programs.

The first challenge faced by offset programs is that they must incorporate a mechanism to overcome the uncertainty that arises because of the nonpoint nature of sources under consideration. While a traditional cap-and-trade program can actually measure the pollution loads associated with the rights that are being transacted, when nonpoint sources are involved the loads can only be estimated. For example, if a farmer is paid to adopt a tillage practice in order to sequester carbon in the soil, it is virtually impossible to know exactly how much carbon is actually stored. Hence, most programs adopt a structure in which sellers of offset credits are paid to adopt a practice with payments tied to the estimated environmental benefits provided. For example, at one time farmers could generate carbon offset credits by committing to continuous conservation tillage for five years with the number of credits generated varying depending on the estimated sequestration achieved, ranging from 0.2 to 0.6 metric tons per acre per year. Obviously, the better the model is, the more certainty there will be that the offset has truly delivered the environmental benefits that are hoped for. More important than precision, however, is that the practice and model do not create *perverse incentives* in which the recipient of the payments can adopt one practice to receive a payment, but make other management choices that have a countervailing effect.

To adjust for the uncertainty that exists in offset programs, most such programs use a trading ratio in which more than one credit must be generated for each offset credit that is used by a point source. Trading ratios have received substantial attention by environmental economists. Interestingly, the conclusion of the economics literature tends to be that trading ratios should be used to incentivize participation of nonpoint sources, meaning a ratio of less than 1:1. This runs exactly counter to prevailing practices in the field where nonpoint sources are typically penalized by ratios of 2:1 or more.

The environmental integrity of an offset program requires that any increase in pollution by a point source is offset by reductions provided by a nonpoint source. However, this only occurs if the offset is additional, that is that it would not have occurred in the absence of the transaction. However, additionality is not always satisfied because many of the practices supported through offsets are implemented even without a payment. Hence, one of the central concerns in such programs is defining criteria for additionality or, equivalently, establishing the *baseline* to which the final environmental consequences will be compared. How this is actually implemented in practice varies greatly. Some programs attempt to estimate *financial additionality* while others simply use actual practices at some point in time to establish the baseline.

Closely related to additionality are the issues of leakage and slippage. Leakage refers to offsetting consequences that result from changes in prices. For example, efforts to reduce deforestation in one region may reduce the global supply of timber, increasing the price and thereby encouraging deforestation elsewhere. Slippage usually refers to more geographically concentrated effects, perhaps by the same landowner. For example, Wu (2000) found that the U.S.

Conservation Reserve Program's payments to encourage farmers to take land out of production may also incentivize farmers to bring other land back into production.

A couple of other issues that arise in offset programs that deserve attention are permanence and stacking. Permanence refers to the extent to which environmental objectives are achieved only if the project is maintained, which is particularly true in the case of carbon sequestration programs. Again, when nonpoint sources are involved ensuring permanence is particularly difficult and requires repeated monitoring. Finally, stacking refers to the question of whether a single management practice can generate more than one type of offset credit. In some cases, stacking can be environmentally beneficial and cost-saving, but in other cases the stacked credits may not satisfy additionality. Hence, each offset program must address the question of stacking and, to date, most have not allowed stacked credits to be used as offsets.

Despite the challenges noted here, offset programs are increasingly being used in a variety of domains. The Clean Development Mechanism program under the Kyoto Protocol is the largest such program. In that program carbon emissions in developed countries can be offset by reductions in developing countries. As of March 2012, the Clean Development Mechanism program had created estimated reductions in greenhouse gases equivalent to nearly 900 million metric tons of carbon dioxide from over 1,400 projects, mostly involving the development of renewable energy. Offset programs to achieve water quality improvements have also grown in number. As of 2009, there were 19 active offset programs to improve water quality, all but one of which was in the United States. Most of these programs seek to reduce nutrient loads by creating incentives for farmers to adopt conservation practices. With their increased use, standards are being established for how to address uncertainty, additionality, leakage, and other challenges. It appears likely, therefore, that policymakers will increasingly adopt offsets as a way to confront difficult environmental problems.

Richard T. Woodward

See also: Climate Change Impacts; Emissions Trading; Nonpoint Source Pollution; Pigouvian Taxes; Water Pollution

Further Reading

Sohngen, B., and S. Brown. 2004. Measuring Leakage from Carbon Projects in Open Economies: A Stop Timber Harvesting Project in Bolivia as a Case Study. *Canadian Journal of Forest Research* 34(4): 829–939.

Wu, Junjie. 2000. Slippage Effects of the Conservation Reserve Program. *American Journal of Agricultural Economics* 82(4): 979–992.

Ostrom, Elinor

Elinor Ostrom (August 7, 1933–June 12, 2012) was an American political scientist and the first female recipient of the Nobel Prize in Economics (2009). She received her B.A., M.A., and Ph.D. all from the Political Science Department at the University of California at Los Angeles (UCLA). For most of her professional career she was a professor of political science at Indiana University, where she co-founded and co-directed the Workshop in Political Theory and Policy Analysis. She has written or edited more than 30 books and 300 articles, and is most well-known for developing the Institutional Analysis and Development (IAD) framework for understanding the effective management of common pool resources.

Ostrom first began graduate work in the mid-20th century when the scholarly understanding of resource categorization was dominated by the Paul Samuelson dichotomy—goods were either private goods or public goods, and as such were most effectively managed either by markets or government. It was not until the influence of Ostrom and others that an understanding gained traction that goods could exist more along a range of type, with pure private and public goods merely the endpoints. This implied that provision of goods could successfully be made along a range of institutions, and not just through markets or government. Ostrom came to focus on common pool resources as a categorization within that range and her work shed enormous light on the qualities and characteristics of successful management institutions of those resources in numerous real-world examples across the globe.

Ostrom first began studying common pool resources in graduate school with an analysis of the water industry in southern California. Over an extensive career she contributed insights to long-term management of a host of environmental resources including forests, fisheries, lands, and water systems, in places across the globe including Nepal, Nigeria, Kenya, Australia, Bolivia, India, Mexico, Poland, and Zimbabwe. Her work challenged the conventional wisdom that common pool resources could not be managed outside of private markets or government regulation. In so doing she highlighted real-world instances of collective self-governance of common pool resources that avoided the tragedy of the commons and effectively managed sustainable resource use. Throughout, Ostrom served as a role model, breaking through many gender barriers that existed in academia at the time.

Ostrom arrived at her research results from a uniquely interdisciplinary perspective. Indeed, the genesis of the workshop she co-founded at Indiana University was to bring political scientists, economists, and sociologists together. Over the years it expanded to include methods, models, and data from other disciplines as well. Ostrom was well-known for the hands-on field work she engaged in—novel at the time—to add detail and depth to her research results. This focus on real-world settings forced her to appreciate the complexities of individual contexts. Perhaps her most important overall research result is that one-size-fits-all policies are not effective. In other words, the institutional rules developed for management of common pool resources, to be effective, should be fit to the specific social and ecological settings on a case-by-case basis. While Ostrom's IAD framework offers general guidelines for institutional development, there are no hard and fast rules to be applied in every context. Policy, and people, are too complex for that.

Lea-Rachel Kosnik

See also: Coase Theorem; Common Pool Resources; Pigouvian Taxes, Property Rights; Tragedy of the Commons

Further Reading

Ostrom, Elinor. 2009. *Beyond Markets and States: Polycentric Governance of Complex Economic Systems.* Nobel Prize Lecture, Sweden.

Outdoor Recreation

Although travel cost models (TCMs) had been used with increasing frequency in the two decades following Hotelling's famous 1947 letter to the U.S. National Park Service, the use of consumer surplus estimates in policymaking did not really take off until the 1970s. At that time the burgeoning environmental movement began to push back against, for example, controversial federal water projects such as the Hell's Canyon Dam on the Columbia River and proposed ski resorts such as Mineral King in California. In both cases, economic studies examining the trade-offs involved with these projects relied heavily upon the TCM to estimate the value of proposed (and displaced) recreation activities to evaluate project benefits and costs. The use of economic analysis, at least for large federal projects and environmental regulations, was further solidified when President Ronald Reagan issued Executive Order 12291, which required benefit–cost analysis (BCA) for all federal decisions expected to have impacts of $100 million or more. Economists have since had a seat at the policy table, and the TCM has proven to be a useful tool to inform policy decisions at the local, state, and national level in the ensuing decades.

Early TCM studies were often used simply to estimate a net economic value for recreation, that is, the value of a recreation trip or a recreation visitor day, so that the previously intangible benefit of recreation could be included in a BCA for a given project. However, it quickly became apparent that estimates of consumer surplus per unit of recreation were insufficient for many policy questions. Both the Clean Water Act and the Clean Air Act required federal and state agencies to improve the quality of water and atmospheric resources. The key policy questions no longer focused on the value of recreation, but rather on the change in value associated with a proposed policy or project. The basic TCM was insufficient to deal with such policy questions. Subsequent development of the TCM—especially the concept of weak complementarity by Mäler and the random utility model by McFadden—allowed researchers to directly incorporate the changes in the quality of a resource and/or its substitutes. The TCM could then be used to generate theoretically defensible estimates of the net economic value of changes in environmental quality at one or many sites.

Motivated by a wide variety of policy questions, the 1980s and 1990s saw a relative explosion in TCM studies focusing on changes in recreation use value associated with changes in environmental quality. Examples include acidic deposition from the atmosphere into lakes, reductions in pollutants, or nutrient loads into water, increasing instream flows to enhance wildlife habitat, health advisories associated with consumption of contaminated fish and wildlife or contact with contaminated water at beaches, loss of wetlands, changes in the quality of hunting and fishing, and, perhaps most infamously, oil spills. The vast majority of these studies were conducted at more or less a local level, examining only a few sites within, say, a county or multiple county area, with relatively few studies conducted at the larger state or provincial, regional, or national levels.

Despite generating a massive body of literature, two problems were immediately apparent for those wishing to use TCM studies for policy analysis. First, environmental quality data collected by natural scientists such as biochemical oxygen demand (BOD) or total suspended solids (TSS) may vary substantially by time of day or season or, crucially, may not be perceived accurately by people. That is, can a recreationist stand at the riverside and estimate the BOD or TSS? The answer is, of course, "No." Instead he or she may only be able to see that the river is clear or not, that aquatic vegetation appears normal or not, or that a desired species is present or not. All of these perceived outcomes may be functionally related to BOD, but it is a leap of faith for the analyst to state that people behave as if BOD correlates to their individual perceptions. Further, different studies used different measures that attempted to capture similar effect: Study A may have used BOD in the recreation demand model, whereas Study B used dissolved oxygen saturation. Why? Because those were the biophysical data available at the study sites. But how can one compare the benefit estimates from studies using two similar, but different, changes in resource quality?

A second problem encountered by those wishing to use TCM analysis is that high-quality travel cost studies can be very expensive. A TCM study necessarily involves talking to recreationists on-site, by mail, over the phone, or via the Internet. Regardless of the method of contact, the survey design must include additional resources to anticipate and adjust for survey biases that will inevitably be encountered regardless of the elicitation method. Given the cost of a TCM study, policymakers may rationally ask if benefit estimates from TCM studies done else-where (for a similar problem and policy) can be applied (transferred) to their lo-cally proposed policy.

As described by Griffiths et al., there has been an increasing reliance upon bene-fits transfer by the federal government to evaluate the costs and benefits of proposed policies (and, by implication, increasing reliance at other levels of government). One factor constraining the use of benefits transfer has been alluded to earlier: even for similar problems and policies (say, oxygen levels in a river or stream), TCM practitioners may not have used comparable measures in their models (BOD vs. dissolved oxygen saturation). The fact that the even similar measures of environ-mental quality are not the same across models complicates the process of transfer-ring benefits from one (or many) study sites to a new site.

Griffiths et al. also address the issue of indicators of environmental quality as measured by physical scientists and the perceptions of environmental quality to which people actually respond. Writing within the context of the Clean Water Act, the authors note that the legislation is aimed at maintaining or improving the *bio-logical integrity* of aquatic resources, and that analysts should value ecological benefits, not merely changes in biophysical measures. If an ecological production function were used to link physical measures of environmental quality to ecological endpoints that can be directly perceived by people, then analysts would no longer need to make that leap of faith in connecting biophysical measures to perceptions. Further, generating a set of standard ecological endpoints (or outcomes that can be accurately perceived by people) for use in TCM studies would greatly ease the dif-ficulties encountered in benefit transfer exercises.

Paul M. Jakus

See also: Benefit Transfer; Clean Air Act; Clean Water Act; Executive Order 12291; Hotelling, Harold; Travel Cost Method

Further Reading

Griffiths, C., H. Klemick, M. Massey, C. Moore, S. Newbold, D. Simpson, P. Walsh, and W. Wheeler. 2012. U.S. Environmental Protection Agency Valuation of Surface Water Quality Improvements. *Review of Environmental Economics and Policy* 6(1): 130–146.

Mäler, K-G. 1974. *Environmental Economics: A Theoretical Inquiry.* Baltimore, MD: Johns Hopkins University Press.

McFadden, D. 1974. Conditional Logic Analysis of Qualitative Choice Behavior, in P. Zarembka (editor), *Frontiers in Econometrics.* New York: Academic Press.

Mendelsohn, R., and S. Olmstead. 2009. The Economic Valuation of Environmental Amenities and Disamenities: Methods and Applications. *Annual Review of Environment and Resources* 34: 325–347.

P

Passive Use Value

Passive use value, also known as existence use or nonuse value, is when someone is willing to give up something in exchange for knowing that an environmental or natural resource exists in its natural state when the person does not actively use or visit the site. Passive use value is one of the more controversial topics in environmental and resource economics.

Consider gray whales. Suppose that you never intend to go whale watching. You have a fear of flying. You don't like driving long distances. You get seasick. Even in your wildest dreams you cannot imagine ever seeing a gray whale surface in the Pacific Ocean. But, you might still value gray whales. If you were asked to donate money to a Gray Whale Protection Fund would you do it? How about a one-time donation of $1? If your answers were "yes" then you have a passive use value for gray whales.

For a public good to have passive use value there are two necessary conditions: uniqueness and irreversibility. If these conditions are not present then the public good in question probably has a small or zero passive use value.

The concept of uniqueness is related to the lack of substitutes. For a good to generate passive use value it must be one of a kind or at least be one of a few of a kind. Goods that generate passive use value are unique ecosystems and natural wonders. Examples of natural resources that might generate passive use value are the Grand Canyon or an endangered/threatened species such as the bald eagle. These goods do not have any or many good substitutes. People will be willing to pay to preserve them even if they think they will never see the resource.

Irreversibility means that once an action is taken you cannot go back. If the Colorado River is dammed and the Grand Canyon fills with water the sights and sounds of the Grand Canyon cannot be restored. Once a plant or animal species is extinct, its genetic material cannot be reproduced. Technology might be available to restore the resource but, for some people who value it, restoration is not fully satisfactory. If development is reversible or a replica is a good substitute, then passive use value is likely to be small.

Another condition for passive use value is that individuals must have some reason, or motive, for valuing the preservation or protection of a public good other than using it. Three possible motives for passive use value are the altruistic motive, the bequest motive, and the intrinsic motive. People might have passive use values because they want to preserve an economic good or resource for someone else. I may be willing to contribute to the Gray Whale Preservation Fund because a family member enjoys whale watching. People might have passive use values because they want to preserve an economic good or resource for someone in the future. A dedicated hiker might be willing to pay more than consumer surplus to preserve his or her favorite wilderness area so that it will be available for his or her great-grandchildren. The word intrinsic means inherent or essential. In the case of natural resources, passive use value might be motivated by the desire to preserve the natural order of things. An environmentalist may wish to protect endangered species because they are important in and of themselves, or for ecological integrity.

To illustrate the economic theory of passive use value more formally, consider the total value framework. The total value framework to environmental valuation acknowledges that some people have passive use value. Total value is equal to use value plus passive use value. In order to understand how total value can be decomposed into its use and existence components, consider the factors that affect utility (i.e., happiness). Utility increases with the consumption of public goods that can provide use and passive use value, such as gray whales, and consumption of all other private goods. If the prices of all other private goods are held constant, we can use income to measure consumption.

If you want to take a gray whale watching trip your use value is defined by a comparison of situations. Utility without a gray whale–watching trip and all of your income is equal to utility with gray whale–watching trips and use value from the gray whale–watching trip subtracted from income. Use value is the amount of money taken away so that you are just indifferent between these two situations.

If you do not want to take a whale-watching trip, your use value from gray whale watching is equal to zero. This does not mean that total value is zero. Many people want to save the whales but they never intend to go whale-watching. Passive use value is the amount of money taken away from income to avoid a specific decrease in the gray whale population that keeps the utility in both situations equal when whale-watching trips in both situations are zero.

The total value of the gray whale population is the sum of use value and passive use value. The formal definition of total value is similar to the definitions of use value and passive use value but the trip-taking assumption is not made. Total value is the total willingness to pay for a change in the resource allocation. Total value must be greater than or equal to passive use value. If zero trips are taken by the individual use value equals zero and total value is equal to passive use value. If one or more trips are taken by the individual then use value must be positive.

Some people argue that passive use values do not exist: "How can you value something if you don't use it?" This argument is not supportable. Economic theory does not rule out passive use value. Indeed, people reveal their passive use value through their own behavior (this is the typically way that people reveal that they have a value for something): people make donations and buy products related to the good or resource that generates passive use value (e.g., reading material). Passive use values are real economic values. Real resources are expended—that is, resources that could be out to alternative uses—to express passive use values. These observations argue for including passive use value in benefit–cost analysis. Yet still, others argue that the tools available to estimate passive use value are not good enough to measure passive use value accurately. This carries weight but it does not reject outright the notion of including passive use values in benefit–cost analysis.

A more pragmatic answer to the question of whether to include passive use value in benefit–cost analysis is to conduct sensitivity analysis. The analyst should attempt to measure passive use value whenever the necessary conditions for passive use value are met. Then conduct the benefit–cost analysis with and without passive use values included. On the other hand, if passive use value cannot be measured then present use value (benefit) estimates as lower bound estimates of total value and recognize that some of the benefits of a policy are not estimated.

John C. Whitehead

See also: Benefit–Cost Analysis; Contingent Valuation; Exxon *Valdez* Oil Spill; Krutilla, John V.; Welfare

Further Reading

Kopp, R. J., 1992. Why Existence Value Should Be Included in Cost–Benefit Analysis. *Journal of Policy Analysis and Management* 11(1): 123–130.

Krutilla, John V. 1967. Conservation Reconsidered. *American Economic Review* 57(4): 777–786.

Rosenthal, Donald H., and Robert H. Nelson. 1992. Why Existence Value Should Not Be Used in Cost–Benefit Analysis. *Journal of Policy Analysis and Management* 11(1): 116–122.

Payments for Environmental Services

Payments for Environmental Services (PES) are a mechanism by which landowners are compensated for the environmental benefits generated by their land management practices. Five key criteria to describe the principle of PES are: (1) a voluntary transaction in which (2) a well-defined environmental service (or a land use likely to secure that service) (3) is bought by a (minimum of one) buyer (4) from a (minimum of one) provider (5) if and only if the provider continuously secures the provision of the service (conditionality).

These criteria cover a wide variety of programs. Examples of environmental services include watershed protection, carbon sequestration, and biodiversity conservation. The buyer of the services may be a national government, using PES as an environmental policy instrument. Alternatively, they may be a private company or a domestic or foreign conservation organization, aiming to provide incentives for others to provide certain environmental services.

Given this wide variety of potential programs, Engel et al. provide three necessary conditions for the design of a genuine PES scheme: (1) the relationship between the type of land use being promoted and the provision of the ecosystem service must be clear; (2) stakeholders must have the possibility to terminate the contractual relationship (it is a voluntary transaction); and (3) a monitoring system must accompany the intervention, in order to ensure that the provision of services is taking place (additionality and conditionality of payments).

PES are one of a set of policy options for obtaining environmental services. They are increasingly being used in preference to regulatory measures such as protected areas, particularly in developing countries, because of their potential to be win-win, i.e., to provide benefits of both environmental protection and poverty alleviation.

PES are close in spirit to the Coase theorem, in which it is argued that socially suboptimal situations (e.g., too little provision of environmental services) can be resolved through voluntary market-like transactions, provided that transaction costs are low and property rights are clearly defined and enforced. In other words, it is possible that individuals, communities, and even supranational entities may be able to negotiate toward efficient provision of environmental goods and services. The creation of markets for trading environmental services thus becomes a potential solution for market failures that lead to the undersupply of these types of services.

Conservation approaches such as PES can be much more effective than indirect approaches with respect to achieving environmental objectives. Some researchers assert that, in contrast to decades of what have been referred to as policies for conservation by distraction (e.g., community development programs, or integrated conservation and development projects) that have only indirect effects on conservation, direct payments such as PES schemes are likely to be (a) institutionally simpler; (b) more cost-effective in delivering benefits to buyers; (c) more effective in generating economic growth among suppliers by improving cash flow, diversifying income sources, and reducing income variance; and (d) provide new sources of finance for conservation.

One of the earliest PES programs was the Conservation Reserve Program (CRP), introduced in 1985 by the U.S. federal government. Under the CRP, eligible agricultural producers receive payments for land retirement and approved conservation practices. Landowners apply for enrollment by bidding to undertake certain activities in return for a specified payment. Offers for contracts are ranked using the Environmental Benefits Index (EBI), which is based on expected benefits to water quality, soil erosion, air quality, and wildlife habitat, as well as the cost of the contract. The highest-ranking contracts are then selected to participate.

Research on the impacts of the CRP suggests that it has reduced soil erosion, a key environmental indicator and that benefit–cost targeting using the EBI is a cost-effective way to achieve the desired environmental outcomes. There are some concerns that the 10- to 15-year contracts for land retirement are not sufficient for the full benefits to be observed. However, many farmers reenroll their land at the end of their contract, and the majority of those who do not enroll are still not expected to bring land back into production.

A newer program, on a similar scale to the CRP, is the Sloping Land Conversion Program. This was introduced in China in 1999, with the dual objectives of soil conservation and poverty reduction. Farm households receive payment in the form of cash, grain, and seedlings in return for converting cropland to forest or grassland. The intention is to convert around 15 million hectares of land. Contracts last between two and eight years, depending on the type of vegetation planted, and all households within each of two broad geographical regions receive the same subsidy level.

Although the program is voluntary in principle, studies have shown that participation is not always voluntary in practice. However, for those that do participate, evidence suggests that the program tends to raise incomes, as the subsidy payment exceeds the opportunity cost of the retired land on average. It is still early to identify the impacts on soil protection, but while the majority of land entered into the program is steeply sloping, there is some misenrollment of low-slope land. This suggests that targeting could be improved.

The Costa Rican Pagos por Servicios Ambientales (PSA) was established as a PES program in 1996. This program grew out of an existing institutional structure of payments for reforestation and forest management, but contains several notable features: (1) most payments are for conservation of existing mature tropical forest with no harvesting allowed, (2) payments are justified and targeted to produce ecosystem services rather than to support the timber industry per se, and (3) funds come from both earmarked taxes and international donations.

Studies of participation in the PSA program have consistently found that participants differ from nonparticipants in important farm-level characteristics that directly affect land use, the PSA program significantly increased participating farm forest cover in a microlevel analysis, and the payments had a positive and significant impact on forest gain at the national level, with reductions in net deforestation. However, research does not conclude that PES contracting has reduced gross deforestation.

Rodrigo Arriagada and Katrina Mullan

See also: Amenity Values of Forests; Biodiversity; Coase Theorem; Conservation Reserve Program; Ecosystem Services; Property Rights; Public Goods

Further Reading

Arriagada, R., P. Ferraro, E. Sills, S. K. Pattanayak, and S. Cordero. 2012. Do Payments for Environmental Services Reduce Deforestation? A Farm Level Evaluation from Costa Rica. *Land Economics* 88(2): 382–399.

Engel, S., S. Pagiola, and S. Wunder. 2008. Designing Payments for Environmental Services in Theory and Practice: An Overview of the Issues. *Ecological Economics* 65(4): 663–674.

Ferraro, P. J., and A. Kiss. 2002. Direct Payments for Biodiversity Conservation. *Science* 298: 1718–1719.

Roberts, Michael J., and Ruben N. Lubowski. 2007. Enduring Impacts of Land Retirement Policies: Evidence from the Conservation Reserve Program. *Land Economics* 83(4): 516–538.

Xu, Jintao, Ran Tao, Zhigang Xu, and Michael T. Bennett. 2010. China's Sloping Land Conversion Program: Does Expansion Equal Success? *Land Economics* 86(2): 219–244.

Peak Oil

The term peak oil refers to the point in time when oil production reaches its maximum (the peak), after which consumption will steadily decline and lead, ultimately, to depletion. The study of peak oil attempts to estimate the peak date, the total amount of available oil, and the date of ultimate depletion. Peak-oil research is based on the surprisingly accurate prediction by M. K. Hubbert in 1956 of the peak of U.S. crude oil production in 1970. Hubbert's parsimonious analysis estimated this peak by fitting a simple logistic distribution (a bell-shaped curve similar to a normal distribution) to observed oil production. Importantly, Hubbert did not include economic variables—such as prices—in his analysis and peak-oil proponents have generally followed his lead. Despite the limited economic analysis, peak-oil proponents have drawn economic conclusions (many of them dire) from their work. These predictions of catastrophe have fueled the efforts to estimate the peak in world oil production. However, peak-oil analysis has not gained widespread acceptance and many of its conclusions remain controversial.

The standard model underlying most peak-oil analysis assumes that oil production follows essentially a random process. To illustrate, think of the world as a giant checkerboard with oil randomly deposited under some squares but not others. Suppose that each year, we explore a number of squares some of which yield oil and some of which do not. Oil production then begins from the oil-producing sites: first ramping up over time, then holding steady at a maximum level determined by internal wellhead pressure, and finally declining to zero. Under this model, oil production should follow a bell-shaped curve: growing over time as more and more sites are developed, but then declining over time as fewer and fewer sites remain to be developed. Importantly, under this model, the peak date can be estimated from observed production. Moreover, under Hubbert's symmetric logistic version of the model, the total amount of available oil and the date of ultimate depletion can also be estimated.

Despite Hubbert's early predictive success, applying the peak-oil model to other regions has been less successful. In particular, while oil production in many regions does exhibit evidence of peaking, many regions do not. For example, Ohio production seems to have multiple peaks, and Iraqi production seems to be at best chaotic.

Moreover, the logistic model of Hubbert does not clearly dominate other models (e.g., exponential or linear) and allowing for asymmetric increases and decreases in production fit the data better. Unfortunately, the more flexible, asymmetric models cannot be used to reliably estimate the peak date, the total amount of available oil, or the date of ultimate depletion.

Despite these technical difficulties, predicting the peak might be important as an indicator of scarcity. Unfortunately, the peak in oil production has little systematic relationship with the underlying scarcity of oil. In fact, it is easy to construct simple examples where an improvement in technology could either hasten or delay the peak. Thus peaking is not necessarily a good indicator of scarcity.

Economics offers an alternative model of depletable resources. This model, originally developed by Hotelling, describes both how oil should be used to maximize the benefits to society and how oil would be used under competitive markets. As with the peak-oil model, Hotelling's model gets some things right and some things wrong. Importantly, simple versions of the model unrealistically predict steadily increasing prices and decreasing consumption. These unrealistic features of the basic model have reduced its applicability; however, relatively straightforward extensions of the model make it more realistic. In fact, recent work shows that by adding realistic features the Hotelling model can be extended to predict peaking in oil production.

The dire economic predictions of the peak-oil analysts follow from assumptions of irreversibility and nonsubstitutability. Once decline starts there is essentially nothing that can be done to reverse it, and because oil is essential to society, declining oil production will lead to a declining standard of living, wars, and famine. However, these predictions following the peak in world oil production may or may not turn out to be true. If the prediction is simply based on a correlation, then there is no scope for policies to affect the outcome. However, if the prediction is based on a causal relationship, then there is scope for policy. For example, if the relationship between peaking and catastrophe is causal, then by delaying oil peaking we may be able to delay or prevent the catastrophe. The case for causality would be strengthened by carefully explaining a mechanism by which peaking leads to catastrophe. The crucial assumption of any such mechanism is substitutability: how quickly can society substitute away from oil to other energy sources or to reduced energy consumption. If we can readily substitute away from oil, then there will be no catastrophe. But if we cannot, then catastrophe may be imminent.

Whether society can substitute away from conventional crude oil is clear: we can. First, much peak-oil analysis focuses solely on conventional crude and ignores heavy crude such as the Canadian oil sands. Second, with the introduction of electric cars, we can substitute even further away from oil to run our cars on natural gas, coal, or even nuclear power. Thus, it is hard to argue that a peak in conventional crude oil production leads to catastrophe and that governments should actively work to delay the peak.

Although oil peaking may not lead directly to catastrophe, there are other issues to consider. First, although substitution is certainly possible, substitution is costly. Substituting from cheaper oil to more expensive electric cars will decrease our standard of living as oil production declines. Second, each of the substitutions given earlier has environmental costs. Coal and heavy crudes have much higher greenhouse gas emissions; natural gas supply is even more limited than oil; and nuclear power has catastrophic risks that rival anything that could be imagined from peak oil. Thus substitution to other resources is fraught with other difficulties.

The catastrophes predicted by peak-oil analysis are unlikely to follow as a direct consequence of a peak in global conventional crude oil production. Nonetheless, there is substantial scope for policies to improve oil markets. Hotelling's analysis points to a number of market failures, for example unpriced externalities from pollution, common pool extraction, excessive private discount rates, market power, and insecure property rights. Each of these market failures leads to oil markets that are not best for society. Similarly, concerns about sustainability remain: how can we meet the needs of current generations without compromising the ability of future generations to meet their needs? Peak-oil analysis can be helpful by heightening attention to these areas with legitimate scope for policy.

Stephen P. Holland

See also: Common Pool Resources; Exhaustible Resources; Hotelling, Harold; Sustainability

Further Reading

Brandt, Adam. 2006. Testing Hubbert. *Energy Policy* 35(6): 3074–3088.

Holland, Stephen P. 2008. Modeling Peak Oil. *Energy Journal* 29(2): 61–80.

Porter, Richard C. 2006. Beyond Oil: The View from Hubbert's Peak/The End of Oil: On the Edge of a Perilous New World/The Long Emergency: Surviving the Converging Catastrophes of the Twenty-First Century. *Journal of Economic Literature* 44(1): 186–190.

Smith, James L. 2009. World Oil: Market or Mayhem? *Journal of Economic Perspectives* 23(3): 145–164.

Pearce, David W.

Born in 1941, David Pearce was a widely respected environmental economist who made major contributions in both theory and policy. He was a prolific researcher (more than 50 books and 300 articles in scientific journals) and also held important policy positions. Professor Pearce was educated at Oxford and the London School of Economics, and from the 1970s until his untimely death in 2005, was one of the foremost European environmental economists, establishing a name for himself when most of the well-known environmental economists were in the United States.

Professor Pearce held academic positions at a number of universities in the United Kingdom, but is probably best known for the contributions he made at the University College of London (1989–2004), where he founded and directed the Centre for Social and Economic Research on the Global Environment, a very influential resource center and the scholarly heart of the graduate program there.

Professor Pearce made contributions in many areas, including valuation of environmental resources, design of economic incentives for environmental improvement, the economics of climate change, the double dividend of environmental taxation, and the environment and economic development. He is best known for his work in benefit–cost analysis of environmental resources and environmental quality, and for his work in sustainability.

His interest in benefit–cost analysis was central to his role as an advisor to the UK secretary of state, where his work lead to the eventually publication of one of his most influential books, *Blueprint for a Green Economy* (1990). He also was a convening author of the economic report of the Intergovernmental Panel on Climate Change (IPCC) and worked extensively with the Organisation of Economic Co-operation and Development (OECD).

Professor Pearce's 1993 book, *World without End*, was extremely important in creating an operational definition of sustainability that could be accepted by both economists and ecologists. Rather than focusing on extractable natural resources as did some neoclassical economists, he transformed the capital theory approach to sustainability, by considering environmental resources that generated a flow of ecological services.

Professor Pearce received a number of honors and awards over his career, with two coming from the United Nations Environmental Program (UNEP) and the European Association of Environmental and Resource Economists. In 1989, the UNEP included Professor Pearce in the Global 500 Roll of Honor for Services to the World Environment, and shortly before his death he received the Lifetime Achievement Award from European Association of Environmental and Resource Economists.

James R. Kahn

See also: Biodiversity; Nonmarket Valuation; Sustainability

Further Reading

Pearce, David W., and Dominique Moran. 1994. *The Economic Value of Biodiversity.* Earthscan.

Pearce, David W., and Jeremy J. Warford. 1993.*World without End: Economics, Environment and Sustainable Development.* Washington, D.C.: World Bank.

Pearce, David W., and Jules N. Pretty. 1993. *Economic Values and the Natural World.* Earthscan.

Pearce, David W., and R. Kerry Turner. 1990. *Economics of Natural Resources and the Environment.* Johns Hopkins University Press.

Pearce, David W., Anil Markandya, and Edward B. Barbier (editors). 1989. *Blueprint for a Green Economy: A Report.* Vol. 1. Earthscan.

Philosophy

Environmental economics is the study of how to make the best decisions that involve or affect the natural environment. As with any kind of decision, people are bound to have differing opinions about what constitutes a best environmental decision, and even environmental economists often disagree among themselves. The difficulty in reaching agreement on whether a decision is best, or even whether it is simply good or bad, derives from the fact that people vary in their ethical stances on which their judgment of the decision is based. Two broad categories of possible ethical stances are biocentrism and anthropocentrism.

In biocentrism, both humans and nonhuman species have inherent value and the value of humans is not given special status relative to the value of nonhuman species. In particular, the value of nonhuman species does not depend on their value to humans. One form of biocentrism is known as the land ethic, which was popularized by Aldo Leopold in 1949. According to the land ethic, humans are members, not masters, of the environment, and it is our duty to promote the integrity, stability, and beauty of the environment. Another, perhaps more extreme, form of biocentrism is known as deep ecology, in which human harm to the environment is acceptable only for satisfying essential human needs.

Anthropocentrism focuses on the value of humans, and nonhuman species have value only through their benefits to humans. In other words, nonhuman species do not have inherent value. There are various ethical stances within anthropocentrism including: egalitarianism, which focuses on human equality and maintaining minimum standards of living; and utilitarianism, which focuses on maximizing total human happiness (utility), with less concern for how it is distributed among individuals.

Anthropocentrism is the dominant ethical stance within economics, and not because it is necessarily the ethical stance held by its practitioners. As social scientists, one of the responsibilities of economists is to maintain a certain level of objectivity, but many of the tenets of biocentrism are difficult to incorporate objectively into the decision process. For example, even if the economist believes that nonhuman species have inherent value, there is no accepted way to measure inherent value, which is important for the purposes of benefit–cost analysis. In the absence of a way to measure them, they are left out of the analysis. (Of course, the paradox is that leaving inherent values out of the analysis is a subjective choice.) On the other hand, there are relatively objective ways to measure values to humans with nonmarket valuation methods (the aggregation of values to individuals into a measure of total value is less objective, however). As another example, it is difficult to see any objective way to determine whether an action promotes the integrity, stability, and beauty of the environment. Some economists, however, and in particular many ecological economists, adopt ethical standpoints that vary from the traditional, anthropocentric one.

Within anthropocentrism, there are many fundamental areas in which the philosophies of economists differ. One of these concerns the appropriateness of using benefit–cost analysis to make environmental decisions. Even supposing that all the benefits and all the costs could be measured in a relatively uncontroversial way, is it always appropriate to implement a policy for which these measured benefits outweigh the costs? For example, should a policy that leads to the extinction of a species be implemented if its benefits outweigh the costs? According to a strict interpretation of benefit–cost analysis, it should be, yet many would feel uncomfortable with its adoption. The general consensus in economics is that a benefit–cost comparison should be one of several inputs into a decision, and that it is more appropriate for relatively small changes. The precautionary principle and safe minimum standards are attempts to qualify the use of benefit–cost analysis when there is uncertainty regarding the implications of a policy or when there is potential for species extinction.

It is not agreed upon that it is appropriate in the first place to assign dollar values to environmental goods and services. Most economists argue that it is, and that doing so helps put benefits and costs of a policy into common units so that they can more easily be compared. But a few economists, and many noneconomists, believe that some values are incommensurable, that is, that they cannot be measured on a cardinal money scale. If true, this would further weaken the strict or dominant use of benefit–cost analysis as a decision criterion.

The relative importance of efficiency and equity is a debate ubiquitous in general economics. While the reason economists tend to focus more on efficiency might only be that it less obviously involves subjective judgments than equity analyses, virtually any normative economic suggestion involves some weighing of efficiency and equity. It is often not explicitly acknowledged, however. This relates to an even more fundamental debate about whether economists should even engage in normative analyses.

Another fundamental debate concerns how to weigh future benefits and costs relative to benefits and costs occurring today. It is generally agreed within economics that future benefits and costs should be discounted, but there is wide disagreement regarding the amount by which they should be discounted. A small change in the discount rate can often have significant consequences on the conclusions of the study. The issue of discounting is particularly relevant to recent debates about appropriate actions in the face of climate change.

Sustainability has become a buzzword recently, but one of the reasons why it is difficult to reach agreement on which sustainable actions to take is that there are many definitions of sustainability that can conflict with one another. What exactly is to be sustained? Human welfare? A minimum standard of living? The environment as it is? Is any damage to the environment allowed? Are different environmental amenities substitutable? We have yet to reach a consensus on these and related questions.

What these philosophical debates all have in common is that they arise from fundamental disagreements that cannot be settled by the accumulation of data or by testing. Generally, in order to settle a disagreement, the parties must agree on a common standard against which to test a proposition. For example, if parties disagree about whether people behave consistent with a personal discount rate of 10 percent, they can gather data to test this since they agree on the definition of discount rate and they agree that people with a discount rate of 10 percent should act in a certain way. But one party cannot argue that economic analysts should use a discount rate of 10 percent because there is no agreed upon standard on which to judge this statement. Even if, after an empirical investigation, the parties find that, indeed, people do behave consistent with a 10 percent discount rate, a party could question whether the appropriate standard is what people tend to do. The standard might just as well be an ethical standard, for example that future and current generations have equal standing.

Economists can partially circumvent these debates by examining how sensitive their analyses are to different beliefs. Generally, however, responsible economists should probably be more explicit about fundamental beliefs that affect their analyses than they have been. However, many might lack the training to even recognize that these beliefs permeate their work in the first place. The fact that there remain fundamental beliefs about which economists disagree is also evidence that, in many respects, economic thinking is not as well-defined as it often first appears to be and that it is often grounded in a less-than-obvious philosophical paradigm.

Matthew G. Interis

See also: Benefit–Cost Analysis; Discounting; Ecological Economics; Nonmarket Valuation; Precautionary Principle; Safe Minimum Standard; Sustainability; Welfare and Equity

Further Reading

Aldred, J. 2006. Incommensurability and Monetary Valuation. *Land Economics* 82(2): 141–161.

Leopold, A. 1949. *A Sand County Almanac*. New York: Oxford University Press.

Ward, F. 2006. Economic Thinking. Chapter 2 in *Environmental and Natural Resource Economics*. Upper Saddle River, NJ: Pearson Prentice Hall.

Pigou, Arthur C.

Arthur Pigou was born November 18, 1877, on the Isle of Wight, and died March 7, 1959, in Cambridge, England. After being educated at Harrow, he went on to study at King's College, the University of Cambridge, where by 1900, he had obtained a first in both the Historical and Moral Sciences Tripos. He was elected as a Fellow of King's College in 1902, where he spent the rest of his academic life. He published over 12 books and contributed to over 100 articles during his career, holding an appointment as Professor of Political Economy for 35 years, having succeeded Alfred Marshall to the chair in 1908. Among his contemporaries, the best-known was John Maynard Keynes, whose lectureship at Cambridge Pigou privately funded until the former was elected Fellow of King's College in 1909.

Pigou is most commonly remembered for placing welfare at the center of the discipline of economics. Based on the premise that utility was measurable, he proposed in *Wealth and Welfare* (1912) that improved economic welfare would result from: an increase in national income, an increase in the absolute share of national income going to the poor; and, a reduction in the variability of national income, especially the share received by the poor. Pigou expanded on these ideas in *The Economics of Welfare* first published in 1920, where he argued that economic welfare will not be maximized if there is a divergence between what he termed the marginal net social product and marginal private net product of economic activities. Importantly, he highlighted the notion of externalities with reference to the possibility that, "costs are thrown upon people not directly concerned, through, say, uncompensated damage done to surrounding woods by sparks from railway engines . . ." (Pigou, 1932, p. 134), and also provided the argument for what is now termed a Pigouvian tax (subsidy), "when competition rules and social and private net product at the margin diverge, it is theoretically possible to put matters right by the imposition of a tax or the grant of a subsidy . . ." (Pigou, 1932, p. 381).

Pigou's analysis of welfare was subsequently displaced by the writings of economists such as Lionel Robbins who challenged his approach as being unscientific on two counts: it was based on utility being measurable, and it analyzed what ought to be as opposed to what is, that is, Pigou's propositions were normative, and hence value-laden. Also, after his death, Pigou's policy prescription for externalities was criticized by Ronald Coase who argued that assignment of property rights would allow negotiation between parties, resulting in internalization of an externality.

Although overshadowed by Keynes' *General Theory*, Pigou also made a significant contribution to macroeconomics. Defining real balances as the sum of the money supply and government bonds relative to prices, he developed the so-called Pigou effect, whereby an economy could escape the liquidity trap. Specifically, if an aggregate demand shock causes unemployment to rise, prices will fall, thereby increasing real balances, raising consumption, and pushing the economy back toward full employment.

Ian Sheldon

See also: Coase, Ronald; Coase Theorem; Externality; Pigouvian Taxes; Subsidies; Welfare

Further Reading

Pigou, A. C. 1912. *Wealth and Welfare*. London: Macmillan.
Pigou, A. C. 1932. *The Economics of Welfare*, 4th ed. London: Macmillan.
Pigou, A. C. 1943. The Classical Stationary State. *Economic Journal* 37(212): 343–351.

Pigouvian Taxes

A Pigouvian tax, introduced by British economist Arthur C. Pigou, aims to correct economic distortions caused by negative externalities, the imposition of social costs on other parties without compensation. Without correction, negative externalities may exceed the socially optimal level. A Pigouvian tax on a good or service that generates a negative externality can restore the optimum by reducing such activities to efficient levels.

In environmental economics, Pigouvian taxes are targeted at negative externalities such as air and water pollution or solid waste. A prominent example includes carbon taxes, imposed on the per unit generation of greenhouse gases such as carbon dioxide that contribute to climate change. Other examples include charges for nutrient loadings in effluent from wastewater treatment plants, and gas-guzzler taxes on low-fuel efficiency automobiles.

Ronald Coase, believed a Pigouvian tax to be unnecessary and, in fact, a suboptimal way to correct the pollution problem. Coase argues that negative externalities such as pollution are reciprocal in that it takes both a polluting party and a receiving party to create the problem. A Pigouvian tax assigns the liability on the polluting party (which they then share via the tax burden sharing phenomenon), and thus there is no incentive for the receiving party to take action to minimize pollution's cost on them by taking defensive action such as filtering dirty air or water or simply moving away. If the costs of the defensive actions are lower than the cost of cleaning the pollution, social costs would be lower if the solution relied more on defensive action and less on the cleanup level dictated by the Pigouvian tax. Coase, skeptical of market intervention, argued the Pareto optimal solution lies in a negotiated outcome between the affected parties where the correct combination of cleanup and defensive action can be agreed upon.

In 1974, Martin Weitzman published an article that contrasted price-based economic mechanisms for correcting negative externalities, such as Pigouvian taxes, with quantity-based mechanisms, such as emissions standards (or tradable permits).

Price and quantity instruments can both lead to efficient outcomes provided that the marginal cost and marginal benefits of pollution control are known with certainty. However, if the marginal cost function is not known ex ante, then the preferred approach to the problem depends on the perceived relative steepness of the marginal cost and marginal benefit functions in the neighborhood of the policy space. If the marginal benefit of emissions control is relatively flat in the range of the policy outcomes considered (i.e., emission reductions have similar marginal values over a wide range of outcomes), a tax is the preferred option as it minimizes the distortion from an uncertain marginal cost function by allowing the pollutant to vary at the fixed tax rate. Alternatively, if the marginal benefit of emissions control is rather steep (i.e., high levels of emissions are very damaging), a quantity-based emissions mechanism, such as an emissions standard, is preferred.

On the innate preferences of some parties for the price or quantity approach, Weitzman opines:

> From a strictly theoretical point of view there is really nothing to recommend one mode of control over the other. This notwithstanding, I think it is a fair generalization to say that the average economist in the Western marginalist tradition has at least a vague preference toward indirect control by prices, just as the typical non-economist leans toward the direct regulation of quantities. (Weitzman, p. 477)

Weitzman goes on to say that the traditional economist's confidence in the superiority of the price instrument may be misguided if it relies on the premise that the proper price to charge is known with certainty, a matter that is typically elusive in practice. The foundation of his article is that uncertainty about the cost and benefit functions underlie the uncertainty about whether the price or quantity approach is preferred. Others have extended the Weitzman framework to consider prices versus quantities in a dynamic setting that is more reflective of actual policy conditions. They show that quantity instruments, such as cap-and-trade with banking and borrowing between periods, can outperform a tax in a multiperiod setting where policies are set in one period and costs and benefits are resolved in subsequent periods. They find that the flexibility of the quantity-based approach allows firms to adjust their emissions abatement to equate expected marginal costs across periods better than a price instrument can.

To this day, many economists still favor the Pigouvian tax (price) approach to a quantity approach, albeit for different reasons than stated by Weitzman, namely because of their revenue-generating characteristics, a consideration heightened by the prevalence of fiscal deficits throughout much of the world. Money raised through Pigouvian taxes can be used to replace distortionary (e.g., income) taxes in the current system and thereby enhance overall economic efficiency (referred to as a double dividend). While usually attributed to the tax approach, it is important to recognize that revenue can also be raised with a quantity-based emissions trading system that sells emission allowances to the regulated community through an auction or other means. The double-dividend hypothesis, however, has been extensively challenged. First, there is the relevant political challenge in ensuring that revenue raised in a Pigouvian tax system will actually be used to reduce distortionary taxes elsewhere in the system. But there have also been challenges based on theoretical grounds given that pollution taxes themselves create distortions in the real net wage. Subsequent research has examined whether Pigouvian taxes create negative *tax interaction effects* with existing distortions that can negate the double-dividend benefits. The results are indeterminate, and depend highly on the type of policy and model specification.

Brian C. Murray

See also: Air Pollution; Coase Theorem; Emissions Trading; Externality; Solid Waste; Subsidies; Water Pollution

Further Reading

Bovenberg, A. Lans, and Lawrence H. Goulder. 2000. Environmental Taxation and Regulation in a Second-Best Setting, in A. Auerbach and M. Feldstein (editors), *Handbook of Public Economics,* 2nd ed. New York: North Holland.

Coase, Ronald H. 1960. The Problem of Social Cost. *Journal of Law and Economics* 3(1): 1–44.

Fullerton, Don, and Gilbert Metcalf. 1998. Environmental Taxes and the Double-Dividend Hypothesis: Did You Really Expect Something for Nothing? *Chicago-Kent Law Review* 73: 221–256.

Murray, Brian C., Richard G. Newell, and William A. Pizer. 2009. Balancing Cost and Emissions Certainty: An Allowance Reserve for Cap-and-Trade. *Review of Environmental Economics and Policy* 3(1): 84–103.

Pigou, Arthur C. 1920. *The Economics of Welfare*. London: Macmillan.

Weitzman, Martin. 1974. Prices vs. Quantities. *The Review of Economic Studies* 41(4): 477–491.

Pollution Abatement Costs

Benefit–cost analysis is a tool used to evaluate the social desirability of a public policy. Suppose, for example, that firms in an industry emit sulfur dioxide (SO_2), which can cause disease in people and acid precipitation, which harms ecosystems. Because these health and ecological effects are externalities of the firms that produce them, government intervention may be justified to correct this market failure. Under the U.S. Clean Air Act, for example, a number of regulations have been promulgated to address sulfur dioxide emissions. Before such regulations are promulgated a benefit–cost analysis (BCA) is typically conducted to determine if, at the stringency of regulation proposed, the benefits of the regulation will exceed its costs.

In a BCA the positive effects of a regulation are the benefits, while the negative effects are the costs. This distinction is sometimes more a matter of convention; the reduction of a benefit is a cost, and vice-versa. Net benefits to society are estimated by subtracting the total costs from the total monetized benefits. Estimating the total cost of a regulation is often characterized as being relatively simple—particularly when compared to the estimation of benefits—however, the estimation of costs can also present some challenges.

It is important to realize that all costs are really opportunity costs. Even when an expenditure is relatively straightforward—when, for example, a firm purchases a piece of capital equipment, such as a scrubber, to control its SO_2 emissions—the real economic cost is the forgone opportunity to use the resources for some other purpose: to buy an alternative piece of equipment, for example, or to increase profits that may be returned to shareholders for them to buy other things. The general objective of the cost side of a BCA is to record the social cost of a regulation; we record all costs, regardless of who bears them by foregoing other opportunities. The total burden on the economy is, then, the sum of all opportunity costs incurred as a result of the regulation.

It is also important to underscore the last part of the previous sentence: "as a result of the regulation." The appropriate measure of cost in BCA is incremental social cost—the additional costs associated with a new or more stringent environmental regulation or policy. One common challenge in estimating costs is determining which among the costs a firm incurs is truly incremental, and thus attributable to regulation. For example, firms regularly invest in new production equipment, and production processes typically becomes cleaner over time, even in the absence of regulation. A firm facing tougher regulation may, then, invest in new capital equipment sooner than it might have otherwise. The analyst must determine how much of such an investment is truly incremental.

While all costs are opportunity costs and social costs, we often categorize them in other ways as well. There are, for example, compliance costs, indirect costs, and transitional costs. Within these categories we might create further distinctions between capital costs, operating costs, administrative costs, and other opportunity costs.

Compliance costs are the expenditures facilities make to reduce or prevent pollution to comply with a regulation. They are usually composed of two main components: capital and operating costs.

Capital costs include expenditures on the retrofit of existing structures or new equipment with the primary purpose of treating, capturing, recycling, and/or preventing pollution. These one-time costs include expenditures for equipment installation and startup. In BCA, capital costs are usually annualized over the period of the useful life of the equipment so that they may be compared with operating costs (see later). An annualized value is the amount one would have to pay in every year so that the net present value of payments equals the original purchase price of the capital equipment.

Operating costs are recurring expenditures on salaries and wages, energy inputs, materials and supplies, purchased services, and maintenance of equipment associated with pollution abatement.

Administrative, enforcement, and monitoring costs are incurred by governments to assure entities comply with regulations. These costs incurred by federal, state, and/or local governments need to be included when estimating impacts of a regulation to calculate the full social costs of a program or rule.

Consumer surplus losses occur when firms' increased costs of production are passed along to consumers in the form of higher prices. As we noted earlier, a reduction in a benefit is a cost. This is an example: to consumers, higher prices represent a reduction in the benefits they derive from consumption. This analysis can be tricky, however: according to economic theory, consumers pay exactly what it costs firms in a competitive industry to produce the last unit they buy. Thus, there is no social cost to reducing consumption on the margin (i.e., for small amounts at existing levels of production). Because consumer surplus losses would only be important if relatively large changes in output result, they are often ignored in BCA.

Regulations can cause dead weight loss beyond the directly regulated market via the regulatory interaction effect as a new regulation in one market can cause additional dead weight loss in other markets. Even when a new regulation introduces a distortion in just one market, it may exacerbate preexisting distortions in other markets. An important example of how a regulation can interact with preexisting distortions can be found in the labor market. Taxes on wage earnings may introduce a large deadweight loss (a social cost that is not offset by revenue raised to meet other social purposes) in the labor market. Regulations that increase the cost of consumer goods effectively drive the after-tax wage still lower; the real wage rate is the rate at which a worker can trade-off hours worked for goods purchased. When this occurs the worker may want to substitute from work to leisure, that is, work even less.

There are two contexts in which the costs of regulation have typically been estimated. Some researchers have looked back at the cost of specific regulations that have already been implemented. In addition, policy analysts often must attempt to predict the costs of prospective regulations. In most instances of both prospective and retrospective studies the focus has been on affected firms' compliance costs, rather than administrative costs or effects on consumers.

In order to estimate the costs of complying with environmental regulation an analyst might ideally perform an econometric exercise. She would gather data on plants operating with and without the environmental regulation in question, control for other factors such as regional differences in input prices or climate, and isolate an estimate of the regulation on costs. This may only be feasible retrospectively, however. Regulation is, virtually by definition, intended to compel or incentivize firms to do something that they are not already doing. There may not be data with which to estimate the effects of regulations that have not yet been imposed. Thus analysts charged with predicting the effects of proposed regulations often avail themselves of other expedients. Engineering studies estimate costs of compliance based on experts' judgments as to what technology is available to comply with the regulation and the costs of its acquisition and operation. One problem with engineering studies is that estimates are usually developed only for a typical plant, and it is often assumed that this entity is already operating efficiently. The impacts on a broader spectrum of real-world plants could be quite different.

A second approach is to survey plants likely to be affected by the regulation and have each predict its costs of compliance. While this approach has the advantage of reaching a representative cross-section of regulated plants, it also has some drawbacks. Since those completing such surveys are often not economists, they may not carefully distinguish incremental costs from routine investment and expenditure, or it may be time-consuming and expensive to assist them in doing so. Perhaps more importantly, survey respondents may have an incentive to respond strategically. That is, a businessperson may feel that she is likely to face a reduced regulatory burden if she overstates her compliance costs. At the very least, she may feel she has little to gain by carefully considering her cost estimates, and may report only a technically feasible way of meeting regulatory requirements rather than going to the effort of identifying the most cost-effective way of doing so.

A number of commentators have suggested that survey respondents do, in fact, most often overstate the costs of regulatory compliance, generally on the argument that those surveyed do not appreciate that improved technology will likely reduce compliance costs. To the extent that regulatory impact analysts rely on such surveys in forming their estimates, they might overstate costs as well. However the academic literature is mixed on this issue. Several studies find that reported abatement costs understate the true costs of abatement while others find the opposite.

Econometric studies are often more feasible in conducting retrospective evaluation of the costs of regulation, both because more relevant data are typically available and academic researchers are often operating under less stringent time constraints than do analysts predicting the effects of regulation under development. In the United States retrospective cost studies are often performed using data from the Pollution Abatement Costs and Expenditures (PACE) survey on pollution abatement-related operating costs and capital expenditures for the U.S. manufacturing sector.

The PACE survey collects data on costs of pollution treatment (e.g., end-of-pipe controls), pollution prevention (e.g., production process enhancements to prevent pollution from being produced), disposal, and recycling. The survey was sent to approximately 20,000 establishments (who are required by law to respond to it) and was conducted annually by the U.S. Census Bureau from 1973 to 1994 (except in 1987) and then again in 1999 and 2005.

The PACE survey contains operating costs and capital expenditures disaggregated by media: air, water, and solid waste; and by abatement activity: pollution treatment, recycling, disposal, and pollution prevention. Total operating costs are further disaggregated into: salary and wages, energy costs, materials and supplies, contract work, and depreciation.

The PACE survey data—both aggregate and establishment-level—have been used to analyze a wide range of policy questions. These include assessing the impact of pollution abatement expenditures on productivity growth, investment, labor demand, environmental performance, plant location decisions, and international competitiveness.

Ronald J. Shadbegian and R. David Simpson

See also: Benefit–Cost Analysis; Benefits and Costs of the Clean Air Act; Clean Air Act; Environmental Valuation; Externality; Regulation; Welfare Economics

Further Reading

Becker, Randy, and Vernon Henderson. 2000. Effects of Air Quality Regulations on Polluting Industries. *Journal of Political Economy* 108(2): 379–421.

Gray, Wayne B., and Ronald J. Shadbegian. 2002. Pollution Abatement Costs, Regulation, and Plant-level Productivity, in W.B. Gray (editor), *The Economic Costs and Consequences of Environmental Regulation*. Aldershot, UK: Ashgate Publishing.

Gray, Wayne B., and Ronald J. Shadbegian. 2003. Plant Vintage, Technology, and Environmental Regulation. *Journal of Environmental Economics and Management* 46: 384–402.

Harrington, Winston, Richard D. Morgenstern, and Peter Nelson. 2000. On the Accuracy of Regulatory Cost Estimates. *Journal of Policy Analysis and Management* 19(2): 297–322.

Morgenstern, Richard D., William A. Pizer, and Jhih-Shyang Shih. 2001. The Cost of Environmental Protection. *Review of Economics and Statistics* 83(4): 732–738.

Shadbegian, Ronald J., and Wayne B. Gray. 2005. Pollution Abatement Expenditures and Plant-Level Productivity: A Production Function Approach. *Ecological Economics* 54: 96–208.

Precautionary Principle

The precautionary principle (PP) asserts that acting to avoid or mitigate threats of uncertain but potentially serious environmental harm should be accorded high priority in public policy. There are many definitions of the PP in the literature, but most of them can be grouped into three broad categories, on a weaker–stronger scale. The thread common to all three categories is the focus on forestalling uncertain future harm. Here are examples of each category, abbreviated and paraphrased in every case, with emphasis added to highlight key differences: uncertainty about harmful consequences *does not justify failure to take precautionary action* (Bergen Declaration 1990), plausible but uncertain harm *justifies precautionary intervention* (UNESCO 2005), and uncertain harm *requires intervention, and the burden of proof is assigned to the proponent* of the proposed risky action (Wingspread Statement 1998).

The PP has two broad categories of potential application: to potential threats from novel interventions (look before you leap), and to possible adverse surprises when systems are overstressed, for example by exploitation and/or pollution, in the course of business as usual (i.e., a stitch in time saves nine). Novel interventions offer an opportunity that is absent in business as usual (BAU) situations—the proposed intervention can be intercepted and tested for potential harm before it becomes embedded in the social, economic, and environmental systems—but if that opportunity is foregone the distinction between novel interventions and BAU disappears and the initial advantage of the novel interventions case, from a risk management perspective, is lost.

It is clear that novel interventions, before the go/no-go decision, provide the most fertile opportunities for precautionary intervention. But suppose we decide to charge ahead and, if necessary, clean up the mess later. Then, having forfeited the opportunity for prerelease caution, precaution can be expressed only by alertness to early warnings of damage and willingness to implement remedies before we can be sure of cause and effect.

Beginning in the 1980s, international conferences, agreements, and treaties endorsed precaution in various guises. Some governments and international bodies have endorsed the PP in principle (e.g., Canada), and some of them have incorporated it into some areas of policy practice (e.g., the European Union). In the United States, there are instances where the PP is applied to protect human health. Pharmaceutical products are tightly regulated by the Food and Drug Administration, which requires evidence of safety and effectiveness before approving drugs for general release. Roughly similar procedures apply to pesticides.

In U.S. environmental matters, the PP remains more of niche consideration: the usual approach to environmental hazards is to wait until there is evidence of damage and then set a regulatory standard. Endangered species laws apply a systematic precautionary approach—threatened species are identified and monitored, and serious protections are provided for the critical habitats of those identified as endangered. For renewable resources (e.g., fisheries), management for sustainability introduces an element of precaution, and restrictions on harvest often are invoked when evidence suggests a possible breach of the sustainability constraint.

Suppose that, among the plethora of objections that have been raised concerning the PP, we were to concede that three must be taken seriously: the PP does not take risk–risk trade-offs seriously, the PP privileges unfounded fears, and the PP stifles innovation.

The first objection could be blunted by specifying the PP carefully so as to direct it toward risks that are in some sense unusually serious. The second challenges us to be more explicit about the kinds of evidence that would justify invoking more or less drastic precautionary interventions. The third can be addressed by specifying a flexible, iterative testing and active learning process that hones in on serious risks while moving less risky innovations toward implementation. A robust PP should explicitly relate damage conditions, knowledge conditions, and remedies. Consider the following:

> Credible scientific evidence of a plausible threat of disproportionate and (mostly but not always) asymmetric harm calls for avoidance and remediation measures beyond those recommended by ordinary risk management.

The call to action is triggered by scientifically credible evidence of a disproportionate and in many cases asymmetric threat, such that the loss from the worst case outcome (even if unlikely) is disproportionately large relative to the gain from the most likely outcomes, and the remedies indicated are not restricted to those that would pass a benefit cost filter even if substantial risk aversion is built-in.

This PP departs from ordinary risk management in at least three distinct ways. First, its approach to risk assessment is open to complex systems thinking, whereas standard risk assessment models tend to be overly reductive; and it is alert to the possibility of systemic risk, whereas standard risk management tends to be too willing to take refuge in the law of large numbers. Second, it is more even-handed in its stance toward diagnostic risks (balancing the desires to avoid false-positives and false-negatives regarding harm and threat thereof) and open to adjusting the evidence requirement to the severity of the threat, whereas standard risk management bends over backward to avoid false-positives. Third, while it is attentive to costs and cost-effectiveness, it explicitly denies any commitment to a utilitarian (e.g., benefit–cost) filter for proposed remedies in the face of disproportionate threats.

A comprehensive precautionary policy would be sensitive to the need for: early warning to reduce the costs of remedies and increase their chances of success; scope for learning to reduce ignorance, narrow the uncertainties, better specify the possible outcomes and probabilities, and develop and test strategies for avoidance, mitigation, and adaptation; affordable remedies, which are helpful in building and sustaining coalitions in support of solutions among contemporaries, and intergenerational commitments to solutions; and specific policies to reduce or mitigate disproportionate negative impacts of precaution on particular locations or socioeconomic groups.

Here we focus on the first two elements: early warning and scope for learning. For novel interventions, a protocol of screening, prerelease testing, and postrelease surveillance (STS) serves as a metaphor for a family of related remedies that incorporate these considerations. STS is feasible if the effects of an innovation can at the outset be confined in space and time. Sequential steps of screening and testing entail progressively less secure confinement as we become more confident that the risks are modest and manageable. Each step ends with a decision selecting one of three options: proceed to general release, continue to the next step in the testing process, or, if the evidence suggests unacceptable risks in the next step, terminate testing and prohibit general release. For risks thought acceptable, research should focus also on risk management, mitigation, and adaptation. Should evidence of unacceptable risk fail to arise during screening and prerelease testing, general release proceeds with much more assurance than if we had simply taken our chances at the outset. Release is followed by a program of postrelease surveillance to check for unexpected harmful consequences—possible but less likely given the extensive prerelease testing—and research on methods of remediating any damage discovered.

This process cannot eliminate all risk but if all goes well, step by step, prohibitions may become pauses, precautionary accommodations may turn out to be temporary, and levels of insurance and self-protection may be adjusted as more is learned. Precaution is directed toward those innovations that present unusual threats, and is therefore a lesser impediment to innovation in general.

Harmful surprises from business-as-usual stresses may pose greater challenges. Economists often assume that there is a broad domain in which BAU stresses can be managed by systematic implementation of policies to internalize externalities, optimize provision of public goods, and to ensure that resource rents are reinvested. Such BAU policies and institutions may be adequate for sustainability problems in many resilient natural resource and environmental systems, but complex systems theory warns us that harmful regime shifts may occur suddenly.

The ultimate goal of precaution is to avoid risk dilemmas, where the threat has gotten so far out of hand that potential harm and costs of remedy are both enormous: we are doomed if we do and doomed if we don't, the time for precaution is long past, and adaptation is the only tenable fall-back position.

Alan Randall

See also: Climate Change Impacts; Regulation; Risk and Uncertainty; Safe Minimum Standard

Further Reading

Bergen Ministerial Declaration on Sustainable Development in the ECE Region. 1990. UN Doc. A/CONF.151/PC/10; 1 *Yearbook on International Environmental Law* 429, 4312.

Randall, A. 2011. *Risk and Precaution.* Cambridge and New York: Cambridge University Press.

UNESCO. 2005. *The Precautionary Principle*. Paris: World Commission on the Ethics of Scientific Knowledge and Technology.

Wiener, J.B., M.D. Rogers, J.K. Hammitt, and P.H. Sand. 2010. *The Reality of Precaution: Comparing Risk Regulation in the United States and Europe*. Washington, D.C.: RFF Press.

Wingspread Statement on the Precautionary Principle. 1998. http://www.gdrc.org/u-gov/precaution-3.html

Property Rights

A property right in the broad (economic) sense refers to the right, consent, or permission granted to an individual that allows that individual to act in a particular way, or, alternatively, the right of an individual to be free from the harm imposed by the actions of others. When referring to physical property such as land or a house, it might mean the right to use that property in a particular way (e.g., to paint your house bright purple), or the right to sell that property to whomever you choose. However, not all property rights are tied directly to physical property. For example, a firm might have a property right allowing it to generate harmful pollution as a by-product of production. Alternatively, individuals might have a right not to be exposed involuntarily to pollution arising from the activities of others.

Where do these rights come from? In short, they come from society. Society determines what is or is not allowed and therefore the property rights that people have. These rights can be defined legally (for example, through laws, regulations, or legal rules and precedents) or they can emerge from accepted social norms. Once defined, society also needs to enforce those rights, that is, make sure that those rights are protected. For example, the enforcement of property rights is a key function of the judicial system, where courts sort out disputes about who is allowed to do what and impose consequences when they find that someone's property rights have been violated. Possible consequences include ordering an individual to stop acting in a way that violates another's rights and/or requiring payment of compensation for damages or losses due to the violation.

Clearly, individuals care about their property rights. More specifically, an individual's utility, income, and/or wealth will depend on the assignment of property rights. For example, if I have a right to use my land in any way that I want, the land is worth more than if I am restricted in how I can use it (or to whom I can sell it). Similarly, a firm that has the right to generate pollution without having to pay compensation for any resulting damages will earn higher profit than a firm that is prohibited from exceeding a certain level of emissions, or must pay compensation for damages if it exceeds that level. Conversely, all else being equal, an individual who has a property right to clean water will generally have higher utility than a person who does not have that right, either because her water will be cleaner or because, if her water is polluted (as a result of someone else's actions), she will be compensated for the resulting damages.

Although individuals clearly care about their property rights, an important economic question is the role of property rights in determining real outcomes, where by real outcomes we mean the actual use of resources in the economy and the resulting goods or bads that are produced. For example, will society have more pollution under one assignment of property rights than under another? Will the land use decisions that are ultimately made depend on the assignment of property rights?

In essence, property rights determine who has to pay and who gets paid when certain activities occur. Although this has implications for the distribution of income, a famous result known as the Coase theorem states that, under certain conditions, it will not affect real outcomes. Coase's key insight is that, if property rights are well defined and individuals can freely bargain (without income effects), then through bargaining they will arrive at a deal that is mutually beneficial. In addition, although the direction of payment (i.e., who pays whom) under the deal will depend on the assignment of property rights, the real outcome that the individuals agree upon will not.

The insight underlying the Coase theorem has wide applicability and has been demonstrated in a number of different contexts where mutually beneficial trades (bargains) can occur. For example, a well-known result states that, in a simple cap-and-trade system where pollution permits are initially distributed free of charge and the permit market is competitive, the pattern of pollution reductions across firms that emerges after trading does not depend on how the permits were initially distributed. Since the initial distribution of permits defines an assignment of property rights (i.e., each permit gives the holder the right to use or sell the permit), this result is a direct parallel to the Coase theorem.

Although the Coase theorem states that, under certain conditions, the assignment of property rights does not affect real outcomes (after bargaining or trade), importantly, in the real world the conditions needed for this result often fail. For example, bargaining will be difficult or costly when the number of polluters or affected individuals is large. In addition, if individuals can make irreversible investment decisions before bargaining occurs, these conditions can fail. In such cases, property rights can affect real outcomes. More specifically, actions by the government that implicitly or explicitly define property rights can, in turn, create incentives that affect outcomes. A classic example is when the government regulates the use of private property, which some argue constitutes a government taking.

In the United States (and many other countries) the government is allowed to seize private property for public use (e.g., to build a school or a road) under its power of eminent domain. However, the Fifth Amendment of the Constitution requires that it pay just compensation to the landowner for this taking. Some argue that the same protection of private property extends to government actions that do not seize private property but rather regulate its use for a public purpose (e.g., prohibiting the cutting of timber on land that provides habitat to an endangered species). Such actions are often referred to as regulatory takings.

As a property rights issue, the question is whether such an action requires that the government compensate the property owner for the loss in the value of the property that results from the restriction on its use. The rule regarding compensation, that is, whether or how much compensation must be paid, effectively defines the property right. There is considerable debate about the appropriate rule, with private property advocates on one side and proponents of government regulation on the other side. Arguments are often based on notions of fairness or justice. However, from an economic perspective, the questions are whether and how the compensation rule affects the incentives faced by the government and the property owner. These incentives determine the decisions that are ultimately made and hence the real outcomes. An economic evaluation of different rules focuses on how they affect economic efficiency, as measured by aggregate net social benefits, rather than on the fairness of the implied assignment of property rights.

The compensation rule can affect the incentives of both the government and the landowner. If the government is concerned more about its own outlays than about the costs borne by society as a whole, then if it does not have to compensate the landowner for his loss, the government will view the regulation as less costly and hence have an incentive to overregulate. This argument has been used to suggest that requiring compensation will lead to better (i.e., more efficient) regulatory decisions. Although true, other compensation rules—such as a threshold rule that requires the government to pay compensation only for regulations that are deemed to be inefficient—can also achieve this goal. In addition, when the government has to pay compensation, it will typically have to raise the necessary funds through some form of taxation that distorts behavior and thereby generates a (deadweight) loss for society. This means that rules that can induce efficient incentives without requiring that the government always pay compensation (such as the threshold rule) will be more efficient, all else being equal.

While some have argued for compensation as a way to curb excessive regulation, most of the economic debate about compensation has focused on its impact on landowner incentives. Landowners can make decisions prior to the government action, and those decisions can be influenced by whether they expect to receive compensation (and the nature of the compensation) if a taking occurs. For example, landowners can invest in their property to improve its value. If they expect to be compensated based on the actual value of their property, they will have an incentive to overinvest since they will not internalize the risk that the private investment will be wasted if a taking occurs. This is analogous to the standard moral hazard effect of insurance. It implies that any compensation that is paid should not be tied to the actual value of the property (thereby rewarding the landowner for additional investment even if a taking occurs). Rather, if compensation is paid, it should be independent of the landowner's investment (i.e., lump-sum).

But what should the level of (lump-sum) compensation be? If the actual value of the property will influence the likelihood that the government will regulate it, then the compensation amount should equal the loss the landowner would incur under the *efficient* (rather than the actual) investment decision. If compensation is less than this, the landowner will have an incentive to overinvest so as to make the property more valuable, thereby decreasing the likelihood of being regulated (and receiving less than full compensation). Conversely, if compensation is more than this amount, the landowner will have an incentive to underinvest to make the property less valuable and increase the likelihood that he will receive the excessive compensation. Thus, only full compensation, based on efficient rather than actual investment, eliminates these distortionary incentives.

Similarly, a landowner might be able to influence (or possibly eliminate altogether) the possibility of regulation by developing his land—for example, filling in a wetland in anticipation of a ban on wetlands development or cutting timber to destroy habitat for an endangered species that might subsequently be protected. As in the previous case, not compensating the landowner if a regulation occurs will create an incentive for the landowner to engage in these preemptive activities.

Kathleen Segerson

See also: Coase, Ronald; Coase Theorem; Emissions Trading; Externality; Pigouvian Taxes

Further Reading

Coase, R. H. 1960. The Problem of Social Cost. *Journal of Law and Economics* 3: 1–44.

Demsetz, Harold. 1967. Toward a Theory of Property Rights. *American Economic Review* 57(2): 347–359.

Hahn, Robert W., and Robert N. Stavins. 1992. Economic Incentives for Environmental Protection: Integrating Theory and Practice. *American Economic Review* 82(2): 464–468.

Miceli, Thomas J., and Kathleen Segerson. 2007. The Economics of Eminent Domain: Private Property, Public Use and Just Compensation. *Foundations and Trends in Microeconomics* 3(4): 275–329.

Public Goods

Pure public goods have two defining features. One is nonrivalry, meaning that one person's enjoyment of a good does not diminish the ability of other people to enjoy the same good. The other is nonexcludability, meaning that people cannot be prevented from enjoying the good. Air quality is an important environmental example of a public good. Under most circumstances, one person's breathing of fresh air does not reduce air quality for others to enjoy, and people cannot be prevented from breathing the air. Public goods are defined in contrast to private goods, which are, by definition, both rival and excludable. A sandwich is a private good because one person's consumption clearly diminishes someone else's ability to consume it, and sandwiches are typically excludable to all individuals not willing to pay.

Many environmental resources are characterized as public goods, including water quality, open space, biodiversity, and a stable climate. These examples stand alongside the classic public goods of lighthouses, national defense, and knowledge. In some cases, however, it is reasonable to question whether environmental resources (and even the classic examples) are public goods in a fully pure sense. With open space, for example, congestion among those enjoying it may cause some degree of rivalry, and all open spaces are not accessible to everyone. Nevertheless, many environmental resources come close to satisfying the definition of pure public goods, and even when not exactly pure, the basic concept is useful for understanding the causes of many environmental problems and potential solutions.

From an economics perspective, public goods are of interest because—unlike private goods—they are a source of market failure. The problem is free riding: individuals have little incentive to voluntarily provide public goods when they can simply enjoy the benefits of nonrival and nonexcludable pubic goods provided by others. To see free riding at work, consider the challenge of constructing a bridge where the societal benefits of doing so would exceed the costs. How successful do you think a campaign would be to finance the bridge with voluntary donations? It is not hard to imagine how such a campaign would fail, because many (if not most) individuals would choose to make no donation, hoping others would contribute enough to finance the bridge for everyone to enjoy. In this scenario, the market failure would be that no bridge is constructed despite the fact that a bridge would make everyone better off.

Seeking to prevent such underprovision of public goods is one of the primary economic rationales for government. While markets allocate private goods efficiently, governmental intervention is usually required for the efficient (or even reasonable) allocation of public goods. Indeed, this explains why goods such as bridges, parks, police protection, and fire departments are usually financed with tax revenues that governments collect. Governments can thus serve as a coordinating mechanism that provides public goods for the benefit of society.

The same public-goods rationale applies to environmental protection. Because individuals and firms face free-riding incentives when it comes to protecting the environment, policies are often put in place to limit pollution, restrict resource exploitation, or create the right incentives to promote or protect environmental quality. Environmental policies that promote economic efficiency are those for which the societal benefits exceed the costs. Social benefit-cost analysis is the tool that economists use to make such determinations. Yet, with most environmental public goods, special techniques are often required to estimate the economic benefits or costs because environmental quality is rarely traded in markets and therefore does not have directly observable prices. For example, there are certainly benefits of improving air quality, but how are such benefits to be quantified?

The answer is various techniques of so-called nonmarket valuation. These range from simply asking people their willingness to pay (or willingness to accept) for changes in environmental quality to various ways of using other markets to infer implicit values for the environment. There are stated-preference techniques that are based on survey methods and include contingent valuation and choice experiments. There are also revealed-preference techniques that use actual market behavior and include the hedonic price method, the travel cost method, and averting behavior.

The notion of public goods is also becoming increasingly important at the international and global levels. Many environmental problems transcend national boundaries, with climate change being the most prominent example, and maintaining a stable climate is essentially a global public good. Yet the efficient provision of global public goods faces an even greater set of challenges. One challenge is that free-riding incentives are even stronger when the number of people involved is larger. While individuals are typically reluctant to incur private costs for public benefits, they are likely to be more reluctant when their contributions feel like a tiny drop in an even larger bucket.

A second, and important, challenge for providing global public goods is that coordination is difficult among sovereign nations. While policies for environmental protection can be passed at a national level, international coordination requires agreements and enforcement among nations, many of which have different interests and rules of law. There are success stories with disease eradication and the Montreal Protocol for the phaseout of chlorofluorocarbons that deplete the stratospheric ozone layer. But real progress to address greenhouse gas emissions globally and mitigate climate change has thus far eluded efforts within the United Nations. While the future architecture of an international agreement for climate change remains uncertain, it is clear that economic theory on public goods is essential for understanding potential reasons for both failure and success.

Matthew J. Kotchen

See also: Coase Theorem; Nonmarket Valuation; International Environmental Agreements

Further Reading

Barrett, Scott. 2007. *Why Cooperate? The Incentive to Provide Global Public Goods.* Oxford: Oxford University Press.

Olson, Mancur. 1971. *The Logic of Collective Action: Public Goods and the Theory of Groups.* Cambridge, MA: Harvard University Press.

R

Recycling

Recycling is the transformation of materials that would otherwise be waste into useful and valuable resources. It represents one part of a waste management plan with the objectives to reduce materials that are discarded, reuse discarded products with little reprocessing, and recover energy from discarded products through incineration. The environmental appeal of recycling is that it has the potential to reduce the quantity of virgin materials required for production, as well as reduce the amount of environmental contaminants. The economic appeal is that recycling can lead to lower production costs when inputs made from recyclable materials cost less than virgin inputs.

Recycling gained momentum in the United States in the 1960s and 1970s through federal legislation designed to manage waste disposal practices nationally. This legislation culminated in the 1976 Resource Conservation and Recovery Act (RCRA). One of the goals of the act was to conserve natural resources and energy through recycling. In 1988, the Environmental Protection Agency (EPA) raised the national goal for waste reduction and recycling from 10 to 25 percent. In 2002 the goal was further increased to 35 percent. In 2009, the EPA transitioned from a recycling goal to a program called Sustainable Materials Management designed to minimize products' environmental impacts over their entire lifecycle.

Awareness of recycling increased in the public conscious in 1987 when the Mobro 4000 barge searched up and down the East Coast looking for a place to dump its contents of waste. The barge had failed to secure a permit for waste disposal before setting sail from New York and therefore was not allowed to unload its contents. This incident raised public awareness of landfill capacity and efforts to reduce capacity constraints, possibly through recycling. In response to RCRA, many low-quality city dumps closed. Larger and more technologically advanced landfills took their place. As of 2009, there were 1,908 landfills in the United States down from 7,924 in 1988. During that same period, the number of curbside recycling programs increased dramatically, from 1,000 in 1988 to 9,000 in 2009 and the recycling rate increased from 10 percent in 1981 to 34 percent in 2009. As of 2012, the EPA estimates that landfill capacity is not constrained at a national level, though there are locations with regional constraints.

Curbside recycling is one of many programs that supply recyclable materials to markets. Others include deposit–refund systems in which a consumer pays a deposit fee for a product at the time of purchase and receives a refund when the product is returned for recycling. Several states have laws that require this type of deposit–refund system for beverage containers and certain automotive parts like car batteries. Another program that provides a supply of recyclable materials is a disposal ban on specific materials. Used motor oil, for example, cannot be disposed of with traditional waste in most states. Drop-off recycling centers, in which recyclers take their materials to a central location for processing, also contribute to the supply of recyclable materials.

The derived demand for recyclable materials comes from several sources. Firms demand recyclable materials when the cost of using recyclable materials as inputs is lower than using virgin material. Firms may also demand recyclable materials if their customers demand products with recycled content. Government policies also can impact the demand for recyclable materials by mandating the percent of recycled content in products and by implementing policies that require government agencies to buy products with recycled content. The interaction of the supply and demand of recyclable materials determines their price in the marketplace. For some recyclable materials, such as aluminum, the price is relatively high, a reflection of the high energy savings of producing new aluminum cans from recycled material rather than from virgin material. For other recyclable materials, such as glass, the relative price is low partly due to small energy savings from the use of recyclable glass compared to virgin materials for new glass products.

Beyond its contribution to the supply of recyclable materials, curbside recycling presents an opportunity to investigate the economics of recycling. An economist would say that recycling is beneficial to society as a whole if the marginal benefits of recycling are greater than or equal to the marginal costs of recycling. The socially optimal level of recycling is the level when the marginal benefits exactly equal the marginal costs. The socially optimal level is said to make society as well off as possible with respect to recycling. Making such a determination requires the measurement of both benefits and costs for recycling programs. In the case of curbside recycling, the benefits could include a reduction in the amount paid for trash collection, a reduction in the use of landfills, the preservation of natural resources, and a feeling of satisfaction for those who participate in recycling efforts. The costs of curbside recycling include individuals' effort to store and deliver recyclable materials, and the expenditures to run and maintain a program for recycling collection and processing.

Studies attempting to measure the benefits and costs find that the cost of curbside recycling programs varies from city to city. Costs have been estimated to be as high as $5.79 (2012 dollars) per household per month to as low as $1.84. The cost variation arises because of differences in program characteristics such as collection frequency and the number of materials collected. The benefits to recycling also vary from location to location and range from $1.59 to $5.81 per household per month.

In some places, the benefits exceed the costs and it is socially optimal to curbside recycle. In other places, the costs exceed the benefits and it is not socially optimal to recycle. If society is interested in using its scarce resources to maximize society's well-being, then it is important to consider the implementation of recycling on a location-by-location basis and only employing it where marginal benefits are greater than marginal costs. Additionally, it is important to note that if some groups in society desire a recycling rate that is higher than the socially optimum rate, then the increased recycling would come at the expense of other members in society.

The economics of recycling are intriguing. The promise of recycling is to save resources; however, the very act of recycling uses scarce resources. If society increases recycling rates with current technology, the marginal costs of recycling will increase while the marginal benefits will decrease. The future of recycling, then, depends on society's ability to lower costs faster for recycling than for production using virgin materials.

Brandon C. Koford

See also: Municipal Solid Waste; Regulation

Further Reading

Aadland, David, and Arthur J. Caplan. 2006. Curbside Recycling: Waste Resource or Waste of Resources? *Journal of Policy Analysis and Management* 25(4): 855–874.

U.S. Environmental Protection Agency. 2010. *Municipal Solid Wast in the United States: 2009 Facts and Figures.* Office of Solid Waste, EPA 530-R-10-012.

Regulation

Businesses produce goods and provide services that we all enjoy. However, in the process of producing these goods and providing these services, businesses frequently generate by-products that harm the natural environment, including humans. In some cases, these by-products represent extremely hazardous pollutants that cause great environmental harm, for example, radioactive waste generated by nuclear power plants. In other cases, these by-products represent merely nuisances that cause only minor harm, for example, noise generated by lawn care providers. Regardless of the scale, the harm generated by any business represents a burden or cost borne by someone else. Since these costs are borne by others, these costs are distinctively different from the costs that businesses normally face, such as the cost of hiring workers or renting buildings. While labor and rental costs are born internally by businesses, the environmentally related costs are born externally. Given this distinction, businesses are free to ignore external costs, leading businesses to make environmentally insensitive decisions due to this negative externality. Consequently, environmental costs are external to the market as a whole. Since the market price does not reflect environmental costs, it is too low, leading consumers to overconsume goods and services that harm the environment.

Fortunately, governments are able to offer regulatory methods for correcting business-related negative externalities. In the United States, major environmental regulation began in 1970 with the creation of the Environmental Protection Agency (EPA). Since then the EPA has implemented various regulatory programs designed to correct business-related externalities, for example the Clean Air Act in 1970. These environmental regulatory programs attempt to reduce the environmental harm caused by businesses. Most regulatory programs restrict businesses' choices directly or indirectly. Other regulatory programs induce businesses to make more environmentally sensitive choices. Regulatory programs directly restrict businesses' choices generally by imposing design standards, such as the requirement to install filters on smokestacks in order to remove particulate matter. Businesses are legally obligated to meet these design standards. When businesses fail to comply, they are subject to penalties, such as fines. Regulatory programs indirectly restrict businesses' choices generally by imposing performance standards, such as the requirement to keep pollution below a certain maximum. Businesses are legally obligated to meet these performance standards and noncompliant businesses face the risk of penalties.

Other regulatory programs induce businesses to reduce their generation of harmful by-products, that is, pollution, generally by placing a price on pollution. In essence, these regulatory programs transform the disposal of pollution into another cost of business. In the same way that businesses must pay their workers for their time, these regulatory programs force businesses to pay society for the use of its natural environment as a means of disposal. Once businesses must pay to pollute, they should lower their pollution. Since efforts to reduce pollution are not costless, no business is expected to eliminate its pollution. Instead, each business identifies the level of pollution that represents the best trade-off between the cost of pollution and the cost of pollution reduction.

A pollution charge explicitly places a price on pollution by charging businesses for each unit of pollution emitted, for example, pound of particulate matter. A program of transferable permits, that is, cap-and-trade, implicitly places a price on pollution. A program caps the aggregate amount of pollution allowable from an identified set of pollution sources (nearly always businesses), issues the number of permits needed to match this cap (generally one permit per pollution unit), and initiates trading among the set of businesses. The buying and selling of permits within a market establishes a market price for the legal right to pollute. Faced with the need to buy permits for the right to pollute, businesses should lower their pollution. Businesses also enjoy the opportunity to sell permits, which may motivate a business to reduce its pollution in order to generate excess permits, that is, number of permits held exceeds the amount of pollution.

The regulatory programs for correcting business-related externalities enjoy synergies with other similar efforts expended by nongovernmental agents, such as investors. In some cases, nongovernmental efforts merely serve to reinforce regulatory programs. For example, even investors who only care about the profitability of businesses may still pressure businesses to improve their environmental management. Environmentally insensitive choices increase the exposure of businesses to regulatory sanctions. If a business repeatedly violates its performance standard, the EPA may impose a large penalty, which lowers profits. Investor pressure prompts business managers to take seriously these possible penalties, thus improving the effectiveness of these penalties for inducing compliance with performance standards.

In other cases, nongovernmental efforts rely on the regulatory programs for generating influence over businesses' environmentally related decisions. For example, across the United States, members of communities located near polluting businesses are demonstrating that they are very interested in protecting their local environment. In several cases, this interest runs so deep that community members are pressuring regulated businesses to exceed their regulatory requirements, such as lowering their pollution to levels below the maxima established by performance standards. Even though the standards are exceeded, they remain important by serving as a reference point for conveying a community's interest and demonstrating a business' response to local community pressure.

In the end, regulatory programs are only effective at reducing environmental harm if businesses respond to these programs. In the time period shortly following the implementation of a regulatory program, a business is constrained by its capacity to evaluate the set of available options for reducing pollution and by its existing resources: management team, workers, building, equipment, etc. Both constraints limit the effectiveness of regulatory programs and inflate businesses' costs of complying with these programs.

Given the time to evaluate its options fully and modify its resources, a business is much better equipped to respond to regulatory programs. Businesses are more likely to identify the best-fitting approach for reducing pollution. Moreover, businesses may hire a new management team, hire additional environmental management engineers, construct a new building, and install more equipment, as well as researching and designing new technologies. All of these efforts improve the effectiveness of regulatory programs and lower businesses' costs of complying with these programs.

According to conventional economic wisdom, all regulatory programs constrain business operations, thus, undermining profitability. However, based on a competing economic perspective, stringent yet flexible environmental regulation may improve profitability. In a dynamic world where opportunities arise frequently and prove difficult to assess in real time, environmental regulation forces businesses to reexamine their operations. In the process, businesses identify opportunities that allow them to comply with environmental regulation and lower production costs or improve product quality. Empirical evidence supports both perspectives, indicating that the ultimate effect of environmental regulation on profitability depends on circumstances.

The flexibility offered by a regulatory program arguably represents the most important circumstance. Design standards offer no flexibility. Performance standards offer flexibility regarding the methods for reducing pollution but not regarding the level of pollution (i.e., cannot exceed the maximum). Emission charges and transferable permits offer full flexibility regarding both method and level.

Lastly, even the threat of environmental regulation may prove effective at correcting business-related externalities. Fearing the (potential) burden of future regulation, businesses may band together, especially in the form of industrial associations, in order to demonstrate to environmental agencies that the businesses are capable of self-regulation, thus preempting government regulation. For example, in 1988 the American Chemistry Council created the Responsible Care program to promote safe, responsible, and sustainable management of chemicals, which may have been designed to preempt government regulation in response to a major industrial accident in Bhopal, India, in 1984.

Dietrich Earnhart

See also: Clean Air Act; Clean Water Act; Emissions Trading; Externality; Monitoring and Enforcement; Pigouvian Taxes

Further Reading

Earnhart, Dietrich, and Robert Glicksman. 2011. *Pollution Limits and Polluters' Efforts to Comply: The Role of Government Monitoring and Enforcement.* Palo Alto, CA: Stanford University Press.

Renewable Energy

Renewable energy comes from the use of nondepletable sources, such as sunlight, wind, or moving or falling water. In the United States, most renewable energy is used to produce electricity. There is considerable public excitement over renewable energy options. They produce electricity with little or no emissions of greenhouse gases and other pollutants and many of them, such as solar, contain the allure of new technology. What is the current status of these technologies? How competitive are they with other technologies? What policies are used to promote them, and what policies should be used to promote them?

According to the U.S. Energy Information Administration, in 2012 roughly 12 percent of the electricity produced in the United States was generated using renewable sources. About 56 percent of that renewable electricity was produced by hydroelectric dams and just below 30 percent came from wind turbines. The remainder came from biomass, geothermal, and solar technologies. Hydropower dams have been around for many decades, but wind energy and solar power have grown rapidly just over the past decade. Wind generation in the United States grew from 6 billion kWh in 2000 to 140 billion kWh in 2012. Electricity generation from solar power in the United States has increased more than fivefold since 2002 and reached about 4 billion kWh in 2012.

The economics of renewable electricity depend on the costs of exploiting the renewable resource and these costs vary by technology and quality of the resource (wind speed and persistence or solar intensity, for example). The economics also depend on the opportunity costs of the other technologies—coal, gas, or nuclear—against which renewables compete. Renewables tend to be very capital-intensive and, with the exception of biomass, fuel costs are very low. In contrast, fuel prices, which can be variable and hard to predict, account for a large share of the cost of fossil fuel generators. Also, unlike fossil fuels, which can be transported from mines or wells to generators at low cost, renewable resources must be tapped where they are found. Many places with abundant renewable resources are distant from populated areas where electricity demand is concentrated, and therefore the cost of transmitting renewable electricity to markets can be substantial. Although renewable costs have come down over time, recent low natural gas prices and technological improvements have also reduced the costs of new natural gas generators. Overall, the average cost of a kWh produced by both wind and solar is typically greater than that of electricity generated using coal or natural gas.

The economics of renewables also depend on the value of the electricity they produce. Unlike most fossil fuel generators, which can vary their rate of electricity output to match demand, some renewables such as wind and solar are available intermittently, as they can only operate when the wind blows or when the sun is shining.

This intermittency affects the market value of wind and solar. Electricity that is supplied during periods of high demand has greater value than electricity produced when demand is low, so the value of renewable power depends on how well resource availability aligns with demand. This alignment varies by resource and region of the country. For example, wind power in the interior plains tends to be more abundant at night when electricity demand is low, whereas in coastal regions, windy periods may overlap more with peak electricity demand in late summer afternoons. Sometimes the amount of wind power generation leads to excess supply and spot wholesale electricity prices can be negative. Some renewables, such as rooftop photovoltaic installations, can be installed on a customer's premise and may generate more power than the customer needs at certain times. The excess generation can affect voltage stability and create other problems for managing the local distribution network.

Given these considerations, intermittency reduces the market value of wind and solar compared to other technologies. Greater access to energy storage, perhaps in the form of plug-in electric or hybrid electric vehicles or compressed air, might help to solve the mismatch between supply and demand. However, adding storage to a power system would affect the value of other technologies as well, and storage may or may not increase the overall value of nondispatchable renewables compared to other technologies.

Renewable technologies currently have higher costs and lower market values than conventional technologies, particularly natural gas. To overcome these economic hurdles, numerous federal, state, and local policies in the United States promote the use of renewables. Since the mid-1990s with a few brief interruptions, the United States has had a federal policy of providing production tax credits for every MWh of electricity generated by wind and other selected renewable sources. Alternatively, investors can claim a federal tax credit for up to 30 percent of up-front investment costs for solar and other technologies. In addition, 30 states plus the District of Columbia have adopted Renewable Portfolio Standards that typically require that renewables account for a minimum (and often growing) percentage of electricity sold in the state. These policies have helped to fuel the recent growth in renewable generation. But they also raise the question, when does it makes sense to use policy measures to promote the use of renewables?

Three rationales present themselves. The first is to counteract the failure of private markets to capture fully the environmental externalities associated with burning fossil fuels to produce electricity. Environmental emissions impose a cost to society in the form of environmental degradation and poor human health. When that cost is not included in electricity prices, electricity producers rely too much on the use of fossil fuels to produce electricity. The optimal policy raises the cost of burning fossil fuels to include those social costs. Policies such as tax credits can partially remedy that shortcoming by reducing the cost of using renewables. However, these policies are inefficient because they do not correct the market failure directly by increasing the private cost of emitting pollution.

The second policy rationale is to correct market failures associated with spillovers in research and development. Private markets produce suboptimal spending on research and development because the benefits of such activity can spill over to others without compensation to the innovator. This market failure is particularly relevant for new technologies, such as tidal or wave power, advanced wind generator technologies, or photovoltaics. These cases represent a clear rationale for government subsidies for research and development, such as the Department of Energy's Advanced Research Projects Agency—Energy (ARPA-E) program.

The third rationale is to correct for underinvestment in learning. There is often considerable learning associated with developing and using new technologies. For example, rooftop photovoltaic system installers may learn how to install systems to operate more efficiently, and wind manufacturers may find ways to improve manufacturing efficiency. Learning can be thought of as an investment; the firm should price to the learning curve by initially offering the product at a low price to increase sales and learn more. However, if firms are not able to capture the benefits of this learning, they would not reduce prices to learn and therefore will underinvest in learning. For example, other installers may observe what the first installer does and capture the benefits of learning. Subsidies for the development or use of the technology are justified if the firms are not able to capture the benefits of their own learning.

Karen Palmer and Joshua Linn

See also: Alternative Energy; Biofuels; Energy Efficiency; Energy Policy; Externality; International Association for Energy Economics; Pigouvian Taxes

Further Reading

Joskow, Paul. 2011. Comparing the Cost of Intermittent and Dispatchable Electricity Generating Technologies. *American Economics Review Papers and Proceedings* 100(3): 238–241.

McVeigh, James, Dallas Burtraw, Joel Darmstadter, and Karen Palmer. 2000. Winner, Loser, or Innocent Victim: Has Renewable Energy Performed as Expected? *Solar Energy* 68(3): 237–255.

National Research Council (NRC). 2009. *Electricity from Renewables: Status, Prospects and Impediments.* Washington, D.C.: The National Academies Press.

Schmalensee, Richard. 2012. Evaluating Policies to Increase Electricity Generation from Renewable Energy. *Review of Environmental Economics and Policy* 6(1): 45–64.

Risk and Uncertainty

Risk to an economist means that we can characterize something that might happen, or might not, using a measurable probability. Uncertainty, in contrast, means we do not even really know the probability that something will happen. Ambiguity is often used to refer to those in-between situations, as when we might have two good scientific estimates of the probability that the earth will be 3°C warmer by the year 2050, but they are different, and we may not know which one is correct. Economists often neglect to explicitly consider the severity of the outcome in the definition of risk, but most other disciplines (e.g., psychology, medicine) do. The severity of a risky outcome nevertheless matters in determining how tolerant we humans are when facing some risk. Betty might be willing to gamble $1 on a lottery ticket because losing results in what appears to be a small loss, but she might at least try to take no gambles at all when it comes to her health.

The very nature of the future involves unknowns. Thus, optimal or efficient resource management, requiring that trade-offs be made between the present and the future, likely involve risk and/or uncertainty. In extraction of nonrenewable or renewable resources, future prices may be uncertain, as well as resource stocks, which are affected by discovery and technological innovation. All economists basically agree that the price of a scarce resource will rise over some period of time. However, few economists would bet on an oil price being higher or lower one year from now. Similarly, coping with climate change can be thought of as an intertemporal resource allocation problem, where the optimal amount of greenhouse gas over time must be determined. Adverse impacts from climate change certainly look likely in the future to most all climate scientists, but the magnitude and exact nature and location of the impacts may be best characterized as uncertain.

Some of us like risk and others have an extreme distaste for it. Our preference for risk in certain situations might vary: if we are sometimes in the former category we are risk lovers, and in the latter category we might be risk averse. In the middle, people might be risk neutral. Economists have formal definitions of these concepts, but the basic idea of risk neutrality corresponds to a required payoff one seeks for a gamble. If I am risk neutral, then I am indifferent between a gamble that will pay me either $1 or $0 with a 50–50 chance, versus being given $0.50, the expected value of the gamble. A risk lover may actually prefer the gamble even if her alternative was to get $0.40 because she loves the thrill, whereas one who is risk averse will only undertake the gamble if given more than $0.50. The economics of decision making under conditions of risk is most transparent when money gambles are involved, but of course many decisions of importance in environmental and natural resource economics do not directly involve money. There is no reason to believe that our preferences for risk involving money gambles carry over to all of the other risks that we face.

Similarly, some people may actually prefer to face uncertainty, some might be neutral about it, and some may be uncertainty, or ambiguity, averse. It is hard to imagine a situation where we might prefer to face uncertainty, but suppose you could know whether you had a slowly progressing, life-threatening disease. Are you sure you would be better off if you knew about it? Some doctors in fact suggest that patients who do not know about their disease are happier, and live longer than they otherwise might. Thus, like risk preference, uncertainty preference is an empirical issue, and it likely varies from situation to situation, or from one to another context.

Behaviors to mitigate or avoid risk, such as those who are risk averse would undertake, are called averting behaviors. For example, consider an individual faced with cancer risks from arsenic in drinking water in the home. The household may choose to mitigate this risk by taking one of several possible measures, such as effective water treatment. We might not observe a member of the household long enough to know if they get cancer, but again we might assume that the mitigation choice helps reveal the preference for risk, and in some settings, the implied monetary value of a risk reduction. Averting behaviors that involve preventative expenditures, like cost of illness measures in the health arena, are thought to be lower bounds on the value of risk reductions. If we see the household spend $2,000 for a water treatment system, and say, $60 per year in upkeep on the system, we begin to get an idea of the lower bound monetary value to the household of reducing risks from the arsenic.

It may seem that if society faces uncertainty, there is no logical way to make a decision or plan for the unknown. Surprisingly, this is not so. People make decisions while facing uncertainty all the time. Recent studies in economics have demonstrated that some frameworks for decision making are consistent with the precautionary principle, which many European countries seem to follow. People may choose to forgo development, for example, even when the benefits of preserving natural habitats are uncertain. Being especially careful (i.e., going forward slowly) in allocating scarce resources can be logical, and supported using sound mathematical modeling known as robust optimal control.

One of the most important questions for policy makers is: Do people really understand risks? If a person were told that the chance that a large portion of the Antarctic's ice would melt by the year 2100 was, say, 1 in 100, would he understand what that means? Would he understand how this probability is different than if he were told the chance was 1 in 1000? How about 1 in 50? Psychologists and economists have considerable evidence that understanding risks is quite difficult for people in general, except in the simplest cases, such as in a fair coin toss. Thus, environmental policymakers may well have to struggle to change societal perceptions about the existence of climate change, and with what chance particular outcomes will unfold.

There is no reason that perceived risks and science-based estimates of risks, based on the average person in a population, should be the same. Consider the risks from cigarette smoking. First, maybe an individual does not have the same sense of the risks of dying from smoking as scientists who study these do. Naturally, one way of explaining why people smoke is that they might be grossly underestimating the mortality risks from doing so. But second, maybe an individual really does not face the same risks as the average person in the population does. If Betty's mother died of heart disease, she is already at a greater risk of getting heart disease than the average person, so her smoking risks may well be different than the typical science-based estimate. For these reasons, people may have their own sense, or subjective probabilities, of risky outcomes.

This example carries over into important energy and resource policy decisions. For example, Riddel and Shaw studied people's willingness to accept compensation to bear the risks of transporting and storing high-level radioactive wastes from nuclear power plants, which are an essential piece of the puzzle in society's decision to adopt nuclear power, say, as opposed to continuing to burn conventional fossil fuels such as coal. They found that people surveyed had subjective probabilities that were thousands of times higher than the risks that scientists estimated, and they clung to those perceptions even when told of the scientific estimates.

W. Douglass Shaw

See also: Asymmetric Information; Averting Behavior; Climate Change Impacts; Natural Hazards; Precautionary Principle; Safe Minimum Standard; Value of Statistical Life

Further Reading

Grijalva, Therese, R. Berrens, and W. D. Shaw. 2011. Species Preservation versus Development: An Experimental Investigation under Uncertainty. *Ecological Economics* 70(5): 995–1005.

Jakus Paul M., W. D. Shaw, T. N. Nguyen, and M. Walker. 2009. Risk Perceptions of Arsenic in Tap Water and Bottled Water Consumption. *Water Resources Research* 45(W05405).

Riddel, Mary, and W. D. Shaw. 2006. A Theoretically-Consistent Empirical Non-Expected Utility Model of Ambiguity: Nuclear Waste Mortality Risk and Yucca Mountain. *Journal of Risk and Uncertainty* 32(2): 131–150.

Slovic, Paul. 1987. Perception of Risk. *Science* 236(4799): 280–285.

Woodward, R. T., and W. D. Shaw. 2008. Allocating Resources in an Uncertain World: Water Management and Endangered Species. *American Journal of Agricultural Economics* 90(3): 593–605.

Rosen, Sherwin

When economists value a McIntosh Apple or a Toyota Prius they turn to the markets for apples and automobiles where product prices give the values of the fruit or vehicle. Behind this reliance is the idea that market prices reflect the preferences and demands of consumers as well as the resources employed and supply costs of producers. When environmental economists value cleaner air in Chicago or cleaner (fewer) hazardous waste sites in New Jersey, however, market prices of these non-market goods are not readily available. Sherwin Rosen made a huge contribution to the field of environmental valuation by offering the insight that markets for these environmental goods do exist, but they are implicit; they are embedded in the markets for goods that we do observe being bought and sold. Environmental economists must do some statistical detective work to get those values. Think about the value of a house. The market price depends on its structural characteristics such as bathrooms and living space and neighborhood characteristics such as safety and air quality. In his 1974 article in the *Journal of Political Economy* titled "Hedonic Prices and Implicit Markets: Product Differentiation in Perfect Competition,"

Sherwin Rosen offered the insight that if air quality varies by location, then an implicit market for air quality exists in the explicit market for houses. The increment in house price due to cleaner air is an implicit market price that reflects the value of the cleaner air. This approach has allowed environmental economists to estimate the value of a wide variety of environmental goods and contribute to benefit–cost analysis that promotes efficient environmental policy. Environmental and urban economists have applied a related approach of his that combines compensating differences in housing prices and wage rates due to cleaner air and other amenities that vary by location to estimate the value of quality of life in different areas. These approaches are just two of many contributions he made during a distinguished career.

Sherwin Rosen was born in Chicago, Illinois, in 1938, earned a B.S. from Purdue University in 1960, and a Ph.D. in economics from the University of Chicago in 1966. He was on the faculty at the University of Rochester 1967–1977 before joining the faculty at the University of Chicago. He was the Edwin A. and Betty L. Bergman Distinguished Service Professor in Economics at Chicago at the time of his death in 2001. He was best known for his work in labor economics and industrial organization. His 1974 article about hedonic prices and implicit prices had at least as great an influence on labor economists as environmental economists and is one of the most highly cited articles in economics. It provided economists a framework for estimating values of changes in mortality risks, values of keen interest to labor and environmental economists alike. Income inequality, gender wage differences, and the economics of superstars are other areas in which he made pathbreaking contributions. He was a fellow of the American Academy of Arts and Sciences, member of the National Academy of Sciences, and was president of the American Economic Association. The impact of his work is still great.

Glenn Blomquist

See also: Environmental Valuation; Hedonic Methods; Value of Statistical Life

Further Reading

Rosen, Sherwin. 1974. Hedonic Prices and Implicit Markets: Product Differentiation in Pure Competition. *The Journal of Political Economy* 82(1): 34–55.

S

Safe Minimum Standard

One of the defining themes of neoclassical economics is its focus on marginal analysis—we should do more of something if the marginal benefits of doing so are greater than the marginal costs. But for many environmental issues, this decision rule leaves us uneasy. This unease is particularly acute for environmental policy decisions that involve uncertainty and irreversibility. The famous ecologist Aldo Leopold said: "The last word in ignorance is the man who says of an animal or plant, 'What good is it?' . . . If the biota, in the course of aeons, has built something we like but do not understand, then who but a fool would discard seemingly useless parts? To keep every cog and wheel is the first precaution of intelligent tinkering." As an example, consider the decision of whether to allow critical habitat for an endangered species to be developed. A strict neoclassical economist would calculate the ecosystem services provided by the species, value those services, and then compare those values to the benefit that would be generated by allowing the critical habitat to be developed. The first objection to this decision rule is that many of the services provided by the endangered species may be unknown. Perhaps the species will provide the genetic resources needed to cure an important disease or to make our crops more disease resistant. Perhaps the species is playing an important, unknown role in the ecosystem, and its loss would result in catastrophic changes to that ecosystem. The neoclassical economist's response would be to calculate the expected value of the ecosystem services provided by the endangered species, and compare that expected value to the benefit from development. But what if we do not know the probabilities? And what if we do not know how valuable the species might be? How would we calculate an expected value?

Ciriacy-Wantrup considered how society should approach natural resources that provide a flow of services, but where that flow could be irreversibly lost if the resource is not protected. Endangered species and biodiversity are the examples that have been discussed the most in academic work, but Ciriacy-Wantrup identified other examples, such as an aquifer that can lose its storage capacity if overpumped, or soils that can be eroded to the point where they cannot rebuild through natural processes. In each of these cases, the resource has a critical zone. If the resource is depleted to the point where it enters its critical zone, it cannot recover and is irretrievably lost. A second feature of these cases is that the future value of the services provided by the resource is not known with certainty, and could be quite large.

Ciriacy-Wantrup argued that in such cases, the resource should be maintained at a safe minimum standard level, a level high enough to safely avoid the critical zone. The concept of a safe minimum standard is intuitively appealing, and is consistent with the precautionary principle. But as a decision rule the safe minimum standard is very conservative. Must all flow resources be protected, regardless of the opportunity cost of doing so? Bishop argued that society should maintain resources at a safe minimum standard unless the costs of doing so are unacceptably large. What constitutes unacceptably large costs is a political decision, but economists have a role to play in helping decision makers understand the true opportunity costs of conserving resources. This approach is similar in spirit to the way that the Endangered Species Act makes exemption decisions. A federal agency is allowed to carry out actions that would result in destruction or modification of critical habitat only if there are no "reasonable and prudent alternatives" available.

Ciriacy-Wantrup and Bishop both argued that the safe minimum standard has a game-theoretic foundation. Specifically, they argued that the safe minimum standard is the minimax-loss strategy in a two-person game against nature. To see this, consider a game where society chooses whether or not to save an endangered species, and nature chooses whether or not loss of the species turns out to be harmful. In such a game, society's safest strategy (the strategy that guarantees the smallest possible loss) is to preserve the species. Ready and Bishop draw a parallel between the preservation of the species and buying an insurance policy.

However, preservation of the resource could also be thought of as risky. Consider the commonly made argument for conserving biodiversity that we do not know which species might provide important genetic information in the future to cure a disease or protect crops from new pests. In that case, preserving the species (or conserving biodiversity in general) is more like a lottery ticket; it costs us something to preserve the species (foregone opportunities), but the future payoff is uncertain. In such a situation, the social strategy that minimizes potential losses is to allow the species to go extinct. If society wants to follow the safest course possible, it should not buy lottery tickets.

There is a game-theoretic foundation for the safe minimum standard, but it does not rely on the minimax-loss decision rule. Instead, it is based on the concept of regret. In a two-person game against nature, regret is defined as the difference between the situation you experience and the best possible situation you could have experienced. If the resource can be thought of as an insurance policy that protects against the possibility that loss of the resource would result in a bad outcome, the strategy that minimizes potential regret is to preserve the species. If the species can be thought of as a lottery ticket that could provide large benefits in the future, the policy that minimizes potential future regret is still to preserve the species.

Is it necessary to find a consistent argument for the safe minimum standard that is rooted in economic theory? An alternative motivation for the safe minimum standard is that from the perspective of sustainability. We are addressing issues where trade-offs are made between material gains for the current generation and maintaining levels of natural resources, reductions in natural resource levels may be irreversible, and loss of the natural resource may (or may not) result in diminished opportunities for future generations. It is in situations like this that the arguments in favor of a strong sustainability rule are most compelling. Adopting a safe minimum standard rule is consistent with the notion of strong sustainability.

Ultimately, the decision whether to maintain resources at safe minimum standard levels is a political one. Public opinion surveys and stated preference valuation studies have consistently shown that the general public supports the idea of preserving endangered natural resources, particularly those whose loss would be irreversible, but that the cost of maintaining a safe minimum standard does matter. It would appear that the public has already accepted the notion of the safe minimum standard, even if economists are still trying to find a motivation for the policy consistent with their theory.

Richard C. Ready

See also: Biodiversity; Ciriacy-Wantrup, S. V.; Endangered Species; Precautionary Principle; Sustainability

Further Reading
Berrens, R. P. 2001. The Safe Minimum Standard of Conservation and Endangered Species: A Review. *Environmental Conservation* 28(2): 104–116.

Bishop, R. C. 1978. Endangered Species and Uncertainty: The Economics of the Safe Minimum Standard. *American Journal of Agricultural Economics* 60(1): 10–18.

Ciriacy-Wantrup, S. V. 1968. *Resource Conservation: Economics and Policies.* 3rd ed. Berkeley and Los Angeles: University of California Division of Agricultural Sciences.

Ready, R. C., and R. C. Bishop. 1991. Endangered Species and the Safe Minimum Standard. *American Journal of Agricultural Economics* 73(2): 309–312.

Schelling, Thomas C.

Thomas C. Schelling (1921–) is an American economist who shared the 2005 Nobel Memorial Prize in Economics "for having enhanced our understanding of conflict and cooperation through game-theory analysis." In academic and policy circles, he is best known for his work on nuclear weapons and arms control, including his 1960 book *The Strategy of Conflict.* In popular culture, his most lasting contribution was introducing director Stanley Kubrik to the ideas that led to the 1964 movie *Dr. Strangelove.*

Schelling has written about climate change economics for over 30 years, including a chapter in a 1983 National Academy Press assessment of the threats of climate change and his fascinating 1992 presidential address to the American Economic Association. In *Strategies of Commitment* (2007), he writes:

> The topics [of nuclear weapons and climate change] are completely diverse: nuclear fission versus infra-red absorption. But the two have much in common, both in the demands they make on diplomacy and in the kind of challenge they pose. Nuclear weapons required an unprecedented reorientation of military thinking that took some decades . . . The global atmosphere is the largest, and may prove to be the most challenging . . . and most long-lasting "common" we must learn to manage, "we" the six billion and more who meteorologically share the planet.

Schelling was an early analyst of many of the central issues in climate change economics and policy, including the challenges facing international negotiations, the costs of inaction, the potential of geo-engineering, and the appropriateness of discounting future costs and benefits.

Regarding international climate negotiations, Schelling puts front and center the free-rider problem in this global tragedy of the commons: "[W]ithout clearly defined obligations backed up by the prospect of sanctions, international cooperation involving potential major sacrifices cannot be sustained." But he is pessimistic about the ability of the international community to create such cooperation: "Sanctions large enough to be effective deserve skepticism. Punishing poor countries will not be attractive; punishing rich countries, or large countries, or powerful countries will [also] not be attractive."

This worries Schelling less than one might think because he is relatively optimistic about the costs of inaction. Although he warns that potential catastrophes may be lurking unseen, he also argues that rich countries will likely be able to adapt ("half of the 14 million Dutch [already] live below sea level") and that the main economic impact will be on agriculture and forestry, which account for a very small share of economic activity in developed countries. Poor countries, which are more dependent on agriculture and less able to adapt, are a bigger cause of concern in his view, but he argues that they have more pressing concerns, such as clean drinking water. He emphasizes the need for caution because of how poorly we can anticipate the needs and lifestyles of people 100 years from now, describing rich-world climate policy as "very much like a foreign aid program with some of the foreigners being descendants who live not on another continent but in another century."

Like most economists, Schelling favors tackling climate change with economic instruments like carbon taxes. Although one might therefore view climate policy and foreign aid as complements—carbon tax revenue could in theory be used to fund foreign aid—Schelling sees them as substitutes, arguing that "[a]batement expenditures should have to compete with alternative ways of raising consumption utility in the developing world" and that is it "logically absurd to ignore present needs and concentrate on the later decades of the coming century."

Yoram Bauman

See also: Adaptation to Climate Change; Climate Change Impacts; Discounting; Tragedy of the Commons; Pigouvian Taxes

Further Reading

National Research Council (US). 1983. Carbon Dioxide Assessment Committee. *Changing Climate: Report of the Carbon Dioxide Assessment Committee*. Washington, D.C.: National Academy Press.

Schelling, Thomas, C. 1992. Some Economics of Global Warming. *American Economic Review* 82(1): 1–14.

Schelling, Thomas C. 2007. *Strategies of Commitment: And Other Essays*. Cambridge, MA: Harvard University Press.

Sea Level Rise

Global sea levels have risen by more than 2 millimeters per year on average since the late 19th century. Climate change and higher global temperatures are likely to accelerate the historical rate of sea level rise over the next century through the melting of ice masses and thermal expansion of the oceans. There are significant uncertainties about the magnitude and speed of future sea level rises given the uncertainty of future greenhouse gas emissions and the human response to changing natural conditions. The Intergovernmental Panel on Climate Change (IPCC) estimates that the global average sea level will rise by 18 to 59 centimeters by 2100 if nothing changes.

Sea level rise projections indicate substantial variability at different locations. Some locations could experience sea level rises higher than the global average, while others could have a fall in sea levels, depending upon the effects of local land subsidence or uplift. For areas experiencing a significant rate of subsidence such as the Mid-Atlantic and Gulf Coast, relative sea level is increasing at a more rapid rate than in other areas. For areas in which uplift is taking place, such as portions of the Alaskan coastline and in parts of the Pacific Northwest, relative sea level has been decreasing. Changes in atmospheric winds and ocean currents also affect regional variations in sea level rises, although these variations cannot be predicted reliably.

Coastal areas in the United States include some of the most developed land and represent a significant wealth of natural and economic resources. Fueled by preferences for coastal locations the population of U.S. coastal counties has exploded over the last several decades, with a growth rate more than double the national average. According to the National Oceanic and Atmospheric Administration, more than 50 percent of the nation's population lived in a coastal zone in 2010, which accounts for less than 20 percent of U.S. land area (excluding Alaska). Population growth in coastal zones has been accompanied by economic development which produced numerous benefits including employment, recreation and tourism, and nature-based commerce and energy.

As the coastal population continues to grow, the relatively dense populations and valuable economic developments have become more vulnerable to risks associated with climate change and sea level rises. Sea level rise affects coastal areas that already face a wide range of natural and human-induced stresses. Long-term sea level rise can cause inundation of low-lying areas, erosion of beaches and shorelines, and increased flooding and storm damage. This combination of population growth and increased vulnerability has been seen as an explanation for the trend of rising insured disaster losses along the U.S. coast.

Given the potentially severe impact on the natural environment and human systems, it is important to understand the implications of higher sea levels for the United States. For example, what are the estimated rates of sea level rise along the U.S. coast, and which ecosystems or economic sectors are most vulnerable to rising sea levels? Are certain regions more likely to experience higher damage than others? How well can we cope with sea level rises, and is there a threshold beyond which certain regions can no longer effectively adapt? Under what conditions could adaptation and mitigation be realized? These are critical questions for decision makers as they assess the implications of sea level rises.

National assessments suggest that the expected rise in global sea levels could have significant impacts for the United States. In general, the Southeast and mid-Atlantic coasts are most vulnerable because of their low-lying topography, high economic value, and rapid land subsidence. Parts of the Northeast, particularly coastal islands in southern New England, are also vulnerable to inundation because of their low-lying and heavily developed land. The West Coast, with the exception of San Francisco Bay and Puget Sound, is generally at lower risk as a large portion of the area is made up of rocks or cliffs.

An economically efficient response to sea level rises suggests that areas should be protected when the value at risk exceeds the costs of protection. A policy that requires all developed areas to be protected is likely to result in negative net benefits. The adaptation strategies will determine building coastal defenses to protect high-value areas and abandoning property and assets in low-value areas. Nevertheless, sea level rises will result in higher infrastructure costs for some coastal development and the inundation of many unprotected coastal areas. A review of the existing literature indicates that estimates of the cumulative impact of a 50 centimeter sea level rise by 2100 on coastal property range from $20 to $150 billion.

These estimates do not reflect the potentially large effect on coastal wetlands, which provide a wide range of services such as habitat for fish and wildlife, opportunities for recreation education and research, and esthetic values. These functions and services are economically and ecologically valuable. As such, the estimated impact shown earlier provides only a limited measure of total economic costs associated with sea level rises. Improving comprehensiveness and accuracy for various policy options is essential for future impact assessments. A comprehensive benefit–cost analysis should inform decision makers if such policy options are justified from an economic efficiency perspective.

Okmyung Bin

See also: Benefit–Cost Analysis; Climate Change Impacts; Coastal Resources; Natural Hazards; Risk and Uncertainty; Wetlands

Further Reading

Intergovernmental Panel on Climate Change, 2007. *Climate Change 2007: The Physical Science Basis Contribution of Working Group I to the Fourth Assessment Report of the Intergovernmental Panel on Climate Change* [Solomon, S., D. Qin, M. Manning (eds.)].

National Oceanic and Atmospheric Administration. 2012. *The Economic Value of Resilient Coastal Communities.* http://www.ppi.noaa.gov/wp-content/uploads/PPI_Ocean_Econ_Stats_revised_031912.pdf

Neumann, J. E., G. Yohe, R. Nicholls, and M. Manion. 2000. *Sea-Level Rise and Global Climate Change: A Review of Impacts to U.S. Coasts.* Pew Center on Global Climate Change, Arlington, VA.

Subsidies

Subsidies are direct payments from the government to individuals and/or firms. These payments can be used to address problems associated with the environment and natural resources, however they are seldom implemented under the principle that in most cases the polluter should pay. Economic theory can guide policy decisions, informing as to when subsidies are appropriate, where they should be levied, and at what level they should be set. Subsidies are most prevalent in energy and technology policy.

Externalities are an example of a market failure. If some cost or benefit is associated with an economic activity that is not borne by the agent undertaking the activity, that cost or benefit is called an externality. Pollution as a by-product of the production of a good is a negative externality associated with an external cost: the producer who emits the pollution is not suffering its costs (to the health of nearby people, for instance). Inoculations are a positive externality associated with an external benefit: the consumer who gets the shot provides benefits to others by exposing them to a reduced risk of disease.

Arthur Pigou formulated the idea that the market failure from externalities can be solved if policymakers internalize the externality, that is, make the producers of the externality face the true price, including the externality. If producers of negative externalities face a tax per unit of the externality equal to the marginal external damages of the externality, then the social optimum will be reached. This tax is called a Pigouvian tax. Similarly, producers of positive externalities can face a Pigouvian subsidy to bring about the social optimum.

Subsidies can be used for both positive and negative externalities. For positive externalities (e.g., research and development for energy technologies), the subsidy is levied per unit of the externality. For negative externalities (e.g., pollution), the subsidy is levied per unit of *abatement* of the externality. If a baseline level is established, then subsidizing producers for each unit abated will achieve the same level of emissions as taxing each unit of abatement.

Externalities can thus be addressed with either taxes or subsidies. If the subsidy rate and the tax rate are equal to each other, then either policy will result in the same amount of total externality. However, these policies will differ in terms of the distribution of the costs and revenues. Taxes generate revenues, and subsidies entail costs. The distribution of those costs or revenues is a question for policymakers to decide, but it does not impact the efficiency of the policy or the overall level of the externality. However, this equivalence between taxes and subsidies will not hold in cases where firms can enter and exit in response to policy. In that case, subsidies encourage entry and taxes encourage exit.

In an environmental context, subsidies are more commonly used to promote the research and development of energy and environmental technologies. These subsidies are actually addressing market failures from two different externalities: the negative externality of the pollutant or the resource use, and the positive externality from research and development itself (e.g., learning spillovers). For instance, the clean energy industry has received extensive federal subsidies over the past several years.

Energy subsidies are prevalent in federal policy, but these subsidies are rarely Pigouvian, that is, they are not intended as a policy instrument to address a market failure caused by externalities nor are they set equal to the per unit external cost or benefit. Instead, these policies are often intended to keep energy prices low for consumers, or to reduce costs for producers. One study estimates that, from 2002–2008, federal energy subsidies for fossil fuels in the United States totaled $72 billion, compared to just $29 billion for renewables. Most of these dollars are attributed to tax breaks for producers, including the Foreign Tax Credit and the Credit for Production of Nonconventional Fuels. About half of the subsidies for renewables went to corn-based ethanol.

Worldwide, energy subsidies look similar. The International Energy Agency has estimated that consumption subsidies for fossil fuels totaled $409 billion in 2010. Oil subsidies represented about half of that amount. That agency claims that for energy subsidies directed at fossil fuels, the costs outweigh the benefits. A complete phaseout of all energy subsidies by 2020 would reduce global energy demand by 5 percent and carbon dioxide emissions by 5.8 percent.

. Subsidies in agriculture and resource policy have been used in the context of brownfield redevelopment, erosion control, loans to farmers, and grants for erosion control. In the future, subsidies could be a part of climate change policy at either the federal or international level, including subsidies for renewable energy sources, carbon emissions trading, or other greenhouse gas mitigation strategies. Climate change is an international issue: greenhouse gas emissions from one nation affect the climate of all nations. Thus, climate policy negotiations occur at an international level. The World Trade Organization (WTO) has limits on what subsidies can be levied by individual nations, and some have argued that climate-related subsidies may conflict with trade rules related to subsidies.

Like taxes and emissions trading, subsidies are a policy tool that change relative prices for consumers and producers, altering incentives so that individual decisions coincide with socially optimal allocations. Subsidies have an advantage over traditional command-and-control policies in that they allow for flexibility among consumers and producers, who may face heterogeneity in abatement costs or preferences. While most subsidies in energy and resource policy today are actually exacerbating the problems of environmental externalities rather than solving them, subsidies can be designed efficiently and can be part of an efficient policy toolkit to address market failures in environmental and resource policy.

Garth Heutel

See also: Brownfields; Emissions Trading; Externality; Pigou, Arthur C.; Pigouvian Taxes

Further Reading

Environmental Law Institute. 2009. Estimating U.S. Government Subsidies to Energy Sources: 2002–2008. September.

Howse, Robert. 2010. Climate Mitigation Subsidies and the WTO Legal Framework: A Policy Analysis. International Institute for Sustainable Development. May.

International Energy Agency, World Energy Outlook 2011 Factsheet.

Sulfur Dioxide Trading

In the 1970s, scientists observed that the acidity of rain falling in higher elevations of eastern United States and Canada was increasing. Sulfur dioxide emissions from coal-burning power plants were implicated as a major cause of this increase. The increase in the acidity of precipitation was later linked to the declining health of lakes, streams, and forests in these areas. During the 1980s public awareness of the problems associated with acid rain grew considerably.

In 1990 the Clean Air Act was amended. Title IV of the 1990 Amendments, the Acid Deposition Control Title, established the Acid Rain Program (ARP). A central feature of the ARP is a cap-and-trade program for sulfur dioxide from large electricity generating facilities, which were mostly coal-fired power plants.

The sulfur dioxide cap-and-trade program is both ambitious in its scope and novel in the context of environmental regulation. In 1990, coal-fired power plants accounted for 56 percent of total electricity generation and 64 percent of sulfur dioxide emissions in the United States. The cap established that environmental quality is scarce by limiting the total amount of sulfur dioxide that these sources could emit. However, the program gave power plant managers the freedom to determine how to reduce their emissions in order to comply with the cap. The ability to use low-cost emission reduction methods to achieve the cap was further facilitated by allowing the plants to sell their share of the cap.

Sources subject to the cap-and-trade program are typically all but the smallest boilers in the continental United States that serve the electricity sector and burn fossil fuels. Heat from the boiler is used to create steam, which is then used by a generator to create electricity. The cap was implemented by allocating a limited number of allowances to the boilers subject to the program. Each allowance allows a boiler to emit one ton of sulfur dioxide. The program was implemented in two phases. Under Phase I, which began in 1995, 263 of the historically most polluting boilers were allocated allowances and required to comply with the program. Phase II began in 2000 and essentially brought all other coal-fired boilers of significant size into the program. Furthermore, during Phase II the number of allowances allocated annually to boilers covered under Phase I was reduced. The program also allowed boilers that would not be affected until Phase II to elect to participate in Phase I, and 182 boilers did so. This feature of the program was intended to encourage boilers that could easily reduce their emissions to become suppliers of allowances during Phase I. Starting in 2010 the annual allocation fell to about 9 million allowances. This annual allocation represents an allowable amount of emissions that is 50 percent lower than the total amount of sulfur dioxide emitted by these boilers in 1980.

The number of allowances a boiler receives is typically based on its total coal use from 1985 to 1987 multiplied by a ratio of sulfur dioxide to coal use. Some sources obtained additional allowances through special provisions of the ARP. For example, plants that installed large-scale pollution controls in the early years of the program received additional allowances.

Critically, a boiler may use allowances allocated to any other boiler for compliance. That is, the market for allowances is national and there are no restrictions on their trade. The U.S. EPA records allowance transactions and potential allowance owners must register with the U.S. EPA, but otherwise the U.S. EPA does not regulate their exchange.

A few months after the end of the calendar year, each boiler in the ARP is required to surrender a number of allowances equivalent to the amount of sulfur dioxide it emitted during the previous year. Once an allowance is surrendered it cannot be used again. Boilers have very rarely failed to have a sufficient number of allowances to surrender.

Allowances have a vintage, which is the first year that it can be used for compliance. For example, allowances with a 1995 vintage can be used for compliance starting in 1995. Furthermore, allowances can be used for compliance in any year after the year of its vintage. That is, boilers may bank allowances for compliance in future years. During Phase I a large number of allowances were banked. The bank accumulated in anticipation of Phase II, when more boilers were brought into the program and the annual allowance allocation to Phase I boilers declined. Allowing allowance banking further reduced the cost of the program by allowing boilers to delay making investments in sulfur dioxide controls. In the early 2000s boilers began to reduce the total number of allowances that were banked. That is, they drew the total size of the allowance bank down and thus the total amount of sulfur dioxide emitted by the boilers in the ARP exceeded their annual allowance allocation in those years.

To preserve the integrity of the cap and incentivize participation in the allowance market, considerable effort is put into monitoring and verifying the emissions of each boiler. Coal-fired boilers affected by the ARP are required to have monitors that continuously measure the amount of sulfur dioxide in their exhaust. Furthermore, every three months they are required to report their hourly sulfur dioxide emissions to the U.S. EPA.

The sulfur dioxide cap-and-trade program contained some innovative features. These include phasing in affected sources, reducing the annual allocation of allowances over time, allowing banking, providing allowances to sources that reduce their emissions earlier than required, and provisions for nonelectricity-generating sources to elect to participate in the program. Furthermore, the program includes an annual auction of a small number of allowances with the purpose of, in part, providing price information to the market. Both current vintage allowances and allowances with a vintage seven years in the future are auctioned. About 2.8 percent of the annual allowance allocation is sold through the auction.

In the first few years of the program allowance trades between boilers owned by different companies were relatively rare. However, as owners of boilers became more familiar with the market, trade between companies expanded considerably and a robust market developed. Firms that provided brokerage and ancillary financial services began to participate in the allowance market, much as they do for other commodity markets. They helped sellers and buyers find each other, reported allowance prices from recent transactions for both current and future allowance vintages, and even provided hedging services by purchasing and selling allowances.

Boilers reduced their emissions in a variety of ways. Many switched the type of coal they burned to coal with lower sulfur content. Coal mined in the western United States has less sulfur content than coals mined in the central and eastern United States, and coal production shifted to the western mines. A few large boilers installed pollution control equipment that captured over 90 percent of the sulfur dioxide in their exhaust. The program also incentivized more incremental methods of emissions reductions such as changing the operation of the boiler and related equipment.

Economists have studied how well the program incentivized innovation in pollution control technology, the influence of local electricity regulators and mining interests on compliance behavior, the performance of the auction, the consequences of allowing Phase II boilers to enter the program in Phase I, and whether boilers banked allowances in a manner consistent with economic theory. During Phase I of the program the market price of an allowance fluctuated between $70 and $200 in current year dollars. These prices are about 10 to 35 percent of the allowance prices forecast for this period by U.S. EPA when Title IV was adopted. The lower than expected allowance prices were mainly attributable to an unexpected decrease in the cost of low sulfur coal mined in the West. Studies of the cap-and-trade program's actual performance conclude that it cost 43 to 61 percent less than alternative regulatory approaches that arguably could have been used to reduce sulfur dioxide instead. Furthermore, studies of the actual cost of the cap-and-trade program conclude that it cost the same or less than was expected at the time of its adoption. However, the benefits of the program have been much greater than was anticipated.

While the intent of the ARP is to reduce the damage caused by acid rain on sensitive ecosystems, the major benefit of the program was to reduce fine particulate matter pollution. Fine particulate matter consists of a mix of chemicals and substances smaller than 2.5 micrometers in diameter. Through chemical reactions in the atmosphere sulfur dioxide is converted into particulate matter. Ambient exposure to particulate matter causes detrimental health effects, including premature mortality. The relationship between particulate matter exposure and premature mortality was not firmly established in 1990. Chestnut and Mills found that the benefits of the ARP exceed its costs by a 40:1 ratio, with the majority of the benefits attributable to reduced premature mortality from particulate matter exposure. Other studies find that the optimal level of sulfur dioxide emissions, a level that equates the marginal benefit of reducing sulfur dioxide to the marginal costs of controlling sulfur dioxide from U.S. power plants, is about 1 to 3 million tons per year, which is about 67 to 90 percent lower than the current annual allocation of ARP allowances.

In the pursuit of reducing ambient levels of particulate matter, the U.S. EPA has adopted regulations that require additional reductions in sulfur dioxide from coal-fired power plants beyond those required by Title IV. The Clean Air Act provides authority for these regulations in sections of the act that address local air quality and toxics emissions. By 2012, these regulations reduced the price of Title IV allowances to less than a dollar.

David A. Evans

See also: Air Pollution; Clean Air Act; Emissions Trading

Further Reading

Burtraw, D., and S.J. Szambelan. 2010. U.S. Emissions Trading Markets for SO_2 and NOx, in Bernd Hansjürgens (editor), *Permit Trading in Different Applications*, pp. 15–45. New York: Routledge.

Chan, G., R. Stavins, R. Stowe, and R. Sweeney. 2012. The SO_2 Allowance-Trading System and the Clean Air Act Amendments of 1990: Reflections on 20 Years of Policy Innovation. *National Tax Journal* 65(2): 419–452.

Chestnut, Lauraine G., and David M. Mills. 2005. A Fresh Look at the Benefits and Costs of the U.S. Acid Rain Program. *Journal of Environmental Management* 77(3): 252–266.

Ellerman, A. Denny, R. Schmalensee, E.M. Bailey, P.L. Joskow, and J.P. Montero. 2000. *Markets for Clean Air: The U.S. Acid Rain Program.* Cambridge: Cambridge University Press.

Evans, D.A., and R.T. Woodward. 2013. What Can We Learn from the End of the Grand Policy Experiment? The Collapse of the National SO_2 Trading Program and Implications for Tradable Permits as a Policy Instrument. *Annual Review of Resource Economics.* 5: 16.1–16.24.

Sustainability

The concept of sustainability plays an important, if contested, role in the related fields of environmental and ecological economics. Historically, environmental economists focused on the use of benefit–cost analysis to identify the efficient allocation of nonmarket goods and services. This had major implications for the conservation of environmental resources, which typically involve complex streams of costs and benefits accruing to diverse sets of stakeholders. In informal terms, benefit–cost analysis involves assigning monetary values to unpriced costs and benefits. When these externalities are internalized, the result is often a conservative approach that involves the sustained provisioning of high-value ecosystem services.

That said, the limitations of benefit–cost analysis were apparent quite early on, as emphasized for example in Ciriacy-Wantrup's work on safe minimum standards. The conservation of natural resources, ecosystems, and biodiversity typically involves significant short-run opportunity costs that are well-defined and that often accrue to politically influential stakeholders. If decision-makers employ high discount rates based on impatience and/or a reliance on short-run planning horizons, the costs of conservation can dominate the perceived benefits in both formal benefit–cost analysis and in practical decision-making. On the other hand, the long-run benefits of conservation are often difficult to gauge because of scientific uncertainty and uncertainty about the preferences and needs of future generations. Ciriacy-Wantrup was concerned that at least some environmental resources might be truly essential to posterity, anticipating the more recent discourse surrounding ecosystem services and their role in supporting human flourishing. As such, he embraced an approach to decision-making in which unique and potentially irreplaceable resources should be conserved unless the costs were judged to be unbearably large. In effect, this approach placed bounds on the application of the benefit–cost approach as a way of managing catastrophic environmental risks under conditions of strong uncertainty.

Ciriacy-Wantrup's framework is similar to the concept of *strong sustainability* that has emerged in the ecological economics literature. Broadly, ecological economics studies the economy and an embedded subsystem of social and ecological systems, adopting a transdisciplinary approach to environmental policy and governance. More specifically, ecological economists emphasize a tripartite approach to managing the links between the economy and the environment, with equal importance attached to the goals of (a) enhanced human flourishing, (b) distributive and procedural fairness, and (c) ecological sustainability. Advocates of strong sustainability see environmental resources as the joint or common property of present and future generations. While the present generation has a right to utilize resources for short-run economic gains, it also holds a duty to conserve the resource base for the enjoyment of future generations. In this framing, the degradation or despoliation of ecological systems would impose a wrongful harm on future generations in the absence of restorative measures, such as the rendering of appropriate compensation. As a rule of thumb, ecological economists are skeptical about the ability of monetary payments to compensate for the loss of ecosystem services over multigenerational time scales. Operationally, then, this approach is in line with Ciriacy-Wantrup's criterion. The depletion of natural resources (say high-quality petroleum resources) carries with it a duty to develop and provide substitutes (e.g., renewable energy technologies) that could generate equivalent services on a sustainable basis. Good policies would then achieve this goal cost-effectively with due attention to equity concerns.

In environmental economics, the concept of *weak sustainability* has received comparatively more emphasis. At a fundamental level, this approach is based on the moral supposition that the utility or well-being of a typical member of society should be maintained or enhanced from each generation to the next. This framework envisions environmental resources as a form of capital that contributes importantly to production and consumption and to the provisioning of nonmarket goods and services. As such, it calls for modeling and accounting techniques that explicitly gauge the value of natural capital stocks and the role they play in supporting the material economy. Weak sustainability, however, views natural capital, manufactured capital, and new technologies (i.e., blueprints used for combining inputs to produce outputs) as appropriate substitutes. Accordingly, it does not call for the conservation of environmental resources as a core policy objective. Rather, the focus is on maintaining the overall productive capacity of the economy and its ability to sustain human well-being in the long run.

Operationally, advocates of weak sustainability often argue that an economy is sustainable if the rate of investment in manufactured capital is at least as high as the monetary value of natural resource depletion. National governments and international agencies have therefore developed accounting frameworks for tracking changes in the monetary value of natural capital stocks. This approach, grounded in the early and important contributions of John Hartwick, is strictly valid only under idealized conditions—it holds for economies in which population, technology, and terms of trade are all constant through time, and where resources are allocated in a fully efficient manner through the correction of all market failures. In the face of population growth, a higher rate of capital investment is needed to achieve weak sustainability, while technological change allows society to derive higher well-being from a given set of capital assets. In theory, then, it is not possible to gauge the sustainability of an economy in the weak sense based on accounting metrics alone. Instead, forward-looking models are required that simulate the coupled dynamics of complex ecological-economic systems.

One interesting theme of the sustainability literature is its emphasis on the endogeneity of preferences and the complex relationship between economic growth and human welfare. Daly and Cobb's Index of Sustainable Economic Welfare (ISEW), for example, corrects a standard measure of per capita consumption for a wide array of social and environmental costs. This indicator suggests that the robust economic growth that occurred in the 1970s through the 2000s led to relatively little improvement in social welfare. This disparity can be explained by two factors—rising inequality and the social costs imposed by greenhouse gas emissions. While controversial in terms of its details, the ISEW indicator is interesting both for the clarity of its rationale and its attempt to provide a comprehensive welfare metric that accounts for a wide array of market and nonmarket goods. Similar results stem from survey research on life satisfaction or happiness, which suggests that relatively little improvement in experienced well-being has occurred in recent decades in the world's advanced industrial societies. This may be in part because economic growth has led to upward pressure on the social norms that define what people understand as the good life. Also, it may be that the gains of increased private consumption have been offset by declines in the quality of social interaction and other factors known to strongly affect happiness. While these results do not undercut the importance and legitimacy of the weak sustainability concept, they do suggest that it is inappropriate to gauge well-being using uncorrected measures of income and consumption.

The concepts of weak and strong sustainability point to a broad and pluralistic approach to understanding and managing the relationship between ecological and economic systems. On the one hand, it is surely salient to construct deep and meaningful measures of well-being plus models that project the welfare implications of environmental degradation over intergenerational time scales. On the other hand, Ciriacy-Wantrup's core arguments remain well taken—in the face of uncertainty, conserving environmental resources is often essential in securing the life opportunities of future generations. This is an area of research and praxis and involves a deep engagement between multiple disciplines and between academic researchers, practitioners, and stakeholders.

Richard B. Howarth

See also: Ciriacy-Wantrup, S. V.; Ecological Economics; Ecosystem Services; Green National Accounting; Philosophy; Precautionary Principle; Safe Minimum Standard; Welfare and Equity

Further Reading

Ciriacy-Wantrup, S. V. 1952. *Resource Economics: Conservation and Policies.* Berkeley: University of California Press.

Daly, Herman E., and John Cobb. 1989. *For the Common Good: Redirecting the Economy toward Community, the Environment, and a Sustainable Future.* Boston, MA: Beacon Press.

Hartwick, John M. 1977. Intergenerational Equity and the Investing of Rents from Exhaustible Resources. *American Economic Review* 67(5): 972–974.

Neumayer, Eric. 2003. *Weak versus Strong Sustainability.* Cheltenham, UK: Edward Elgar.

T

Technological Innovation

Technological innovation can lower the cost of achieving climate mitigation objectives. As such, understanding the links between market conditions, policy context, and technological innovation is important. Innovation relates to both the invention of new climate change mitigation technologies (CCMTs) as well as their adoption in the marketplace by firms, households, and other market participants. Examples include energy-efficient appliances, renewable energy technologies, carbon capture, and storage. In developing countries some of the most significant mitigation opportunities relate to technologies that also yield important local environmental and health benefits (e.g., improved indoor cooking stoves). The benefits of such technological innovation can be supported by organizational innovations that encourage the more efficient use of such technologies, as well as substitution between different economic activities (e.g., between transport modes).

Unfortunately, in the context of CCMTs there are at least three reasons to expect that innovation will not be optimal in the absence of public policy interventions. First, the costs associated with greenhouse gas emissions (GHG) are externalized by the emitter, resulting in insufficient incentives for the invention and adoption of mitigating technologies. Innovation will bend in the direction of GHG-emitting technologies since they are not priced. Second, there are important positive information and knowledge spillovers associated with the invention and adoption of CCMTs, which mean that the benefits are imperfectly captured by investors. This results in a slower rate of innovation in CCMTs (and other technologies) than would otherwise be the case. Third, many of the most important GHG-emitting sectors exhibit additional market failures (e.g., imperfect competition, network externalities, split incentives, etc.), which can adversely affect innovation in different ways. For example, there can be important barriers to entry and exit in the electricity or transport sectors.

The first problem is specific to CCMTs, and requires a targeted policy of internalization. All climate policies impose a price on polluting, whether implicitly or explicitly. The change in opportunity costs of emitting GHGs then translates into increased cost of some factors of production, and thus incentives to innovate in a manner that saves on the use of these factors. Clearly the choice of policy instrument has an effect on innovation. Different measures of equal stringency (i.e., with equivalent environmental objectives) may have very different effects on both the rate and direction of innovation.

In the theoretical literature a strong case has been made for the use of market-based instruments (e.g., taxes, emissions trading), rather than direct regulation (e.g., technology-based controls) in order to induce innovation in CCMTs. The hypothesis is that if more prescriptive policies are applied, technology invention and adoption decisions are constrained by the precise characteristics of the standard. Thus, in order to induce search for the optimal technology to meet a given environmental objective, governments should seek to allow for more flexibility in their policy regimes when this can be achieved at reasonable administrative cost.

Unfortunately, the empirical evidence on the benefits of market-based instruments to promote the development of CCMTs is scant. This may be due in part to the greater difficulty associated with assessing the innovation impacts of more flexible policy instruments. Indeed, the very nature of the advantages of flexible market-based instruments gives rise to difficulties associated with assessing the innovation effects of their implementation: the innovations induced can take on a myriad of forms and come from a myriad of sources. In many cases the climate change mitigation benefits of a particular technology may have been incidental to the motivation for its development and adoption. Nonetheless, recently there has been increased empirical evidence to support the theoretical findings that flexible market-based instruments are more innovation-friendly.

The second and third problems should be addressed primarily through more general policy framework conditions that are not specific to CCMTs. Support for basic research, protection of intellectual property, higher education policy, and other measures will at least partially overcome the positive information and knowledge externalities. Similarly, general structural policy conditions such as competition policy will help to ensure that market failures are obviated.

Given the long-run and potentially catastrophic impacts associated with climate change increased attention has been paid to the need to induce breakthrough (or radical) innovations in CCMTs, such as advanced nuclear power, third-generation biofuels, and even geo-engineering innovations. There are good reasons to think that the mere pricing of GHGs will not be sufficient to call forth the kinds of innovation needed to stabilize concentrations to safe levels, even if knowledge and market failures are addressed. Indeed, it is significant that assumptions about the timing and cost of backstop technologies are often the most important determinants of macroeconomic modeling assessments of the costs of climate change mitigation.

Since the timeframe for the development of breakthrough technologies is long, the predictability of the policy framework is vital. For example, investments in R&D for breakthrough are (approximately) irreversible. The costs of such investments cannot usually be recovered should policy (or market) conditions change. As a consequence policy uncertainty can serve as a significant brake on invention.

Moreover, with respect to adoption, many of the most GHG-intensive sectors have long-lived capital, for which investment decisions are only reversible at great cost or after a significant lapse of time. Adoption will also be slower than optimal.

The uncertainty of the policy framework is also partially a consequence of the global nature of climate change. Since all countries benefit from GHG mitigation irrespective of the location of emission, investors need to assess the credibility and viability of policy initiatives against a backdrop of unpredictable international negotiations. For this reason, increased attention is being paid to the use of international technology-oriented agreements as a complement to emissions-based agreements. Such agreements can result in more efficient allocation of invention efforts as well as encourage the wider global diffusion of knowledge and technologies.

Nick Johnstone

See also: Adaptation; Climate Change Impacts; Emissions Trading; Pigouvian Taxes

Further Reading

Carraro, C., E. DeCian, L. Nicita, E. Massetti, and E. Verdolini. 2010. Environmental Policy and Technical Change: A Survey. *International Review of Environmental and Resource Economics* 4(2): 163–219.

Jaffe, A. B., R. Newell, and R. N. Stavins. 2002. Environmental Policy and Technological Change. *Environmental and Resources Economics*, 22(1–2): 41–69.

Johnstone, Nick, and I. Hascic. 2012. Policy Incentives for Energy and Environmental Technological Innovation: Lessons from the Empirical Evidence, in J. Shogren (editor), *Encyclopedia of Energy, Natural Resource, and Environmental Economics*. Amsterdam: Elsevier.

Popp, D. C., R. G. Newell, and A. B. Jaffe. 2009. Energy, the Environment, and Technological Change. NBER Working Paper 14832.

Tolley, George S.

George S. Tolley is an exponent of a Chicago tradition of confidence in the power of economics to provide insights into behavior and useful prescriptions for public policy. His influence on environmental policy has been mostly as a university professor, advisor, and producer of scholarly and applied research. A notable exception was his tour of duty as deputy assistant secretary and director of the Office of Tax Analysis at the U.S. Treasury for 1974–1975. More typical was his service on the National Academy of Sciences Committee on Automotive Pollution, the Energy Engineering Board at the National Research Council, and various advisory boards and commissions for Illinois and Chicago, and consultant to the Agency for International Development and World Bank. With his rare combination of talent for explaining economic insights into pros and cons of different policy options and ability to have noneconomists embrace his economic ideas as their own, he has been able to influence environmental policy for the better. Major funding from the National Science Foundation and U.S. Environmental Protection Agency for grants dealing with urban pollution, amenities, visibility, and health effects of air pollution provided him the means to carry out ambitious research programs that facilitated access to decision makers. He shared what he learned through publication of many peer-reviewed journals articles and more than 20 books. Five books dealt with environmental economics and policy and one other has been particularly influential. *Valuing Health for Policy: An Economic Approach* has been read and cited by both environmental and health economics since its publication in 1994. This book is one of only 10 references listed in the guide to implementing Executive Order 12866 Economic Analysis of Federal Regulation that governs benefit–cost analysis of major environmental regulations.

George Tolley earned his B.A. from American University in 1947 and his Ph.D. in economics from the University of Chicago in 1955. He has held regular and visiting faculty positions at North Carolina State University, Purdue University, University of California—Berkeley, and the University of Chicago where he has been most of his career and at which he is professor emeritus. He is a fellow of the American Association for the Advancement of Science and is the honorary editor of the journal *Resource and Energy Economics*, which he founded and edited from 1978 to 1998. He received an honorary doctor of sciences degree from North Carolina State in 2006. He has been a practicing economist for more than 60 years and is still responding to the demand for his services.

Glenn Blomquist

See also: Air Pollution; Health

Further Reading

Blomquist, Glenn C. 2002. Economist and Editor George S. Tolley: A Special Issue in His Honor. *Resource and Energy Economics* 24(1): 3–11.

Tolley, George S., Donald Kenkel, and Robert Fabian. 1994. *Valuing Health for Policy: An Economic Approach*. Chicago: University of Chicago Press.

The White House, Office of Management and Budget, *Economic Analysis of Federal Regulations under Executive Order 12866.* http://www.whitehouse.gov/omb/inforeg_riaguide. Accessed May 31, 2013.

Toxics Release Inventory

Information disclosure is rapidly becoming a widely used policy mechanism to induce self-regulation of pollution by firms. The Toxics Release Inventory (TRI), mandated by the Emergency Planning and Community Right to Know Act of 1986, is one of the earliest examples of a policy to disclose environmental performance information about firms to the public. It mandates that all manufacturing facilities with toxic emissions above a threshold level submit information about their annual on-site releases, off-site transfers, pollution prevention activities, and recycling and other disposal methods of over 650 toxic chemicals to the U.S. Environmental Protection Agency (EPA). The EPA then makes this information publicly available, thereby providing investors and consumers, community and environmental groups, and government regulators unprecedented access to information about environmental quality and the ability to monitor the environmental performance of facilities. The annual release of the TRI figures generates national and state news reports of the facilities and locations with the largest toxic releases.

Characterized as the third wave of environmental regulation, information disclosure programs like the TRI appeal to regulators because they engage private citizens and the market in environmental regulation and could save the government money and time in drafting and implementing new regulations for a large number of pollutants. Although emissions reported to the TRI are not directly penalized, these emissions are frequently linked to other pollutants covered by an array of pollution laws, including hazardous waste, clean air, clean water, and toxic substances legislation. The TRI focuses attention directly on the underlying releases of toxic chemicals into the environment and the efforts of firms to reduce these releases through pollution prevention practices, on-site and off-site recycling, and re-use. It allows consumers and investors to signal their preferences about a facility's environmental performance through product and financial markets and thereby creates incentives for facilities to self-regulate their environmental performance. By engaging the public in previously unprecedented ways, the TRI has changed the costs and benefits of polluting to firms and has reduced the transactions costs for the public to exercise its property rights to the environment.

Reported emissions of toxic chemicals nationally have fallen dramatically from when the TRI began in the late 1980s. This decline in reported releases, however, must be interpreted with caution for several reasons. First, TRI data are self-reported, and a lack of understanding about reporting requirements and incomplete and inaccurate reporting no doubt exists, especially in the early years of the program. Second, even with completely accurate reporting, TRI releases only focus on a subset of all chemicals and pollutants, and some reduction in reported releases may mask substitution to other nonreported substances. Despite these concerns, the general conclusion is that the TRI has encouraged firms to reduce their toxic releases to avoid negative publicity and appeal to different constituencies such as investors, community groups, and government regulators.

Investors have used information about a firm's toxic releases to proxy for the productivity or innovativeness of a firm as well as to proxy for the risk from lawsuits and liabilities and greater scrutiny by regulators. A facility with high TRI releases may therefore not be as attractive to investors as one with lower releases. A number of studies find that publicly traded facilities with higher TRI releases than expected (based on their economic sector or past behavior) experience lower stock market valuations when TRI data is released. Facilities with the largest negative returns were found to subsequently reduce their emissions more in the future.

Information in the TRI is also utilized by community groups to track the behavior of facilities in their neighborhood and to uncover problems of environmental justice. By providing information about a wide class of toxic chemicals across many economic sectors for communities across the country, environmental groups and activists are able to document the health of their communities and can compare the level of emissions against community characteristics. In doing so, several studies find evidence that emissions of toxic chemicals are highest in areas that are racially diverse, poor, less well educated, and less politically active. There is some evidence that firms in these areas, especially those areas that are more likely to engage in collective action, respond to these community pressures and reduce their emissions.

Information in the TRI also impacts how firms interact and engage with government regulators. While the majority of TRI releases are not subject to explicit regulatory guidelines, firms can use their TRI emissions to signal their environmental credentials to regulators. Evidence that regulators receive such signals is supported by the fact that firms with lower TRI emissions face fewer delays in receiving new permits and are targeted for inspections at a lower rate. The TRI is also used as a vehicle for the government to promote other policies or government priorities. For example, the TRI facilitated the implementation of the National Pollution Prevention Act, which established a national policy encouraging voluntary efforts to prevent and reduce pollution at its source. As the act requires firms to report their pollution prevention activities geared toward toxic chemical releases to the TRI, government regulators harnessed the power of the market to encourage firms to voluntarily engage in self-regulation practices. Another example of the TRI being used to promote government priorities relates to the voluntary 33/50 program. Launched in 1991, this program challenged firms to voluntarily reduce their emissions of 17 toxic chemicals by 33 percent (relative to a 1988 baseline) by 1992 and 50 percent by 1995. The potential to track progress in emissions reduction and adoption of pollution prevention practices likely limited incentives to free-ride and contributed to the effectiveness of the 33/50 program in inducing voluntary adoption of pollution prevention practices, participation in the program, and reducing toxic emissions.

The TRI is a groundbreaking policy within the wider information disclosure approach to environmental regulation. By providing information about environmental pollution to the public, the TRI allows different constituencies to express their demand for environmental quality and has created opportunities for firms to engage in self-regulating practices. The TRI has served as a model for other toxic chemical registries in countries around the world as well as in the development of other pollution registries such as the Greenhouse Gas Reporting Program.

Madhu Khanna and Keith Brouhle

See also: Environmental Justice; Hazardous Waste; Information Disclosure; NIMBY and LULU

Further Reading

Cohen, Mark A., and W. Kip Viscusi. 2012. The Role of Information Disclosure in Climate Mitigation Policy. *Climate Change Economics* 3(4-1250020): 1–21.

Hamilton, J. T. 2005. *Regulation through Revelation: The Origin, Politics and Impacts of the Toxics Release Inventory Program.* Cambridge: Cambridge University Press.

Khanna, M. 2001. Economic Analysis of Non-Mandatory Approaches to Environmental Protection. *Journal of Economic Surveys,* 15(3): 291–324.

Trade Policy

Over the past two decades, there has been considerable debate about the connection between trade and environmental policy. A specific concern of the environmental lobby has been that with increased trade liberalization, governments will not be able to set appropriate environmental policies, due to the fact that they may be constrained in their use of complementary trade policies by World Trade Organization/General Agreement on Tariffs and Trade (WTO/GATT) rules. A key implication drawn from this is that, without the ability to apply border measures such as tariffs, industries in countries that apply tough environmental standards will be hurt either through loss of market share or their total displacement to countries with weaker environmental standards, thereby creating pollution havens.

The ongoing policy discussion on how to address climate change is clearly characterized by this same set of concerns. Developed countries, including the United States and the European Union (EU) member countries, are pursuing national efforts to reduce carbon emissions. In doing so, the expectation is that their energy-intensive industries will face increased costs of production. As a consequence, much of the proposed climate legislation also includes some type of border measure targeted at energy-intensive imports, popularly referred to as carbon tariffs. The argument for such border measures is twofold: first, there will be carbon leakage, that is, production by domestic energy-intensive industries such as steel will simply be replaced by production in countries with less restrictive climate policies; second, there will be a reduction in competitiveness of firms in those industries most affected by domestic climate policies.

The inclusion of border adjustments in proposed climate legislation can be rationalized as follows: by utilizing import tariffs (export subsidies) on all energy-intensive traded goods, carbon leakage is reduced (competitiveness restored) by worsening the terms of trade for countries that do not implement tough climate policy. While there is considerable debate among legal observers as to whether such border measures will be treated as trade-distorting under current WTO/GATT rules, the principle for their use is actually well-founded in the literature on origin versus destination-based taxation systems. As long as a domestic tax is applied uniformly across all goods, and what are legally termed border tax adjustments (BTAs), are set no higher than the domestic tax, there will be no effect on relative prices.

In the case of BTAs for domestic climate policy though, it is likely that they will only be applied to a small set of energy-intensive industries, including steel, aluminum, and paper production, in which case relative prices could be affected. Notwithstanding this, the WTO/GATT has rules in place on the level at which BTAs can be set: GATT Article II: 2(a) allows members of the WTO to place on the imports of any good, a BTA equivalent to an internal tax on the like good. However, under GATT Article III: 2, the BTA cannot be applied in excess of that applied directly or indirectly to the like domestic good, that is, they have to be neutral in terms of their impact on trade, their objective being to preserve competitive equality between domestic and imported goods. In addition, with respect to exported goods, WTO/GATT rules allow rebate of the domestic tax on the exported good, as long as the border adjustment does not exceed the level of the domestic tax, it is not regarded as an export subsidy under the GATT Subsidies Code. In other words, the key underlying principle of the WTO/GATT rules is that a border measure cannot be used to provide domestic firms with a competitive advantage, that is, allowing BTAs for domestic climate policy would be motivated not by environmental concerns, but to ensure that competitive equality in international trade is preserved.

While the principle of border adjustments is recognized in the WTO/GATT rules, their application will likely be complex legally in the case of climate policy. Specifically it is unclear whether a BTA will be allowed on imports of a final energy-intensive good such as steel, when domestic climate policy directly affects a nontraded input into steel production, such as electricity, which is not physically present in the final good. It could be argued that if a carbon tax on electricity production is designed to ensure that the price domestic consumers pay for an energy-intensive product such as steel reflects the social cost of producing steel, then a BTA on imported steel should be permitted. Importantly though, if a BTA is constrained by WTO/GATT rules to restoring competitive equality between domestically produced and imported steel, it should be based on the implied tax on domestic steel production. In other words, the appropriate benchmark for BTAs is the carbon content of domestic steel production, and not that of imports. Interestingly a precedent has already been set for this: BTAs levied on U.S. imports of goods that contain ozone-depleting chemicals (CFCs) are set with regards to the CFC content of U.S.-produced goods and not that of imports.

This discussion clearly highlights the tension between environmental lobbyists who regard trade policy as a means of pursuing environmental goals, and trade policy analysts who are concerned about the potential for protection through border measures for domestic environmental policy. This is borne out in recent empirical work by the World Bank, which evaluated the effects, by 2020, of three border measures targeted at developing country imports, if Organisation of Economic Co-operation and Development (OECD) countries were to unilaterally reduce their 2005 level of carbon emissions by 17 percent in 2012. These results show that a BTA based on the carbon content of developing country imports would have a significantly trade-distorting impact compared to a BTA based on the carbon content of domestic production. In addition, a BTA for both imports and exports based on the carbon content of domestic production would be the least trade-distorting outcome, a result that bears out the analysis of origin versus destination based tax systems. However, the latter would likely be difficult and complex to implement, suggesting that no border measures might actually be the best policy if countries want to avoid costly trade disputes in applying their climate policies.

Ian M. Sheldon

See also: Carbon Pricing; Externality; International Environmental Agreements; International Trade

Further Reading

Mattoo, A., A. Subramanian, D. van der Mensbrugghe, and J. He. 2009. Reconciling Climate Change and Trade Policy. CGD Working Paper, 189, Washington, D.C.: Center for Global Development.

Messerlin, P. A. 2012. Climate and Trade Policies: From Mutual Destruction to Mutual Support. *World Trade Review* 11(1): 53–80.

Tragedy of the Commons

First introduced by Garret Hardin in a 1968 *Science* article of the same name, "The Tragedy of the Commons" has become synonymous with society's overuse of common pool resources. Common pool resources are resources that can be used by a large group of individuals, but are not owned by any one individual. These resources have features of both private and public goods. As with public goods, access is open to all. Because a rationing mechanism is not used to prohibit access by potential users of the resource, these goods are characterized as nonexcludable in provision. But as with private goods the benefit is enjoyed individually. Because use by one individual diminishes the quantity or quality of the resource available for others, these goods exhibit rivalry in consumption. Examples of common pool resources include fishing grounds, public forests, groundwater aquifers, nonrenewable energy resources, and the atmosphere.

According to Hardin, the *tragedy* arises when the characteristics of common pool resources are coupled with individual self-interest. Left to their own devices, humans will overuse the commons because the individual benefit exceeds the cost paid by that individual. Costs imposed on other users by an individual's own use are ignored. Self-interest provides a compelling incentive to continue to use the commons, even if continued use by all may lead to depletion. Hardin used the parable of a common pasture shared by self-interested herdsmen to describe this incentive and the resulting unsustainable outcome. He suggested that the tragedy manifests itself today in overgrazing on national lands, overfishing in the world's oceans, and overuse of national parks. The Tragedy of the Commons has been used to explain species extinction, water supply depletion, climate change, and other environmental threats. Many forms of pollution are likewise understood by considering the individual utility calculations associated with using the commons as a means of disposal.

Hardin ascribed the underlying cause of the tragedy to exponential population growth, an issue to which he dedicated much of his essay. Population growth, Hardin argued, was one of a special class of societal problems: those without technical solutions. Suggesting that a world with finite resources can support only a finite population, Hardin inferred that population growth must at some point equal zero. Noting that the associated maximum population level would be uncomfortably compromised, Hardin suggested that the optimal population level is below this maximum. He proposed that a laissez-faire approach to human reproduction cannot be expected to result in the optimal rate of population growth.

Hardin did not just describe the dilemma in his essay, he suggested solutions. Appeals to conscience are decidedly not among those suggestions. In fact, Hardin argued that appeals to conscience will tend to eliminate from the human race those who have a conscience. His logic is simple. Those who voluntarily restrain themselves from overexploiting the common resource will receive fewer resources. Those who do not succumb to appeals to conscience will gain more resources. Those with more resources will outcompete those with fewer, and will produce offspring with similar tendencies.

If people cannot be convinced to voluntarily restrain themselves from overgrazing, what can be done? One possibility is privatization of public resources. Enclosure laws that converted common grazing areas to fenced, individually owned parcels led to better stewardship of the land because each landowner had a private incentive to maintain his own property. Some find this market approach appealing, but it cannot easily be applied to oceans, the air, or other widely dispersed commons. Hardin preferred the coercive power of laws, arguing that rules that limit our freedom, but to which we have mutually agreed, can help us avoid the tragedy of the commons. He admitted that regulation has its drawbacks, but argued that we must do something and all other available mechanisms are worse.

It is interesting to note, as Hardin did, the contrast between the prevailing sentiment of the *Tragedy* and that which Adam Smith noted in *An Inquiry into the Nature and Causes of the Wealth of Nations* (1776) regarding the outcome of individual self-interest in the context of markets. Smith can be interpreted as suggesting that individual interest can lead to maximum social benefit, which stands in stark contrast to Hardin's suggestion that individual interest leads to ruin. Understanding that Smith's proposition applies in the context of market goods, while Hardin's thesis applies to common property helps us see that both positions hold merit.

The Tragedy of the Commons is easily seen as an application of the Prisoner's Dilemma, whereby the actions that each individual is compelled to undertake due to self-interest result in suboptimal conditions for society at large, thereby implying that cooperative action would be preferred. According to Hardin, because individuals behave opportunistically, to avoid the tragedy, use of the commons must be governed by some form of regulation, including private property rights, resource allocation, or taxation.

While Hardin's simple examples and unflinching language are compelling, his essay is not without controversy or criticism. We do observe examples of sustained, cooperative use of common pool resources. In recent years, behavioral economists have chipped away at the starkest assumptions about self-interest on which some of Hardin's claims rest, providing arguments against the inevitability of overuse. Elinor Ostrom (winner of the Nobel Prize in Economic Sciences in 2009) argued that collective institutions and polycentric governance could serve as an effective alternative to government control or privatization of the commons. Ostrom presents numerous case studies illustrating that collective rules and norms can achieve environmentally sustainable and economically efficient outcomes for common pool resources.

In addition to misjudging the capacity of communities to establish and enforce rules for governing the commons, Hardin underestimated the impact that technology would have on crop yields. Hardin also did not foresee the impending declinations in population growth that would result from advances in health care and social welfare systems in developed nations. In later years, Hardin wrote that he should have specified that the tragedy followed from *unmanaged* commons. The commons can be managed sustainably, and in his original 1968 essay Hardin advocated for rules designed to manage the commons.

Kate Krause and Peter W. Schuhmann

See also: Common Pool Resources; Externality; Hardin, Garrett; Public Goods

Further Reading

Hardin, G. 1968. The Tragedy of the Commons. *Science* 162(3859): 1243–1248.

Ostrom, E. 1990. *Governing the Commons: The Evolution of Institutions for Collective Action (Political Economy of Institutions and Decisions)*. Cambridge: Cambridge University Press.

Smith, A. 1937. *The Wealth of Nations*. New York: Modern Library.

Trans-Alaskan Pipeline

The Trans-Alaskan Pipeline System (TAPS) transports crude oil from the Prudhoe Bay oilfields on the North Slope of Alaska to the Port of Valdez and the world oil market. The pipeline system, constructed from 1975 to 1977, is an engineering marvel covering over 800 miles. Crossing sensitive environmental terrain, including mountain ranges, earthquake zones, and permafrost, the pipeline opened to drilling the environmentally sensitive North Slope, which is home to vast herds of caribou. The pipeline features prominently in some of the most important environmental developments in the United States.

Vast oil discoveries on the North Slope were first announced in 1968. The timing was important for two reasons. First, oil prices doubled between 1970 and 1973 increasing pressure for rapid development of the North Slope. Second, environmental concerns also increased during this period; the National Environmental Policy Act (NEPA) was passed in 1969. Importantly, NEPA required an environmental impact assessment of large-scale projects, and the TAPS was one of the first test cases for NEPA.

The environmental impact assessment for the Trans-Alaskan Pipeline was conducted by the Department of the Interior. It identified short-term impacts (e.g., erosion and noise during construction), operational impacts (e.g., discharge from tanker ballast, oil releases from tank cleaning, heat loss melting permafrost and causing instability), long-term impacts (e.g., increased public access from roads, disturbances of fish and wildlife habitat), and cultural impacts (e.g., oil revenues and outside contact accelerating cultural change on the Native communities). It also warned about the likely danger of marine and terrestrial oil spills and included the prescient statement that "The salmon and other fishery resources of Prince William Sound would be especially vulnerable to such spills." The impact assessment was highly controversial and invited public comment and court cases.

NEPA required the evaluation of alternatives to the project. One viable alternative was a Trans-Canada land route, which would have avoided earthquake zones and risky marine transshipment. Moreover, this alternative would have delivered the oil to the more lucrative Chicago market. In fact, the Trans-Canada route may have dominated the Trans-Alaska route based on both economic and environmental concerns.

NEPA's performance in this important test case was mixed. In the end, the U.S. Congress exempted TAPS from NEPA and rejected the Trans-Canada alternative. This congressional settlement also resolved Alaskan Native land claims and conserved large tracts of Alaskan wilderness. Despite the exemption, NEPA likely did affect the actual construction of the pipeline, which featured technological innovations to reduce the risk of earthquake damage and to lessen the impact on the permafrost.

Without TAPS, the 1989 Exxon *Valdez* oil spill would not have occurred. This costly spill heightened attention to the environmental dangers of economic development, and the concept of existence value and the contingent valuation method were developed as the subsequent court cases attempted to calculate the damages to the Prince William Sound.

TAPS makes further oil development on the North Slope of Alaska possible. In particular, opening the oil deposits in the Arctic National Wildlife Refuge (ANWR) would make use of TAPS. Without TAPS, the coastal breeding ground of the caribou in ANWR would not be as threatened.

The future of TAPS is highly uncertain. The maximum daily throughput is over 2 million barrels per day. Current production is only 700,000 barrels per day and declining. In addition, global climate change may melt sections of the permafrost which supports the pipeline. Although the future of the TAPS is uncertain, TAPS has played an important role in the development of environmental and energy policy.

Stephen P. Holland

See also: Contingent Valuation; Exxon *Valdez* Oil Spill; Passive Use Value; Peak Oil

Further Reading

Alexander, V., and K. Van Cleve. 1983. The Alaska Pipeline: A Success Story. *Annual Review of Ecology and Systematics* 14: 443–463.

Brew, David A. 1974. *Environmental Impact Analysis: The Example of the Proposed Trans-Alaska Pipeline.* Geological Survey Circular 695, United States Department of the Interior, Reston, VA.

Busenberg, George J. 2011. The Policy Dynamics of the Trans-Alaska Pipeline System. *Review of Policy Research* 28(5): 401–422.

Cicchetti, Charles, and A. M. Freeman. 1973. The Trans-Alaskan Pipeline: An Economic Analysis of Alternatives, in A. C. Enthoven and A. M. Freeman (editors), *Pollution, Resources and the Environment.* New York: W. W. Norton & Co.

Department of the Interior. 1972. *Final Environmental Impact Statement Proposed Trans-Alaskan Pipeline.* Washington, D.C., vols. 1–6.

Travel Cost Method

The travel cost model is a revealed preference method for estimating the economic value of changes to the accessibility and quality of environmental resources. Typically the method is applied to outdoor recreation. For example, imagine an oil spill generating acute environmental impacts along a shoreline that results in beach closures. Beachgoers must find alternative, less desirable destinations or activities in lieu of visiting the closed beaches. The travel cost model can be used to quantify in monetary terms their losses. Alternatively, the satisfaction that recreators derive from visiting a lake will depend in part on the lake's water quality. If a policy intervention reduces the quantity of pollution loadings into the lake, its water quality will improve and visitors' recreational experience will be enhanced. In response, recreators will likely take more trips to the lake, and the travel cost model can be used to monetize the benefits generated by the quality improvement.

In a 1947 letter to the National Park Service, Harold Hotelling suggested the logic behind the travel cost model. The National Park Service was interested in measuring the recreational benefits arising from the parks it managed. Unlike traditional marketed goods, visitors to these parks paid at most a minimal entry fee that was administratively set. Because the price of admission was not determined by the interaction of supply and demand for park services, traditional approaches to welfare analysis were thought to be inappropriate. Hotelling recognized that entry fees were only a small fraction of the total cost of visiting a park. In particular, visitors must travel from their homes to the park and, in the process, incur travel costs. These costs include out-of-pocket expenses (such as gasoline and other automotive operating costs) as well as travel time. Indeed, the degree to which people are willing to bear these costs and travel long distances to desirable national parks is a strong indication of the recreational value they provide. By exploiting the variation in visitors' proximity to parks and opportunity costs of travel time (i.e., what they would be willing to pay to avoid an hour traveling to a recreation destination), one can trace out a demand curve for trips to a park as a function of travel costs. This demand curve shares the same properties as demand curves for marketed goods, and thus can be used to generate the value arising from changes in the quality and accessibility of recreational resources.

A recreational demand curve for a particular recreational site can be illustrated graphically with the horizontal axis measuring the quantity of recreational trips and the vertical axis measuring the price of a trip, or the travel cost. The relationship between the quantity and price of recreational trips obeys the law of demand, implying that as travel costs rise, ceteris paribus, consumers take fewer trips. The recreational trip demand curve slopes downward. And if travel costs were sufficiently high, the demand for trips would fall to zero. Consider the possibility that access to the site is closed, perhaps due to an oil spill. Prior to the spill, our representative individual would incur a particular travel cost to visit the site. At that price, she was willing to take a certain number of trips. After the spill, her quantity of trips falls to zero, and the price that would make her freely chose that quantity is found where the demand curve intercepts the vertical axis. The *consumer surplus* generated by those trips equals the triangular area below the demand curve and above the price. This area represents the difference between her *maximum* willingness to pay for the trips and what she actually paid. Stated different, the consumer surplus represents what she would be willing to pay for the right to visit the site at the current price. With the site closure, she loses her ability to visit the site and therefore experiences an economic loss. The monetary value of that loss is equal to the consumer surplus.

If we were to add up the consumer surpluses across all visitors to the affected site, we would have an estimate of the total economic loss arising from the closure.

Now consider a policy that improves the quality of a recreational site. After the quality improvement, the desirability of the site increases, and thus our consumer demands more trips. This increase in demand corresponds to an outward shift in the demand curve. Assuming our consumer incurs a constant per trip travel cost, her quantity of trips increases and her consumer surplus increases by the trapezoid between the demand curves and above the per trip travel cost. That area represents her maximum willingness to pay for the quality improvement. Aggregating these *changes* in consumer surplus across the affected population of recreation generates an estimate of the total willingness to pay for the quality improvement.

A maintained assumption of the travel cost model is that all value generated by the recreational site is tied to the recreational *use* of the recreational site. In other words, if consumers do not consume a particular site, they do not value changes in its accessibility and quality. Karl Goran Mäler called this assumption weak complementarity, and in the context of traditional marketed goods like televisions and houses, seems intuitive and plausible. For unique recreational resources such as the Grand Canyon or Yosemite National Parks, the assumption is more troubling, as it rules out passive use values and other use related values that may not be tied directly to recreation. In these cases, the welfare estimates generated by the travel cost model should be interpreted as a lower bound to the total value generated by the resource. In some cases, these lower-bound estimates may be sufficiently informative for policy purposes, but if not, the analyst should consider other nonmarket valuation approaches, such as stated preference methods.

Roger H. von Haefen

See also: Contingent Valuation; Nonmarket Valuation; Outdoor Recreation; Welfare

Further Reading

Freeman, A. Myrick. 2003. *The Measurement of Environmental and Resource Values,* 2nd ed. Washington, D.C.: Resources for the Future.

Hotelling, Harold. 2000. Letter to A. E. Drury, National Park Service, dated June 18, 1947, republished in Frank Ward and Diana Beal, *Valuing Nature with Travel Cost Models,* Northampton, MA: Edward Elgar.

Mäler, Karl Goran. 1974. *Environmental Economics: A Theoretical Inquiry*, Baltimore, MD: Johns Hopkins University Press.

Tropical Rain Forests

Tropical rain forests are located between the Tropics of Cancer and Capricorn, primarily in developing nations within Central and South America, West and Central Africa, and Southeast Asia where annual rainfall averages more than 2,500 mm.

These forests cover only a small part of the earth's surface, but yet contain well over half of the world's terrestrial plant, insect, and animal species providing biodiversity levels unmatched by any other biome.

Tropical deforestation increased from approximately 7.75 million hectares per year in the 1920s to a height of approximately 14.67 million hectares in the early 1980s, to the recent level of approximately 7.43 million hectares per year through to 2010. The rate of deforestation has been the highest in Asia for the last three decades (1.1%, 2.9%, and 4.1% in the 1980s, 1990s, and 2000s, respectively) with Latin America and Africa behind this figure with annual losses between 0.7% and 2.1%, but also increasing over this time period. In absolute terms the total amount of primary forest lost has been greatest in Brazil, India, and Mexico, totaling over 374, 261, and 132 million hectares by 2005, respectively. The largest source of tropical deforestation is the conversion of primary forest to cropland and pasture.

Tropical deforestation is of global concern because these ecosystems are critical for hydrological and carbon cycles, provide habitat for rare species, and generate local and regional benefits including soil and erosion control and nontimber and timber forest products. These ecosystems have environmental impacts that reach far beyond political borders. For example, approximately 8 trillion tons of water evaporates from Amazonian forests each year affecting atmospheric circulation and precipitation patterns that span continents and hemispheres.

The public good characteristics of tropical forests create a market failure that motivates economic policy aimed at forest protection and sustainable use. Unlike temperate forests, because of the inherent low fertility of the soils and slow growth rate of tropical timber species, tropical forests are often treated as a nonrenewable resource in policy. Policy analysis distinguishes between the sources, immediate causes, and underlying causes of deforestation to better identify the appropriate targets for policy and develop the means for which these effects can be empirically measured. The sources of deforestation are described as the land uses that replace forest cover (such as agriculture, ranching, plantations, and urban land) and the activities that result in loss of forest cover (such as charcoal production and logging at high intensities). Policies to address the sources of deforestation target landowners, firms, and households. The immediate causes of deforestation include the set of existing choices as determined by agent characteristics and other exogenous factors (including tax incentives, market prices of goods produced on cleared land, laws, and regulations) that can be confounded by population dynamics. Policies to address the immediate causes of deforestation target regional markets, transportation, and marketing infrastructure. The underlying causes of deforestation include the macroeconomic policies that promote or support deforestation through the design and implementation of specific laws and regulations (such as migration policies, industry level subsidies, and other government policies that directly or indirectly impact deforestation rates). These policies affect the immediate causes of deforestation and the sources of deforestation through regional and national markets that are impacted by social, political, and cultural norms and technological ability. Policies to address the underlying causes of deforestation target macroeconomic conditions and/or national and international markets.

Efforts to reduce deforestation and preserve biodiversity are often complicated by government policies that encourage economic development (such as road, dam, and settlement projects) to address poverty, foreign debt, and international trade deficits. Agricultural subsidies, tax breaks, and illegal logging have also contributed to forest clearing in many nations. Thus, given the inherent trade-offs between deforestation and development, strategies to reduce deforestation rates face the challenge of encouraging preservation while respecting national sovereignty to advance populations and tap natural resources for economic development. Some market-based interventions include timber certification programs, roundtables on sustainable production (such as for acai and palm oil), and moratoria (e.g., on beef).

At the local level, polices are focused on the sources of deforestation. In this case, government and nongovernmental organization policy goals can be divided between those that aim to stabilize agriculture (such as shade farming and agroforestry) and policies that seek to increase returns of the forest (such as the harvest of nontimber forest products including rubber and native fruits and nuts). Government support for ecotourism can address the sources, immediate and underlying causes by providing employment opportunities for local peoples as well as creating a national revenue source supported by federal preservation and park designations.

Internationally, programs that provide monetary incentives for developing countries to avoid deforestation and reduce deforestation rates are the most promising option to date. These programs that fall under REDD and REDD+ (Reducing Emissions from Deforestation and Forest Degradation). REDD "is an effort to create a financial value for the carbon stored in forests, offering incentives for developing countries to reduce emissions from forested lands and invest in low-carbon paths to sustainable development." These payments are made for conservation (or avoiding deforestation), sustainable management of forests, and the enhancement of carbon stocks.

Jill Caviglia-Harris

See also: Biodiversity; Exhaustible Resources; Offsets; Public Goods

Further Reading

Angelsen, A., and D. Kaimowitz. 1999. Rethinking the Causes of Deforestation: Lessons from Economic Models. *World Bank Research Observer* 14: 73–98.

Betts, Richard A., Yadvinder Malhi, and J. Timmons Roberts. 2008. The Future of the Amazon: New Perspectives from Climate, Ecosystem and Social Sciences. *Philosophical Transactions of the Royal Society B: Biological Sciences* 363(1498): 1729–1735.

Food and Agriculture Organization of the United Nations. 2012. State of the World's Forests. Rome: FAO/UNEP.

Malhi, Yadvinder, J. Timmons Roberts, Richard A. Betts, Timothy J. Killeen, Wenhong Li, and Carlos A. Nobre. 2008. Climate Change, Deforestation, and the Fate of the Amazon. *Science* 319(5860): 169–172.

Nepstad, Daniel C., Claudia M. Stickler, Britaldo Soares-Filho, and Frank Merry. 2008. Interactions among Amazon Land Use, Forests and Climate: Prospects for a Near-Term Forest Tipping Point. *Philosophical Transactions of the Royal Society B: Biological Sciences* 363(1498): 1737–1746.

UN-REDD. 2009. "About the UN_REDD programme." http://www.un-redd.org/AboutUNREDDProgramme/tabid/583/Default.aspx. Accessed March 22, 2013.

U

United States Society for Ecological Economics

The United States Society for Ecological Economics (USSEE) is one of several regional professional organizations within the broader scope of the International Society for Ecological Economics (ISEE). USSEE and the other regional ecological economics organizations provide a venue for intellectual exchange and collaboration on issues related to the theory, policy, and implementation of sustainability and sustainable development. USSEE consists of interdisciplinary scholars and practitioners who seek to develop integrated solutions to our most pressing economic, social, and environmental problems, and who care about the well-being of the earth. Other regional ecological economics societies represent ecological economists in Africa, Australia–New Zealand, Brazil, Canada, Europe, India, Latin America, and Russia. All ecological economics societies hold professional meetings that serve as a forum for exchanging information, presenting cutting-edge research results and advancing practical solutions toward an ecologically sustainable and economically viable future.

Ecological economics is the science of sustainability, which is predicated on the notion that environmental problems are complex, nonlinear, and require transdisciplinary approaches to solving them. This integration of economic, social, and ecological systems brings together scholars and practitioners from a variety of natural and social science disciplines. The common goal of ecological economists is to enhance theoretical understanding and practical solutions for achieving long-term economic and social well-being, without undermining the absorptive, regenerative, and resource capacity of the natural environment. The focus of the USSEE is on developing new approaches to understanding our economy and its dependence on the biophysical systems that govern life on earth. USSEE is intentional about advancing dialogue across different disciplines, backgrounds, and professional contexts to address pressing social and ecological problems. The society is particularly interested in identifying concrete solutions and actions to bring about a more just and sustainable future.

The USSEE is a membership organization, and USSEE members are also members of the International Society for Ecological Economics. A portion of annual dues paid to the ISEE contribute to USSEE initiatives and activities.

The USSEE was founded in 2000. Its past presidents have been Robert O'Neill (2000–01), John Gowdy (2002–03), Barry Solomon (2004–05), Karin Limburg

(2006–07), Sabine O'Hara (2008–09), Jon Erickson (2010–11), and Valerie Luzadis (2012–14).

The board of directors of the USSEE establishes policy for the society and is responsible for the fulfillment of the stated purposes of the society. Officers of the society include the president, president-elect, immediate past president, and secretary-treasurer. The USSEE board of directors is comprised of eight individuals, drawn from the president, president-elect, immediate past president, secretary-treasurer, four at-large members, and one student member. The positions of president-elect and immediate past president are vacant every other year for periods of one year so that the two never simultaneously serve on the board. The at-large members, student member, secretary-treasurer, and president-elect are elected by a direct vote of the USSEE membership.

The USSEE's biennial conferences provide a national and international forum to focus on the latest issues in ecological economics and to share information about new developments and activities. Biennial conferences provide opportunities for students of ecological economics to present their research and to engage with scholars in the field. Students are represented in the USSEE board, and the society provides financial aid and volunteer opportunities to students to enable participation in meetings to present work and share ideas for the future. USSEE biennial conferences are held in odd-numbered years, and ISEE conferences are held in even-numbered years. The inaugural conference for the USSEE was held in Duluth, Minnesota (2001), and subsequent conferences have been held in Saratoga Springs, New York (2003), Tacoma, Washington (2005), New York (2007), Washington, D.C. (2009), East Lansing, Michigan (2011), and Burlington, Vermont (2013).

In between conferences, USSEE board and members work to advance knowledge in ecological economics through publications, higher education, workshops, blogs, and other formal and informal communications. *Ecological Economics* is the long-standing transdisciplinary journal of the ISEE. The journal is concerned with extending and integrating the study and management of nature's household (ecology) and humankind's household (economics). This integration is necessary because conceptual, academic, and professional isolation have led to economic and environmental policies that are mutually destructive rather than reinforcing in the long term. USSEE previously sponsored the publication of *Ecological Economics Reviews* as a special issue of the *Annals of the New York Academy of Sciences*. A related journal is slated to be published by Springer under the title of *Reviews in Ecological Economics*. The USSEE also supports regular webinars related to ecological economics, edited collections of papers from biennial conferences, and regular posts to an online blog highlighting education opportunities, publications, general discussion topics, and related job postings.

The USSEE honors scholars and practitioners in ecological economics through the Herman Daly Award, which is given in honor of Herman Daly, one of the visionaries who founded the field of ecological economics. The award is designed to recognize individuals who have connected ecological economic thinking to practical applications and implementation of solutions that are sustainable in scale, equitable in distribution, and efficient in allocation. The award is given in conjunction with the USSEE biennial conference. Past recipients of the Herman Daly Award include David Batker (2003), Mathis Wackernagel (2005), Gretchen Daily (2007), John Gowdy (2009), Juliet Schor (2011), and Annie Leonard (2013).

The USSEE also provides leadership in curriculum development at the undergraduate, graduate, and continuing education level in a range of academic fields such as environmental science, environmental studies, ecological economics, policy, management, law, and ethics. Outside of academia, our members engage in intellectual exchange and communication about the full scope of ecological economics, including analyses and positions about the economic, social, and environmental crises we face as a nation and globe, as well as the policy options available for addressing them effectively.

The USSEE plays a key role in setting the research agenda for ecological economics in the United States, and in communicating the development of effective economic, social, and environmental policies. In engaging scholars, practitioners, and policymakers as its members, the USSEE is committed to advancing research and analysis as well as identifying policy tools and practical solutions that can be implemented at the national, state, and community levels.

Robert B. Richardson

See also: Association of Environmental and Resource Economists; Ecological Economics; Fisheries Economics Associations; International Association for Energy Economics

Further Reading

Costanza, Robert, John H. Cumberland, Herman E. Daly, Robert Goodland, and Richard B. Norgaard. 1997. *An Introduction to Ecological Economics*. Boca Raton, FL: CRC Press.

Daly, Herman E., and John B. Cobb, Jr. 1994. *For The Common Good: Redirecting the Economy toward Community, the Environment, and a Sustainable Future*. Boston, MA: Beacon Press.

Daly, Herman E., and Joshua Farley. 2010. *Ecological Economics: Principles and Applications*, 2nd ed. Washington, D.C.: Island Press.

Ehrlich, Paul R. 2008. Key Issues for Attention from Ecological Economists. *Environment and Development Economics* 13(1): 1–20.

Røpke, Inge. 2005. Trends in the Development of Ecological Economics from the Late 1980s to the Early 2000s. *Ecological Economics* 55(2): 262–290.

University Economics Departments

Many economic programs offer doctoral degrees with a specialty in environmental and resource economics and/or agricultural economics. University of California at Riverside, University of New Mexico, and University of Wyoming were among the first (1969, 1974 and 1975, respectively) to begin offering the environmental and resource economics field as part of their doctoral degree in economics. However, students seeking a doctorate in economics with a field in environmental and resource economics have a host of universities to choose from including both traditional economics departments and agricultural economics departments.

Agricultural economics departments are listed on the Agricultural and Applied Economics Association website (www.aaea.org) and individual department websites. Graduate programs in economics are listed on the American Economic Association website (www.aeaweb.org), individual department websites, and are also obtained from email correspondences. Some departments provide flexibility to the student to choose a field without limiting the choices offered by the program.

The agricultural economics departments that offer a Ph.D. in the field of environmental and resource economics are (in alphabetical order): Arizona State University, Auburn University, Colorado State University, Cornell University, Iowa State University, Kansas State University, Michigan State University, North Carolina State University, Ohio State University, Oklahoma State University, Oregon State University, Pennsylvania State University, Purdue University, Texas A&M University, Texas Tech University, University of Arizona, University of California at Berkeley, University of California at Davis, University of Connecticut, University of Georgia, University of Florida, University of Illinois, University of Maryland, University of Minnesota, University of Missouri, University of Nebraska, University of Rhode Island, University of Tennessee, University of Wisconsin, Utah State University, Virginia Tech University, Washington State University, and West Virginia University.

The economics departments that offer a Ph.D. in the field of environmental and resource economics are (in alphabetical order): Arizona State University, Auburn University, Clemson University, Colorado School of Mines, Colorado State University, Cornell University, George Washington University, Georgia State University, Harvard University, Iowa State University, Michigan State University, North Carolina State University, Oregon State University, Rensselaer Polytechnic Institute, Stanford University, SUNY Binghamton, Texas Tech University, Tulane University, University of Arizona, University of California at Riverside, University of California at San Diego, University of California at Santa Barbara, University of Colorado, University of Connecticut, University of Delaware, University of Hawaii, University of Kentucky, University of Maryland, University of Miami, University of Michigan, University of New Mexico, University of Notre Dame, University of Oregon, University of Rhode Island, University of Tennessee, University of Texas,

University of Utah, University of Washington, University of Wyoming, Vanderbilt University, Virginia Tech University, Washington State University, West Virginia University, and Yale University.

Many schools appear in both the agricultural economics and economics lists. In these cases, a Ph.D. in environmental and resource economics is offered through both programs, either as a separate or joint program.

Economists and prospective students are interested in how academic departments fair relative to others in research productivity. Such rankings serve as an aid in benchmarking research productivity, aligning perspective graduate students with Ph.D. programs, or in matching job candidates with potential academic employers. In the field of environmental and resource economics, studies provide rankings for economics departments based on faculty research productivity in *Journal of Economic Literature* (JEL) Category Q, Agricultural, Resource and Environmental Economics. Rankings are typically based on quality-weighted publication measures such as citation impact scores. Other methods of department rankings include surveys of faculty, graduate student placements, and journal article page counts in select journals.

Using faculty publications between 1985 and 2010 provided in the Econlit database and quality indicators provided by the Social Science Citation Index (SSCI) and Research Papers in Economics (RePEc) in JEL category Q, the top agricultural economics programs are (in ranked order): University of California at Davis, Iowa State University, University of Maryland, University of California at Berkeley, Cornell University, North Carolina State University, Purdue University, University of Illinois, University of Minnesota, Michigan State University, University of Wisconsin, Ohio State University, Texas A & M University, Oregon State University, Washington State University, and Utah State University.

The top economics departments are (in ranked order): Iowa State University, University of Wyoming, North Carolina State University, Yale University, Harvard University, University of California at Santa Barbara, SUNY Binghamton, University of Rhode Island, Massachusetts Institute of Technology, Stanford University, University of Colorado, University of Connecticut, Georgetown University and Rensselaer Polytechnic Institute.

There are differences in the top departments in the subdisciplines of JEL category Q. In JEL category Q1—agriculture, agricultural economics departments dominate the top 10 based on total productivity in this field. The top 10 departments are (in ranked order): University of California at Davis, Iowa State University, Purdue University, Cornell University, North Carolina State University, University of California at Berkeley, University of Illinois, University of Maryland, Michigan State University, and University of Minnesota.

In the other JEL subdisciplines, Q2—renewable resources and conservation, Q3—nonrenewable resources and conservation, Q4—energy, and Q5—environmental economics, there is a mix of agricultural economics and economics departments in the top 10. The top departments in the field of renewable resources and conservation are (in ranked order): University of Wyoming, University of Maryland, University of California at Davis, University of California at Berkeley, Iowa State University, North Carolina State University, University of Illinois, Cornell University, University of Minnesota, and Ohio State University.

The top departments in the field of nonrenewable resources and conservation are (in ranked order): University of California at Berkeley, University of Maryland, University of California at Santa Barbara, University of Wyoming, University of California at Davis, University of Minnesota, University of Wisconsin, Cornell University, Purdue University, and University of Colorado.

The top departments in the field of energy are (in ranked order): University of Wyoming, Cornell University, Iowa State University, University of California at Davis, Harvard University, University of Minnesota, University of California at Berkeley, Purdue University, University of California at Santa Barbara, and Texas A&M University.

The top departments in the field of environmental economics are (in ranked order): University of Wyoming, University of Maryland, University of California at Santa Barbara, Michigan State University, University of California at Berkeley, University of Illinois, Iowa State University, University of California at Davis, Oregon State University, and Cornell University.

While schools may be ranked differently according to their productivity, statistical analysis indicates that there may be minimal difference between groups of schools.

Therese C. Grijalva and Clifford Nowell

See also: Journals

Further Reading

Grijalva, Therese C., and Clifford Nowell. 2008. A Guide to Graduate Study in Economics: Ranking Economics Departments by Fields of Expertise. *Southern Economic Journal* 74(4): 971–996.

Grijalva, Therese C., and Clifford Nowell. 2012. What Interests Environmental and Resource Economists? A Comparison of Research Output in Agricultural Economics versus Environmental Economics. *Agricultural and Resource Economics Review* forthcoming.

Smith, V. Kerry. 2010. Reflections—Legacies, Incentives, and Advice. *Review of Environmental Economics and Policy* 4(2): 309–324.

User Cost

In resource and environmental economics, dynamic resource models pertain to the study of how the amount of a resource—the stock of the resource—changes over time. Stocks can change due to natural processes (fish are born and die, seepage of rainfall recharges a groundwater aquifer, and so forth), and due to human intervention (people catch fish, pump groundwater, mine coal). The purpose of these models is to examine the economics of harvest and extraction.

Although the element of time is a fundamental feature of a dynamic resource model, it is only a necessary feature of dynamic modeling. The sufficient characteristic—what makes a model dynamic in an economically nontrivial way—is that use of the resource today changes the amount available in the future. Solar and wind energy are renewable resources in the sense that they change over time, but they are not depletable—their availability in the future does not depend on their use today—and so there is no classical dynamic element to their use. By comparison, for instance, extracting a unit of groundwater today reduces the amount of groundwater in the future. It follows that dynamic resource models pertain to exhaustible resources and renewable, depletable resources.

The economic significance of this simple physical dynamic of resource use—that each unit extracted today implies one less unit available for the future—lies in its implication for economic cost. The economic cost of extracting a resource is not only the production cost of extraction. It includes the opportunity cost imposed on the future because one more unit extracted today means one less unit available in the future, and so the value of the resource stock in the future will be lower. This opportunity cost is known as the user cost.

This cost will strike many readers as intuitive, but it is worth considering a simple exercise to illustrate it. Suppose you are on a deserted island and a friend mails you a cake (how you end up on an island alone, with a friend who knows you are there and won't save you, but manages to get a cake to you, is left to your imagination). The cake will mold on day 3, but until then—for the two days starting with the delivery of the cake—it is perfectly good. It is small enough that you could eat it all on day 1 and still enjoy the last bite. How would you divide your consumption of it across the two days?

Most people would say they would divide the cake roughly in half across the two days, and almost everyone would leave at least some of the cake for day 2. In this example, the cake is an exhaustible resource stock for which the extraction cost is zero. The impulse to divide the cake (divide the stock) across two days reflects the opportunity cost of current consumption described earlier. Every bite taken on day 1 is one less bite available on day 2.

The only difference between the opportunity cost in this cake exercise and the opportunity cost in most dynamic resource models is that in the former the opportunity cost arises strictly due to the finiteness of the stock—again, one bite taken today is one less bite for tomorrow—whereas in most resource models the opportunity cost arises because a reduction in the size of the stock left for the future increases the cost of extraction in the future; in other words, the cost is not due to the finiteness of the stock per se, but rather due to the higher cost associated with a smaller stock. For fishing, the full economic cost of catching fish today is not just the cost of catching fish, but includes the cost imposed on the future because leaving fewer fish to the future will increase the cost of catching them. Similarly, for groundwater the full economic cost of groundwater extraction is the cost of pumping water plus the cost imposed on the future because each unit of water extracted today means higher pumping costs in the future. For coal, the economic cost of mining is the current extraction cost plus the opportunity cost imposed on the future because as the stock is drawn down, extraction costs rise.

At the margin, this opportunity cost that is imposed on the future by current extraction is often called the marginal user cost. The full marginal cost of current extraction is the current marginal extraction cost plus the marginal user cost.

From the perspective of economic efficiency, a resource should be exploited only if it provides at least some value to people: fish are harvested because people like to eat them, coal is mined because people want the energy embedded in it, and groundwater is pumped because people want to drink it, irrigate their crops, and water their lawns. Denoting this benefit at the margin by marginal benefit, the economically efficient rate of use of a resource stock is characterized by the condition that the marginal benefit of current extraction is equal to the marginal cost of current extraction, which includes the marginal user cost.

This fundamental equation of efficient dynamic resource use is the source of a number of insights about the economically efficient rate of resource extraction. Here is the first: current extraction is lower than would be predicted by a static model that ignores the implication of current extraction on future benefits. In a static model where the future is ignored, efficient extraction is identified as the quantity where the marginal benefit of the last unit extracted is just equal to the current marginal extraction cost of the last unit. In a dynamic setting, though, it is understood that the marginal cost of extracting the last unit includes the opportunity cost arising because the unit could be used in the future instead, that is, the marginal user cost. This additional cost causes current extraction to fall.

The impact of the discount rate in a dynamic resource model is communicated via the marginal user cost. The higher the discount rate the lower the marginal user cost, because the net benefit of exploiting the stock in the future is lower. Applying this understanding brings one to a second insight. Because the marginal user cost depends on the discount rate, with a higher discount rate implying a lower marginal user cost, the optimal rate of current extraction increases with an increase in the discount rate.

The implication for the efficient rate of exploitation of a resource stock over time is very different for an exhaustible resource and for a renewable, depletable resource. For an exhaustible resource the marginal cost of current extraction is always rising over time because the resource stock is always falling over time. This brings us to a third insight concerning the efficient use of an exhaustible resource over time. Because the marginal benefit of current extraction is downward sloping (think of the cake example, where the first bite is more satisfying than the last bite), and marginal cost is rising over time, it follows that the extraction of an exhaustible resource falls over time. In other words, more of the resource stock is extracted in the current period than next period, more of the resource stock is extracted next period than the period after, and so on.

For a renewable resource stock the dynamics are more complicated. In the typical case there is a stock level at which extraction satisfies the economically efficient rate of use and satisfies a biological or physical condition that extraction is just equal to the replenishment of the stock. For example, in the case of a fish stock this stock level is where the efficient harvest is just equal to stock growth, and in the case of a groundwater stock this stock level is where the efficient extraction of water is just equal to recharge from rainfall. At this stock level the stock does not change over time; extraction equals stock replenishment period after period. This stock level is called the steady-state stock level, because the stock level remains steady over time.

What happens when the stock is not at its steady-state level? When the stock is above this level, the marginal cost of extraction is lower, both because the marginal extraction cost is lower and because the marginal user cost is lower (when the stock is relatively large, the cost imposed on the future by taking one more unit today is relatively low). It follows that extraction must be greater than replenishment, causing the stock to fall to the steady-state level. When the stock is below the steady-state level, a similar logic compels the conclusion that the stock must rise to the steady-state level. We arrive at a fourth insight. In the typical case, the efficient rate of extraction of a renewable resource results in a steady-state stock level where extraction just equals stock replenishment.

A final insight is indicated by the second and fourth insights. The steady-state stock level for a renewable resource depends on the discount rate. The higher the discount rate the lower the steady-state stock level.

Resource economists have expanded the analytical framework of dynamic resource models well beyond the simple models discussed here. But the logic of all such models is consistent, reflecting the fundamental understanding that extracting a unit of a resource stock imposes a cost on the future.

Bill Provencher

See also: Common Pool Resources; Discounting; Exhaustible Resources; Groundwater

Further Reading

Keohane, Nathaniel O., and Sheila M. Olmstead. 2007. Managing Stocks: Natural Resources as Capital Assets, Chapter 6 in *Markets and the Environment*. Washington, D.C.: Island Press.

V

Value of Statistical Life

Life is precious. Environmental economists are keenly aware of this fact and also that human life is affected by environmental quality. Health is affected by a variety of factors. Biological factors such as genetic endowment and age, lifestyle factors such as diet and exercise, and health care such as inoculations and medications along with pollution are all factors that affect health. Environmental economists continue to contribute to the evidence that exposure to air pollution, water pollution, and toxic substances pose risks to life. Their main contribution, however, is a conceptually sound framework for valuing changes in risks to health and estimates of values of those changes.

The basic idea is straightforward: values of life are reflected in trade-offs individuals are willing to make. The values are the amounts that individuals trade for small changes in their own probabilities of living. Paying higher rent for an apartment that is located farther away from a Superfund site gets a reduction in exposure to toxic substances and reduction in risk. Paying for a basement ventilation system gets a reduction in risk due to exposure to radon. Working for lower pay at a job that has less risk reflects a similar trade-off. Each of these situations involves a trade-off between money and small changes in mortality risks. Such trade-offs are common in everyday life. Typically trade-offs are between an amount such as $70 per year and a change in annual risk of death such as 0.00001. For ease of comparison among various situations involving small changes in risk, it is common practice to divide the amount of money by the change in risk. This standardized, unit (0–1) change value of $7 million is often referred to as a value of statistical life. The reason is that the situation can be thought of another way. Consider a group of 100,000 people and that it is known that eight will die due to exposure to pollution, but the identities of the individuals who will die are unknown. It is also known that each person is willing to pay $70 for a reduction in pollution that would reduce to number of deaths to seven. Thinking of the situation this way, the value of the unknown, statistical life is the number of individuals times the amount per individual, or $7 million. These values are vital. They are used in benefit–cost analysis of environmental regulations. Since 1981 benefit–cost analysis has been required of all major federal regulations in the United States by Executive Order of the president, where permissible by law. It is not unusual that reductions in mortality risks are the most important benefits in the economic analysis for environmental regulations.

Although individuals trade health risk for other desirables on a regular basis, trades are not as easily observed as trades of stocks on Wall Street or purchases of fruits and vegetables at a grocery store. Markets for trading money and health risks rarely, if ever, exist. Consequently, economists have engaged in detective work to uncover situations in which there is sufficient information to infer values of the risk changes. Much of the evidence comes from the labor market. Different jobs have different working conditions. If similar workers have choices between jobs which are the same except for work-related risk of death and pay, then market equilibrium implies that workers who choose riskier jobs are compensated by higher pay. Through statistical analysis that explains differences in pay by differences in worker characteristics and job characteristics, economists isolate these risk-compensating wage differences. These trade-offs yield estimates of values of small changes in mortality risks, that is, values of statistical life.

Additional evidence about trade-offs comes from decisions made by consumers. Different houses have different characteristics, some of which depend on location. Through statistical analysis that accounts for differences in house prices by differences in structural, neighborhood, and environmental characteristics and information about the effect of environmental quality of health, the trade-offs between housing prices and mortality risks can be estimated. Different motor vehicles have different characteristics, one of which is inherent safety. Through statistical analysis that explains vehicle prices by characteristics such as associated fatal crash rates, trade-offs between money and fatality risks can be estimated. Related analyses of highway travel speeds and motorist use of safety equipment reveal trade-offs between valuable time and fatality risks and also yield estimates.

Yet another source of estimates of values is constructing realistic survey or experimental situations and asking individuals directly if they would make the specified trade-offs. Contingent valuation constructs a market-like situation in which individuals can state what trade-offs they are willing to make between their own money and small changes in mortality risks. The situation might be asking how an individual would vote for a referendum that would reduce air pollution from electric power–generating plants, reduce fatality risks, be accompanied by a specified amount added to each utility bill, and be implemented by the relevant government authorities and electric company if a majority supports the referendum and is willing to pay. Advantages of contingent valuation are that the situations can be designed to closely match risks associated with exposure to pollution and to value risks about which the typical individual does not have much information beforehand. These advantages are strengths compared to values revealed through statistical analysis of worker or consumer choices. A concern about contingent valuation is that estimates could be unreliable because the situations are hypothetical; individuals might not really support and pay as they say. Skeptics still exist, but more than 40 years development of stated preference techniques has yielded ways to mitigate hypothetical bias and produce reliable estimates of values of changes in mortality risks.

Many studies of worker choices in labor markets, consumer choices in product markets, and citizen choices in constructed experimental and contingent markets have produced a sizable body of evidence on trade-offs that show how much individuals are willing to pay for changes in mortality risks. The typical value for adults falls in a range from $2 to $12 million (2012 U.S. dollars). This information has guided decisions about environmental policy and proven useful despite what may appear to be a wide range. In economic analysis of regulations the U.S. Environmental Protection Agency (EPA) now tends to use an average value of about $8 million, again measured in 2012 dollars. In other words, if an environmental regulation is expected to benefit 100,000 people by reducing each person's risk of death by 0.00001, then EPA uses a value of about $80 per person for the reduction in risk, and this benefit of the regulation is valued at $8 million for the group of beneficiaries. The agency also uses a range of values to determine the sensitivity of estimates of total social net benefits to this value.

Although environmental economists have a clear understanding of the meaning of value of statistical life, the EPA has become sensitive to meanings that have been misconstrued by others who are interested in environmental policy. In contrast to ordinary trade-offs involving small risks, others have envisioned noncomparable situations such as the amount a captive can offer to avoid certain execution, a situation that is quite different from environmentally related changes in risk. To promote clearer understanding, the EPA is considering new terminology. The new term would be values of mortality risks, where the standard unit, for convenience of comparison, would be the value of a 0.00001 change per person per year. In other words, the small changes in mortality risks would be standardized to one in a million.

Something to keep in mind is that no single value exists that is universal for all individuals in all circumstances. Trade-offs that individuals are willing to make for changes in mortality risk are expected to be different among individuals. They could vary because of ability to deal with exposure to pollution, health status, family situation, religion, income, or age. Values are expected to increase over time with real income growth in a country, and values are expected to be higher in richer countries than poorer countries. One of the more intriguing findings of recent research is that trade-offs appear to vary with age and that parents appear to value reducing risks to their children more than they value reducing their own risks. Although caution is warranted due to the small number of studies, indications are that the values for children are substantially higher. Evidence of trade-offs that senior citizens are willing to make is less clear and policy implications are controversial. At this time the EPA usually uses one value for all, regardless of age, income, or other personal characteristics of the beneficiaries.

The values environmental economists use for policy analysis are based on trade-offs that individuals are willing to make between small changes in mortality risks and money. They do not use an ad hoc measure such as foregone earnings that would generate no or low values for improvements for children, retirees, or others who do not work in the formal labor market. Use of values of statistical life, or values of mortality risks, inferred from observed or stated trade-offs is the way in which environmental economists incorporate the preciousness of mortality risks into economic analysis of regulations that reduce exposure to air pollution, water pollution, and toxic substances. In this way, small changes in risks to life are treated as precious, but not priceless.

Glenn Blomquist

See also: Averting Behavior; Contingent Valuation; Executive Order 12291; Health; Hedonic Price Method; Nonmarket Valuation

Further Reading

Cameron, Trudy. 2010. Euthanizing the Value of Statistical Life. *Review of Environmental Economics and Policy* 4(2): 161–178.

Cropper, Maureen, James K. Hammitt, and Lisa A. Robinson. 2011. Valuing Mortality Risk Reductions: Progress and Challenges. *Annual Review of Resource Economics* 3: 313–336.

Executive Office of the President, Office of Management and Budget. 2013 Draft Report to Congress on the Benefits and Costs of Federal Regulations and Agency Compliance with the Unfunded Mandates Reform Act. http://www.whitehouse.gov/sites/default/files/omb/inforeg/2013_cb/draft_2013_cost_benefit_report.pdf. Accessed June 6, 2013.

Water Conservation

Water conservation has subjective meanings: some define it as an unmitigated good, that is, a reduction in water loss, waste, or use. Others define it as a reduction in measured water use, which may, if forced, actually reduce utility. A third group will note that measured water conservation in one place may increase water use on an unmeasured margin; for example, the conserved yield from lining an earth canal may be used to irrigate golf courses when it formerly recharged aquifers. Regardless of the definition, water conservation can be encouraged with price or nonprice instruments. Price increases reduce quantity demanded; non-price instruments can shift the demand curve.

Water prices are more often directed at cost recovery than water conservation. They vary with location and use. A farmer pays one price to receive water from an irrigation ditch, a family pays a different price to receive drinking water at its tap, an organization might pay a variety of prices to buy water that is then left to flow in-stream for environmental purposes. Prices may be found in an auction, determined by the average cost of utility service, or set through an administrative procedure. An increase in price often results in a reduction in quantity demanded, but the elasticity of this response varies with the price level, use of water, availability of substitutes, and incidence of water prices (i.e., who actually bears their burden). Incidence results from political or regulatory decisions to use block prices, social tariffs, sectorial cross-subsidies, regulatory exemptions, and other adjustments. These adjustments target particular goals, but they also distort consumption decisions and conservation investments.

Suppose for simplicity that it costs $1 to receive one cubic meter of drinking water (265 gallons), a number that is close to $3 per ccf (hundred cubic feet of water, or 748 gallons). Wholesale water buyers usually pay far less for water (e.g., $100 for 1 million liters, or 0.81 acre foot) because the water is neither suitable for drinking nor typically pressurized for 24/7 delivery through a distribution system.

A 20 percent price increase, from $1.00 to $1.20 per cubic meter, may be too low for retail users to notice. The same percentage increase may produce a noticeable response from a farmer who can pump his own groundwater or no response from a farmer who needs water to finish his crop.

These responses can be attributed to sliding up a demand curve to a point of lower quantity demanded. A direct increase in water conservation (a decrease in water consumption) results from shifting the demand curve inward. Shifts occur—all else being equal—from changes in income, technology, or taste. Most of these are beyond the control of the utility. Higher income increases direct and indirect water demand, via respective increases in irrigated landscaping or meat consumption; environmental awareness reduces demand by lowering consumption of all resources. Utilities can encourage inward shifts by subsidizing replacement of water-intensive appliances or landscaping; "education" on the value of water can lead people to shut off faucets while brushing their teeth. Utilities can reinforce changes in taste by ensuring that water prices are high enough to remind consumers of its scarcity. Note that the net conservation impact of each response is affected by offsetting forces. A low-flush toilet may take two flushes to clear the toilet bowl. Low-flow showerheads may lead people to shower more to remove soap or merely enjoy their virtue. Others may wash their car more often. These responses will not be easy to predict in cases where people lack a water meter or do not receive feedback on their water use very often, due to our psychological tendency to put more weight on virtuous acts and less weight on vices.

Water meters, in fact, improve water conservation by making volumetric pricing relevant (nonzero price elasticity) and triggering a behavioral response to measurement of use. Smart water meters that deliver consumption data on short intervals inside one's house strengthen this response by increasing the frequency with which price signals are received and behavior is noted. They also make it easier to spot leaks and change prices in response to surges or drops in demand. It is possible to promote water conservation without meters by mandating the installation of high-efficiency appliances, banning outdoor watering, or educating people to use less, but these command-and-control methods are less efficient than meters. A higher price for metered water will reduce use; a mandated low-flow showerhead in the guest bathroom does little. That said, meters may not be efficient where the opportunity cost of water use or price of water is low relative to the cost of installing meters. In those circumstances, it makes sense to ignore water use or rely on nonprice mechanisms, respectively. A master meter on a multifamily building and some neighborly coercion may be more efficient than meters on each apartment.

Rebound effects can be even stronger with wholesale or bulk water consumption. Farmers who install drip irrigation systems often divert conserved water to other crops or other land parcels (Ward and Pulido-Velazquez, 2008). Such diversions must be put into the proper context. For example, dividing off-stream use into consumed water, nonconsumed recoverable water, and nonconsumed, nonrecoverable water will clarify that consumed water reductions may be beneficial while reductions in recoverable water that reduce return flows—thereby impairing the rights of downstream users—may not be. Meters that reduce diversions at the trunk canal give farmers an incentive to minimize or eliminate tailwater flows that previously percolated into groundwater or flowed downstream to neighbors and ecosystems. Meters or higher prices for thermoelectric or industrial users can make it cost-effective to invest in recirculating cooling systems or closed-loop processes.

These investments may not be socially efficient if they are exceptions to an otherwise lax attitude to conservation (in a service area or watershed where industry shares water with urban and agricultural users) for two reasons. First, conservation investments may conserve water at a high cost per unit. Second, investments may crowd out or distort substitutions to or from labor, energy, capital, and other resources.

People often want examples of successes and failures in water conservation. Las Vegas is a notable failure, not because of its program to subsidize lawn removal (and thus reduce water used for outdoor irrigation), but because it charges one of the lowest prices for water in the western United States (about 30 cents per cubic meter) at the same time as the threat of imminent water shortage is used as a justification to spend $800 million to bore a deeper third straw intake into Lake Mead. For examples of successes, consider how Australians dramatically reduced their water consumption—mostly through demand reduction—in the middle of their 10-year drought, or how water managers in Santa Barbara used a combination of very steep prices and public awareness to reduce demand by 50 percent in the middle of their 1987–1991 drought; demand returned to 60 percent of pre-drought levels when water supplies returned and prices were reduced.

David Zetland

See also: Groundwater; Jevons, William Stanley; Regulation

Further Reading

Brean, H. 2012. Worker Killed, Another Injured at Lake Mead Third Intake Construction Site. *Las Vegas Review Journal*, June 11.

Loaiciga, H. A. and Renehan, S. 1997. Municipal Water Use and Water Rates Driven by Severe Drought: A Case Study. *Journal of the American Water Resources Association* 33: 1313–1326.

Ward, F. A. and M. Pulido-Velazquez. 2008. Water Conservation in Irrigation Can Increase Water Use. *Proceedings of the National Academy of Sciences* 105(47): 18215–18220.

Zetland, David. 2011. *The End of Abundance: Economic Solutions to Water Scarcity.* Mission Viejo, CA: Aguanomics Press.

Water in Development

Most readers of this entry probably woke up this morning and turned on a tap to get water for their first cup of coffee (or tea) or reached into a refrigerator for a beverage. Unfortunately, for billions of people around the world, obtaining drinking water is much more challenging. It probably involves a family member walking a few miles, standing in line to collect just one jerrycan of water from an unreliable public source, hauling this awkward container all the way home under the unrelenting sun, storing the water in a somewhat clean vessel, and finally maybe filtering and or boiling some of the water to provide for several family members. Does economics have any insights on these two very different realities, that is, why an environmental resource such as water is obtained and consumed in such strikingly different ways around the world?

While water is an essential input for agriculture and various manufacturing and other industries, we focus on the use of water for drinking and human consumption because the benefits (for human health) relative to costs are perhaps most striking. Additionally, many of the arguments discussed later also apply to the demand for and supply of water in agriculture and industry in the developing world. We do not need a lecture on how to resolve the diamond–water paradox, the fact that diamonds are less useful but more expensive than water, to realize that willingness-to-pay for clean sufficient regular water (i.e., high demand primarily because of health benefits) usually exceeds the costs of supply. Thus, the task of providing abundant, clean, and reliable water to large populations was tackled head on by planners in the United States, Europe, and many newly industrialized countries. Western governments decided early in the development process to invest in centralized water treatment plants from where water is distributed through a network of underground pipes to individual houses, each of which have meters to compute consumption and generate bills to partially cover the operating costs. Unfortunately, it has been virtually impossible to replicate this strategy in much of the developing world because of a combination of reasons related to (a) lack of resources, including information, (b) tropical ecology and climate, leading to frequent and high incidence of diseases (including water-borne diseases), and (c) historical factors influencing governance and institutional evolution (or the lack thereof). More recent studies offer deeper reasons for why policy analysts appear to have consistently overestimated benefits and underestimated the cost of supplying clean water in developing countries.

On the demand side, the common assertions are that developing country citizens are either simply too poor to pay for clean water and or misinformed about the dangers of drinking water contaminated with microbial and other pollutants. Further probing suggests at least four deeper and complementary reasons for low realized demand. First, households exposed to contaminated water also face a host of environmental and other exposures such as high levels of air pollution. Thus, even if they pay for clean water, their health may not noticeably improve because of myriad exposures. Second, even noticeable improvements in health might not translate into higher human capital returns because of missing educational and labor markets—that is, a healthy bright future worker may have limited earning potential. Third, without clear market signals, the potential user may pay too much attention to other preference modifiers including sociological factors such as peer pressure (i.e., because everyone else in their community is consuming water from traditional sources) or to psychological drivers such as high discount rates or risk aversion that lead to a down weighting of future uncertain benefits. Finally, demand may be low for the service that is delivered (few hours, low volume, contaminated water) than the conceived service subject to benefit–cost analysis for planning.

On the supply side, costs are likely underestimated for at least three reasons. First, for all intents and purposes water supply is a quasi-public good that requires costly coordination among users leading to high transaction costs for sustained provision. For example, if *all* households in a remote village do not make timely financial or labor contributions, the system will break and maintenance and upgrading will cease. Second, improving public source water quality leads to limited health benefits, unless accompanied by other complementary (but costly) behaviors such as safe water handling and handwashing by a majority of households. Prevention and infection externalities dominate and make household coordination unlikely and/or very costly. Finally, dysfunctional governance and weak accountability result in inefficient implementation, with corruption as a primary source of leakage or high effective unit costs of delivery.

Thus the academic and practitioner communities are working hard at filling our knowledge gaps regarding many of the demand and supply questions surrounding water. Applied economists are conducting field experiments and/or relying on quasi-experiments around the developing world to understand, for example, how provision of information on the quality of drinking water changes demand and how community-level social capital and collective efficacy reduce the average cost of water supply. Drawing on some of these findings, increasingly, donors and aid agencies have broadened their objectives from a narrow focus on physical infrastructure to sustainable service provision through three types of programs. First, donors have focused on helping utilities reduce costs and increase revenues to become financially viable, thereby improving and extending service delivery. Second, we have witnessed a rise in large-scale projects in which corporate entities, with private equity, assume operating risk and/or develop under a license or contract to deliver water. The third reform approach puts the community front and center of the planning, design, implementation and operations processes, and replacing career bureaucrats with qualified technocrats as project guides. This philosophy is typically captured in reflecting community needs through participatory planning, decentralized delivery, cost sharing (typically 10% of capital and 100% of operations costs) and strengthening local institutions. The jury is still out, that is, there are few rigorous impact evaluations, on whether these reforms will remove the large disparities in drinking water needs around the world.

Subhrendu K. Pattanayak and Jie-Sheng Tan-Soo

See also: Averting Behavior; Health

Further Reading

Olmstead, S. 2010. The Economics of Water Quality. *Review of Environmental Economics and Policy* 4(1): 44–62.

Pattanayak, S. K. and A. Pfaff. 2009. Behavior, Environment and Health in Developing Countries: Evaluation and Valuation. *Annual Review of Resource Economics.* 1: 183–222.

Whittington, D., W. M. Hanemann, C. Sadoff, and M Jeuland. 2009. The Challenge of Improving Water and Sanitation Services in Less Developed Countries. *Foundations and Trends in Microeconomics* 4(6): 469–607.

Water Pollution

The economics of water pollution is complicated by several features. Water pollution causes externalities or third party effects—in this case, usually (and literally) downstream effects. Unless those external costs are internalized by the polluter, there will be downstream effects. Rivers and lakes or surface water, groundwater, and oceans are all at risk for water pollution. Additionally, there are multiple sources of water pollution that require different solutions or policies. These sources include point source pollution, nonpoint source pollution, atmospheric deposition of pollution, groundwater contamination, and ocean pollution. Finally, the pollutants entering the water bodies may be either fund pollutants or stock pollutants. The environment has some absorptive capacity for fund pollutants. Common examples are nitrogen and phosphorous—not harmful in small quantities, but they can cause eutrophication in larger quantities. Stock pollutants, on the other hand, are those for which the environment has little to no absorptive capacity. These are persistent pollutants that accumulate in water bodies and in the food chain.

Point source pollution can be traced back to a specific discharge pipe and, as such, is easier to control and to monitor. The timing of pollution can also be determined with some accuracy. Pollution control authorities have focused (until recently) control efforts on point sources such as sewage treatment plants and production facilities such as paper mills.

Nonpoint source pollution is pollution that runs off the land when it rains. Runoff from farms, roads, golf courses, and residential lawns are included in this category. Predicting the timing and quantity of nonpoint source pollution is difficult, so until recently, this type of pollution was ignored. Now, however, nonpoint source pollution accounts for a majority of water pollution. Recent attention has focused on regulations and incentives for controlling nonpoint source pollution.

Groundwater contamination usually results from toxic or harmful substances leaching into underground aquifers. For oceans, the main sources of pollution are ocean dumping and oil spills. Oil spills from tankers and from offshore drilling sites are not uncommon. Ocean pollution from trash is becoming a large problem in certain areas where plastics are accumulating.

Water bodies are also becoming polluted when air pollution falls to the ground. This is called atmospheric deposition and occurs either when it rains (wet deposition) or when pollutants get heavy and fall to the ground (dry deposition). Air pollutants like sulfur dioxide cause acid rain and heavy metals such as mercury (a by-product of burning coal and trash) contaminate water, and are found in fish tissue. Most freshwater and many saltwater fish are listed with fish consumption advisories for children and women of childbearing age due to mercury contamination.

Traditionally, water pollution control policies have relied on command and control, or regulation limiting the amount of pollution discharged into a water body. Early examples in the United States include the 1899 Refuse Act (a part of the broader Rivers and Harbors Act) and the Water Pollution Control Act of 1948. The Water Pollution Control Act of 1948 included both regulations on waste discharges and economic incentives in the form of subsidies for the construction of wastewater treatment plants. Subsidies lowered the cost to municipalities of building expensive wastewater treatment plants that might not have been built otherwise. The 1972 amendments to the Water Pollution Control Act, or the Clean Water Act (CWA), gave the EPA authority over setting effluent limits for water quality protection. The CWA requires that dischargers of pollutants obtain permits called National Pollutant Discharge Elimination System (NPDES; http://cfpub.epa.gov/npdes/) permits for their discharges. Other, more recent policies include the Safe Drinking Water Act of 1972, the Total Maximum Daily Load (TMDL) program of the Clean Water Act, and laws on ocean dumping.

Most of these policies rely on expensive command-and-control regulations. The regulations do not offer flexibility or cost-effectiveness, but are based on industry-wide or technology-based standards. Recently, however, watershed-based trading (or water quality trading) has gained attention as a way to achieve a standard at lowest cost. Pollution trading of any kind relies on the idea that polluters (facilities, factories, sewage treatment plants, etc.) tend to have very different costs for pollution control. Trading works if there is enough variation in costs that high-cost sources can buy allowances from lower cost of control sources. If high cost of abatement sources buy allowances at less than their marginal cost of cleanup and low-cost sources sell for higher than their marginal cost of cleanup, the same standard can be reached, but at a lower total cost.

Many trades have taken place across similar types of polluters (e.g., point source to point source). But watershed-based trading may also be an appealing option for point sources who have already been forced to clean up a significant portion of their discharge, so much so that additional treatment could be extremely expensive. If those point sources instead subsidized the treatment of a nonpoint source, the same reductions could be met at much lower cost. For example, the marginal (additional) cost of abatement rises with abatement. Imagine two sources, one point source that is half-way up its own marginal cost schedule, and a nonpoint source that has not cleaned up at all. The nonpoint source may have higher overall marginal costs of cleanup, but is not yet on the curve (abatement = 0). In this case, the total cost of abatement is lowest if the nonpoint source cleans up the next unit, rather than the point source. An example is Lake Dillon, Colorado. Lake Dillon was experiencing excess phosphorous pollution. The sewage treatment plant opted to build a buffer around a local golf course to keep phosphorous from fertilizer out of the lake, rather than build additional sewage-based treatment.

Some watershed-based trading, however, relies on complicated ambient trading ratios, which restrict trades. The Long Island Sound nitrogen trading program in Connecticut functions more like an ambient tax than an ambient trading program. The ambient trading ratios change with distance north and east of the hotspots in Long Island Sound. As such, the price is not determined by the market, but is set by the state. Still, a tax program offers an incentive for pollution control and is more cost-effective than a strict regulation. This program is expected to save $200 million, or 20 percent over the life of the program compared to command-and-control approaches.

While rarely used for water pollution control in the United States, effluent charges, or taxes, have been used extensively in Europe. Some of these are combined with effluent standards while others are used as incentives for firms to reduce pollution more than the standards. Most recently charges have been used for heavy metals.

Policies related to oil spills rely heavily on the legal system, but oil spills, in particular the Exxon *Valdez* spill of 1989, opened the door for nonmarket valuation methods such as the contingent valuation method to become valid tools for natural resource damage assessments.

For ocean pollution, the complexities include enforcement and the vast expanses the pollution can travel. Oil spills, toxics, and plastics pollution in the ocean are all harmful to marine life and to beach recreation. While liability for an oil spill might be obvious, sources of plastic pollution are many and diffuse.

Do the benefits of water pollution control policy exceed the costs? The evidence is mixed. The benefits of water pollution control policy are tricky to estimate and policies that rely on command and control are expensive to implement. Co-benefits from air pollution control policies further complicate the measurement of benefits. For example, policies aimed at reducing sulfur dioxide emissions from coal-fired power plants have reduced emissions considerably. These reductions have also improved water quality conditions.

Using cost-effective policies would help reduce costs considerably while leaving benefits unchanged. Moving toward policies that utilize economic incentives will help. Water quality trading is one step in that direction. Economic incentive approaches offer flexibility and can stimulate change.

Lynne Lewis

See also: Clean Water Act; Contingent Valuation; Externality; Exxon *Valdez* Oil Spill; Groundwater; Nonpoint Source Pollution; Offsets; Regulation

Further Reading

Griffiths, C., and W. Wheeler. 2005. Benefit–Cost Analysis of Regulations Affecting Surface Water Quality in the United States, in Roy Brouwer and David Pearce (editors), *Cost Benefit Analysis and Water Resources Management*. Northampton, MA: Edward Elgar.

Ohlmstead, Sheila M. 2010. The Economics of Water Quality Trading. *Review of Environmental Economics and Policy* 4(1): 44–62.

Tietenberg, Tom, and Lynne Lewis. 2012. Water Pollution, Chapter 18 in *Environmental and Natural Resource Economics*, 9th ed. Upper Saddle River, NJ: Pearson.

Welfare

Welfare economics is the study of social well-being. If one's utility, or happiness, rises then one enjoys a welfare improvement (and vice versa). Social welfare is a function of all individual welfare levels. In environmental and resource economics, with its focus on market failures, welfare economics is often used to consider whether society is better or worse off in response to government policy. The early welfare economists, such as Arthur Pigou, thought that utility could be measured by assigning numbers to units of happiness so that welfare could be compared directly from one person to another. Economists realized that such cardinal utility measurement was not feasible and came to favor ordinal utility. Ordinal utility means that individuals can rank bundles of goods and services from the most preferred to the least preferred.

Using the notion of ordinal utility, one way to judge if a reallocation of resources improves social welfare is to determine if it improves the well-being of at least one member of society without making any other members of society worse off. If it does then the policy is called a Pareto improvement (named after the Italian economist Vilfredo Pareto). The Pareto criterion has come to be viewed as very strict. Very few, if any, policies make no one worse off. Under the strict Pareto criterion, a policy that takes one dollar from the richest person in society and gives it to the poorest person in society would not be an improvement—the richest person is worse off by one dollar. Alternatively, a potential Pareto improvement is a policy that passes the compensation test—it has benefits greater than costs such that the winners could compensate the losers so that the losers are no worse off than before the policy. The compensation need not actually occur to pass the potential Pareto test.

Benefit–cost analysis, a method used to calculate and compare monetary gains and losses, is the practical application of welfare economics. The concept of economic surplus is the basis for the theory of economic benefit and cost measurement. Considering a market good, for example a car, the consumer's economic surplus is the difference between what the consumer is willing and able to pay and the market price of the car. The consumer may be willing and able to pay the manufacturer's suggested retail price of $35,000. However, if the negotiated price is $31,000 then the consumer surplus is $4,000—the difference between the consumer's maximum willingness to pay and the market price. The consumer surplus is a monetary measure of the net benefit that the consumer gained from the transaction.

Goods that are not sold in markets, such as water quality, also provide consumer surplus. Consider an angler who is willing and able to pay $5 for each additional fish caught per trip. If an environmental regulation leads to a water quality improvement, and the improvement enables the angler to catch two additional fish beyond his usual catch, then the consumer surplus per trip increases by $10.

Producer surplus is the difference between what the business firm is willing to accept in exchange for the product and the additional cost of producing that unit of the product. It is measured as the difference between the revenue earned by business firms and the variable costs of production (i.e., the sum of marginal costs). Producer surplus is equivalent to profit if the fixed costs of production are zero. With environmental regulations that negatively affect business firms, the loss of producer surplus is a measure of the cost of the policy.

Consumer surplus is usually a good approximation of what is known as an exact welfare measure. Consumer surplus is not exact because of income effects. Consider a price reduction that leads to an increase in consumption of a market good. As the price falls, the amount of money available to spend on all goods, including the one whose price has fallen, increases. This is a form of the income effect on demand. As income increases the demand for a product increases for normal goods and decreases for inferior goods. In the same way, a price decrease will lead to a positive change in income available for spending, which might further increase the amount consumed of the good whose price has changed (if it is a normal good). On the other hand, a price increase will lead to a negative change in income available for spending, which might further decrease the amount consumed of the good whose price has changed.

Consumer demand has both income and substitution effects. A demand function with income effects is known as a Marshallian (named after the economist Alfred Marshall) demand function. Exact, income-compensated or Hicksian (named after the economist John Hicks) demand functions are preferred for welfare analysis because they focus on the substitution effect. The substitution effect is the change in quantity demanded that arises solely due to the willingness to pay for more or less of a good, not due to a change in the ability to pay (i.e., the income effect).

Exact welfare measures include compensating and equivalent variations and surpluses. The compensating variation is the amount of money an individual would need to obtain the initial utility level after a price change. When a policy leads to a price decrease the compensating variation is the willingness to pay to obtain the price decrease. When a policy leads to a price increase the compensating variation is the willingness to accept compensation for the price increase. In both cases the utility level with the price change and after income is adjusted by the compensating variation is equal to the utility level before the price change.

The equivalent variation is the amount of money an individual would need to obtain the subsequent utility level after a price change. When a policy leads to a price decrease the equivalent variation is the willingness to accept compensation to forgo the price decrease. When a policy leads to a price increase the equivalent variation is the willingness to pay to avoid the price increase. In both cases the utility level with income adjusted by the equivalent variation and the price change is equal to the utility level that would result after the price change.

In environmental and resource economics it is often the case that a policy will change a nonmarket good instead of a market price. In this case there are compensating and equivalent surpluses. The compensating surplus is the amount of money an individual would need to obtain the initial utility level after an environmental quality or resource quantity change. When a policy leads to a quality or quantity increase the compensating surplus is the willingness to pay to obtain the increase. When a policy leads to a quality or quantity decrease the compensating surplus is the willingness to accept compensation to avoid the decrease. In both cases the utility level with income adjusted by compensating surplus and the quality or quantity change is equal to the utility level before the quality or quantity change.

The equivalent surplus is the amount of money an individual would need to obtain the subsequent utility level after a quality or quantity change. When a policy leads to a quality or quantity increase the equivalent surplus is the willingness to accept to forgo the increase. When a policy leads to a quality or quantity increase the equivalent surplus is the willingness to pay to avoid the decrease. In both cases the utility level with income adjusted by equivalent surplus and the quality or quantity change is equal to the utility level after the quality or quantity change.

The differences in exact welfare measures are subtle but important. The correct measure is a function of the implicit property rights to the environment. If those who are affected by the policy feel that they have a property right to the original level of price, quality or quantity then the compensating measures are appropriate. If those who are affected by the policy feel that they have a property right to the subsequent level of price, quality or quantity then the equivalent measures are appropriate.

Total economic value is the decomposition of willingness to pay and willingness to accept into use value and passive use value. Use value is the willingness to pay for a change in the resource allocation that results from on-site or direct use of the environment or natural resource. Use value can derive from consumptive or nonconsumptive use. Consumptive use is when the resource is extracted from the natural environment. Examples include hunting and fishing (catch and keep) and mining. Nonconsumptive use value is when the resource is enjoyed but not extracted from the natural environment. Examples include hiking and wildlife watching. Passive use value is the willingness to pay (or accept) for the resource reallocation that does not lead to changes in behavior.

John C. Whitehead

See also: Benefit–Cost Analysis; Nonmarket Valuation; Passive Use Value; Pigou, A.C.; Welfare and Equity

Further Reading

Banzhaf, Spencer H. 2010. Consumer Surplus with Apology: A Historical Perspective on Nonmarket Valuation and Recreation Demand. *Annual Review of Resource Economics* 2: 18.1–18.25.

Bergstrom, John C., 1990. Concepts and Measures of the Economic Value of Environmental Quality: A Review. *Journal of Environmental Management* 31(3): 215–228.

Boadway, Robin W., and Neil Bruce. 1984. *Welfare Economics.* New York: B. Blackwell.

Randall, Alan, and John R. Stoll. 1980. Consumer's Surplus in Commodity Space. *American Economic Review* 70(3): 449–455.

Willig, R. D. 1976. Consumer's Surplus without Apology. *American Economic Review* 66(4): 589–597.

Welfare and Equity

Welfare in economics means either the well-being of individuals or the aggregation of individual welfare into the well-being of society. One of the great philosophical questions, and a question of everyday political importance, is whether a society's welfare will be improved following a reallocation of resources. This question appears regularly: is society better off by switching energy production methods; by educating more people; by putting more criminals in jail? The question can also be asked in hindsight (retrospectively): were we made better off by an action? Economics has reached a carefully qualified answer in theory and applies practical methods that are severely limited versions of that theory through benefit–cost analysis. It is the problem of a bridge between welfare and a sense of fairness or equity, which is unresolved by more exactly answering the question of social welfare.

What economists call efficiency is maximizing the welfare of society when it is assumed that such welfare depends on the sum (a very specific form of aggregation) of the welfare of individuals who only care about themselves. Society views each of these individuals as equally important. Economists further assume that each person receives the same additional welfare from added income. The result is that applied welfare analysis, called benefit–cost analysis, generally adds benefits or subtracts costs from affected individuals regardless of their position or characteristics within the society, especially, but not limited to, their income status.

While the default social welfare analysis based on the earlier assumptions is transparent to those knowledgeable of these assumptions, it may give undue credence to a result said to be efficient when these assumptions are not generally viewed as being globally accepted. In addition, the well-known Arrow impossibility theorem establishes that an aggregate social welfare function cannot exist without violating seemingly reasonable criteria.

These assumptions may not be so burdensome if perfectly competitive markets are universal. Generations of economists have learned the first welfare theorem of economics, that a society with perfectly competitive markets will achieve an efficient social outcome. However, the confounding (and somewhat more restrictive) second welfare theorem of economics states that a completely different but still efficient market outcome can result if there is a change in the distribution of income. Thus efficiency, the well-being of a society, is not uniquely determined without consideration of the distribution of income.

The many sources of market failure such as externalities, imperfect competition, and incomplete markets with uncertainty removes the presumption that even a market-based society begins at an efficient point. Further, it would be convenient if policy proposals were of the win–win–all win type; in this case it is clear that society would be better off taking the action (called a Pareto improvement in honor of Vilfredo Pareto, the economist who first formalized the criterion). The problem results when virtually all changes involve both some winners and losers. If the winners fully compensated the losers, then the win–lose problem is changed into a win–win problem. In the absence of such compensation, a potential for compensation may exist, but uncompensated outcomes with both winners and losers may not qualify as a clear improvement.

The default approach taken in benefit–cost analysis is termed the (Kaldor-Hicks) potential compensation criteria. In effect, analysts state that society's welfare is improved if the winners could potentially compensate the losers although such compensation is not required. Hence the potential exists for a policy that benefits the rich at the expense of the poor but may be assessed as efficient.

If social welfare is assessed using a transparent but likely incorrect set of assumptions assuming equal social welfare and equal marginal utility of income across individuals, how can equity concerns be integrated into applied welfare analysis? Several supplemental analyses to basic welfare analysis have been advanced, and new approaches are being investigated.

A supplemental analysis can be done for a subgroup of concern. The subgroup might be disadvantaged youths receiving training in an employment program, those people below some income level, a minority, the government, or the residents of a smaller area such as a state or locality. An analysis can reveal whether the identified subgroup appears to gain or lose from an action, and a decision-maker can choose whether or how to take such a result into consideration regarding a project. Further, legal constraints or policies may suggest that some group should not be made worse off as the result of a policy action. A subjective, but explicit, weighting can be applied to the gains or losses of identified subgroups. The most common application is to weight gains or losses received by different income groups according to assumptions about the incremental utility (satisfaction) from income. The U.S. Census Bureau reports poverty information by weighting information using such Atkinson weights, which imply a ratio, such as 2:1 or 4:1, between those in low- or high-income groups. The World Bank and the UK government have supported weighting approaches at various times. Alternative weighting approaches such as those based on relative marginal tax rates, relative income, or more complex measures such as the Lorenz curve have been suggested. New analysis is pursuing the concept that equity is a value some individuals place on the well-being of others, which should not be treated any differently than other values included in a welfare analysis. There are theoretical complications as to whether double counting may occur when preferences are of a particular form, but survey research is beginning to investigate and quantify the monetary value people place on the well-being of others. General equilibrium or multimarket analysis, as has been carried out in regard to allocating the legal right to emit pollution, has also indicated a fairly direct trade-off between efficiency and equity when property rights are being allocated.

Few topics divide analysts as much as does the debate about the separation of efficiency and equity, the equity assumptions of benefit–cost analysis and methods to integrate equity into an analysis.

Scott Farrow

See also: Benefit–Cost Analysis; Welfare

Further Reading

Farrow, Scott. 2011. Incorporating Equity in Regulatory and Benefit–Cost Analysis Using Risk Based Preferences. *Risk Analysis* 31(6): 902–907.

Foster, J., and Sen, A. 1997. On Economic Inequality after a Quarter Century, in Sen, A. (editor). *On Economic Inequality, Expanded Edition.* Oxford: Clarendon/Oxford Press.

Harberger, Arnold. 1978. On the Use of Distributional Weights in Social Cost–Benefit Analysis. *Journal of Political Economy* 86(2:2):S87–S120.

Lave, Lester. 1996. Benefit–Cost Analysis: Do the Benefits Exceed the Costs? in Hahn, R. (editor), *Risks, Costs, and Lives Saved.* Cambridge: Cambridge University Press.

Loomis, John. 2011. Incorporating Distributional Issues into Benefit Cost Analysis: Why, How, and Two Empirical Examples Using Non-Market Valuation. *Journal of Benefit-Cost Analysis*, 2(1): Article 5.

Scarborough, Helen, and Jeff Bennett. 2012. *Cost–Benefit Analysis and Distributional Preferences: A Choice Modeling Approach.* Cheltenham, UK: Edward Elgar.

Wetlands

Wetlands are areas that are permanently or seasonally saturated with water such that they embody distinct ecosystems characterized by vegetation adapted to moist soil conditions. There are many types of wetlands classified by scientists because the water associated with wetlands can be freshwater, saltwater, or mixtures of the two; and also because the water can be flowing periodically or permanently. As a result of this diverse definition, wetlands provide a considerable array of important environmental functions. Common wetland types include bogs, fens, marshes, and swamps, with many further subtypes within these classifications.

Wetlands have featured prominently in environmental research because they provide a number of important ecosystem services such as water purification, flood control, recreation, habitat, carbon sequestration, and shoreline stability. The diversity of wetlands types has led wetlands to be considered the most biologically diverse of all ecosystems because they provide habitats to a wide range of plant and animal life. However, despite their environmental importance wetland systems are more degraded than any other ecosystem on the planet according to the UN Millennium Ecosystem Assessment. This has led to significant international conservation efforts such as the Ramsar Convention, which is an international agreement to stem wetland loss and increase awareness of wetland values. This convention has been signed by over 160 countries.

The extent of wetland loss and degradation is somewhat controversial due to the lack of historical wetland inventory data as well as changing procedures for the classification of wetlands. However, it is generally agreed that wetland degradation has occurred in virtually all parts of the world. For example, early estimates of wetland loss in the United States suggested that by the mid-1970s 46 percent of the wetlands present at the time of settlement have been lost. Recent research has continued to document wetland decline in North America, although there is some evidence that the rate of loss has slowed.

The reasons for wetland losses are complex. The main contributing factor in North America and other parts of the world has been agricultural expansion where wetlands have been drained to increase cultivated area and to remove wetlands as obstacles to farm machinery. This has been particularly important in the prairie pothole region of central North America, which represents the breadbasket of the continent. Other factors include urban developments, forestry expansion, mining, and climate change.

The linkage between wetland loss and agricultural expansion on private lands, coupled with the important ecosystem services provided by these ecosystems, has led to some innovative policy developments. Hence wetland conservation has been of considerable interest to environmental economists. The central policy issue is that most wetland services are enjoyed by the public at large, whereas the costs of maintaining wetlands has fallen on the owners of the lands where wetlands are located. Furthermore, many wetland services cannot be captured as income by wetland owners as the services generate economic benefits that accrue primarily off-site. The picture is further complicated by the fact that many of the economic values of these services are not reflected in markets; or in cases where they could be captured in markets, they are not directly linked to the particular wetland being examined.

This conservation issue has generated the concept of no-net-loss, which attempts to balance losses with reclamation, mitigation, and restoration efforts such that the total acreage of wetlands in a specific area does not decrease, but remains constant or increases. Thus, this approach is similar to an offset system where a cap is placed on wetland areas and any losses are offset by the restoration of previously existing wetlands or the creation of new ones. In the wetland case, landowners or organizations who restore or create wetlands can offer these as credits to developers who in the process of completing projects, which remove wetlands, are required to provide compensating wetlands to satisfy the no-net-loss requirements. The creation of surplus credits under a no-net-loss rule has led to the development of mitigation banks, which have become free-market enterprises that collect wetland credits and offer them for sale to developers. Economists find this policy approach attractive because the banking provides economic incentives to landowners and organizations to protect or restore environmental assets while providing developers with a bank of existing credits. Under sufficient regulatory oversight the banked wetlands to be used for compensation can be preapproved, which can save developers time and money in seeking credits for required compensation—thus wetland banks are able to provide services at lower costs.

No net loss policy which employs wetland area as the measure of loss and compensation is relatively simple to implement. However, this area approach does not guarantee no net loss of wetland function and/or ecosystem service provision. For example, compensating loss of wetlands in rural agricultural areas with equivalent areas of urban storm water retention ponds may not replace lost wildlife habitat or water filtration services but might generate considerably higher recreation and flood control services. This raises the issue of assessing losses and compensation in terms of wetland function. However, this would be extremely costly to implement because each wetland would then have to be assessed with respect to its ecological function or ecosystem services provided.

Understanding the economic value of wetlands is complex due to questions regarding the presence or absence of the wetland(s) or the presence/absence of the ecosystem services the wetland(s) provide. The values associated with wetlands have perhaps been one of the most studied ecosystem values by economists and has involved the application of different methods to different spatial configurations of wetlands (i.e., individual wetlands or all wetlands in a defined geographic area). Accordingly, a wide range of economic valuation estimates exist in the literature.

Attention by economists recently is on the value of wetland services. Some of these are relatively easy to measure; for example, the prices or incomes earned from market activities associated with wetlands, such as commercial fishing and hunting and the harvesting or collection of natural products (e.g., herbal medicines, fuel wood). Another approach involves the costs of replacing some services (e.g., water quality improvement) with human-made engineered solutions (e.g., water treatment plants). For many wetland services, however, market information or replacement costs do not exist requiring the application of nonmarket valuation methods. The services that would require these approaches involve unpriced recreational use, scenic amenities, passive use, or existence values associated with wildlife or aquatic life associated with wetlands, or other types of preservation benefits.

Peter C. Boxall

See also: Biodiversity; Ecosystem Services; Nonmarket Valuation

Further Reading

Dahl, T.E. 2011. Status and Trends of Wetlands in the Conterminous United States 2004 to 2009. U.S. Department of the Interior; Fish and Wildlife Service, Washington, D.C. 108 pp.

Ghermandi, Andrea, Jeroen C.J.M. van den Bergh, Luke M. Brander, Henri L.F. de Groot, and Paulo A.L.D. Nunes. 2010. Values of Natural and Human-Made Wetlands: A Meta-Analysis. *Water Resources Research* 46: W12516.

ABOUT THE EDITORS AND CONTRIBUTORS

Editors

Timothy C. Haab is the chair of the Department of Agricultural, Environmental and Development Economics at Ohio State University. Timothy has served as coeditor of the *Journal of Environmental Economics and Management*, which is the flagship journal of the Association of Environmental and Resource Economists. He is the coauthor of *Valuing Environmental and Natural Resources* (Edward Elgar, 2002), and he and Whitehead are coauthors of *Preference Data for Environmental Valuation: Combining Revealed and Stated Approaches* (Routledge, 2010). Haab is also the author of more than 40 peer-reviewed journal articles. Haab received his Ph.D. from the University of Maryland in 1995.

John C. Whitehead is the chair of the Department of Economics at Appalachian State University. He is an associate editor of the *Journal of Environmental Management* (2010–2013) as well as *Marine Resource Economics* (2007 – present). He has served on the board of directors of the Association of Environmental and Resource Economists and is a past-president of the Socioeconomics Section of the American Fisheries Society. Whitehead is the author of more than 80 peer-reviewed journal articles, and he and Haab are coauthors of *Preference Data for Environmental Valuation: Combining Revealed and Stated Approaches* (Routledge, 2010). He received his Ph.D. from the University of Kentucky in 1990.

Contributors

W. L. (Vic) Adamowicz
University of Alberta

David A. Anderson
Centre College

Lee G. Anderson
University of Delaware

Rodrigo Arriagada
Pontificia Universidad Católica de Chile

Maximilian Auffhammer
University of California, Berkeley

Kenneth A. Baerenklau
University of California, Riverside

Yoram Bauman
Sightline Institute

Robert P. Berrens
University of New Mexico

Okmyung Bin
East Carolina University

Richard C. Bishop
University of Wisconsin—Madison

Glenn Blomquist
University of Kentucky

Peter C. Boxall
University of Alberta

Keith Brouhle
Grinnell College

Scott J. Callan
Bentley University

Richard T. Carson
University of California, San Diego

Jill L. Caviglia-Harris
Salisbury University

Paul E. Chambers
University of Central Missouri

Janie M. Chermak
University of New Mexico

Todd L. Cherry
Appalachian State University and
CICERO Center for International
Climate and Environmental
Research–Oslo

Richard Crume
U.S. Environmental Protection
Agency

Jim DeMocker
U.S. Environmental Protection Agency

Mark Dickie
University of Central Florida

Chris Dockins
U.S. Environmental Protection Agency

Dietrich Earnhart
University of Kansas

David A. Evans
U.S. Environmental Protection Agency

Mary F. Evans
Claremont McKenna College

Scott Farrow
University of Maryland, Baltimore
County

Nicholas E. Flores
University of Colorado Boulder

Michael Giberson
Texas Tech University

Gwendolyn L. Gill
University of North Carolina Charlotte

Charles W. Griffiths
U.S. Environmental Protection
Agency

Therese C. Grijalva
Weber State University

Peter A. Groothuis
Appalachian State University

Timothy C. Haab
The Ohio State University

John M. Hartwick
Queen's University

Martin D. Heintzelman
Clarkson University

Garth Heutel
University of North Carolina at
Greensboro

Stephen P. Holland
University of North Carolina at
Greensboro

Frances Homans
University of Minnesota

Richard B. Howarth
Dartmouth College

Bryan Hubbell
U.S. Environmental Protection Agency

Matthew G. Interis
Mississippi State University

Paul M. Jakus
Utah State University

Robert J. Johnston
Clark University

Nick Johnstone
Organisation for Economic Co-operation and Development

James R. Kahn
Washington and Lee University and Universidade Federal do Amazonas

Matthew E. Kahn
University of California, Los Angeles

Madhu Khanna
University of Illinois

Lynne Kiesling
Northwestern University

Catherine Kling
Iowa State University

Brandon C. Koford
Weber State University

Lea-Rachel Kosnik
University of Missouri—St. Louis

Matthew J. Kotchen
Yale University

Kate Krause
University of New Mexico

Jamie B. Kruse
East Carolina University

Craig E. Landry
East Carolina University

Sherry L. Larkin
University of Florida

Lynne Lewis
Bates College

Joshua Linn
Resources for the Future

John B. Loomis
Colorado State University

Kelly B. Maguire
U.S. Environmental Protection Agency

David M. McEvoy
Appalachian State University

Mike McKee
Appalachian State University

Daniel L. Millimet
Southern Methodist University

Tanga McDaniel Mohr
Appalachian State University

Mark A. Moore
Simon Fraser University

O. Ashton Morgan
Appalachian State University

Katrina Mullan
University of Montana

Brian C. Murray
Duke University

Jason H. Murray
University of South Carolina

Jim Neumann
U.S. Environmental Protection Agency

Douglas Noonan
Indiana University-Purdue University
Indianapolis

Catherine S. Norman
Johns Hopkins University

Clifford Nowell
Weber State University

Karen Palmer
Resources for the Future

Ian Parry
International Monetary Fund

George R. Parsons
University of Delaware

Mark D. Partridge
The Ohio State University

Robert H. Patrick
Rutgers University

Subhrendu K. Pattanayak
Duke University

Krishna P. Paudel
Louisiana State University

Daniel R. Petrolia
Mississippi State University

Daniel Phaneuf
University of Wisconsin

Paul R. Portney
University of Arizona

Bill Provencher
University of Wisconsin

Alan Randall
University of Sydney

Richard C. Ready
Pennsylvania State University

Robert B. Richardson
Michigan State University

Mary Riddel
University of Nevada, Las Vegas

Michael J. Roberts
University of Hawaii

Randall S. Rosenberger
Oregon State University

James Roumasset
University of Hawai'i, Mānoa

Jayjit Roy
Appalachian State University

Jonathan Rubin
The University of Maine

Abdoul G. Sam
The Ohio State University

Kurt E. Schnier
University of California, Merced

Peter W. Schuhmann
University of North Carolina Wilmington

Kurt Schwabe
University of California, Riverside

Peter M. Schwarz
University of North Carolina Charlotte

Jason Scorse
Monterey Institute of International
Studies

Roger A. Sedjo
Resources for the Future

Kathleen Segerson
University of Connecticut

Ronald J. Shadbegian
U.S. Environmental Protection Agency

W. Douglass Shaw
Texas A&M University

Ian M. Sheldon
The Ohio State University

Jay P. Shimshack
Tulane University

Jason F. Shogren
University of Wyoming

Erin O. Sills
North Carolina State University

Nathalie Simon
U.S. Environmental Protection
Agency

R. David Simpson
U.S. Environmental Protection
Agency

V. Kerry Smith
Arizona State University

Martin D. Smith
Duke University

Brent Sohngen
The Ohio State University

Sarah L. Stafford
College of William and Mary

Mark C. Strazicich
Appalachian State University

Jie-Sheng Tan-Soo
Duke University

Laura O. Taylor
North Carolina State University

Jennifer A. Thacher
University of New Mexico

Janet M. Thomas
Bentley University

Tom Tietenberg
Colby College

George Van Houtven
RTI International

Roger H. von Haefen
North Carolina State University

Christian A. Vossler
University of Tennessee

Christopher A. Wada
University of Hawai'i, Mānoa

Diana Weinhold
London School of Economics

Amanda L. Weinstein
University of Akron

William J. Wheeler
U.S. Environmental Protection Agency

John Whitehead
Appalachian State University

James Wilen
University of California Davis

Richard T. Woodward
Texas A&M University

Mine K. Yücel
Federal Reserve Bank of Dallas

David Zetland
Aguanomics.com

INDEX

Note: Page numbers in **boldface** reflect main entries in the book.